PENGUIN BOOKS

KEITH RICHARDS

Victor Bockris is the author of *Ali: Fighter, Poet, Prophet*; *With William Burroughs: A Report from the Bunker*; *Making Tracks: The Rise of Blondie*; *Uptight: The Velvet Underground Story*; and *Warhol*, which is also published by Penguin. He was born and educated in England but now lives in New York.

VICTOR BOCKRIS

Keith Richards
THE BIOGRAPHY

PENGUIN BOOKS

PENGUIN BOOKS

Published by the Penguin Group
Penguin Books Ltd, 27 Wrights Lane, London w8 5TZ, England
Penguin Books USA Inc., 375 Hudson Street, New York, New York 10014, USA
Penguin Books Australia Ltd, Ringwood, Victoria, Australia
Penguin Books Canada Ltd, 10 Alcorn Avenue, Toronto, Ontario, Canada M4V 3B2
Penguin Books (NZ) Ltd, 182–190 Wairau Road, Auckland 10, New Zealand

Penguin Books Ltd, Registered Offices: Harmondsworth, Middlesex, England

First published in Great Britain by Hutchinson, an imprint of Random House UK Ltd, 1992
Published with additional material in Penguin Books 1993
1 3 5 7 9 10 8 6 4 2

Copyright © Victor Bockris, 1992, 1993
All rights reserved

The moral right of the author has been asserted

Set in 9.75/12.25 pt Monotype Sabon
Typeset by Datix International, Bungay, Suffolk
Printed in England by Clays Ltd, St Ives plc

Except in the United States of America, this book is sold subject
to the condition that it shall not, by way of trade or otherwise, be lent,
re-sold, hired out, or otherwise circulated without the publisher's
prior consent in any form of binding or cover other than that in
which it is published and without a similar condition including this
condition being imposed on the subsequent purchaser

For the women,
in particular Anita Pallenberg,
Linda Keith and Sheila Oldham.

I've lived my life in my own way,
and I'm here because
I've taken the trouble
to find out who I am.

KEITH RICHARDS

Contents

CONTENTS

List of Illustrations

Acknowledgements

James Michener once told me the key to being a writer is to maintain a sweet relationship with yourself. This is particularly true, I would think, in biography. I write out of love, admiration, and humor, but that doesn't make the writing easier than if you were writing out of hatred, disgust, and irony. Either way, you find yourself alone, stumbling around in the dark.

For being my lifeline during the three years it took to write this book, deepest thanks to Lisa Krug, Andrew Wylie, Miles, Stellan Holm, and Robert Dowling.

For assistance in constructing and writing the book, thanks to Ann Patty, Steve Messina, and Lydia Buechler at Poseidon in New York, Paul Sidey and Ingrid von Essen at Random House in London, and my collaborators Lisa Krug, Mim Udovitch, and Robert Dowling.

For interviews with the author I am especially grateful for their generosity and enlightenment to Anita Pallenberg, Linda Porter (née Keith), Sheila Oldham, Terry Southern and Albert Goldman. For outstanding interviews with or articles about Keith Richards, I wish to thank Mandy Aftel, Stanley Booth, Roy Carr, Barbara Charone, Adrian Deevoy, Bill Flanagan, Chet Flippo, Bill German, Robert Greenfield, Kurt Loder, Lisa Robinson, and Charles Young. And for outstanding images, Bob Gruen, Michael Cooper, and Gered Mankowitz.

For inspiration, information, and insanity I acknowledge the aid and collaboration of Penny Arcade, Price Abbott, Gini Alhadeff, Isabelle Bannon, Jessica Blue, William Burroughs, Mary Beach, Roberta Bayley, David Bourdon, Bobbie Bristol, Isabelle Baudron, Annie Bingham, Rosemary Bailey, Heiner Bastian, Ted Berrigan, David Courts, James Carpenter, Tei Carpenter, Jim Carroll,

ACKNOWLEDGEMENTS

Jonathan Cott, Diego Cortez, John Dunbar, Liz Derringer, Ed DeGrazia, Rick Derringer, Marriane Erdos, Kim Evans, Gisella Freisinger, Mick Farren, Marianne Faithfull, Steve Finbow, Ed Friedman, Raymond Foye, James Grauerholz, Allen Ginsberg, Craig Gholson, Bob Gruen, John Giorno, Art and Kym Garfunkel, Dr. Joseph Gross, Bill German, Liz Gibbons, Emma Hall, Debbie Harry, Clinton Heylin, Richard Hambleton, Terry Hood, Susan Hill, David Heymann, Mary Harron, Anthony Haden-Guest, Václav Havel, Paula Igliore, Fred Jordan, Baird Jones, Ray Johnson, Becky Johnston, Jose at 380 Copy Shop, James Karnbach, Mark Kostabi, Justin Krug, Laura Kronenberg, Lawrence Krug, Maria Lexton, Lydia Lunch, John Lindsay, Richard Lloyd, Carl Laszlo, Benjamin Lefeyre, Seaver Leslie, Christopher Makos, Legs McNeil, Taylor Mead, Earl McGrath, Steve Mass, Tom Mershon, Charles and Diana Michener, Stewart Meyer, Annabelle McCall, John Michel, Gered Mankowitz, Gerard Malanga, Toshiko Mori, Philip Norman, James Nares, Glenn O'Brien, Uschi Obermeier, George Plimpton, Linda Porter, Claude Pelieu, Caz Phillips, Peter Moritz Pickshaus, Robert Palmer, Bill Prince, Marcia Resnick, Josef Rauvolf, Doris Richards, Chantal Rossett, John Richardson, Jonathan Riley, Walter Stedding, Ingrid Sischy, David Schmidlapp, Chris Stein, Terry Spero, Dieter Steiner, Frances Schönberger, Tim Schultheiss, Liza Stelle, Aram Saroyan, Stuart Samuels, Kate Simon, Joe Stevens, Gus Van Sant, John Telfer, Lynne Tillman, John Tytell, Jeffrey Vogel, Jan van Willigen, Christopher Whent, Peter Wise, Michael Watts, Rebekah Wood, Lee Williams, and Susan Williams.

I

Gimme Shelter
1943–1956

Hitler had me marked!

KEITH RICHARDS, *from an interview with Charles Young, 1988*

On December 18, 1943, at the height of the Second World War, while air raid sirens wailed and flak exploded over the streets nearby, Keith Richards was born a war baby in Livingstone Hospital, Dartford, Kent. At the age of thirty-three, his mother, Doris Dupree Richards, bore the only child of her marriage, which lasted twenty-seven years, for the express purpose of avoiding wartime work. As during most of Keith's childhood, his father, Bert Richards, who was thirty-six when his son was born, was absent for the event, having been called up to serve as an electrician in the army. "I don't remember World War Two at all," Keith said on the subject of being born in a crossfire hurricane, "nothing except the sirens. I can hear them today in the old movies on TV and the hair on the back of my neck goes right up and I get goose bumps. It's a reaction I picked up in the first eighteen months of my life . . . I was born with those sirens." He was also born to the sound of music. Doris would jump up and cut a few fast steps around the room whenever she heard a hot sound on the radio. She spent the majority of her pregnancy bopping to the popular violinist Stephane Grappelli and the big band sound of Billy Eckstine and the singer Ella Fitzgerald. Keith was in good musical company from the outset.

Dartford, a small industrial town just sixteen miles southeast of London, was on the German bombing corridor between the southeast coast and the capital, an area nicknamed "the Graveyard." When Keith was six months old, in June 1944, the Germans unleashed their unmanned V-1 airplanes from bases in France. An eighteen-foot-long metal cylinder with two small wings packed with explosives, the V-1, or "Doodlebug," could fly below the level detectable by radar and reach England in one hour. Once it had reached its destination, the Doodlebug would cut dead its motor, which sounded not unlike a washing machine, and drop out of the sky on its target. This was, in part, the brilliant invention of a man who would go on to become an architect of the U.S. space program and a major fan of the Rolling Stones, Wernher Von Braun. For eighty days it caused devastation to the British without cost to the Germans in bombers or pilots. Sixty thousand British civilians lost their lives as a result of German bombing raids during the Second World War. The inhabitants of London and "the Graveyard" (also known as "Doodlebug Alley") were the hardest hit. "It was," according to one of them, "as if we had a plague of giant hornets going over all the time. The noise was terrific. Shrapnel used to fall all around us like rain. Across the middle of Kent the noise of fighters, guns, and bombs was an almost continuous crazy chaos."

Before the two and a half months of daily V-1 raids ended, Keith and Doris were evacuated to Mansfield in Nottinghamshire, which was out of the direct line of fire, and also where Keith's father, Bert, was recuperating in an orthopedic hospital. Bert had been out of England only once and that was, as Keith later put it, "to get his leg blown up in the Anglo-American tour of Normandy." Shortly after their departure, Keith's cot in the Richardses' Dartford home at 33 Chastillian Road was destroyed by a Doodlebug.

"There was a great brick through the cot," his mother recalled. "People were killed in the house next door and the one opposite." Years later, Keith, who has a revisionist tendency to infuse his childhood years with the drama that characterized his adulthood, would tell a friend, "Hitler dumped one of his V-1s on my bed! He was after my ass, you know that! I was out shopping with my ma ... and no house was left when we returned. The rocket went straight into my room!"

The Richards house was damaged, but not in fact flattened, and shortly after the war the family returned to it and to what was left of Dartford. His first memory was being carried out into the garden, pointing up at an airplane, and his mother saying, "Don't worry, that's a Spitfire!"

Conditions in postwar Britain were grim. "To look back at all was to look back in anger—and in grief," wrote David Thomson in *England in the 20th Century*. "So men looked forward, damning the recent past perhaps too completely, and shunning so vehemently the errors of the past that they were apt to commit an entirely new set of errors of their own. Uppermost in their minds was the desire for fuller social justice, a lessening of class differences, and greater security and peace." The Richards family hovered uncomfortably on the borderline between the lower and middle classes in a society in which class was perhaps the chief controlling factor. Food was allocated on a strict system of rationing that severely limited anything considered luxurious, such as candy, as well as such basic staples as milk, orange juice, eggs, and meat. "I was eleven before I could buy candy whenever I wanted," Keith said of the rationing, which continued in Britain until 1954. By the time Keith was three or four years old, he was already inured to a household dominated by poverty. Bert Richards worked as a foreman in an electronics factory in Hammersmith, London. "He'd worked his way, been there ever since he was twenty-one or so," Keith recalled. "Always been very straitlaced, never got drunk, very controlled, very hung up. We just about made the rent. My dad worked his butt off in order to keep the rent paid and food for the family. The luxuries were very few. There wasn't a lot of chances for someone, the way I grew up."

The real problem of the Richards family was not, however, poverty so much as the differences between Keith's parents. Doris and Bert Richards were joined in a temperamental misalliance that by the time of Keith's appearance on the scene was based more on a tongue-biting tolerance and the pursuit of separate interests than on the mutual bonds of family life.

RICHARDS: "My great-grandfather's family on my father's side came up to London from Wales in the nineteenth century. My grandfather, my father's father, Ernest Richards, was a Londoner. He was the mayor of Walthamstow, a working-class borough in East London. They liked him so much they made my grandmother [Elizabeth] mayor after he died. They were solid socialists, helped organize the Labour party in England. The Red Banner and all that.

It wasn't cool to be a socialist back then. The Tories used to hire thugs to beat and assassinate people. It was the height of fame for the family. They were very puritan, very straight people. Both dead now. But then you come to Gus: my mother's father, Theodore Augustus Dupree. He was a complete freak. He used to have a dance band in the thirties, played sax, fiddle, and guitar. The funkiest old coot you could ever meet. My mother's family was very artistic, all musicians and actresses. My grandparents [Gus and his wife, Emily] had seven daughters and the house was filled with music and skits all the time. My grandfather was a saxophone player before he took up guitar. He got gassed in World War I and couldn't blow anymore. My grandmother used to play piano with my grandfather until one day I think she caught him playin' around with some other chick, and she never forgave him, and she refused ever to touch the piano again. I think she's even refused to fuck him since then. Very strange. That side of the family came to England from the Channel Islands. They were Huguenots, French Protestants who were driven out of France in the seventeenth century. So I come from a weird mixture. Very stern on one side, and very frivolous, gay, artistic on the other."

Bert was close to Keith during his early years, taking him to play football on nearby Dartford Heath, imbuing the son with admiration for his "athletic" father. But throughout the majority of his son's childhood, Bert Richards was the prototypically absent father. A small, shy man, he arose regularly at 5:00 A.M. to attend to his low-paying job as a foreman in an electrical plant in Hammersmith, London. From there he returned to his bomb-damaged house at 6:00 P.M., where he collapsed into an armchair in the lounge and remained there wrapped in an unapproachable silence until he retired to bed. Bert was not an unaffectionate man, but Keith saw that "it wasn't possible to be that close to him because he didn't know how to open himself up."

The dominant parent in Keith's formative years was undoubtedly his mother. Both Keith and Doris have described their relationship as close. Though 33 Chastillian Road lacked a telephone and a refrigerator, the Richards family possessed a radio, and the lively Doris sang along and danced to the popular American artists.

According to his mother, Keith sang with her to the radio and from the age of two had perfect pitch. Soon he was correcting her if she wandered sharp or flat. Coddled within the largely female world of the Duprees, Keith preferred to stay in and spend his time drawing and reading rather than playing football or fighting. English and history were his favorite subjects. In these pursuits he was encouraged by a small public library, only three blocks from his house.

"With six aunts, he was a bit spoiled, and he really was a sweet-looking kid," Mrs. Richards said. "Chubby and sturdy—and always with a red nose and a stark white face. But Keith was a bit of a mother's boy, really. He was such a crybaby. When he first went to school [at the age of five] I went to meet the teacher. She said he had been in a terrible state all day. I had to carry him home. He was frightened that maybe I wasn't coming to get him. Once I got him home he had a high temperature. When he started school he used to get panic-stricken if I wasn't there waiting for him when they all came out."

At the age of five, Keith also began to attend the Saturday matinee movies regularly, although usually alone. This first glimpse of a world beyond the confines of his family and the aftermath of the war offered a series of startling vistas to the sheltered boy. British culture in the postwar years was straddled by two giant influences: On the one hand there was the strangely glamorous horror of the Nazis, with their mad, evil faces and flash uniforms. On the other was the more tangible presence of America, represented by the 110 American army bases throughout Britain.

Although he would retain a lifelong fascination with the Nazis, in an attempt to dream up his own paradise he plunged into a love affair with the United States. Soon Keith had read every book on America he could put his hands on in the local library and it was said among his relatives that he knew more about his adopted country than his native one. When one of his aunts moved to California and sent him a map of the state, it became his most treasured possession.

Hollywood film stars, especially Roy Rogers and Errol Flynn, were much more vibrant than their English counterparts, such as John Mills and Richard Attenborough. Keith played World War II games in the machine-gun bunkers across from the marshes along the river Thames, and in comparison to these desolate slabs of concrete beneath England's slate-gray skies, he found the panoramas of sun-blasted badlands in American westerns exhilarating. Keith became, as he later told friends, "an incredible dreamer." He saw himself riding through the badlands of South Dakota wearing a white Stetson, strumming a guitar. But with his physical world in near ruins and his emotional world in a figurative cold war, Keith was growing up a fearful, timid child whose sensibilities, gone underground for self-protection, were being compressed into a dense internal core that would serve as a source of both protection and hostility all his life.

In September 1951, Keith left infants' school and began to attend Wentworth Primary: "They had just finished building a few new schools by the time we'd finished the first one so we went to a new one nearer to where we lived. That's where I met Mick, 'cause that's where he went too, Wentworth Primary School. He also lived around the corner from me, so we'd see each other on our tricycles and hang around here or there." Doris remembered meeting Mick at school, but noted that Keith never invited him home, something he rarely did with any playmate. "We weren't great friends, but we knew each other," recalled neighbor and fellow revisionist Michael Jagger, who was the same age and lived only two blocks away from Keith on Denver Road. "He used to dress in a cowboy outfit, with holsters and a hat, and he had these big ears that stuck out. I distinctly remember this conversation I had with Keith. I asked him what he wanted to do when he grew up. He said he wanted to be like Roy Rogers and play guitar."

One teacher at Wentworth Primary found Keith "a straightforward type of person. He laughs when he is happy, cries when he is sad. There is no problem in trying to find out what is going on inside his mind. He's open, frank." "He was a bright, attentive boy," recalled another, "especially responsive to words and language, who had a mischievous wit that made even the teachers laugh." He liked tennis and cricket. According to the writer Edward Luce, when Keith was seven he was given a saxophone "which (for a short time) he took everywhere with him. As the instrument was almost as big as he was, people felt sorry for him when he struggled along the street with it." But despite these occasional flashes of charm, Keith remained essentially a solitary, stay-at-home child. Small for his age and socially timorous, he tended to avoid peer interaction and to prefer the safe company of his aunts and mother. From the age of eight to thirteen, Keith accompanied his father every summer weekend to their tennis club, where he would watch him play and fill in as ball boy. Doris thought he was lonely. While living on Chastillian Road, he spent a lot of time alone in a tent he erected in the back garden, reading, drawing, and painting, which, as he saw it, became "my whole life." The family's annual summer holidays, two weeks camping on the Isle of Wight or at a holiday camp in Devon where he reluctantly donned costumes for the fancy dress balls, did little to broaden his social or cultural horizons.

Keith was, however, the beneficiary of a wider cultural heritage through the tastes and influence of his maternal grandfather, Gus Dupree. Where Bert Richards was the archetypal British stoic, lower-middle-class subdivision, Gus Dupree was that other much-loved stereotype, the working-class British eccentric. Gus and his family of seven daughters lived in London, and Keith and Doris would visit regularly for a few days at a time. Keith's first memory of London was "huge areas of rubble and grass growing."

"He was one of those cats who could always con what he wanted," Keith explained. "And from living with all these women, he had such a sense of humor, because with eight women in the house you either go crazy or laugh at it."

Gus introduced Keith to the British music hall humor of such popular stars of the day as Max Miller, Arthur English, and [Keith's favorite] Jimmy James, who epitomized the top-hatted, alcoholic, stage-door Johnny. Gus also took him to the films and Victoria Palace shows of the Crazy Gang, who would come to have a lasting influence on British humor, culminating in Monty Python, and, surprisingly, on Keith's vision of the longevity of the Rolling Stones. According to theater historian Stephen Dixon, "The Crazy Gang consisted of three very different and highly skilled double acts who got together every so often from the early thirties onwards but also continued to function successfully away from the gang . . . The style of comedy for which [the Crazy Gang] is best remembered [was] outrageous audience involvement in which indignity after indignity was heaped upon the paying customers."

In 1954 the Richards family, due a new house since the V-1 smashed Keith's crib in 1944, left 33 Chastillian Road for number 6 Spielman Road on the brand new Temple Hill Estate. England's struggle to rebuild its shattered cities resulted in a series of aesthetically and organically disastrous housing estates, offices, and schools. Poorly built, with few amenities for their inhabitants, these were distinctly repetitive, boxlike structures, more like cells than forms following function. Keith was whisked away from a world that, if drab, had at least become safe through habit, and was set adrift on a landscape that looked to him as alien as the moon.

The move to Spielman Road, where Keith would spend the balance of his childhood and teen years, was threatening and disorienting. Although he had acquired some of the habits of a loner, he missed the boys he had played with on Chastillian Road. "In 1954 my family moved to this fucking soul-destroying council estate at completely the other end of town," Keith explained. The Temple Hill Estate looked like "a disgusting concrete jungle of horrible new streets full of rows of semidetached houses." The fact that few people had moved in yet and most of the buildings were empty only made it more alien. "Everyone looked displaced," Keith thought. "Everybody was wondering what the fuck was going on. Until the middle fifties, everything was just the war. 'Why can't we ... ?' 'The war.' The war went on for years. They said it finished in '45. About '56 for me ... The feeling of how are we going to get out of this hole? We've won two wars and we're dying." Keith blamed his father for the move. "My dad really had no sense of taking a gamble on anything. And because he wouldn't take a chance on anything, he wouldn't try to get us out of there, which is what eventually did my mother in as far as he was concerned."

In 1955, only one year after the shock of the move, Keith confronted the eleven plus examination. This comprehensive exam, a scholastic manifestation of England's tendency to preserve rigid class distinctions until 1971, attempted to direct the eleven-year-old child toward his or her ultimate professional destiny, based on a score that admitted the student, in descending order of scholastic achievement, to either grammar school, technical college, or secondary modern school. The test only drove Keith further into himself. He had begun to resent school as much as he resented his new home. As he saw it, the eleven plus was "a big trauma, because this virtually dictates the rest of your life as far as the system goes." While Keith, who was neither an academic achiever nor a dunce, was sent to Dartford Technical College, his more privileged and driven schoolmate Mick Jagger, whom he would not see for six years, was sent to grammar school.

RICHARDS: "In those days there was an inverted snobbery. One was proud to come from the lowest part of town—and play the guitar too. Grammar school people were considered pansies, twerps."

Dartford Tech, on the other side of town from the Temple Hill Estate, required a long bus ride back and forth, and even at age eleven Keith was still nervous about going on his own. If he missed the bus he panicked because there wasn't another one, and he would often stop to visit Doris, now the manager of a local bakery, on his way to school. After a while he switched from taking the bus to riding his bike to school, but that too had its problems. Jagger recalled seeing Richards riding by on occasion, although Keith never stopped to acknowledge his old friend. He was usually pedaling as fast as he possibly could in an attempt to elude the gang of boys who had taken to chasing him home every day.

Perhaps because of the them-against-us attitude engendered by the war, English schoolboys judged each other largely on how well they fought and which gang they joined. This was made poignantly clear in the testimony of one boy in a BBC interview who explained: "I would rather get hurt and be put in the hospital than refuse to fight, whether the geezer is ten times bigger than me, because if I lose face in front of me mates, well, that is it, I mean. I have got no right to say anything." Keith Richards was born a Sagittarius. According to his chart, he could not "abide any form of restraint," was "highly strung," and was in "danger of nervous breakdowns if under any prolonged strain." Considering that he would eventually base his adult existence on belonging to a gang, it is curious that Keith "didn't want to know" about the idea. His mother thought it was just a combination of Richards shyness and Dupree arrogance. Regardless, gangs were the predominant mode of organization among English boys in the forties and fifties and Keith's attitude soon caused him a lot of aggravation.

The world of the English schoolboy was sexually charged, violent, and cruel. In the 1950s English teenagers were segregated by sex at school and took much longer to get acquainted sexually than their American counterparts. English boys went through their most sexually potent years reacting to each other rather than to the opposite sex. Consequently, any boy with the slightest hint of androgyny became the target for the pent-up sexual energy of his peers. Such was Keith's fate at Dartford Tech. "I got my ass kicked all over the place," he remembered. "I learned how to ride a punch."

Soon he was feigning illness and taking every opportunity to cut school in order to avoid fighting. He did, however, obey the schoolboy code of silence, and never said anything—that would have been a sign of softness Keith could not allow himself. Doris noticed him coming home with cuts and bruises on his knees and face, but was not sure whether Keith had cut himself in carpentry class or had been beaten up by one of the class bullies. Evidently willing to let him handle matters himself, she did not inquire.

During his second year at Dartford Tech the bicycle route to and from school took him through a desolate, gang-ridden area of town. The daily gauntlet became a nightmare of immense proportions that preyed on his mind day and night. It was at this dark moment of his childhood that a brilliant explosion occurred which turned his life, as Keith recalled it, "zoom! From black and white to glorious Technicolor."

2

Connection
1956–1961

Rock and roll hit England like Hiroshima!

KEITH RICHARDS, *from an interview with Charles Young, 1988*

If Keith's early childhood was lonely, his teen years teemed with the vital activity that would connect him to the music that was starting to pulse through England.

British people, and particularly the men who controlled the British music industry, maintained a great distrust of anything or anyone who was not from the British Isles, and what got their backs up more than anything was music from America. There was, for example, an English folk movement that shrilly insisted every folk song sung in England be a British song about a British subject. But in the 1950s American movies and American music seemed to overwhelm the English culture, leading as prophetic an observer as George Orwell to snap, "Evidently there are great numbers of English people who are partly Americanized in language and, one ought to add, in moral outlook." Consequently, a reactionary anti-American sentiment in the postwar British music establishment drove the growing number of rock and roll enthusiasts underground—into small clubs and dance halls. Often, the British record companies and music promoters supported local entertainers at the expense of superior international ones.

At this time the idea of being a pop singer was not especially appealing to British teenagers. The world of pop seemed impossibly distant and too American to be made over by the British. The strongest musical trend developing in England was folk music. Skiffle, a simple, folky, slowed-down precedent to rock and roll, developed with remarkable rapidity. The most significant influences, however, came from America. Elvis, Little Richard, and Jerry Lee

Lewis had the clubs and dance halls rocking. "The need for British teenagers to identify, to latch onto a musical culture that was more immediate and exciting than the 'light music' of the day was remarkable," wrote Iain Chambers in *Urban Rhythms*. "When Lonnie Donegan notched up his first hit with 'Rock Island Line' in January, 1956, he was launching his solo career, and the whole skiffle boom, with a song that had been recorded by the Weavers. The songs of Leadbelly and Woody Guthrie started to be sung in bars and clubs all over Britain, as a generation began to fantasize that they weren't sitting in Croydon or Rochdale, but were out there with Woody, waiting for a freight train, riding the rails with lonesome hoboes, gazing down on the Grand Coulee Dam, or peering out of the prison bars as the Midnight Special thundered past. Pop fashions often seem silly once they are gone, but the skiffle boom of the fifties was a great era for music, and of vital importance in the development of the British music scene." Keith was twelve when the first wave of rock and roll, spearheaded by Bill Haley, Elvis Presley, Jerry Lee Lewis, and Buddy Holly, hit England. Rationing had ended in 1954, and by 1956 English teen-agers were primed to erupt from the controlled depression of the postwar years. The film *Blackboard Jungle* sounded the clarion call. "I was rocking away, avoiding the bicycle chains and the razors in those dance halls," Keith remembered. "The English got crazy. They were really violent then, those cats. Those suits cost them a hundred fifty dollars, which was a lot of money. Jackets down to here. Waistcoats. Leopard-skin lapels. Amazing. It was really, 'Don't step on my blue suede shoes.' It was down to that." For the first time since moving to Spielman Road he felt that there was a reason to live. "We were very conscious we were in, like, a totally new era. Rock and roll changed the world. It reshaped the way people think. It was almost like A.D. and B.C. and 1956 was the year one."

The spirit of rock and roll appeared to have an immediate effect upon Keith, for at age thirteen the shy boy who had said that he didn't want to join any kind of clique became a star singer in the school choir and the extroverted leader of his Boy Scout patrol.

RICHARDS: "Believe it or not, it was the Beaver Patrol. That was a commando unit, that patrol, compared to what the Boy

Scouts were supposed to be about. I was in the Scouts for about two years, and I learned an awful lot about how to live out there in the woods. Certainly that's what I wanted to learn. But every year they had these huge gatherings of us Scouts from all over the country, like summer camp—a jamboree. And at one of them I smuggled in a couple bottles of whiskey. Soon afterwards there were a couple of fights that went down between us and some Yorkshire guys, and so I was under suspicion. All the fighting was found out after I went to slug one guy but hit the tent pole instead, and broke a bone in my hand! A few weeks later I had some dummo recruit come in, a kid just offensive to me in every way, and I punched him out, so I got thrown out. I couldn't imagine going on with it anyway, but I learned certain aspects of leadership from that."

In 1956, the choirmaster at Dartford Tech, Jake Clair, a man whom Keith has never forgotten, discovered that the twelve-year-old Richards possessed a beautiful soprano and recruited him for the school choir. At first Keith didn't think anything of it. "Religion only came for me as a singer in a choir," he said. "All it meant to me was you could get out of physics and chemistry." The Richardses were atheists. Doris didn't approve of vicars; she told Keith they were all dirty old men. However, Jake Clair worked hard on Keith and two other boys, Spike and Terry, who would become his friends and in a sense his first group. Soon Clair had the trio singing so well they started entering interschool competitions. On several occasions they ended up singing in London at the Royal Festival Hall, and, in an astonishing crowning achievement, walking up the aisle at Westminster Abbey singing the "Hallelujah" chorus from Handel's *Messiah* for the young new queen, Elizabeth II, whose coronation in 1953 had offered depressed England hope of a new Elizabethan age. He saw himself, Spike, and Terry as the biggest hoods in the school—they all wore tight jeans underneath their cassocks. Keith used this tough, arrogant confidence to push himself to the front of the stage. It was his "first taste of show biz."

Richards's rebellion extended to the school uniform, a cap with a badge on it, a blazer with a badge on it, and a pair of big gray flannel trousers, which he hated as much as his cassock. "I refused to go to and from school with those fucking clothes on. I used to wear two pairs of pants to school, a very tight pair and a very baggy pair which I would just put on as soon as I got near the school, because they would just send you home if you had tight pants on."

A dramatic change in Keith's life came when his voice broke at fourteen and he was, as he saw it, "thrown out of the choir." The choirmaster said, "You're the best soprano I've had in a long time, but it's gone now, your career is over." He got very resentful and, with all the force of his newly minted hormones, started "fucking up royally at school," talking in a block-hard, closed voice that neither asked for nor gave quarter and relished exclamations, such as "Bollocks!" and "Fuck off!" "I think that's when I stopped being a good boy," he said, "and started to be a yob." According to Bert Richards, "After that he became a loner, and I knew from very early on that nothing was going to hold him."

Keith continued to assert himself physically. Turning to his friend Spike, he asked for advice about how to handle the boys who were harassing him on his way home. "Spike told me the only thing to do so that I'd never get hassled again was the very next one who tried, just let him have it," Keith recalled. "So that was that. The nearest thing was this old bicycle chain that I just happened to have in my saddle bag."

RICHARDS: "I've never thought of myself as brave. When I'm confronted with a situation, there seems to be only one thing to do. And I think that maybe that's because I've never been a big guy. Because of my birthday, which is in December, I would always, through the weirdness of the English educational system, be virtually a year younger than the class I was in. When you are six, seven, eight, or nine, a year is a long time, so I was always the little guy."

Meanwhile, the relationship with his father became increasingly strained. Ever since they had moved to Spielman Road, as Doris saw it, Bert had acted as if Keith was in the way. For Bert there were no outlets in music, alcohol, laughter, or the company of others. The only pleasure he seemed to take was in sports. Consequently, the only approbation Keith could have received from Bert during his passage through puberty would have come from sports.

However, Keith showed signs of rebellion when he stopped accompanying Bert to his tennis club, and when Bert and Doris went to watch Keith play football they were greeted by the spectacle of their only son sprinting in the opposite direction as soon as he saw the ball coming toward him. Keith keenly disappointed his dad. "Sports were OK when I played ordinary football," Keith explained. "That went on until I was thirteen, and, though I wasn't really much good at it, I quite enjoyed the idea of getting out of the classroom into the open air. But when we switched over to rugby football . . . well, that was too much. Much too rough for me. I couldn't see much sense in crashing into one of your mates and maybe getting hurt, just for the sake of winning a match."

Richards thought going to school was "completely wrong for me." He hated the workshops where they taught him to make machinery and carpentry classes in which everything had to be measured to within a thousandth-of-an-inch accuracy.

RICHARDS: "When you think that kids—all they really want to do is learn, watch how it's done and try to figure out why and leave it at that. You're going to school to do something you wanna do, and they manage to turn the whole thing around and make you hate 'em. I don't know anyone at school who liked it. I wanted to get the fuck out of there. The older I got, the more I wanted to get out. I just knew I wasn't going to make it."

He didn't. He did three years, but at the end of the third year, which coincided with having to leave the choir, "I fucked up so much they made me do it again. Which was really just to humiliate me." He would stay in school for the next two years, but he never graduated.

It was at this juncture, according to Keith, that his grandfather Gus Dupree recognized something in him and started to develop it. "I had lost all formal contact with music and might have lost interest in it except for my grandfather Gus," Keith said. "Since I was three I used to think his guitar lived on top of the piano. In fact, it had always been kept in its case, but every time he knew I was coming over, he would for some reason take it out, polish it up, display it. He never pushed it on me. He never said, 'You should do this.' He would just leave it there as sort of an icon, just resting against the wall on top of the piano. He never forced it on me, he just let me discover how beautiful that guitar was."

By the time Keith was fourteen he was regularly visiting his grandfather. First he would give Keith a good meal and then Keith would stare at the guitar. Finally he plucked up the courage to ask Gus if he could hold it. "I guess he caught me at the point where I was transferring my interest from singing to playing. I don't know what he saw in me, but whatever it was, he created it." Gus showed him the rudiments of the instrument and encouraged him to play. Keith stumbled through a version of "Malagueña." "It must have been just appalling," Keith remembered. "But every time he would say, 'OK, OK!' and pretend he liked the way I played it. It was like, 'Wow, I'm turning my granddad on!' Which is an amazing way of teaching. I don't know what he saw in me. Actually, whatever it was, he created it in me."

Apart from offering Keith attention and encouragement, Gus also took him into the world of musicians. Richards remembered these visits vividly: After the lessons Gus would take Keith on tours of the music stores, in which he was well known and welcomed, on the Charing Cross Road. Sitting in the back of Ivor Marantz's guitar store for hours, smelling the varnish and the boiling glue, Keith was as enchanted as if he were in "some alchemist's laboratory."

By 1959 Keith was going out of his mind at Dartford Tech. In one final fit of disobedience, half an hour before the end of school on the final day of his fourth year, he went over the wall with some mates, hopped onto a motorcycle, and took off "in search of chicks!" He didn't find any. What he did find was a very irate headmaster greeting him with the school's final condemnation: That's it, you're expelled!

However, Keith was lucky. Once the headmaster had gotten over Keith's act of defiance, he had to admit that Richards's drawings showed talent and he arranged for Keith to get a place in that nearby citadel of learning, Sidcup Art College, situated between Dartford and London. As Keith remembered it, "When I went to art school in 1959, people were just starting to grow their hair and loosen up. You got in there on the favor of the headmaster. He says, 'You takin' anything? What you on?' And you're about fifteen or sixteen and you don't even know what the fuck they do in art school. You have this vague picture of naked ladies sittin' around. Drawing them . . . 'Well, I'll try that.'"

If timing is everything in rock and roll, Keith Richards walked into art school at the perfect moment. The legendary British music business that had fueled vaudeville and early Hollywood had never been healthier than it was in the late fifties. There were some fifteen hundred small clubs and dance halls scattered around the British Isles. Union rules made it hard for foreign entertainers to work in England, so a large number of English jazz bands, folk singers, and pop musicians of one kind or another packed them year-round. Selling tickets to their shows generated a nice piece of cash for the promoters. But by the late fifties there was so much money (everything being relative) to be made in the U.K. music biz that a viciously competitive scene had developed and the music itself suffered. British jazz, always something of a dubious notion anyway, was dying. The pop field was weak. Folk was strong but not showing signs of growth. As the decade neared its end people began to gather in groups, centring on the ban-the-bomb movement, but splitting into smaller factions such as the folk movement, the trad-jazz movement, and the poetry movement. Some of the characters in these movements ended up eking out an existence teaching at art schools. English music needed a new seedbed, and in the late fifties and early sixties it found one in the nation's art colleges, which became productive cultural institutions.

The students were also a lively group. The minimum age at which a child could leave school was raised to fifteen in the 1950s, and in order to keep a lot of youngsters out of the work force while the government tried to integrate the returning army into the economy, large numbers of middle-class and working-class children were encouraged to go on to some higher form of education. For the first time in their history, English children had their own social identity—as teenagers.

Between 1959 and 1962 John Lennon, Ray Davies, Pete

Townshend, Jimmy Page, Ron Wood, and David Bowie had just left, were in, or were about to enter British art schools. Almost every school contained at least one of the men who would go on to become the first generation of pop musicians. At Sidcup Keith met Dick Taylor, who would, after playing in the proto-Rolling Stones, go on to form another big English group in the sixties, the Pretty Things.

As soon as Keith got to art college he was so mesmerized by the music scene he discovered there that he seemed to completely forget about the naked ladies. Everybody was into Brigitte Bardot, jazz, American folk music, and black rhythm and blues. Duchamp, Picasso, the abstract expressionists, Charlie Parker, and Jack Kerouac were heroes. Diet pills were prevalent. When Keith Richards entered Sidcup he was an internally boisterous but externally quiet fifteen-year-old with no apparent prospects. When he left in 1962, he would be a guitarist in London's hottest band, the Rolling Stones.

Art school was completely right for Keith. Most of the teachers were, in his view, drunks, freaks, and potheads who didn't care what the kids did. And music was a major theme. The rich mixture of the jazz of Miles Davis, the folk music of Bert Jansch and John Renbourn, the blues of Muddy Waters, and the infant British rock they were spawning made for an exciting course of study. The dormant student found himself burning the candle at both ends. He started learning how to play a variety of different songs from the other students. "There were a lot of better guitar players at school than me," Keith remembered. "But then I started to get into where it had come from. Broonzy first. He and Josh White were considered to be the only living bluesmen still playing. I thought, 'That can't be right.'"

It wasn't long before Keith came across the sound that would become his calling card. The Chicago R&B music infected Keith and set a musical precedent for his career.

RICHARDS: "It was about 1958 that I first heard John Lee Hooker, at about the same time that I cottoned onto Muddy Waters and the other Chicago blues guys. I would have been around fifteen or sixteen, I was at art school, and records were passing around between aspiring guitar players and bluesmen—

bored sixteen-year-old white kids. I think it was the fact that we were searching out these records that brought us together—we found we weren't the only ones in the world that listened to that kind of music. I learned those John Lee Hooker chords, which are very strange shapes, and it immediately affected everything I did since."

As Albert Goldman pointed out in his book on John Lennon, the English rock stars who went to art school all developed in the same way, "by taking the raw material of rock and roll and subjecting it to the techniques that English art schools had inherited from the pre-war avant-garde." Richards would always say that he looked at music like painting, taking silence as his canvas. According to David Courts, a longtime friend of Keith's who went to art school shortly after he did, "A crucial thing you learn when you have to draw anything is that the big difference between looking at something and seeing it is looking at the juxtapositions of the lines rather than just seeing the overall image. You see the parts of what goes into the image. So you're not just looking at it—there's a much more powerful input of the image . . . where it's really going into the memory bank. With musicians, when they are listening to a bit of music, actually noting what the bass players are doing, in a very similar way they are not just looking at it, they are seeing what it is made up of."

A basically impractical lad when it came to money, Keith, of course, had no funds to buy the essentials for his new world. "I used to pose in front of the mirror at home. I was hopeful. The only thing I was lacking was a bit of bread to buy an instrument. But I got the moves off first, and I got the guitar later," he recalled. His ace in the hole was his live-in collaborator on anything musical, Doris. It was a snap to get her to help him buy his first guitar. She insisted she was willing to buy it only if he promised to take it seriously, but she was probably just as eager to acquire the instrument as Keith was. The two of them went out and got him an acoustic (a Rosetti) for seven pounds. Keith simultaneously talked Doris into lending him the money for a record player, and ended up with one of those old windup 78 RPM machines with needles that could scar a record for life.

Keith began practicing with the passion of a man who has fallen in love. He discovered that he could get the best acoustics sitting at the top of the stairs or standing in the bath, and he religiously took up his position every afternoon. "I probably learned more off records than anything else," he said. "I'd spend hours and hours on the same track—back again and back again. I'd learn the chords and how songs were put together. I practiced every spare minute— just because I wanted to be good at it. I loved doing it." He also spent a lot of time playing for Doris in the kitchen. "At the time he was getting into Elvis Presley records and he'd sit for hours and just play," she recalled. "He never went out. He'd say, 'I don't want to go out, all I want to do is practice.'" It was from this regime that the musical motor of the Rolling Stones—an appropriated, testosterone-crazed conflation of American rock, black rhythm and blues, and white country and western music—was initially derived, and with a vengeance. "Keith used to play country and western music beautifully, just like Johnny Cash," his mother remembered. "He'd sit on his own for hours listening to country and western records and then play them. His father thought I was encouraging him too much."

Bert wasn't too keen on his son's new passion. As soon as he got in he'd mutter, "Stop that bloody noise." But Doris felt differently. "With Keith I think it was a gift," she said. "Keith said he could play straightaway and didn't need tuition. He'd tell me, 'If you're taught it inhibits you and you play like you're taught and I want to play as I feel.'"

If Richards's home became his rehearsal studio, art school became his laboratory. It was now that he started to choose his own masters from among the vast assortment of artists from Woody Guthrie to Elmore James. Everybody in art school had acoustic guitars, so they leaned more toward doing Jack Elliot and Josh White imitations, but the sound of rock had already planted its tentacles deep inside Richards, and he was drawn to Chuck Berry.

"Chuck Berry has been called 'folk poet of the '50s,' 'the major figure of rock and roll' and 'the single most important name in the history of rock'," wrote Arnold Shaw in his insightful *The Rockin'*

'50s. "Musically, Berry came from the opposite direction of Presley to meet almost at the crossroad of rockabilly. As Presley was a Memphis white singing guttural, bluesy black, Berry was a St. Louis black singing country white. When he came to Chicago he was singing, in his words, 'Nat [King Cole] and [Billy] Eckstine with a little bit of Muddy [Waters].' In fact, his clean-cut enunciation occasionally caused him to be taken for white as Presley was taken for black."

RICHARDS: "To me, Chuck Berry's style is one of the loosest and most exciting to play, and more than anything else he has the knack for turning a twelve-bar progression into a commercial song. The songs were totally unknown and totally unexpected. I had to figure them out for myself. I used to absolutely slavishly copy Chuck Berry. I practiced every spare minute."

"Keith was *obsessed* with Chuck Berry," Taylor remembered. "Even in those days he could play most of Chuck's solos. Really, it was staggering because Keith had this natural talent which was way above what you'd expect from a lad who'd never played with a band."

Near the end of his first year at Sidcup, Keith bought an electric guitar in exchange for a pile of records. It was a really cheap F-hole guitar, but he bought a Japanese pickup and stuck it on and improved the sound, and got a little beat-up radio for an amplifier. His guitar soon started acting as a social passport. His relationship with Dick Taylor flourished. For Richards, Taylor was both a teacher and a conduit into acceptance. "Once I learned guitar, things like drawing and painting, which had been my whole life since I was a kid, just took second place," he recalled. "Rock and roll got me into being one of the boys."

"There was a lot of music being played at Sidcup," Taylor recounted, "and we'd go into the empty classrooms and fool around with our guitars. During school we'd play in the cloakroom, which was next to the principal's office. He'd come in and go absolutely spare. But they really didn't give a fuck."

One of his teachers, Brian Yates, said that if Keith had worked as hard on his art as on his guitar he could have been a brilliant student. "Dick Taylor was a more serious musician than Keith,"

Yates said, "and from what I heard of their music, his playing was superior to Keith's. He had better technique, and their sessions often consisted of Dick showing Keith how to do certain things on the guitar."

Unbeknownst to Keith, Dick was playing in a band with Mick Jagger at the same time he was playing with Keith. "Mick wanted to have a regular group, so he organized a little band with two kids from Dartford Grammar, Bob Beckwith, Alan Etherington, and me," Taylor recalled. "We called ourselves Little Boy Blue and the Blue Boys [Little Boy Blue was Sonny Boy Williamson's pseudonym] and we tried to play rhythm and blues the way we heard it on Chuck Berry records and other records of black blues performers. We were a group for about two years and we took turns practicing at one another's houses. Keith was a loner and always seemed to be quiet. He was an absolute lout, but a really nice lout. Keith really was the school's rocker. I sometimes played with him in one of those classrooms, but it never occurred to me that he'd be interested in playing with our group."

Not only was Richards developing as a rock and roll player, but he also began to create his own image, another essential ingredient in any rock star.

DICK TAYLOR: "When I think of Keith at college, I think of dustbins burning. We used to get these baths of silk-screen wash, throw them over the dustbins, and then throw on a match. The dustbins used to explode with a great *whoomph*. He was a real ted, just a hooligan, and I used to really like him for that. I remember once the art school took us on a trip to Heal's, the furniture shop, because we were studying graphic design and they wanted us to see well-designed furniture. And Keith was sitting on this really nice sofa worth hundreds of pounds and quite casually dropping his cigarette in it and burning a hole and not giving a monkey's ass about it. And going around ripping off ashtrays and lamps and things. In order to stay up late with our music and still get to Sidcup in the morning, Keith and I were on a pretty steady diet of pep pills, which not only kept us awake but gave us a lift. We took all kinds of things—pills girls took for menstruation, inhalers like Nostrilene, and other stuff. Opposite the college, there was this little park with an aviary that had a cockatoo in it. Keith used to feed it pills and watch it stagger around on its perch. If we were feeling bored, we'd go over and feed another upper to Cocky the cockatoo."

With all the requisite equipment now in place, Keith picked up his first live gigs through an art college connection: "There was another cat at art school called Michael Ross, who desperately wanted to be Gene Vincent. I was really hung up on Gene Vincent and I used to have to play guitar for this guy. He decided to form a country and western band—this is real amateur, Sanford Clark songs and a few Johnny Cash songs, 'Blue Moon Over Kentucky.' I was roped into this weirdo country band for a while."

The domestic performing scene had been left with two weak musical strains—trad jazz (white revivalist traditional jazz) and British pop, a diluted, commercially motivated spawn of Elvis Presley. Nineteen sixty-one saw the British success of such smooth crooners as Matt Monro and the continuing success of Pat Boone. Cliff Richard and the Shadows continued to dominate the British pop scene. Mr. Acker Bilk, the short, fat Dixielander, was the unlikely star of the trad-jazz scene. Keith found the popular trad dance, the stomp, in which "everybody tried to break the ceiling to a two-beat," very tame. "When Fabian and Bobby Vee and those early controlled idols came along," he said, "it seemed like rock and roll was on rationing. There was only one thing to do: start your own band."

3
Sing This All Together
1961–1963

The triangular flow of energy between Brian, Mick, and myself was the thing the Stones ran on. It was this conflict and interchange of allegiances which was the basic emotional engine of the Stones . . .

KEITH RICHARDS, *from an interview with Mandy Aftel, 1974*

One morning in the spring of 1961, during his second year at Sidcup, Keith was on his way to college when he spotted his old friend Mick Jagger, who had also developed an interest in music—although he had no idea of making it his profession. He was attending the London School of Economics, where he was studying to be a journalist or a diplomat. "In a small town like Dartford," Richards said, "if anybody's headed for London or any stop in between, then in Dartford station you're bound to meet." They met on their way to school, on the train. The first thing Keith noticed was the records Mick was carrying. He had *The Best of Muddy Waters* and Chuck Berry's *Rockin' at the Hops*. The records were unavailable in England at the time—Jagger had ordered them directly from Chess Records in Chicago. Keith was impressed. Their common interest in the blues led to an immediate friendship, and Keith invited Mick for tea that afternoon.

MICK JAGGER: "At that time in England the whole thing was meeting someone who shared your point of view. Not simply your musical point of view, but someone who was also your friend."

When Jagger arrived at Spielman Road later that day, Richards heard for the first time the artist who was to become his Rosetta stone. Although Berry had long been his musical model, Muddy Waters was now introduced as a spiritual guide: "He [Jagger] started playing me a few records here and there," Richards recalled, "but when I eventually got to hear Muddy Waters, it all fell into place for me. He was the thing I was looking for, the thing that pulled it all in for me. When I heard him I realized the connection between all the music I'd heard. He made it all explainable. He was like a codebook. I was incredibly inspired by him as a musician. He was more than a guitar player, more than a singer, more than a writer. It was all him. He was the hoochie-coochie man." At the end of their first session together, Jagger, who was still playing with Dick Taylor in Little Boy Blue and the Blue Boys, said, "Come and join the group."

The magnetism between these two disparate characters was instant and mutual. Though they shared geographical roots, their closeness also grew from the complementary nature of their temperamental differences. Whereas Keith was the genuine working-class article, wrapping a mantle of rebellion around the obdurate inner core of a loner, Mick was obedient to his parents' wishes that he pursue his education, and was goal oriented, the type of teenager whose endeavors have been sufficiently rewarded that they taught him the kind of enterprise that led him to write to Chicago for the records he wanted to hear.

The exchange of influences was personal as well as musical. At the time there was a subtle revolution in attitudes towards class distinctions among kids. Whereas before the war a working-class boy like Richards would not have been welcome in the home of a middle-class boy like Jagger, the breakdown in class values as a result of the war combined with rock and roll to break through the barrier. Although Keith felt he was moving up in the world by visiting Mick's house, Mick felt that they were instantly, intuitively close because they came from the same mental and geographical place. Keith, he said, was born his brother by different parents by accident.

"Compared to Keith, Mick's an extremely insecure person," commented one friend. "To be with Keith is great fun because he's relaxed and he's always having a good time. You could be sitting talking to Mick and if another person comes in the room he changes completely, becomes very closed off. I think this is because his mother never gave him the proper appreciation. She has no idea who her son is. Keith's mother always doted on him. His friends said that behind every great man is a doting mother."

"Keith never really got on with my husband," Doris recounted. Bert had tried to be strict, "but he kind of gave up on me," said Keith, "I think because of my mother, who had this tendency to give in to me, especially as I got older. I disappointed him incredibly. I turned out to be a Dupree instead of a Richards." When Keith refused to even consider getting a job, tension between father and son mounted. "I wasn't going to art school for three years just to work in some fucking place pushing a pencil around lettering until I graduated to using the T square."

In the musical classification system current in England—jazz and folk were for the serious musician or listener; pop and rock and roll, although quite different, were roped together under one condescending label, "popular"; and rhythm and blues was arcane— Little Boy Blue and the Blue Boys opted for the last, choosing their name because they wanted to be associated with the Chicago blues songs of the Chess records Jagger was collecting. But, as Keith later pointed out, they were also out-and-out rock and roll fans from the start: "Little Richard was the first guy that really drilled Mick and I into the wall with 'Good Golly, Miss Molly.'"

Dick Taylor, who was the base of the band's triangle and hung out with Keith and Mick a great deal, recalled, "Keith and Mick were always the ones. Mick always liked Keith's playing. As various people dropped out, were ousted, whatever, it was the combination of Keith and Mick that lasted. Mick really was behind Keith quite a lot."

In fact, the two hit it off so well they began acting, talking, and dressing alike, laying the foundations of both their music and images. "Mick liked Keith's laid-back quality, his tough stance, his obsession with the guitar," remembered Taylor, "and Keith was attracted to Mick's intelligence, his dramatic flair, his streak of ambition. Even then, I feel, they were experiencing the beginning rapport that would be so important to their future."

Nonetheless, Keith, seventeen, continued to accompany his parents on their annual summer vacation in Devon. In the summer of 1961 Mick joined them, and there Keith and Mick performed in public for the first time in a pub, as an Everly Brothers-style duo. As soon as Keith started playing, everyone fell silent. Afterward, as Keith stood at the bar and bathed in the glow of applause, his ambition and business sense emerged. "I wish," he whispered to his mother, "we had a manager."

In March 1962—by which time they had managed to acquire better equipment and had developed their sound—the Blue Boys read an ad in a music paper announcing the opening of an R&B club in London, and decided they had to attend. A week later, Keith found himself driving up to London. It was, he recalled, "my first trip into the big town just to have some fun."

Keith's ambitions took on new meaning the day in March 1962 that he and his Dartford gang walked into the dirty, damp basement of the Ealing Club and beheld England's first electric R&B band, Blues Incorporated, featuring Alexis Korner on guitar, Cyril Davies on harmonica, and Charlie Watts on drums, playing for some two hundred hard-core souls who constituted almost the entire British R&B community. To Richards, who was just eighteen, the visit was electrifying. The room was small and packed with a like minded group of misfits who wanted to play. Plus, Korner's band sounded amazingly hot.

Richards and Jagger attended the club regularly and became friendly with Korner, who ran it as well as playing there and who, at thirty-three, was considered the father of the English blues. They visited his home and met some of the other Ealing enthusiasts. The other men who frequented the club—Eric Clapton, Eric Burdon, Jack Bruce, Ginger Baker, Paul Jones, Ron Wood, Long John Baldry, Dave Davies, and Jeff Beck to name but a few—would go on to form, among other groups, the Yardbirds, the Kinks, the Animals, Manfred Mann, Cream, the Faces, and the Pretty Things. Suddenly, Keith realized, "I was in the union without a card!"

"We were the first generation that wasn't drafted," explained the musician Dave Clark. "The thing about getting drafted when you were eighteen was that that's the most important time of your life for freedom of expression. For so many, that period was cut short, and you were told what to do, where to go, who to be. Then you got out of the service, got married, and worked a job in a factory. That was it. Had the government not stopped the draft, there would have been no Dave Clark Five, no Beatles, no Stones."

It was Korner's habit to let anyone who had the courage get up on the bandstand and have a blow. Soon Jagger and Richards were ready to perform. Backed up by Alexis and Charlie Watts, they tore through Chuck Berry's "Around and Around." But when the number was over, Cyril Davies congratulated Jagger, then turned his back on Richards without a word. Like many of his contemporaries, Davies believed that the blues should only be played in a jazz form. Richards's rock and roll Chuck Berry style was an insult to his ears. Also, Korner and Davies were looking for a charismatic young singer to front them. They thought Jagger, who impressed them with the way he tossed his hair, might be their man.

Sitting in the audience, Dick Taylor had felt around him a general resentment of Richards's sound. "They didn't seem to understand what you were doing," he remonstrated.

"Fuck 'em," Keith replied. "They'll learn."

The rejection hurt, but Keith had become adept at shielding himself. What he found harder to handle was Jagger's growing relationship with Korner. Whenever they went to the club—and at first they always went together—Mick was always asked to sing, and he was soon regularly doing three numbers, whereas Keith was essentially asked not to play. And on the few occasions when he managed to creep on stage with Mick, Alexis would hustle him off after the first number.

RICHARDS: "I probably played really diabolically then, but I was still a better guitar player than Alexis ever was. I mean, I love Alexis and the kind of music he lays down, he's really good at it, but the kind of music we were getting into then—well, he wasn't one hundred percent behind it. He was tryin' to force somethin' that wasn't really in him. It got to the point where after three or four weeks we'd go down and Mick'd say, 'Let's do "Roll Over Beethoven"' and Alexis would suddenly plunge one of his metal thumb picks through his string and say, 'Oh, sorry, old chap, I think I've busted a string—you carry on,' because he knew he couldn't keep up with that kind of beat."

In May, Korner invited Jagger to join Blues Incorporated, and he accepted. Jagger later played down his commitment to Blues Incorporated, but his move into Korner's band signaled the end of the Blue Boys.

RICHARDS: "Mick would be invited on some of these deb dates that Alexis copped occasionally through, uh, kissing the hem of some lady-in-waiting, just because he was a bit of a freak and they loved the response . . . getting all these chinless wonders coming up, 'Ay seay, cheppie, can yew play "Moooon Rivah"?' to Alexis and Cyril Davies, can you imagine? But I never had any desire to join the band; that band drove me crazy, quite honestly. I thought it was just a very, very amateurish attempt by a lot of middle-aged men, ya know?"

ALEXIS KORNER: "Mick had a very different kind of showmanship, and he was different from the very beginning. One of the most interesting things about Mick as a personality, and it's a very delicate subject, is the enormous impact he has made on the world when it comes to male identification. He's basically helped to alter the whole idea of what it is to be male. He personally may not have done it, but his example has been a very, very strong one. I think you can imagine just how shocking Mick was in the early days when you consider that the kind of theatricality which Mick uses is not really the kind of mannerism which you easily identify with the male role in the theater. It's more of a kind of Marilyn Monroe thing. And, frankly, it was wildly embarrassing first time round with it.

"Mick was very, very involved in what he was doing, but he realized that one of the very few ways of retaining your sanity when you're that committed is with the ability to laugh at yourself. It's an English tradition to be disrespectful . . . we rather enjoy poking fun at things. And Mick simply took this a bit farther . . . finding the absurdity not only in the world but in his own life as well. He always had a rather nasty laugh, so he's carried it farther."

While Jagger was singing for Korner, a twenty-year-old from Cheltenham who also frequented the Ealing Club, Brian Jones, invited Keith to audition for a band he was putting together. Keith jammed with Brian and three other technically proficient Ealing enthusiasts, Ian Stewart on piano, Brian Knight on vocal and harmonica, and Geoff Bradford on guitar. The musical rapport between Jones and Richards was immediate, but the other players were less enthusiastic about "the Chuck Berry expert." When Richards brought Jagger and Taylor to a few sessions, Bradford and Knight started ragging Jones about hanging around with a bunch of rock and rollers. After one terrific row between Richards and Bradford, Keith was sure that Brian was going to kick him out of the band in favor of Geoff, who was a fine guitarist. Instead, Brian immediately turned on the complainers and delivered one of the bullish broadsides for which he was to become renowned: "Fuck off, you bunch of bastards!" he snarled. "You're a load of shit! I'm going to get it together with these guys." Bradford and Knight walked out to form a respected band, Blues by Six, leaving the new configuration of Jones, Stewart, Richards, Jagger, and Taylor.

That summer and fall, Brian Jones became the major catalyst in Keith's life. The exchange was mutual, for while Jones pressed records by T-Bone Walker and other jazz blues musicians on him, Richards turned Jones on to Chuck Berry and Jimmy Reed, pointing out that it was "all the same shit, man, and you can do it." Still, the way Keith saw it, Brian was miles ahead of him. Whereas he and Mick were still living at home with their moms and hadn't taken any steps toward turning professional, Jones had been expelled from school and had his own flat, a variety of jobs, and an illegitimate child.

RICHARDS: "I'd just met Brian, and I went round to his apartment—crash pad, actually, all he had in it was a chair, a record player, and a few records, one of which was [by] Robert Johnson. He put it on and it was just astounding stuff. When I first heard it, I said to Brian, 'Who's that?' 'Robert Johnson.' I said, 'Yeah, but who's the other guy playing with him?' Because I was hearing two guitars, and it took me a long time to realize he was actually doing it all by himself. You think you're getting a handle on the blues and then you hear Robert Johnson—some of the rhythms he's doing and playing at the same time, you think, 'This guy must have three brains!' To me he was like a comet or a meteor that came along and, BOOM, suddenly he raised the ante, suddenly you just had to aim that much higher.

"But Brian was also much more together. He was already out of school—he'd been kicked out of university and had a variety of jobs. He was already into living on his own and trying to find a pad for his old lady. Whereas Mick and I were still living at home. When we met Brian he was the only one around really interested in forming a band. Mick and I were just interested in playing."

Despite Jagger's continued doubts about making music his profession and Stewart's impression that Richards and Jagger "were a couple of Piccadilly panhandlers" and Jones was "a flake," there was a chemical spark among them that kept their twice-a-week rehearsals going through the summer. Keith had just about had it with Spielman Road, and the room in which they rehearsed, a bare storeroom above a pub in London's Soho, became his spiritual home. Attending the London School of Economics continued to be Jagger's first priority and singing with Korner his second, but Richards had reignited their musical partnership by pulling Mick into Brian's loosely formed band.

RICHARDS: "We were rehearsing three times a week—no gigging, we didn't dare. We'd go down to Alexis's club once a week to see what they were doing. 'It's coming,' we'd tell 'em. 'We'll be gigging soon.'"

Brian, Keith, and Mick had quite different intellects. The three together would add up to a rounded, comprehensive team musically and socially, but Jones was to drive a wedge between Richards and Jagger deeper than Korner had.

ALEXIS KORNER: "Because of Brian's particular insecurity, he was very heavy on everyone else's insecurities. Obviously I dug Brian, but he could be very mean, just plain evil, like twisting words and finding a way of saying something that would hurt without it sounding like it at the time. Brian made sure that if he was being ironic—even if the words sounded strange—you knew."

RICHARDS: "We were really a team, and there were periods when we had a ball together. But there was always this incredible conflict between Brian, Mick, and myself where it was imbalanced in one way or another. There was always something between Brian, Mick, and myself that didn't quite make it somewhere. It started out with Brian and I being more friendly because we were completely dedicated to the idea of getting this band together. Also, Brian and I were the sort of people they were glad to kick out.

They'd say. 'You're nothin' but bums, you're gonna end up on skid row.'"

Jagger soon attracted Jones's attention by seducing his girlfriend. At first this breach of trust caused an enormous upheaval. The girl left and Brian lost the flat she had been paying for. The upshot was that Brian became close to Mick. It was then that Keith first noticed how Brian would switch from one friend to another, unable to relate to two people equally at the same time. "Maybe it was in the stars," Keith said. "He was a Pisces. I'm Sagittarius and Mick's Leo. Maybe those three can't ever connect completely all together at the same time for very long."

Competition became the mother of their invention. The combination of Brian's need to divide and dominate and Jagger's lack of commitment to the band produced a persistent fear that they were on the verge of breaking up. Far from sapping the group's energy, this fear actually lent their music much of its edge. When not destructive, it proved inspirational. It made them even more hostile and arrogant, fragmented their music, and created an image of rejection that would represent a definitive departure from anything that had come before them in British culture. The blatant sexuality of Jagger and Jones and the rebel attitude of Richards would soon strike fear in the hearts of middle-class parents everywhere. As the British jazz singer and writer George Melly noted, they "felt themselves part of a crusade. They were going to preach the blues and they were going to live the blues too."

"I had not turned out to be anything like what my dad wanted," Keith said. "He must have been horrified to see what a thug he'd produced in me. The time came when I had to fly the coop. It was either him or me: 'I'm leavin'! I gotta go!'" In October 1962, Richards, Jagger, and Jones moved into a dingy second-floor flat in a three-story house, 102 Edith Grove, just off the King's Road in West London's World's End.

In order to cover the rent they had to take in three boarders—two London School of Economics students described by Keith as "the straightest people you've ever seen in your life" and a former best friend of Jones's, Richard Hattrell.

The two-room flat, with a bathtub in the kitchen and a common toilet on the next landing, soon became the prototype of a hippie crash pad. "It was filthy!" Keith said. "It was disgusting! Mold growing on the walls." Individually christened balls of spit and snot stuck to the walls. There were smoke smudges on the ceilings from candles. Filthy clothes, half-eaten food, stubbed-out cigarettes, broken crockery, guitars, and amplifier wires covered the floor. The smell was appalling.

RICHARDS: "The top floor was two guys trainin' to be school-teachers. They used to throw little bottle parties up there, all dancing around to Duke Ellington. Downstairs was living four old student-teacher tarts from Sheffield, Nottingham, and Liverpool! 'Allo, dahlin'. 'Ow are ya? All right?' They got roped into doing the cleaning and occasionally got knocked off for their trouble. Real old boots they were. They used to sort of nurse people and keep us together when we really got out of it, but they had no sympathy for what was going on on our floor."

Such a living arrangement—six boys in two rooms—was not that uncommon among students. It might have been OK had it not been for Jones. He lifted money from the students whenever he wanted to buy drink or cigarettes, rehearsed at all hours, and let Keith, who had no money to contribute, stay there full-time as his guest.

DORIS RICHARDS: "I was surprised at Keith's sudden departure. I used to do everything for him and I was afraid that when he left home he would be helplessly lost. I worried about Keith because of that awful place in Edith Grove. They'd stay in bed all day because they had no money for the heater, food, or anything. They'd say, 'Do have a cup of tea.' They'd look for the tea, then spend a lot more time hunting round until they could find a cup. If you got one with a handle on it you were lucky. I just marveled at it all. How these boys could leave home and live in an indescribable place like this was beyond me. I offered to wash their shirts. I soon wished I hadn't. They'd send about a dozen to me and it looked as if they'd been strewn all over the garden during a rainstorm. If someone had thrown a bomb in the place, it couldn't possibly have been any worse."

Shortly after Keith left home, Doris and Bert broke up; Keith would not see his father again for twenty years. His mother took a second husband, Bill Richards (Richards is a common name in that part of England), whom Keith resented. In the wake of his sudden separation from his parents, and in the context of the perverse ties forming between Jagger and Jones, Keith's commitment to music intensified. "Even though the first wind had gone out of rock and roll," he said, "we were not about to let this motherfucker go. I'm only eighteen, and already people ain't hearin' this music anymore, and it had lit up my life! Now, one way or another, I had to keep the flame alive." But Keith's attachment to his group of friends was primarily emotional. When Keith left his mother and took up with Brian and Mick, he was replacing one dysfunctional family with another. For the isolation of his upbringing, this new family was to substitute a new, selective isolation among a few initiated peers. Though the membership of this private club would change a little over the years, the habit of interacting with a limited, carefully culled group would last the rest of his life.

After considering many names, Brian decided to call their group the Rolling Stones in homage to Muddy Waters's song "Rolling Stone." Although the name was derided by many, who thought it sounded like a circus act, it emphasized their commitment to the emotional music. Waters explained: "When I sing the blues, when I'm singing the real blues, I'm singing what I feel. When I sing the blues it comes from the heart, from right here in your soul, an' if you singing what you really feel it come out all over. It ain't just what you saying, it pours out of you. Sweat runnin' down your face."

Edith Grove, where they lived from October 1962 to September 1963, was the womb from which the Rolling Stones' music and way of life was born. From October through December, Richards and Jones honed the group's sound listening to records, talking about the music, and trying to play it for upwards of eight hours a day. This was harder work than it might sound, because they were studying some of the greatest guitar players of the century—Robert Johnson, Muddy Waters, Elmore James, Chuck Berry—and unbeknownst to them, many of these men had tuned their instruments in ways neither Brian nor Keith knew about. For instance, Keith discovered from the twenty-four-year-old Glaswegian Ian (Stu) Stewart that the pianist behind Berry, Johnnie Johnson, had a great influence on Chuck, and that many of Berry's songs were written in piano chords. Or, as Berry himself would later insist to Richards, "Several of my songs were accelerated on record, the tape velocity upping the key from A to C."

RICHARDS: "Brian and I worked on guitar together intensely, just trying to figure out how in the hell these guys from Chicago got this beautiful sound and interplay. To me, one guitar by itself is not that interesting. It's how one guy reacts to another that I find far more interesting to listen to than even Segovia. The Rolling Stones are basically a two-guitar band. That's how we started off. And the whole secret, if there is any secret behind the sound of the Rolling Stones, is the way we work two guitars together. We used to sit around and play guitar all the time. It was the cheapest way to keep warm. And that went on for ages. For the first six months the Rolling Stones never actually played a gig. They just rehearsed and rehearsed."

IAN STEWART: "They were young enough to be influenced in the heart rather than the head. What they worked out was a synchronization of playing that the guitarists in the other bands didn't have. Instead of one guitar playing lead and the other playing rhythm guitar underneath him, which was the usual way, Keith and Brian were more of a piece, alternating as leads, taking turns soloing, blending."

In order to heat the place, they had to stuff coins into the gas meter. As often as not, Keith and Brian were reduced to staying in bed all day to keep warm. Brian figured so prominently in Keith's life that no picture of Richards could have been composed without an answering shot of his soul mate. They'd spend hours making faces at each other. "Brian was always best at that," said Keith. "There was a particularly horrible one he could do by pulling his face down at the corners and sticking his fingers up his nostrils. He called it 'doing a nanker.'"

IAN STEWART: "During this period, Keith and Brian developed a relationship as close as their guitar playing, and I sensed that Jagger was beginning to feel left out, jealous, resentful of Brian.

Mick didn't have much to contribute, since his guitar playing and his attempts at the harmonica were pretty feeble, but he had a lot of ambition and vanity and he was damn smart, and I could see him looking at Brian in a way that was a little bit menacing. I could sense back then the beginning of Mick's desire to distance Keith from Brian. When people live together all the bloody time they begin to develop virtually their own language and you're never sure whether you're getting through to them or whether they mean what they say or whether they're laughing at you all the fucking time. I used to think they were fucking insane at times."

When you put emotional cripples together, you often get powerful results.

RICHARDS: "There was this period of about two months in '62 where Mick was doing quite a few gigs with Blues Incorporated to the exclusion of rehearsals with the embryonic Rolling Stones. Brian particularly was feeling that Mick was just after as much bread as he could get—uh, two pound ten a week—and because he [Brian] was a stickler for rehearsals he felt that to a certain extent Mick was deserting us—which was, to any rational person, rather silly because the Stones weren't working at all.

"Brian and I had decided that this rhythm and blues thing was an absolute flop. We weren't going to get away with it. We were going to do an Everly Brothers thing and we spent three or four days in the kitchen rehearsing these terrible songs. Then we decided we'd write a song too. The song sounded like a 1920s musical—just the weirdest kind of song. Brian was utterly impossible to write a song with. He would dominate anything he was into—there was no way you could suggest anything. Then Brian wouldn't make a decision about chord changes, where the changes should go. And he said that Mick had to sing it. Mick just couldn't get around it. At the time Mick could only sing a twelve-bar blues."

The chaotic setup, the pressure, the competition inevitably led to explosive emotional outbursts. Richard Hattrell, who had originally been lured into the scene by Brian with an invitation to join the band but was rapidly reduced to roadie, was the first victim.

RICHARDS: "Dick was like a complete puppy to Brian. The guy

was about five foot three, very fat, and wore thick spectacles, and he would do anything for Brian. Brian, Dick, and me would walk to a Wimpy Bar to eat and Brian would make Dick walk ten yards behind. It was freezing cold, the worst winter in a hundred years, and Brian would say, 'Give me your overcoat,' and he gave Brian his army overcoat. 'Give Keith the sweater,' so I put the sweater on. 'Now you walk twenty yards behind us.' And off we'd walk to the local hamburger place. Then Brian would say, 'No, you can't come in, give us two quid. Now wait here.' This cat would stand outside the hamburger joint while we went inside and ate."

RICHARD HATTRELL: "What really compounded our troubles was the severity of that winter. It was a pisser—paralyzing amounts of snow, the temperatures constantly below zero that froze all the water pipes in our flat, thereby cutting off the sink and toilet. Keith's responsibility was getting the coins to feed the electric heater. He wasn't very conscientious, and we'd usually run out of coins and really freeze. We were really like some kind of outlaw band out of Dickens."

RICHARDS: "We had to become petty pilferers. We'd go to the pads where we knew there'd be parties on and await the opportunity to examine the inside of the fridge. That was a high spot, because it meant we could get a drink or two, or at least a snack. If no one was looking we'd try to lift a couple of eggs or something, then hide them away so we could get away with them without them breaking. Or we'd walk in sayin', 'Hello, how nice, we'll help you clean up,' and we'd steal all the bottles and whatever food we could find lying around and run for it."

Richards always maintained that nothing got to him because he didn't give a fuck about anything, but he had a much more complex character than he liked to pretend. According to a handwriting analysis conducted by the International Psychology Service in Paris in 1964, he was a practical, cheerful, nervous person with a fanciful imagination who was sensitive and artistic and who lived spontaneously. His weakness came from being dependent on collaboration. "He lacks confidence and tends to be easily influenced," the analysis read. "He attaches too much importance to other people's opinions. He's lively and non-conformist and lives in a world of fantasy but is anxious and tends to shy away from reality. He feels secure in a group and is borne along by it. His identification with the group protects him."

Keith had not seemed naturally aggressive as a child, but under the tutelage of Brian Jones, the young man who liked to feed drugs to a cockatoo for fun, was showing his sadistic streak. He now joined Jones in the constant ragging of Hattrell, whom they finally got rid of in an act of brutality that would become commonplace as their relationship evolved.

RICHARDS: "It ended up with us stripping him off and trying to electrocute him. That was the night he disappeared. It was snowing outside. We came back to the pad and he was in Brian's bed. Brian for some reason got very annoyed that he was in his bed asleep. We had all these cables lyin' around and Brian pulled out this wire: 'This end is plugged in, baby, and I'm coming after you.' Brian ran after him with this long piece of wire cable that's attached to this amplifier, electric sparks, chasing around the room, and he ran down the stairs out into the street with nothing on, screaming, 'Don't go up there, they're trying to electrocute me.'"

The sexual electricity among Brian, Keith, and Mick fueled the triangular flow of energy. Brian was the most promiscuous, not to say profligate, having already fathered two children. In his teens Jagger had been seduced by a slightly older girl, and he had been sexually active since. Richards saw himself as the kind of boy girls stuck their tongues out at as he was being thrown out of a club. He had never had a girlfriend. As they continued to weave the web of love and hate that would dominate their lives in the years to come, on the coldest nights, for warmth, Brian, Keith, and Mick slept in the same bed (without any sexual activities taking place). "Space was so limited," Jones claimed, "that we even had to regulate our breathing."

Living in such close quarters and operating defiantly outside the status quo, the surviving members of the Edith Grove commune developed relations along the lines described by the sociologist Lionel Tiger in his seminal book *Men in Groups*: "In certain groups, such as of adolescents, and for certain activities, such as hunting, fishing, or warfare, social process is 'charismatic' rather than stratified. This is to say, it tends towards equality, lack of systemized allocation of privilege, rank, etc., and towards a free-flowing camaraderie which—significantly from our point of view here—is seen to have a 'homosexual tinge'—though not necessarily erotic. ('Homosexual' refers to male camaraderie and esprit rather than to specifically erotic contacts)."

The Rolling Stones' creative method was the consumption and rejection of people as fuel for their work. Keith was always attracted to unusual, antisocial underdogs. "The crazy chemistry of the people was what kept us going," he said. They needed each other—as scapegoats, rivals, catalysts, fellow travelers, and friends. Now that Hattrell was gone they needed another catalyst. A young printer named Jimmy Phelge, who moved in shortly thereafter, opened up another dimension in the Richards-Jones-Jagger ménage.

RICHARDS: "Phelge was the sort of guy who would meet you on the stairs of your slum with his streaked Y-fronts on his head and nothing else, and he'd say, 'This is Phelge—welcome home. Unfortunately I haven't made enough money this week to help chip in with the rent, so instead I'll entertain you and be as disgusting as possible for the whole week.' And he'd be spitting at you. It wasn't a thing to get mad about. Covered in spit, you'd collapse laughing."

Sometimes Phelge would nail up the door to the toilet while a visitor was in it, then lower a tape recorder through the window to capture the moment when his victim couldn't get the door open.

RICHARDS: "Every time someone would come into the bog I'd switch the tape recorder on and go around to the bog door and knock, and they'd say, 'Wait a minute,' and then you'd get these conversations going through the door, followed at the end by the flushing of the toilet, which sounded on tape like applause, and then the next person would come in. It's incredible what people say while they're taking a crap. It was the funniest thing. You'd get people muttering, 'Whoa, I need that! Ooooooh! Just made it! Mmmmmm! Larvely!'"

If Richards's reaction to Phelge was to pick up his experiments with sound and apply them to his own ribald humor, which was of the toilet variety so prevalent among the British, Jagger's reaction was even more revealing.

RICHARDS: "Phelge was going through this incredible scene at the time—everybody went through it in a way. Mick went through his first camp period. He started wandering around the house in a blue linen housecoat, wavin' his hands everywhere—'Oh! Don't!'—a real King's Road queen for about six months. Brian and I immediately went enormously butch, sort of laughing at Mick. That switching around confusion of roles that still goes on. Brian and I used to kid the piss out of him. But Mick stayed on that queen kick for about six months."

The emergence of Jagger's camp side was to have two vital results. On the one hand, he would develop the androgynous, homoerotic element of his personality as a performer and marry his imitation of the King's Road queen to his version of a black rhythm and blues singer. On the other hand, it would bring him to a crossroads in his relationship with Jones. No one can really know what happened sexually between Jones and Jagger at Edith Grove, since the one is dead and the other chooses not to remember, but, according to Anita Pallenberg, Jones would later insist that there was a brief sexual liaison between them during this time. Whether Jagger really did have a sexual liaison with Jones, or whether Jones was winding her up, we shall never know. Pallenberg, who would go on to have relationships not only with Jones but also with Jagger and Richards, and who is arguably the most qualified outsider to judge the dynamic among them, believes that this was the event that triggered Jones's eventual banishment from the group. According to her, Brian upset the triangle's balance by going to bed with Jagger.

ANITA PALLENBERG: "I only know that Brian did break up a lot of things by actually going to bed with Mick. And I think Mick always resented him for having fallen for it. In later years there have always been rumors about Mick being gay, but then it was as if Brian violated Mick's privacy by revealing his weak side. So that was probably why he resented him.

"Brian was always a perfectionist in the way he was talking, choosing his words. He did want to catch your attention when he was speaking, to captivate you. Then he had the way he moved, and his hair, which was captivating, and I'm sure the Stones fell for it. Keith in a cynical way, maybe. Mick, he fell for it. Brian broke that barrier and Mick never really forgave him for it. Brian was so far ahead of them you wouldn't believe it. Here are Mick and Keith trying to learn how to be sex objects—they were still schoolboys, and Brian already had two illegitimate children. Also, Brian was the one who did the hustling, getting people together and believing it, I mean really knowing it, unlike Mick, who couldn't make up his mind whether he wanted to be an accountant. Brian was saying in the earlier days, 'Look, it's going to happen!' At the same time he had it in his hands so that he could control it, so he used to control it. And when they found out he was right, that they did make it, instead of appreciating what he did, they resented it. And that's when Brian's doom really started. They had a vendetta, Mick and Keith, a real vendetta."

Speculation on the homoerotic bonding at the core of the Rolling Stones was not confined to the Jagger-Jones duo. The Beatles became friendly with the Stones in the spring of 1963. Paul McCartney told a friend that the first time John Lennon went around to see Mick and Keith at Edith Grove, they were in bed together (but were not actually doing anything). John reported back: "I'm not sure about those two, you know. What d'you think?" Paul said they were never sure. He also said that the first time Mick and Keith came backstage to see them they couldn't believe that the Beatles were wearing stage makeup. It really freaked them out. The next time they saw the Stones play, Mick was all made up like a transvestite.

Despite the strange closeness, their essential character differences were already evident.

ALEXIS KORNER: "Of Brian, Mick, and Keith, Keith was the most open. Brian was interested in portraying himself as any of the fantasies he had of himself. Mick was always very deliberate about the way he presented himself. Keith was the least interested in portraying himself as something other than he was. Keith is a man of belief and Mick is a man of fear. Mick works on fear, that driving thing, 'What if I fuck up?' It is a lot easier to be like Keith than it is to be like Mick."

Though Jones was still the undisputed leader of the Rolling

Stones, as Jagger turned on him Richards began to doubt him too, admitting that although Jones was brilliant when he had an instrument in his hands, he was actually something of a flake. Brian was not above stealing from Keith when he was asleep. "He was such a beautiful cat in one way," Richards said, "and such an asshole in another." Introducing him to fellow guitarist Eric Clapton that winter, Keith exclaimed, "This is Brian, he's the schizophrenic!"

When the Stones first started trying to play in London clubs in the winter of 1962, they met with an almost blanket rejection from the white revivalist traditional jazz establishment. According to the British writer Mick Farren, "The old jazzers, who both disliked the Stones' music, appearance, and attitude and at the same time felt threatened by them, did everything they could to block their progress. The influence of this old guard extended deep into both the press and the music business." Snapped one uptight promoter, "Forget them, by the time we're finished with that little lot they won't get a job in any club in England."

As Richards and Jagger's partnership strengthened, they developed a pattern of latching onto the most powerful person on the scene, soaking up his influences, and then discarding him. When they first went to the Ealing Club they looked up to Alexis Korner as "the Guvnor." Within three weeks they were laughing at him. The two of them latched onto Brian Jones as the-greatest-person-they-had-ever-met, but a year later they were taking the piss out of him. Jimmy Phelge's humor had held sway at Edith Grove for months, but now they had grown tired of him.

The club owner Harold Pendleton reluctantly allowed the Stones to play the Thursday night intermission for Cyril Davies at London's leading venue, the Marquee, but they soon lost this coveted gig. Davies, a notorious drinking man from the old school, turned upon them viciously one night in front of the audience and told them they were bloody awful and to fuck off. When the astonished Keith, who had developed a real affection for Cyril, saw how much Harold Pendleton was enjoying the group's public humiliation, he snatched up his guitar and swung it at the club owner's head in an act that would characterize his response to criticism of his band. Luckily he missed, but the Rolling Stones were banished from playing the most influential club in London for some time to come. In the freezing winter of 1962, there were periods of real despair at Edith Grove.

RICHARDS: "In a way, when we started the band, there was not much prospect of even making the band pay for itself. It might have lasted six days—we never knew from one week to another. If we couldn't come up with the rent for the joint once in a while, we would have been forced to dissipate or sell off the equipment, and that might have been the end of the band. This pad was getting so screwed up, for like six months we used the kitchen to play in, just rehearse in, because it was cold, and slowly the place got filthy and started to smell, so we bolted the doors and locked them all up, and the kitchen was condemned. Then one night I got back rather worse for wear from drink and found I was locked out, so I smashed a window in order to get in. That woke Phelge, Mick, and Brian and also let in a cloud of London smog. The window never got mended and the London weather continued to seep in the rest of the time we were there. I was also responsible for breaking the only piece of functional apparatus in the place—Brian's trusty old record player. One night I plugged the leads into the mains through a damp socket and the whole contraption exploded in my face. I didn't dare to tell him. I just said it had packed up like everything else in that damned hovel."

But their real problem was not having a decent drummer or bass player. In December they replaced Dick Taylor with Bill Wyman. At first Wyman seemed to be an odd choice.

BILL WYMAN: "They didn't like me, but I had a good amplifier, and they were badly in need of amplifiers at that time! So they kept me on."

"He was a real London Ernie," Richards said. "Brylcreemed hair and eleven-inch cuffs on his pants and huge blue suede shoes with rubber soles." But after a dubious start Bill started to play a strong, swinging bass line that Keith felt he could walk on and things began to pick up. In January 1963, Charlie Watts joined them.

RICHARDS: "The R&B thing started to blossom. Charlie was in the other band playing with us on the bill in a club. He'd left

Korner and was with the same cats Brian had said 'Fuck off' to about six months before, Blues by Six. We did our set and Charlie was knocked out by it. 'You're great, man,' he says, 'but you need a fucking good drummer.' So we said, 'Charlie, we can't afford you, man,' because Charlie used to love playing but he always had to do it for some economic reasons."

CHARLIE WATTS: "They were working a lot of dates without getting paid or even worrying about it. And there was me earning a pretty comfortable living, which obviously was going to nose-dive if I got involved with the Rolling Stones. But I got to think about it. I liked their spirit and I was getting very involved with R&B. So I said, OK, yes, I'd join. Lots of my friends thought I'd gone raving mad."

Watts was a curious mixture of fashion plate and serious jazz devotee from the old school. The two people in the world he would have most loved to be were Stravinsky and Fred Astaire, yet as a drummer he aspired to be Art Blakey, Max Roach, or Elvin Jones, who, as a member of the John Coltrane band, revolutionized jazz drumming in the sixties. "When I play I might try to do something like Elvin Jones," he said. "You'd never recognize it, but I've sat there with the Stones and imagined I was him." Most rock drummers played as hard as they could. Watts was a purist, flicking his snare stick with his wrist, not hitting the drums hard at all. He even played the bass drum with his relaxed heel on the floor.

RICHARDS: "I'm probably the most drummer-influenced guitarist around. There's an undefinable thing about drummers. A lot of cats have good hands, and they might be making all the right moves, and playing incredible paradiddles and shit, but it's like the playing just keeps going down the runway and never takes off. Whereas with Charlie, you suddenly realize that you're floating a few inches above the ground."

Though Watts was a superb musician, the Rolling Stones did not follow the drummer's lead the way most rock groups do.

BILL WYMAN: "Every rock and roll band follows the drummer. If the drummer slows down, the band slows down with him or speeds up when he does. That's just the way it works—except for our band. Our band does not follow the drummer; our drummer follows the rhythm guitarist, who is Keith Richards. It's probably a matter of personality. Keith is a very confident and stubborn player. Immediately you've got something like a hundredth-of-a-second delay between the guitar and Charlie's lovely drumming, and that will change the sound completely. That's why people find it hard to copy us. Now I'm not putting Charlie down in any way for doing this, but on stage you have to follow Keith. You have no way of not following him. The tune is basically worked out, but it changes all the time, it's very loose. So with Charlie following Keith, you have that very minute delay. When you actually hear that it seems just to pulse. You know it's right because we're all making stops and starts and it's in time—but it isn't as well. The net result is that loose type of pulse that goes down between Keith, Charlie, and me. That's what we think the reason is for our sound."

Charlie entered the Stones' world more intimately than Bill did. He started spending weeks at a time at Edith Grove, listening to Brian and Keith play and soaking up their attitudes and influences. He admired Keith's style, characterizing him as "the classic naughty schoolboy who hated the head boy," and loved him for it.

RICHARDS: "Most people don't know what a band is. The musicians are there to contribute to the band's sound. The band isn't there for showing off solos or egos. A lick on a record—it doesn't matter who played it. All that matters is how it fits. The chemistry, to work together like that, has to be there. You have to work on it, figure out what to do with it. But basically it's not an intellectual thing you can think up and just put there. It has to be there. You have to find it. Suddenly everybody knows just what they've gotta do. And those are the magic moments. Suddenly you sort of feel like you're ten feet tall and you're not touching the ground. That's what I've always lived for—that moment when a band just clicks in. You may go eighteen hours without even taking a pee, it's just such tremendous fun. Like, 'Yeah, man! That's it, man!' It might not even be, you know? But at that time, it was it. To me, to put four or five guys together and just boom, let it go, when that happens, it's just the pinnacle. It's one of the purest pleasures I know. I mean, it ain't gonna hurt nobody. It's not even gonna hurt you. It's just pure pleasure."

CHARLIE WATTS: "It was more of a family than a band, 'cause I'd never been in a band longer than three months. When the Stones asked me to join they talked in terms of band commitment, so I thought, 'This'll go on for a year and the next year fold up.'"

Ian Stewart's boogie-woogie piano was an equally important element in the group. "He was part of the core," Eric Clapton noted, "the rhythm section, the keyboard man. He really knew the early stuff, the actual blues, the boogie-woogie." Brian also made an addition when he learned how to play the mouth organ like Muddy Waters's harmonica player, Little Walter. By now Mick Jagger had combined the mannerisms of Jones and Richards, Berry and Waters, Jimmy Phelge and Hayley Mills (a teenage English actress to whom he bore a startling resemblance). Jagger's image would take the Stones out of the specialist world of English R&B and transform them into icons who offered English boys an astonishing new way to be erotic: the image was so uniquely British it would take the American competition four years to come up with anything close to rivaling its impact.

In February and March 1963, the Rolling Stones Mach I, as Richards would come to call them, began to play around London several nights a week.

RICHARDS: "It was the beginnings of Beatlemania. The first Beatles record came out. They've got harmonica. We'd heard they did Chuck Berry songs, but being a pop star did not even come into the realm of possibilities. We saw no connection between us and the Beatles; we were playing the blues, they were singing pop songs dressed in suits. They were an encouraging sign in a new trend in popular music, but to be in the charts, or to be pop stars—we were almost a reaction against all that. We were hip not to be pop stars, it was like the only dignity we had left. Then suddenly, everyone was lookin' round for new groups, more and more groups were being signed, and Alexis Korner got a record contract. He'd gotten so big he'd split from his club gig. Who gets his spot? None other than ... the Rolling Stones. Now we start making just enough bread to stay alive. And we're getting these places raving."

Pinpointing the moment the London R&B scene took off, Iain

Chambers wrote in *Urban Rhythms*: "The music of the British R&B groups was, for the existing standards of pop, extreme. It was certainly not welcomed and accepted in the manner that the Beatles had been. The 'sartorial' style of many of these white groups—long hair, scruffy clothes, an unkempt and 'lived' appearance—was also understood to be the manifesto of bohemian sentiments. Now the rhetoric of a previously restricted enclave, and its social, moral and political disaffiliation, begins to enter the popular culture. The expression of a select few was now transposed to a wider screen where it would connect to a far broader pulse than ever before.

"The inward-looking, self-sufficient image of these groups, apparently fed by their fierce loyalty to the blues, had quickly acquired the edge of male rebelliousness. Most obviously, the blues-indebted Stones sound, and their socially provocative stage and public personae, marked an important breaking away from the traditions that ruled pop and popular music in general. It tended to take the form of reducing the ironic cast of the blues to a blatant obsession with male sexuality. This was the heart of the musical and cultural outrage represented by a group like the Rolling Stones."

"It was simply a matter of atmosphere," recounted one promoter, Vic Johnson. "Those boys seemed in a world of their own as they pushed out this supercharged music, which electrified the whole place. The kids watching had never sampled this sort of thing and they didn't know what to make of it at first, but by the end of the evening they knew all right. They knew they'd heard a violent sound that knocked most of the trad groups right off the scene. They were playing the blues, but they weren't an academic blues band. The Rolling Stones were more like a rebellion."

"If the Stones hadn't been successful, I'd probably never have gotten the chance," said Rod Stewart. "They cleared the way for a lot of other bands, too, just making it possible for that kind of music to be played."

In March they started playing the residency in Giorgio Gomelsky's Crawdaddy Club in Richmond that would shortly lead to their attracting a manager and a record contract. Although the Crawdaddy Club was far from the Marquee and the Soho clubs that traditionally formed the nucleus of the London avant-garde music scene, word of mouth about the Stones' act spread rapidly. Within two weeks they were packing the place, and Gomelsky, who had an informal managerial association with them, became their first outspoken champion.

GIORGIO GOMELSKY: "They did Jimmy Reed really well—it's not so much that Jimmy Reed is difficult, it's the timing, the tempo. The beat is very important: It's got to be a fast/slow thing . . . and to keep the tension is not easy and Keith knew that inside out. Keith is not a great guitar player by any imagination, but he is a great rhythm guitar player because he always gets right on the right feel. Keith has never grown up, in my opinion. He's always at war! He's too much! He's a rubbery kind of person, he bounces off anything, he comes back. Nobody knows how he does it, he's always there, he's great! He's a very great character. If you went to make circus characters out of the Stones, he would be the clown who is being beaten up but gets up again. Keith was the rhythm guitar player. He was putting out the fucking energy."

In one of the first intelligent discussions of the band's emergence Alan Beckett wrote in the *New Left Review*: "Some of their earliest work—the Chuck Berry numbers for instance—was pleasant, but unremarkable. Some was downright bad when you looked at it in relation to the original. Thus, 'I Just Want to Make Love to You' was frantic and had none of the power and dignity of the original, while the Bo Diddley-style number, 'Mona,' was overadorned and generally in complete contradiction to the simplicity and relaxation of the latter artist's music. Other early pieces, however, are perhaps the most important work in this idiom ever performed in Britain; good examples are their versions of Howling Wolf's [Willie Dixon number] 'Little Red Rooster' and Slim Harpo's 'King Bee.' Because no attempt was made to reproduce the specific mannerisms, these works were effective translations rather than replications of something essentially foreign. *In these pieces the erotic narcissism became a possibility in English life . . .*"

Nik Cohn, who has done some of the best writing about this period, recalled the Stones' appeal at the Crawdaddy vividly: "they lay down something very violent in the lines of rhythm and blues. They were enthusiasts then; they cared a lot about their music . . .

They were mean and nasty, full blooded, very testy, and they beat out the toughest, crudest, most offensive noise an English band had ever made . . . Naughty but nice, they were liked by the Aldermaston marchers and hitchhikers, beards and freaks and pre-neanderthal mods everywhere. Simply, they were turning into the voice of hooliganism . . . Keith Richards wore T-shirts. All the time he kept winding and unwinding his legs, ugly like a crab; he was shut in, shuffling, the classic school drop-out. Simply, he spelled Borstal."

Another early witness was the recording engineer Glyn Johns, who would work with them extensively in the future: "The first time I heard them I'd never seen anything like it. I just thought they were fantastic. What attracted me to them was the way they played rhythm and blues. I had never heard a white man sing like Jagger, let alone an Englishman. I was knocked out. There was something different about them. There was the music, of course, but it was also them—they didn't look like the pop stars we were brought up on. They were not terribly goodlooking. In fact, they were pretty ugly. And their attitude—for the time they were incredibly rebellious, and very strange. It was just their appearance, their clothes, their hair—their whole attitude was immediately obvious to you as soon as you saw them playing. It was just a complete *pppprt* to society and everybody and anything."

Or, as the American rock critic Jon Landau commented. "The Stones were the first to say, 'Up against the wall, motherfucker,' and they said it with class."

4
Under Assistant West Coast Promo Man
1963

If you want to make rock and roll your career, you have to have a certain equilibrium between your personality and your ego and your physical makeup—the three things you have no control over. Then you have to have a certain balance to be able to deal with anything that's thrown at you. And anything you throw yourself into, you better get yourself out of.

KEITH RICHARDS, *from an interview with Bill German, 1987*

Keith and Mick couldn't possibly have chosen anyone better as their next catalyst than Andrew Loog Oldham. A skinny nineteen-year-old mod who had worked as a madcap publicist for the dress designer Mary Quant and was a part-time PR man for the Beatles' manager, Brian Epstein, Oldham was a twenty-four-hour-a-day bag of nerves who saw himself as a Phil Spector, the British version of the "teenage tycoon shit." "He was calculatedly vicious and nasty, but pretty as a stoat," wrote George Melly. "He had enormous talent totally dedicated to whim and money." According to Richards, he was "a fantastic bull-shitter and an incredible hustler." His mind was best described by his favorite book, *A Clockwork Orange*, as "a nice quiet horrorshow." *Loog* rhymed with *droog*. According to his girlfriend, Sheila Klein, "He was very entertaining, very funny in terms of performing. He would perform to an imaginary audience—or a real one—all the time. Andrew was on twenty-four hours a day." "We just had the same basic desire to do something—a hustling instinct," Oldham recalled. "I wasn't coming on with a cigar and a silk suit going, 'Listen, kids.' I was the same age as them. We talked the same language."

In May 1963 Oldham became their manager. The Stones had

made a handshake agreement with Giorgio Gomelsky that he was their manager, but they were impatient and found his vision limited. Gomelsky was extremely upset when he found out they had screwed him. The Stones, according to Jagger, felt they were too good and important to let things like that get in their way. The photographer Gered Mankowitz, who would become friends with Oldham and the Stones' semi-official photographer in the midsixties, saw Andrew as "one of those people who is capable of bringing people together, a catalyst. He was very stimulating, very funny. Able to be incredibly cruel. Very cutting. He had an enormous talent for hearing the right thing—he had great ears—and understood the nature of the business, understood the nature of media as it was then. He was an extraordinary bloke."

"I knew what I was looking for," Oldham said. "It was sex, the sex that most people didn't realize was there. Like the Everly Brothers. Two guys with the same kind of face, the same kind of hair. They were meant to be singing together to some girl, but they were really singing to each other."

During the summer of 1963 Oldham cut into the band like a poker player shuffling his deck. Ian Stewart would have to be flushed out because "he didn't look right for the part." Jones would have to be relieved of his illusion that he was the band's leader. Jagger would be featured as the front man and sex symbol, and Richards had to cut the s off his name because *Keith Richard* looked more pop. For the next fourteen years, Keith would be known by this stage name. Ian Stewart agreed to stay on as their road manager and continued to play on their records and sometimes on stage.

RICHARDS: "He was always the perfect counter for all the bullshit we had to go through. This is where Brian starts to realize that things have gotten beyond his control. Before this, everybody knows that Brian considers it his band. Now Oldham sees Mick as being a big sex symbol, and he wants to kick Stu out, and we won't have it. And eventually, because Brian had known him for longer than we, and the band was Brian's idea in the first place, Brian had to tell Stu how we'd signed up with these people, and how they were very image-conscious, and Stu didn't fit in. If I'd been Stu I'd

Although the landlady at Mapesbury Road, Mrs. Yalouris, remembered them as very nice boys who never caused any trouble or made noise, Oldham's abrasive personality was outrageous to the British music business. He might come into the office of a very proper gentleman such as the chairman of Decca Records, Sir Edward Lewis, to discuss a contract and suddenly put his feet up on the desk! On another occasion, he became so impatient in a traffic jam he leapt out of the car and ran across the roofs of all the stalled cars in front of him. Oldham's irreverent make-it-up, fuck-everybody, let's-just-do-it attitude electrified Richards and Jagger and summed up British rock and roll in 1963. "The resistance to the band in the music business was incredible," Oldham said, "but we managed to turn that into a positive factor." They did it primarily by scaring people they despised with the same kind of callous, terrifying attitudes of the teenage gangs in *Clockwork Orange*.

RICHARDS: "There was a time when Mick and I got on really well with Andrew. We went through the whole *Clockwork Orange* thing. Brian never liked Andrew, but he knew that Andrew could help the band more than anyone else. Andrew pulled the right strokes as far as the public relations were concerned, at just the right time. And it worked like clockwork. Nothing was planned. It just fell into place and Brian was resigned to the fact that Andrew was a necessary part of the general noncommunicativeness."

The power base in the band shifted to the Richards-Jagger-Oldham triangle. As Oldham saw it, they were bonded together as much by their work as by their need to keep themselves in the public eye. For them there was no private life. Everything they did was dedicated to the creation of the Stones.

Oldham's financial backer, Eric Easton, inspired Keith's affection because he had played the organ in the dying days of British music hall vaudeville in the 1950s—at the same time as his beloved Crazy Gang. As soon as he had signed them, Easton launched them on a series of one-nighters in ballrooms and clubs in the hinterlands of London that was their first step on the road that would take them out of the smoke and into the glare of the world stage.

RICHARDS: "It was difficult for the first few months. The British end of rock and roll was run by these strong-arm promoters, which meant that you played three or four ballrooms a night, forty-five minutes on stage, get off, jump into the car, you're driven to another one, back to the other one for the second show, and you wear these shitty little suits that they advance you the money for and charge you later, plus wear and tear, and if you don't make the gig, they break your fucking leg. [Heavy accent:] 'Because Moe is not going to stand for any fookin' nonsense, my boy, I'm telling you. Like, this is Lou, this is my bruvver Johnny; don't ask this bloke's name.' I kind of lived in dread of having fingers broken. It's never been a sweet business.

"We were known in the big cities, but then you got outside into the sticks, they don't know who the fuck you are and they're still preferring the local band. That makes you play your ass off every night, so at the end of two-hour-long sets, you've got them. That's the testing ground, in those ballrooms where it's really hard to play. The local youths in places like Wisbech had heard of the Rolling Stones but had no idea what to expect. To start out with, most of them, especially the boys, just gawked. You could sense the hostility from the guys. The chicks were just amazed. They were trying to make up their minds. By the end we always had them, by at least three or four numbers. No matter where we played we had them. They were always bopping about."

At the end of September 1963 they embarked on their first national tour. Incredibly, the headliners were some of their greatest heroes and biggest influences: Bo Diddley, creator of the seminal "hambone" rhythm, the Everly Brothers, and Little Richard. If the Stones had wanted to go to a rock and roll graduate school, they couldn't have hired better instructors.

For Keith, playing on the same stage as Little Richard was "the most exciting experience of my life." Watching Bo Diddley and the Everly Brothers was a nightly education in how to build and hold an audience. Richards and Jones were particularly drawn to Diddley, literally sitting at his feet night after night talking and playing music.

BO DIDDLEY: "It was my first engagement in England. Me, Brian, and Keith became jug buddies; what we call jug buddies is that we drink out of the same jug. They were nice to me then, like brothers. I don't mean black brothers, I mean brothers period. Togetherness. And it was really unique. These people showed me hospitality of another country."

Touring clarified their image. Keith was particularly pissed off about having to wear the outfit Oldham had chosen for the band, which reminded him of his school uniform. He quickly destroyed his jacket by dumping chocolate pudding and whiskey on it or leaving it on the dressing room floor.

RICHARDS: "It's funny people think Oldham made the image, but he tried to tidy us up. Andrew wasn't ahead of us in that respect from the beginning—the press picked up on us only when we'd personally got rid of those dogtooth jackets and the Lord John shirts. It was only then that Andrew realized the full consequences of it all and got fully behind it. After that the press did all the work for us. We only needed to be refused admission into a hotel and that set the whole thing rolling. Andrew exploited our image. He wasn't totally on the right track. He nearly fucked us up with those jackets."

Oldham now realized that the low road was the only road. Between the fall of 1963 and summer of 1964 Oldham, aided by the times and the Stones' talent and enthusiasm, performed nothing short of a miracle of exploitation. Seizing upon the fact that the Beatles had achieved their extraordinary success by turning themselves into acceptable teen images with neatly combed hair, suits, and ties, Oldham hit upon the idea of creating the Stones as their mirror images. It is hard to imagine how vitally important clothes were in England in the early sixties. They were in a sense the only political statement the masses could make. Thus the Rolling Stones only had to enter a restaurant with their long, unkempt-looking hair, tight pants, which accented the crotch and ass, and without ties to literally cause a sensation in the following day's newspaper. In retrospect it was an easy game, but at the time they were inventing a new breed, and Oldham's intuitive sense of soundbites was ahead of its time. His greatest coup was to fashion a series of sloganlike statements that alienated the old and commanded the adoration of the young. Billing the Stones as the ugliest group in Britain, he unleashed the polarizing challenge "Would You Let

Your Daughter Go Out with a Rolling Stone?," which summed up their approach. "People say I made the Stones," Oldham recalled. "I didn't. They were there already. They only wanted exploiting. By the time I got through planting all that negative publicity, there wasn't a parent in Britain that wasn't repulsed by the very sound of their name."

Oldham hit on the axiom "The Rolling Stones are not a band so much as a way of life." It was the line that best described the band's existence, as well as its impact.

RICHARDS: "I reckon there are three reasons why American R&B stars don't make it big in Britain. One, they're old; two, they're black; three, they're ugly. This image bit is very important. It was the image they wanted. We were very hip to the image and how to manipulate the press. When people made these kinds of irresponsible remarks it just drew the fans more firmly to our side."

At the center of the music and hype was the button of sex. On that first national tour Richards later recalled that he could feel the energy building night after night until it finally exploded in "a sort of hysterical wail, a weird sound that hundreds of chicks make when they're coming . . . They sounded like hundreds of orgasms at once. They couldn't even hear the music, and we couldn't hear the music we were playing."

RICHARDS: "Maybe it had to do with World War II or some other social and political thing, but teenage girls needed that sort of frenzy. It was like a mating thing. Surprised as you are that chicks in Sheffield and Doncaster are like going berserk over you, you have a little bit of room to maneuver because for a while only you know that something is going down. It happened so fast that one never had time to really get into that thing, 'Wow, I'm a Rolling Stone.' We were still sleeping in the back of this van every night of the most hard-hearted and callous roadie I've ever encountered, Stu. From one end of England to the other in Stu's Volkswagen bus. With just an engine and a rear window and all the equipment and then you fit in. The gear first, though."

The writer Nick Kent, who would become a major figure in promoting Keithmania in the 1970s, first saw the Stones perform in Cardiff when he was twelve years old.

NICK KENT: "The Stones were second on the bill that night, but you could see the whole audience change when the Rolling Stones came on. These young girls just became wild and violent and made this weird, bestial sound. It was an electrifying experience. I had front-row seats and this girl from the third row threatened me with a stiletto so I immediately sat in the third row.

"After the show I went backstage to meet them. You have to understand the Stones looked so weird that all the girls were frightened of them and they were particularly frightened of Jagger because he had those lips and you didn't see guys like that with long hair in early 1964. Brian Jones was the most nicely middle class, and there were like five girls backstage who were totally enchanted but also very frightened. They all went to Brian, but they were looking at Jagger, who was standing next to them with the attitude, 'OK, talk to me. What you talkin' to that cunt for?' Meanwhile Keith Richards had passed out on the sofa with a bottle of beer in his hand and I went over to get his autograph and he belched in my face."

RICHARDS: "We knew we had become successful when we did that first tour. You know a month or two in front of anyone else that it's happening because you're there every night watching the way the audience is reacting and suddenly there's little girls on the street dressed in their best clothes. I was nineteen when it started to take off and just an ordinary guy—chucked out of nightclubs, birds'd poke their tongues at me, that kind of scene—and then suddenly, Adonis! And you know this is so ridiculous, so insane. It was really a bugger. It makes you very cynical. But it's a hell of a thing to deal with. It took me years to get it under control."

As Iain Chambers pointed out in *Urban Rhythms*, "As the shock effect of parading a blatant male sexuality (although frequently crossed with the contradictory signs of long hair and 'effeminate' dressing) sank in, existing conventions were everywhere affected. Proposing music as the direct extension of a sexual body, white R&B became a potential instrument of cultural revolt. The translation of black R&B and soul into white pop thus involved—particularly in the Stones' case—an explicit sexual strategy intent on dismantling the prevalent sentimental and romantic ties that dominated pop and Tin Pan Alley . . . The contradictory musical and cultural outrage represented by the Stones was destined to transform them, first in England and subsequently in the United States, into the decade's sonorial metaphor for white metropolitan youth rebellion."

The rivalry for leadership that had begun with the arrival of Oldham continued. Jones felt the slow transfer of power to Jagger.

RICHARDS: "You don't realize it on stage, but the strength of the spotlight on the singer is so much brighter than that on the rest of the musicians. The focus of attention is paid so much on the singer that no matter how much you want to upstage the singer, you can't possibly do it. Brian really got off on the trip of being a pop star. Suddenly, from being very serious about what he wanted to do, he was willing to take the cheap trip. And it's a very short trip. He was a contradiction in blond. He was the only guy in the world who thought he could take on Mick as the head onstage personality. 'All the chicks liked me better than Mick.' You know, one of those confidences. And it went on for so long."

As Bill Wyman pointed out in his aptly titled memoir *Stone Alone*, "You had to be tough to be in the Stones." Keith and Mick kept the others under submission by spritzing them with acerbic gibes. While they failed to penetrate Wyman, they began to pulverize Jones. Keith and Mick called him Mr. Shampoo because of his obsession with clean hair. Both did caustic impersonations of his defects—his short legs, which he camouflaged with high-heeled boots, his bull neck. "The faint-hearted or ultra-sensitive would not have stood the gibes that poured from Mick and Keith," Wyman wrote. "They had to have someone to poke fun at, not always in a humorous way, often spiteful and hurtful. They *had* to have a scapegoat or a guinea-pig."

Oldham might have seen the boys as the droogs in *A Clockwork Orange*, but they would have fit better into William Golding's *Lord of the Flies*. Like the Stones, the novel's marooned English schoolboys established a dominant order and then split into competitive, lethal units. Seeing the chink in Brian's armor, Oldham delivered a decisive blow by revealing during the tour that Jones was receiving five pounds a week more than the others. "Everybody freaked out,"

Richards recalled. "We said, 'Fuck you!'" As a result, Brian Jones lost his position as leader of the band.

"Brian got exactly what he was asking for," Stewart explained. "He'd been an asshole to everyone."

One musician who toured with Richards recalled that Keith already displayed the behind-the-scenes leadership qualities that would emerge publicly in the 1970s: "He knew the power he had, but he was quiet and reserved. They were acting out their characters in those days and their characters really became what they are. I watched him on tour a lot and he never really strayed away from being Keith Richards. Keith doesn't ever really change. He's the same guy all the time."

Richards described his first year on the road as "a hard school." When he started he told *Beat International* that he "used to wish I could have had a screen between me and the audience. I just wanted to play, not put on any showmanship." Nevertheless, he soon developed a style that became a model for guitar players on both sides of the Atlantic. Grabbing his guitar and threading his way over tangled wires through backstage crowds to his position, Keith would raise his hand above his head, ready to hit the opening chord as the curtains parted. He would play with his back to the audience as he focused on Charlie, or he might crouch down to hit a particularly intense chord. Occasionally he'd break into a maniacal grin and run backward, or dart across the stage behind Mick to interact with Brian. All of the gestures were executed with an entirely appropriate dramatic flourish. In this way, Richards invented an image of the guitar player that has been imitated ever since. Pete Townshend was among the first to admit, "I pinched my arm-swinging movement from him." "Keith really is a kind of self-contained performer," Albert Goldman commented. "His moves are invariably graceful, well struck, and he makes sense of the body rhetoric that is the most classic, most fitting to a guitar rocker. He's the discus thrower of rock. He's perfect."

5
Lady Jane
1963–1964

It *was* a magical time because I actually managed to turn my little
juvenile fantasies into a way of life.

KEITH RICHARDS, *from an interview with Kurt Loder, 1987*

In the fall of 1963, just before moving into Mapesbury Road, Keith
met and fell in love with his first girlfriend. Just seventeen, Linda
Keith, who joked that she had been a groupie for John Lee Hooker
since she was eight, came from a respectable middle-class family in
Hampstead. Mick was seeing Chrissie Shrimpton, sister of the
supermodel Jean. Brian Jones, though not the faithful type, was
living with Linda Lawrence. The girls were members of that inspir-
ing group who nurtured the emerging British rock stars of the
1960s. Eric Burdon of the Animals remembered Linda as "one of
the great free floating spirits" of the era. According to Andrew's
girlfriend, Sheila Klein, "Linda was stunning-looking. She knew
how to attract a lot of attention and she was just going for
everything. She was working at that time at *Vogue* as an assistant.
She was just about to be a successful model. She was quite original-
looking in what she wore, and quite intense."

Music was still, and in fact would always be, Keith's emotional
priority, and the important events in his life from this time are
almost all related to playing. "He certainly wasn't a quiet man to
live with," she said. "But I liked the fact that he was so involved
with music, that it was such a prevailing part of his and my life."

At first the relationship was idyllic. They formed a twinlike unit,
dressing, acting, talking alike. Linda found Keith a kind, warm, and
considerate lover. Her relationship with him was more intimate
than Jagger's, and she saw him as "shy, introverted, very appealing,
lacking in confidence. He didn't like his appearance." Though

outwardly gregarious, Linda too was shy, introverted, and insecure—as full of contradictions as Keith. She believed in him, developed an absolute passion for his music, and became his muse.

Linda had all the attributes that most appealed to Keith in a woman: With the dramatic looks of a rock and roll Elizabeth Taylor (who was then starring in *Cleopatra*), she was passionate about R&B, and impatient to embark on every available experience. Above all, she was so strong she would prove to be more than a match for Keith. Shortly after they met, Linda moved into Mapesbury Road.

LINDA KEITH: "At the outset we were certainly in love with each other. We were good friends as well as being together. He was a lonely person. I felt that he had been a very lonely child. He talked about his childhood and there was unhappiness there. I had the feeling that he was relieved that it was in the past and that something was happening to him in his life which didn't involve the same ingredients his childhood had."

While Richards learned to live on the road, he also learned how to record. In June 1963 Eric Easton got the Stones a recording contract with Decca Records which included its American subsidiary, London Records.

RICHARDS: "We all looked at each other with a bit of dismay because there was no precedent for anybody lasting. You shot up there and you were gone. There was no way you could believe that it was gonna last for anything more than another two years. So, for us, it was like, 'Oh, man, this is great, makin' records—but that means it's the beginning of the end.'"

British recording studios were primitive and the men who worked in them were for the most part middle-aged. To them a yob like Keith was beneath consideration. He was to do what he was told. At first Oldham was not much help. Unlike Phil Spector, he knew nothing about music or recording technology.

RICHARDS: "When the Beatles and ourselves started, the record business was a fairly small business. There were only two major labels in England and they belonged to companies who made their money with other things, with guidance systems for missiles and stuff like that. It was the same in America: RCA made heavy ship satellites and the like. The record company divisions were just a write-off for these companies. Their whole reason to be was to lose money.

"When rock and roll took off, it became clear that music could be an enormous money spinner on its own. The main thing that the Beatles and ourselves started off with was that we, and because of that the others that followed us, controlled the artistic content of the record. No interference."

The Stones began recording at night when the Decca executives wouldn't be around. They learned as they went along. Their first U.K. single, "Come On," went to number twenty-one. Its follow up, "I Wanna Be Your Man," reached number twelve, but owed its success as much to its composers, John Lennon and Paul McCartney, as it did to the Stones. Their debut U.K. extended-play 45, which featured four songs, was released in January 1964 and was a success, going to number fifteen on the singles charts. But the first sign that the Rolling Stones were going to emerge from the pop pack as an identifiable unit came with the release of their third single, "Not Fade Away," in February 1964. Keith had been playing the Buddy Holly number over and over again on his acoustic guitar at Mapesbury Road. He sped and funked it up. "When he revamped the riff back to the rawness of the Bo Diddley rhythm which Buddy Holly had originally copied," wrote the British critic Martin Elliot, "he conceived the Rolling Stones sound and style. From the first opening chords, played on an acoustic guitar, Keith gave the song its feel and instant appeal." By March "Not Fade Away" reached number three on the charts. It was their biggest success to date. It was also their first single released in the U.S., where it went to number forty-eight.

By the time they toured England again in January 1964 on a double-headlining bill with the Ronettes (then at the height of their fame) their concerts had turned into riots. Night after night the audience would erupt from every direction. Some charged the stage, some threw themselves from the balcony, others ripped at their clothes, screaming at the top of their lungs. Policemen and nurses with stretchers ferried the injured to ambulances. The screams, rushing bodies, and poorly amplified equipment created a cacophony that was in many ways reminiscent of the blitz.

BILL WYMAN: "We used to do three bars of the first song before the whole place just fell to bits and they poured on stage and they broke all the guitars. Every single day over a period of six months—every day a riot."

RICHARDS: "It was like they had the Battle of the Crimea going on, people gasping, tits hanging out, chicks choking, nurses running around with ambulances. You're 30 feet up. You have everyone down there. It's already a kind of submission—like sacrificial lambs. You have people looking up with exposed throats—and it's very primal shit. You took your life in your hands just to walk out there. I was strangled twice. It was living *A Hard Day's Night*—climbing over rooftops with chief constables who don't know their way, getaways down fire escapes, through laundry chutes, into bakery vans. It was all mad. We ended up being like the Monkees without even realizing it."

From 1964 through 1967 the images of the Stones' concerts around the world were telegraphed in newspaper wordbites like "Ambulance men carried out hysterical teenage girls in straitjackets . . . The performance was stopped by police after ten minutes because of rioting teenagers . . . Three thousand fans rioted as the Stones flew in . . . Police armed with batons knocked down rioting fans. West German newspapers described the European premiere of the Rolling Stones as 'hell broken loose' and a 'witches' cauldron.' Someone threw some bombs where the British group, known in Vienna as the 'Mushroom Heads,' were playing . . . Police hurled tear-gas . . ." "I need an army to protect me," said Richards, who was almost crushed to death, strangled, knocked unconscious, or electrocuted on at least six occasions. "I meet thousands of people. When I get home my suitcases are always full up with rubbish given me by fans."

Despite the fact that it took all his energy to keep performing, in accord with the public's and Andrew Oldham's wishes, Keith started talking as if he were the greatest Lothario in England. Interviews referring to this period are peppered with references to sucking and fucking groupies at orgies, although, according to Bill Wyman, Keith only had sex with six women between 1963 and 1965.

Keith boasted of having an affair with the lead singer of the Ronettes, Ronnie Bennett, on the Stones' January 1964 tour of England, claiming it had been one of the few times there had been any competition between him and Mick over a woman. As he told it, he ended up with Ronnie, and Mick had to settle for another Ronette, her sister Estelle. The bemused Bennett, who claimed to be a virgin so devoted to her fiancé and mentor, Phil Spector, that she had turned down a serious erection from John Lennon only a week earlier, certainly had a good understanding of Keith—"He was not so much shy as he was quiet, very to himself in his own room in his own world; he really is a bit of a softie"—but she claims she never had an affair with him.

Eric Clapton, who says he fell in love with Ronnie on a Yardbirds tour, recalled that he was "heartbroken" to see her shortly thereafter with Keith. And Andy Warhol also noted that Ronnie appeared to be spending a lot of time with Keith in New York during the Stones' first visit later that year. However, Ronnie is insistent in her biography that she maintained her virginity until she was wed to Phil. Perhaps Linda Keith had the best assessment of the situation.

LINDA KEITH: "Everyone was always telling me that this affair was going on. Keith always denied it, but I was in this trio with Chrissie and Sheila and apparently their men, Andrew and Mick, were with the other two girls. I must say I was never totally convinced that Keith was having an affair with Ronnie. I thought it might have been slightly wishful thinking on his part. I always went along with it because it seemed like a safe route for a girlfriend to take, to accept the affair was going on rather than to say, 'No, he wouldn't do a thing like that.' It always sounded so idiotic. We didn't have that sort of relationship, and I'm sure that he would have felt that he would be in hot water with me, so I don't know that we ever discussed it. I think part of me was rather surprised because he just wasn't overtly sexual, he wasn't sexually confident. Had he pulled off an affair with her I think I might have been marginally impressed."

By now it was becoming difficult for the Stones to find relief from the glare of fame. Hordes of pubescent girls stood outside Mapesbury Road day and night, carving Keith's and Mick's names into the walls and doors and writing their own names and phone numbers all over their new car, a Ford Consul. "Keith lives here" is still faintly visible on one wall twenty years later. Their neighbors on the quiet middle-class street started to shoot baleful glances at them, eliciting Richards's hatred. "They had some funny habits, but it was them who stared at us," he said. "We had to creep in and out of the place."

Profiles of them began to appear in teen magazines. Keith's answers to the standard pop-star questions revealed both his sense of humor and his identification with the underdog. What is your stage name? "Valerie Masters." What are your parent's names? "Dirt and Boris." Who are your greatest heroes? "The Great Train Robbers and Christine Keeler."

On the road, Richards's room became the hub of the band's communal life. If he wasn't actually playing, which he did most of the time, Keith was always listening to some good music. Much like Muddy Waters in personality, he seemed to naturally draw dependents around him. "It's such a weird thing, because you're in a little bubble on your own," Keith said. "It's not so much that you're going to places, but places come to you." Keith's hotel rooms took on his personality as he draped the lamps with scarves, put on some funky R&B, stuck pictures on the walls, lit up a cigarette and poured himself a drink. In this "bubble" he constantly worked on his music. Charlie thought he was like a bedouin, capable of setting up or striking camp in an instant.

RICHARDS: "A lot of people have said Keith Richards is the Stones. It's far more subtle than that. There's no way that you can say that any one person is the band and the rest are just padding. It is such a subtle mix of characters and personalities and how to deal with each other, and if it works right you never think about it yourself, because there's always the fear that if you analyze it you'll blow it. So you don't really wanna know.

"They're such a weird collection of guys—the most unlikely people to be a good rock and roll band. Hell, half of them hated the idea of being a rock and roll star in the first place. It was always embarrassing to them; they wanted to be serious artists. And when you're living and working with people like that, it's very difficult if you're phony.

"We developed a style between us, a lot of it to do with the fact that for many, many years on stage I couldn't hear us at all, so I'd be forced right up against Charlie's drum kit in order to hear the beat, and the only thing that he could hear was me with my amp right next to him. That's all he needed to hear in dire circumstances to keep it together. I mean, here you are, the chicks are screaming and the band has no PA, you've very soon got to develop a way of playing where it didn't matter if we heard the voice or the bass, although of course it's preferable if you can. It was just Charlie and me. My playing would have been totally different if I hadn't gone through that with Charlie. I developed more and more of the rhythm things and drum licks because that's really all I was playing to."

During many harrowing experiences suffered by the Stones, Keith seemed to have his own strong survival instinct. His ability to withdraw to a closely defended inner core dated back to his early childhood, and allowed him to combat any threat by any means necessary. Brian, whose constitution was declining along with his influence, began to miss some gigs; Keith, on the other hand, had extraordinary stamina, helped along by the amphetamine pills that had enlivened his art school days.

RICHARDS: "Usually drug taking in music starts off on a very, very mundane level—just keeping going to make the next gig. They're nothing I'd recommend to anybody, drugs, but it's a musician's life—it's very difficult to get anyone to understand. It's an underworld life, anyway. Musicians start to work when everybody else stops working and wants some entertainment. If you get enough work, you're working three hundred fifty days a year because you want to fill up every gig. And you reach a point very early on when you're sitting around in the dressing room with some other acts in the show and you say, 'I've gotta drive five hundred miles and do two shows tomorrow and I can't make it.' And so you look around at the other guys and say, 'How the hell have you been making it for all these years?' And they say, 'Well, baby, take one of these.' Musicians don't start off thinking, 'We're rich and famous, let's get high.' It's a matter of making the next gig. Like the bomber pilots—if you've got to bomb Dresden tomorrow, you get, like, four or five bennies to make the trip and keep yourself together. 'Do you want me to crash this sucker, or do you want me to stay awake?' 'Here, squadron leader, open up your mouth and I'll pop a couple of these blighters in.' I'm sure it was really good speed those fuckers got as well. Government issue. That's how it starts out, and it's usually speed. And once you've got past that, the next question is an escalation.''

Richards's visual training had taught him to see the elements of a piece, take them apart, and reassemble them in a different manner; the first standout success this method achieved was the Rolling Stones' first U.K. album, which was released in April 1964. It had been recorded earlier in the year between performances and was cobbled together by Oldham from completed studio tracks, out-takes, and demos. Richards was determined to make every track on the album as good as a potential single. Although Oldham is listed as the record producer in the studio, Richards became the Stones' *de facto* producer. Oldham produced the all-important package and the hype to sell it.

RICHARDS: "I had a lot of good times with Andrew and I dug it. He'll say the same—he learned from us too. Maybe that was one of the good things about it. It probably wouldn't have been so interesting and so raw otherwise, y'know. In fact, it may not even have made it if we'd have used a producer who was 'experienced,' one of the 'old school.' We were very happy all that time and never, ever thought of using anybody else. In fact, the only outside help we got, funnily enough, came directly from Andrew wanting to be England's Phil Spector, so Spector and Jack Nitzsche, who was really his right-hand man, were around an awful lot. Jack Nitzsche in particular helped us enormously in a very unobtrusive way.

"A first album can be incredible. All that energy . . . unbelievable! It's almost sad in a way, because you know it can only be a once-ever experience, just building up and then finally letting out all that energy in one blast.

"I still listen to that album. The enthusiasm there is obvious I think, because that was our first chance to do what we'd been trying to do for two years, so just being there was a total turn-on.

We had all these numbers we had been playing for ages and at that point they were just ready to be got down in the studio."

The album was a smash success. It knocked the Beatles off the top of the U.K. charts, and stayed there for three months, selling a then-phenomenal one hundred thousand copies. The musician and critic Roy Carr wrote: "From the opening high-octane power surge of 'Route 66' right on through to the very last cymbal crash on 'Walking the Dog,' this album exudes a frenetic primal magnificence and a total commitment to the music that only a band of enthusiastic young activists, dedicated to 'spreading the word,' could hope to create."

"Keith and Brian's guitars meshed impeccably," wrote another critic, "creating a definition in action of rock and roll."

While Jones took up harmonica as his instrument of expression, Richards stuck with his guitar. He had, noted one observer, "an unnerving ability continuously to improve his guitar virtuosity."

"His playing was raw and raunchy with unrelenting energy," acknowledged Chuck Berry. "My playing captured the spirit of teenage rebellion in the 1950s, and Keith, to his credit, updated it with a 1960s sound. The music started sounding hotter, more dangerous. He'd push out the same feeling I'd given it, without ever losing that adolescent soul."

Richards was pleased with the album but was also acutely aware of the distance between their live sound and what he was achieving on vinyl. He had come up against the limits of British recording studios and realized that the band would have to go to America to find people who would understand the sound they wanted.

Keith's first visit to the United States, on a Rolling Stones tour in June 1964, was at first a dream come true.

RICHARDS: "We thought, 'This is the payoff!' We got to fly to America, just to get there! To cats like Charlie and me, America was fairyland. Nobody in our lives had a way of getting there, even once, just for a visit! Forget it, no way. To be paid to go there and play to Americans, we were shitting ourselves.

"Nobody realizes how America blew our minds. I can't even describe what America meant to us. How can you measure it? We were all enthralled and turned on with the idea of being in America, fairyland, do you know what I mean? Once I got to the Astor Hotel it became a blur that day because we just went berserk. First cab to Harlem . . ."

But the two-week tour turned out to be something short of a dream. The Stones were regularly humiliated (on television by Dean Martin) and insulted (particularly by policemen), and their concerts were sparsely attended. They were even berated from their own side of the Atlantic as one English politican said, "Our relationship with the United States runs the risk of getting considerably worse as soon as the Rolling Stones arrive in America."

On one occasion, a cop came backstage to the dressing rooms and ordered the band members to pour their drinks down the toilet.

RICHARDS: "The thing is, I wasn't actually drinking any whiskey, the other two were drinking whiskey and Coke, and I was drinking Coca-Cola. He told them to pour it down the bog, and I refused to pour mine down because I said, 'Why the fuck is an American cop telling me to pour the national drink down the bog?' The cop pulled a gun on me. Very strange scene to me, a cop ordering me at gunpoint to pour a Coke down the john.

"What made matters worse was finding it almost impossible to have sex. We noticed a distinct lack of crumpet, as we put it in those days. It was very difficult, man, for cats who had done England, scoring chicks right, left, and center, to come to a country where apparently no one believed in it. We really got down to the lowest and worked our way up again. In New York or L.A. you can always find something, but when you're in Omaha in 1964 and you suddenly feel horny, you might as well forget it.

"Suddenly we were brought down, bang, everybody saying, 'What a fuck-up, we've blown it.' America was still very much into Frankie Avalon. There wasn't any thought of long-haired kids. We were just entertainment-business freaks with long hair, just like a circus show. In the middle of the country, forget it. We were playing to empty places. But those empty towns, that's where you learned your craft—how to put on a show when there's a hundred people in a place that seats five thousand. You play to those few and the joint's rocking, and everybody has forgotten about all those empty seats, this vast cavern that we can see as we're looking at this wedding party down front. You manage to create this whole new environment. That's what stopped us from turning into pop stars then, you were always having somebody hittin' you in the face, 'Don't forget, boy.' Then we really had to work hard in America and it really got the band together. We'd fallen off in playing in England 'cause nobody was listening. We'd do four numbers and be gone.

"If Dean Martin listened to us a little more he wouldn't have been quite so flippant. At the time it was like a deadly insult, but all it did, all those things, they only went to make us want to prove ourselves more so we'd come back and bite your head off. That was all they did, they steeled you. That's what toughens you up."

Despite the Stones' overall impression that they had fallen in America, their first U.S. album, *England's Newest Hit Makers*, released that month, went to number eleven on the U.S. charts. Clearly they had some fans in America, like the girl at Kennedy Airport whose reply to the question "Why do you like the Stones?" was "Because ... Keith is beautiful, and because ... they're so ugly, they're attractive." The writer Jonathan Cott reflected, "Even in that early, undifferentiated surge of rock groups that announced the English rock 'n' roll renaissance, it was easy to distinguish the Stones from the Dave Clark Five, Freddie and the Dreamers, the Kinks or the Beatles. No other group presented (or has presented) that eerie quality combining the hustling menace of the spiv, the coolness of the dandy, and the unpredictable amorality and frivolity of the Greek gods. And from the moment they landed in America, those soul survivors of British imperialism, these half-scruffy, half-exotic exiles on Main Street naturally and exuberantly took the role of devil's advocate for what was beginning to be thought of as the Love Generation."

When they checked into Chess Studios in Chicago for two days of recording sessions, conducted by Ron Malo, on June 10 and 11, it was like arriving in the promised land. Keith was amazed. Chess had the best machinery and reproduction he had ever experienced: "At first it was almost unbelievable, because at the time the studio was pretty much as it had been through the fifties. Ron Malo—the same engineer who had been doing Muddy's stuff, and Howlin' Wolf for the last few years—did our session. And there was some incredible music going on in back. One day I'd like to produce discs for myself, so I reckon anything I can learn now that we get the chance to travel around a lot is worthwhile. Those studios in Chicago were the greatest. They don't even worry about having a tea break at precisely the right time. They just go on with it until the disc is exactly right."

The lesson the tour was teaching in the fleeting nature of fame in the music business was underscored in Chicago. "Muddy Waters was in Chess Studios in 1964 and he was painting the goddamn ceiling—'cause he wasn't selling records at that time," Keith said. "That throws you a curve, 'ere's the king of blues painting a wall."

"We were unloading our van and taking the equipment in, amps, guitars, mike stands, et cetera, when this big black guy comes up and says, 'Want some help here?'" recalled Bill Wyman. "And we look around and it's Muddy Waters. He starts helping us carry in the guitars and all that. It was unbelievable. The awe we all had for something like that. As kids we would have given our right arms just to say hello to them—and here's the great Muddy Waters helping to carry my guitar into the studio. I mean, it was unreal."

RICHARDS: "It was another of those slaps around the face. He wasn't selling records. And at the same time he was a real gentleman. I would have expected a 'get out of here, white trash' reaction. But those guys were gentlemen, they saw wider than the music business. They immediately nurtured us, and had no reason to know that, because they had, in a year or two they'd be selling more records than they ever had in their lives."

Yet more unreal, Muddy Waters credited the Rolling Stones with helping to bring R&B out of the closet and into the home. "When I started out," he said, "they called my music 'nigger music.' People wouldn't let that kind of music into the house. The Beatles started, but the Rolling Stones really made my kind of music acceptable. I really respect them for opening the doors for black music. I'll tell ya, the guitar player ain't bad either."

The affirmation continued on the second day, when Chuck Berry walked into the studio while they were recording "Down the Road

Apiece." "I stood outside there for a while when you were doing the last number," he told them. "It was great. You got a real great sound going. Swing on, gentlemen."

Shortly after returning from the U.S., the Stones embarked on a summer tour of the U.K. The wear and tear of life on the road was clearly beginning to take its toll even on the stalwart Richards. During the tour, Keith and Mick's new flat at 10A Holly Hill in Hampstead, which they had recently moved into (leaving Andrew at Mapesbury Road), was robbed. That same month Keith had a painful accident during a go-cart race in the Channel Islands. On the opening night in Blackpool, the day their fourth U.K. single, "It's All Over Now," recorded at Chess studios, went to number one, he came close to being seriously injured when he had a run-in with some drunk Glaswegian yobs who'd punched their way to the front of the stage and begun spitting at Brian.

When Keith went over to give their leader, a guy with a particularly large head, a warning, the gang began spitting on him. Ian Stewart, who was from Glasgow and knew how violent Glaswegians could be, watched in horror as Keith started having words with them: "Keith can't stand being booed. He was saying 'Fuck you' and they could hear him." Stu, who had become an expert in the getaway in the year of Stonesmania, figured they'd be off after one more song. Roy Carr, who had preceded the Stones on stage and was watching from the wings, would later describe the incident: "Suddenly a large globule of catarrhal saliva flashed through the air, hung momentarily in the glare of the spotlight, and then hit Richards. Without any hesitation, the outraged guitarist retaliated by smashing the Cuban heel of his Chelsea boot down hard on the knuckles of the lout, then, after taking one quick step backwards, savagely ploughed the toe of his boot into the nose of his adversary." Instantly all the other band members dropped their instruments and ran off stage. Keith stood his ground, glaring down at the hooligans. Ian Stewart was surprised they didn't get hold of Keith's leg and pull him off the stage: "He wouldn't be here now if they had. I just pushed him and said, 'For fuck's sake, get out of here while you're still alive.' Keith still thought he was God and he could kick one of these guys and get away with it."

The opposite side of Keith's personality was revealed when, while he was still on tour, Linda Keith was in a terrible car crash. Returning from a Druid festival in Stonehenge, she went through the windshield of a car. As soon as Keith got off the road, he went straight to the hospital to visit her. She recalled Keith's reaction as one of the most important things that ever happened to her: "I was in the hospital near where the accident happened. My face was messed up so badly my parents and brother had come to the hospital and failed to recognize me. I wasn't allowed mirrors and I was frightened about what had actually happened to me. Keith came to the hospital and saw me, and he leant down and kissed me on my face, and—at that moment I will never forget—showed me that I wasn't a monster, and I wasn't revolting. And that was Keith."

6

As Tears Go By
1963–1965

Mick and Keith were incredibly close and very seldom argued as far as I could tell. Andrew was intense, jumpy, nervous, neurotic—"Let's do it, let's be, let's run, let's do it!" Keith liked Andrew and the three of them, Andrew, Keith, and Mick, had a good time.

LINDA KEITH, *from an interview with Victor Bockris, 1989*

Just as Richards and Jagger had taken everything they could from Jones, since moving to Mapesbury Road they had concentrated on learning everything they could from Oldham. One day in the summer of 1963 Andrew informed the astonished duo that they had to start writing their own songs. "If you take your favorite parts from three hit songs and combine them you're bound to get a hit," Oldham kept saying.

RICHARDS: "For me, definitely the greatest contribution Andrew made was locking me and Mick in the kitchen for a day and a night and saying, 'I'm not letting you out until you got a song . . .' He put it to us: 'You're gonna be dependent upon other songwriters, other people, for all the material you need! From now on you're gonna be more and more dependent. If you get used to that, you'll never get any original material, so come on, let's get it all together. Anybody can write a pop song. I'll lock you in the kitchen!' It was a shock to us. We'd never even thought about it. Andrew literally forced Mick and I to start writing songs. My first reaction was 'Who do you think I am, John Lennon?' At that time, for me, songwriting was somebody else's job. My job was to play guitar and that's what I wanted to do. I didn't think I'd be a songwriter any more than I'd be a nuclear physicist on the side. It was a different area of operation. But Andrew showed me, and what I firmly believe is if you can play an instrument you can write a song. Andrew presented the idea to us, not on any artistic level, but more money. That was the pressure of business. That was a very astute observation of Andrew's. It was very obvious once he put it to us."

It was a year before Richards and Jagger wrote anything stamped by their dual character, but they found success almost immediately in marketing their original songs. Another Decca artist, George Bean, recorded a Jagger-Richards single in 1963. Gene Pitney's version of an early effort, "That Girl Belongs to Yesterday," went to number seven on the U.K. charts. "Tell Me" was on their first album and was their second single in the U.S., where it went to number twenty-four.

That Richards and Jagger could write together soon became a given. After they tried it a couple of times, it was obvious to both of them that this was something they could do together, and they quickly staked out their positions. "Keith always had a lot of talent for melody from the beginning," Mick said. "Everything, including the riffs, came from Keith."

The transition was hard at first. "We were making the same mistake as most white kids who get hung up on the blues," Keith said: "We'd become elitist, although we used to despise the so-called purists. So we needed to reconcile all this with our own past and where audiences were at. And everything we've done since then has been a reconciliation."

They found their voice with two Stones classics written in the summer and fall of 1964. "As Tears Go By" and "The Last Time" revealed the soft and hard sides of Richards and Jagger and staked out the territory of teen angst they would make their own. While Keith and Mick had been desperately failing to come up with some Rolling Stones music, a directive from Oldham to do something opposite finally ignited their creative chemistry. In an attempt to branch out à la Phil Spector, Oldham planned to launch onto the pop scene an angelic-looking convent-school girl named Marianne Faithfull. He asked Jagger and Richards to write a song for her that would conjure up brick walls, high windows, and no sex, and was credited as co-composer. "It was," noted one critic, "their first real song in the sense that it sprang wholly from within themselves, stamped unmistakably with a shared character."

Marianne Faithfull, who would become a powerful influence on the Richards-Jagger collaboration, had a keen perception of the Stones when she recorded the song in the summer of 1964. On the one hand she found them "horrible people—dirty, smelly, spotty." The recording itself, she said, was "all done in half an hour ... it was very strange because they wouldn't speak to me. There was Andrew and Mick and Keith and friends and I just went in and did it. I was quite staggered that they wouldn't even give me a lift to the station."

On the other hand, she soon found herself drawn to Keith. "I was too scared to go up and talk to Keith, of course. And he was much too shy to talk to me. But I liked him. Very much. Keith was a sort of insecure person with a very reflective, intuitive side, which is a very important part of being an artist, and that's what you have to have, that ability to sort of just go in. And that's what I saw. What I felt was just a sort of natural respect. And then when I knew him I could see that side to him in knowing him and seeing him work and the songs he would write, and the way he had a much more sensitive understanding of music. And I think that's why he liked Brian Jones—they had that sort of thing in common."

In August their second U.K. extended-play 45 went to number seven on the singles charts. By September, Faithfull's recording of "As Tears Go By" was in the British top ten and Richards and Jagger were being heralded as the next Lennon and McCartney. Lest there be any doubt of the value of Oldham's contribution, one critic who used the pseudonym Jimmy Phelge wrote: "Had it not been for Andrew Loog Oldham's imagination, perspicacity, and sheer bloody-mindedness, Mick Jagger and Keith Richards would not, in all probability, have ever gotten around to writing together. In which case the Rolling Stones would never have made the quantum leap from snotty South London blues combo to the Greatest Rock & Roll Band Who Ever Drew Breath. By becoming the catalyst (or was it midwife) at the birth of the Glimmer Twins (as they would later become known) he'd radically and irrevocably reshaped the Stones' destiny—having effectively and irretrievably banished Brian Jones to a supporting role and restructured the power base and the rhythmic dynamics of the band in the process."

Both men were surprised by their success. "Something clicked," Richards recalled. "We didn't shout about it much in the early days. It was a good partnership. We never seemed to be short of ideas. We both happened to like the feeling of actually creating something." "We never dreamed of doing that ourselves," said Jagger. "It's fun as long as you can work with someone to bounce off. You can't bounce off your old lady like you can your songwriter."

Actually, the Stones had two writing arms. Apart from the Jagger-Richards credits there were also group compositions registered under the pseudonym Nanker Phelge, a name that combined Brian's term for the disgusting faces he and Keith used to make and the surname of their old Edith Grove catalyst.

Songwriting was also one of the more lucrative pursuits in the music business. Not only does the songwriter earn more royalties than the other members of the band, but selling the publishing rights to the song is the only way to earn any real money in the early days of a career. According to Bill Stephen in *Musician* magazine, "The publishing deal can be more important than the record deal and, should you have a hit tune, far more lucrative over the long run, particularly if your song gets covered by a famous artist." By now Richards was banking more money than he had time to spend.

On returning to England from a second U.S. tour in November 1964, the Stones released the follow-up single to "It's All Over Now." Almost as if they knew they were about to take off into an altogether different realm and wanted to pay one last homage to their roots in Chicago, they chose an obscure, unassailably noncommercial Willie Dixon number, "Little Red Rooster," characterized by Keith as a "pure barnyard blues," rather than plunging ahead with the most commercial sound they could find. Much to the surprise and delight of all concerned, it leapt onto the U.K. charts at number one (a feat previously performed only by Elvis, and Cliff Richard).

RICHARDS: "Singles were all-important then. You put yourself on the line every three months and therefore it had to be distinctive or else. At that time, releasing 'Little Red Rooster' was our distinction, the only way we could set ourselves apart from every-thing else that was going on."

By that time their career was going global. "Tell Me" was number one in Sweden and Denmark. "Not Fade Away" was number one in Greece. "It's All Over Now" was a top-ten hit in Denmark and also reached number one in Germany, Holland, and Sweden. All their records were selling rapidly in most European countries and the Commonwealth, and the American market was opening up. As "Little Red Rooster" held the number-one spot, Keith and Mick hashed out "The Last Time" at Mapesbury Road, their first song that felt good enough to produce as a Rolling Stones single in Britain. "In retrospect, Mick and I learned really quickly," Keith said. "It seemed a long time at the time—sort of, 'Do we have the balls to give this to the rest of the boys to play?' Until we came up with 'The Last Time.' Then we said, 'Yeah, this one we won't be ashamed of giving to the rest of the Stones, so let's try this for a single.'"

"My vision of Keith is that he was constantly strumming the guitar, but it wasn't to find the music that was within himself—in a way, almost, it was to find the music that was out there," said Linda Keith. "It evolved all the time, it was moving ahead." Meanwhile, they continued to produce successful albums of mostly R&B covers with a few Jagger-Richards and Nanker Phelge composi-tions shoehorned in. In December 1964 their second U.S. album, *12 × 5*, went to number three.

Keith was living at full throttle, rocking around the clock, playing music, attending parties, looning about with Andrew, running amok. The first indication that he had started staying up for days at a time without sleep came on November 19 when he collapsed after performing on the British television show *Ready, Steady, Go!* Accord-ing to Wyman, "He hadn't slept for five days and was thoroughly exhausted." But most of the time he had real stamina, at least real enough to allow for continuing musical growth in a time of intense activity. In 1964 the Stones had done five British tours, two American tours, and two European tours. In mid-December 1964, "Heart of Stone," composed by Jagger and Richards, became the group's fifth U.S. single. It went into the top twenty. Richards thought it ironic that slow ballads rather than rock and roll characterized their initial success in America.

In January 1965 their second U.K. album, *The Rolling Stones No. 2*, went to number one. Keith's acne-scarred face, which was featured front and center surrounded by the brooding amphetamine glares of the group, was seen as a purposeful Oldham stroke that only made the fans more empathetic. "I'm glad I'm not the only person in the world with pimples," wrote one. "Just goes to show I guess even stars get spots. So you're human after all!"

They recorded "The Last Time" on February 17 and 18, 1965, at RCA Studios in L.A. "I'd say . . . maybe sixty to seventy percent of our output was recorded in the States during 1964, and by 1965 just about everything was done there—either in L.A. or Chicago," said Keith. Dave Hassinger, who engineered the sessions, noted that Jagger and Richards made all the decisions in the studio—the other three were only peripherally involved. Oldham, too, deferred to them.

The hierarchy in the studio had reached its final form. Keith and Mick were in charge. By now Keith's position as the band's producer had become an unspoken rule. As Hassinger described it, after a playback everybody looked at Keith, and if he was smiling they knew they had a good take. There was never any discussion. Behind the scenes, however, everything was not so copacetic. Wyman complained that Jagger and Richards had a monopoly on songwriting credits and, in turn, the lucrative royalties.

"The Last Time," released in early March, was the first Jagger-Richards composition to appear on the A-side of a single in Britain. As one critic described it, "What lifted 'The Last Time' out of the ordinary was the four-note phrase by Keith Richards that slithered through the lyric with a malign, unignorable persistence, like migraine rendered into sound." The night of its release, the Stones played on the TV show *Ready, Steady, Go!* Frenzied fans stormed the stage. On March 18, "The Last Time" went to number one in the U.K. In the U.S. it reached number nine. In April, their third U.S. album, *The Rolling Stones, Now!*, went to number five. Richards and Jagger had perfected a formula and pinned an audience. "They had a terrific aim on the junior high mentality which pervaded rock from the start," said Albert Goldman. "But the Stones took that kind of juvenile orientation and turned it around on its nasty side, particularly among the boys of that age group, with one finger up their nose and one up their ass wanking it. That seemed to me pretty much the center of gravity for the Stones."

For years Jagger was credited in the media as the Stones' main songwriter. It was little known that the early Stones originals were primarily Richards compositions. When he was at school Keith appeared to have a bad memory, but he discovered that he kept bits of songs in his head and could produce them at will. Occasionally he taped his riffs, but for the most part he just relied upon the tape recorder in his brain. Clearly Richards needed Jagger to pull these songs out of him. Sitting knee to knee in vans, planes, trains, dressing and hotel rooms, Jagger and Richards would play old blues numbers and then take off into their own compositions. Keith played his riffs slowly over and over again and made sounds that only Mick, who would translate them into lyrics and often speed up the beat, appeared to understand. It was, Keith said, like making love.

7
Satisfaction
1965

We realized that there was a whole different thing in the works, because it became obvious that you could expand this thing. And what made that possible was that we managed to export it—which was the most *blinding* thing to any musician at that point. I mean, before that, you had to be the biggest dreamer in the world to think that you could export this stuff to America.

KEITH RICHARDS, *from an interview with Kurt Loder*, 1987

On the night of May 9, 1965, Keith awoke in a hotel room in Clearwater, Florida, with a riff running through his mind, and he quickly recorded it on a cassette tape.

RICHARDS: "I dreamt this riff. That was the first time it had happened to me. I just woke up, picked up the guitar, and ... 'I can't get no ... satisfaction ...' It was very funny 'cause that night I was so tired, I pushed the button and I got the guitar and I ran through the sequence once. On the tape you can hear me drop the pick and the rest of the tape is me snoring. The only way I found it again was, the next morning I checked out my gear, and the tape was at the wrong end. It had played all the way through. How had that happened? Had somebody come in during the night—Mick or one of the boys—and said, 'Fuck you, Keith Richards, piece of shit'? I rewound to find out what had happened.

"'Satisfaction' was the biggest hit we've ever had and it just came boing bang crash, and it was on tape before I felt it. People say they write songs, but in a way you're more the medium. I feel like all the songs in the world are just floating around, it's just a matter of, like, an antenna, or whatever you pick up. So many uncanny things have happened. A whole song just appears from nowhere in five minutes, the whole structure, and you haven't worked at all. You're playing and you're bored stiff and nothing's happening, oh, dear, and you go out and 'ave a joint or something—euhuh! There it is. It's just like somebody tuned in the radio and you've picked it up. Some people equate good work with being difficult to do, but a lot of the time it's the easiest thing. It just sort of flashes by you so quick that people virtually tell you. You didn't even see it yourself."

The next day they flew to Chicago for a three-day recording session at Chess Studios, but failed to turn Keith's riff into an acceptable track. On the fourteenth they flew to L.A. for a two-day session with Dave Hassinger at RCA. Richards had begun to use cocaine as well as speed to stay awake. On the fifteenth they worked for fourteen hours recording six new songs, including "Satisfaction." By the sixteenth they had completed their next album, *Out of Our Heads*, and their most famous single. Ironically, Richards, who felt so sure he knew how the band should sound, did not agree with Charlie, Bill, Stu, Hassinger, and Oldham that it was the best thing they had ever done.

RICHARDS: "If I'd had my way, 'Satisfaction' would never have been released. The song was basic as the hills and I thought the fuzz guitar thing was a bit of a gimmick. So when they said they wanted it as a single, I got up on my hind legs for the first time and said, 'NO WAY!'"

When the decision was put to a vote, Jagger sided with Richards, but they were outnumbered, and four weeks after Keith had dreamed the initial riff, "Satisfaction" was released as their seventh U.S. single. "Opening with Keith Richards' menacing fuzz-tone riff and sung with an insinuating, calculated slowness by Jagger, the smoldering sound of 'Satisfaction' summed up the frustrations of the sixties in a new emotional language: an ironic blend of blues, R&B and Motown rock that the Stones had been working on since 1962, now powered with the driving infusion of soul music," wrote one critic: "'Satisfaction' was the first of Keith's monolithic riff transformations: the model, matrix and masterpiece for all the future Stones' gold from 'Get Off of My Cloud' to 'Miss You.' 'Satisfaction' was the greatest of the Stones' inner-city hymns— blues words with a soul sound in a rock song," concluded another.

On July 10 "Satisfaction" became their first American number one. By then Keith and Linda were on vacation in the south of France.

LINDA KEITH: "I think that Keith enjoyed his stardom and success thoroughly. When 'Satisfaction' went to number one in America he was excited. There was so much status invested in him that his confidence increased, although status that comes from the outside rather than from the inside can leave one frail as well. He was really enjoying the success, the money, the kudos, not in any showy way, not in any flash way, but in a sort of appropriate way."

That summer "The Last Time" was number one in Australia, Germany, Malaysia, New Zealand, Denmark, France, Italy, Turkey, Greece, Spain, Yugoslavia, and Hong Kong. On August 20 "Satisfaction" was released internationally and went to number one in Britain, Turkey, Greece, Finland, South Africa, Argentina, the Philippines, Lebanon, Israel, and Bermuda. Their album *Out of Our Heads*, which contained three Jagger-Richards and four Nanker Phelge songs, went to number two in the U.K. and number one in America.

During 1965 Richards and Jagger wrote "Get Off of My Cloud," "Play with Fire," "Blue Turns to Grey," "What a Shame," "The Under Assistant West Coast Promotion Man," "The Spider and the Fly," "One More Try," "The Singer Not the Song," "Gotta Get Away," and "I'm Free." The band sold ten million singles and five million LPs, and earned more than five million dollars on the concert circuit. And Keith Richards went from being the least well-known member of the Rolling Stones to being a man whose music never stopped playing on the planet twenty-four hours a day 365 days a year. If Willie Dixon can be said to have been the man most responsible for turning the rural impulse of Muddy Waters, Howlin' Wolf, and the other blues legends into the urban and varied music that found an audience and became an influence on future generations, as Peter Watrous has written in *The New York Times*, then Keith Richards can be seen to have been the man who picked up where Dixon left off, "using savage or stately riffs, smooth horns or rhythmic stop-time figures to make the blues new and worth listening to again." Richards went beyond the traditional blues and synthesized his own experiences into a new form of socially reflective pop song. He has succeded better than anyone else in his time at making, as Watrous wrote of Dixon, "something people might remember, something that could stand out in the onslaught of fresh images and language of modern life." "Looking at it over the years, I suppose that the Rolling Stones somehow reverberate to some currently universal vibrational mode," Richards said. "Music has always seemed streaks ahead of any other art form or any other form of social expression. After air, food, water, and fucking, I think maybe music is the next human necessity. People think music is a luxury. In actual *fact*, music is a necessity, because it's the one thing that will maybe bring you up and give you just that little bit extra to keep on going." When *Newsweek* portrayed the Stones as a "leering quintet" best known for its "tasteless themes" and, in general, dirty lyrics, such as "I can't get no satisfaction, I can't get no girlie action," Richards said, "It was then I realized what Lenny Bruce was talking about."

As writing songs became easier, recording them became more difficult. The Stones toured incessantly between 1963 and 1966, doing more gigs per year than any other band (in 1965, for example, they did two American tours, two European tours, two British tours, and one Australasian tour). They were moving around the world so fast that they had to shoehorn in sessions between concerts. They might, for example, fly into L.A. for two days on their way from Australia to Europe to record a single and some album tracks. "Get Off of My Cloud" was recorded this way on September 6 and 7, 1965. In November it went to number one in America and England, but Richards felt that the production was not up to par.

RICHARDS: "It's difficult to realize what pressure we were under to keep on turning out hits. Each single you made in those days had to be better and do better. If the next one didn't do as well as the last one, everyone told you you were sliding out. After 'Satisfaction,' we all thought, 'Wow, lucky us. Now for a good rest . . .' And then in comes Andrew Oldham saying, 'Right, where's the next one?' It got to be a state of mind. Every eight weeks, you had to come up with a red-hot song that said it all in about two minutes, thirty seconds."

Linda Keith felt that Keith was being pulled away from his R&B

roots by Jagger's and Jones's quest for pop stardom. She thought Keith's own stuff, his voice, his sense of the song should be in the forefront, that Keith should play his own music, that at the moment that it became commercial Richards began to lose control of his music.

The business of rock and roll was brutal. Record companies were run more like cartels than legitimate businesses. Rock stars were inevitably young, inexperienced, and constantly in a state of nervous tension or euphoria. Rock and roll tours generated large sums of cash quickly. Every parasite and creep in the area attached himself to the bands. Between 1963 and 1965 the Rolling Stones had generated millions of dollars, but very little of it had found its way into their bank accounts. At the time that his music was selling around the world, Keith was being paid fifty pounds a week. When he returned to London from the States in September 1965, he moved into the Hilton Hotel, but soon had to evacuate because he couldn't afford it. Just as great black musicians from Muddy Waters to Little Richard had been ripped off for millions so were the Stones robbed blind by everybody.

Although Keith often said that he wasn't interested in money as long as they had enough to keep the show on the road, it is not by coincidence that he has been one of the top earners in rock and roll for the last thirty years. When the promoter Robert Stigwood allegedly refused to pay the promised percentage of the receipts for a 1965 Australian tour, Richards accosted him in a London nightclub and, according to rock journalist Keith Altham, "started to beat the shit out of him. Every time Stigwood tried to get up, Keith would belt him again. 'Keith,' I said, 'why do you keep hitting him?' 'Because he keeps getting up,' he said."

In 1965 the Stones replaced their manager, Eric Easton, with Allen Klein. Richards was the driving force in their decision.

RICHARDS: "Eric Easton was just too tired. We couldn't get anything done. He wasn't all that young, and after the strain of our last two U.S. tours, he couldn't make the third one. In fact, he was ill. You think, 'What the fuck do we need him for?' . . . Because that's the way it was. Onward."

Andrew Oldham had discovered an American manager named Allen Klein who was buying up the British rock groups like cheap real estate and producing a lot of fast cash for them. With his gangster image and his bottom-line-accountant's ability to ferret out money where no one else could find it, Klein was an ideal match for Richards. When they met in London's Hilton Hotel, there was an immediate recognition. Despite Klein's diabolical clothes and his squat frame, Keith was impressed by his insistence that he would get them out of their poorly negotiated contract with Decca and get them a million-dollar advance on a new contract.

When Klein had asked Oldham at their first meeting who made the records, Oldham had pointed at Keith. Klein recognized Richards as a songwriter on a par with Bob Dylan and Paul Simon. He paid particular attention to Jagger, feeling he needed to be dealt with "like a chick." Within a year, Klein promised Richards and Jagger, they would both be millionaires. On Jagger's twenty-second birthday, July 26, 1965, the band congregated at Oldham's office at 138 Ivor Court en route to the meeting with Klein at the Hilton Hotel. When Wyman suggested that they be represented by a lawyer, Keith leapt up, screaming, "Don't be so fucking mercenary. We've got to trust someone."

RICHARDS: "I was saying, 'Let's turn things around. Let's do something.' We had to get someone who'd make it work or fuck it up once and for all."

What impressed Richards about Klein most was his gangster image. A short man with a pugnacious face and the schlub body of a character who spends most of his time bent over financial reports, Klein, who posed in photographs with a shotgun, wearing sneakers and a T-shirt, like a movie version of a mob boss, appeared to be nothing short of a genius to his clients. Within a week of agreeing to be represented by him, the five Rolling Stones, with the full support of Oldham, who was finding it difficult to take care of their finances, found themselves in the office of the chairman of Decca Records, Sir Edward Lewis, standing behind Klein's chair. Klein blasted Lewis with profanity, threats, insults, and bottom line demands.

RICHARDS: "He said, 'All we want you to do is get yourself a pair of shades and just stand behind me in a row while I talk. Whatever you do, don't say a word, don't open your mouth.' We just stood there. He put the case, 'You're going to do this, you're going to do that,' and they crumbled in front of our eyes, those hard-boiled English lawyers, they just *shuuush*. And we came out with the best record contract, so that impresses a guy. He did a good job."

Between 1963 and 1965, the Stones' royalties from London and Decca Records totaled around 250,000 pounds. Klein renegotiated an advance of 1,000,000 pounds for U.K. and foreign rights and 1,800,000 pounds for American rights. Their take on the Klein-run 1965 winter tour of the U.S. was forecast to be an unprecedented two million dollars. In the beginning, Richards and Jagger saw Klein as the next greatest-person-they-had-ever-met.

RICHARDS: "Klein was young and he knew what was happening. We decided on an American as our new business manager because, let's face it, when you're handling worldwide transactions, America is the only place to work from, and we did so much business there it was very useful to have a man on the spot. We kept in touch by phone."

Klein explained that in order to protect them from the British tax system, he would channel their money through New York, but he neglected to mention that it wasn't going into the account of their British publishing company, Nanker Phelge Music, but into the account of Nanker Phelge USA, a company he controlled. The way the contract was written, all monies the Stones earned went into Klein's account, and he didn't have to give them a cent of it for years unless he wanted to. And for the next five years, during which time the Stones were for the most part broke, in debt, or "waiting for a big check," he didn't want to. Instead, he lent them money. Consequently, while they were able to maintain the luxurious lives of rock stars, none of them ever had large sums in their own names, and they remained all the more dependent on him.

From 1965 to 1968 the band were happy with the association and looked upon Klein as an avuncular protector and hero. Oldham stayed on board as catalyst-publicist and the Stones sailed into 1966 blissfully unaware that they had been hoodwinked by one of the greatest operators in the music business. Richards, Jagger, and Oldham were out of their depth with Klein, whose Christmas cards reportedly once read, "Though I walk through the valley of the shadow of death I shall fear no evil, for I am the biggest bastard in the valley." But at first they couldn't see this any more than they had been able to see how the record company was taking advantage of them. They were always on the road or under pressure to produce a record. There was no time to think about, let alone check up on, such matters. In all fairness, it must be said that Klein got them much better deals than Easton. It was Klein, Richards pointed out, who turned them into a global phenomenon. In 1966 and 1967 Klein gradually replaced Oldham as the third mind in the group. The Stones' lack of judgment was perfectly understandable. Klein appeared to be exactly what he said he was—on their side. He got them vast sums of money, restructured their business globally, and shepherded them through three years of prosperity during which they would generate two hundred million dollars. However, his primary aim was to make a fortune for himself. Before he had finished with them, Klein would gain publishing rights to their most lucrative creation—all the songs from 1963 through 1969—and the Stones would lose what Richards subsequently believed was in the neighborhood of fifteen million dollars.

Whatever detractors say about Allen Klein, he had a bigger vision of the Rolling Stones' global potential than anybody else.

The first thing Klein did was launch the Stones on a forty-two-day tour of the U.S. with more publicity, more protection, and higher fees than ever before. A cobbled-together album of outtakes and rejects called *December's Children* was released to coincide with the tour. Keith was pissed off at the transparently commercial nature of the product and grumbled that they never would have dared foist it off on their English fans. But in America, where its release was accompanied by a twenty-five-foot-high billboard in Times Square, the album stormed up the charts, reaching number four, and the concerts were sold out.

The tour was efficiently run. The Stones had their own airplane, and they were often on it before the audience left the auditorium.

They usually arrived in the next town between 4:00 and 5:00 A.M., slept through the morning, gathered in the afternoon for publicity sessions, and spent the balance of the day waiting to go on, but touring was still arduous and violent enough for the Stones to maintain their up-against-them philosophy. Knickers and gifts were thrown on stage every night with notes: "Call me, I'm hot for you." Animosity from the authorities increased in direct proportion to their sexual effect on the fans. From October to December 1965, everywhere they went in America the Stones experienced incredulous revulsion from policemen, sheriffs, hotel clerks, and waitresses. People spat on them. Everything was right on edge all the time. Everybody was in a constant state of fear. "I've never been hated by so many people I've met as in Nebraska in the midsixties," Keith recalled. "You could tell they just wanted to beat the shit out of you."

"They did a great job making people hate them," said their new U.S. tour manager, Mike Gruber. "Their image was built and manufactured but they fit the part. Keith was the image. The Stones were him; it jumped out of his body the first time I saw him." Keith was always fighting to defend the Stones. When someone called the group a bunch of faggots during the New York stop on the tour, Keith booted him in the mouth.

By the end of 1965, Richards and Jagger were beginning to express an increasingly chauvinistic attitude toward women in their songs. "It was almost as if women in all their contradictory human-ity symbolized the conditions of life that were the ultimate target of the Stones' anger," noted one critic.

RICHARDS: "It was all a spin-off from our environment ... hotels and too many dumb chicks. Not all dumb, not by any means, but that's how one got. You got really cut off."

They started recording *Aftermath* at RCA Studios in Hollywood on December 3, 1965, while grinding through the last four days of the tour. They spent up to twenty-one hours at a stretch working on the album. They were all so exhausted that Oldham wouldn't let anyone leave the studio to go to a restaurant because they would fall asleep. Jones let Richards down by getting sick on the road and showing up for sessions too out of it to work.

Keith found Brian's behavior beneath contempt. He enjoyed getting high, drinking, and partying, but never to the extent that it interfered with his work. Brian's incapacity was particularly annoying because Keith had come to depend upon him as a guitar partner, and under pressure to produce an album between gigs Richards was facing twice as much work. Keith's sole consolation was that he learned a lot from having to play most of the guitar parts on *December's Children* and *Aftermath*.

Ironically, when Brian did manage to make it to the *Aftermath* sessions in good enough shape to play, he made some of his greatest contributions to a Stones record.

RICHARDS: "Brian would be down on his back, lying around the studio with his guitar strapped around him. Then he would contribute amazing things. Suddenly, from nine hours of lying there (or often not being at the sessions at all for two or three days, which would really get up everybody's back), he'd just walk in and lay some beautiful things down on a track (piano, harpsichord), something that nobody'd even thought of."

Keith had other problems on the tour. At the Sacramento concert on December 3, the band had just launched into "The Last Time" when Keith ran up to his microphone to sing the chorus. Finding it facing in the wrong direction, he banged it with the neck of his guitar. There was a blinding flash. He was thrown by an electric shock and landed, unconscious, on his back. Before Keith hit the ground, Jagger, who had dropped his own mike, was running toward him. Wyman swiftly unplugged Richards's guitar as medics rushed out from backstage and the curtains closed. An eerie silence filled the hall. The confused audience wondered what was happening. The Stones stood around helplessly looking down at their fallen leader, who they all believed was dead. "It was very frightening," recalled Gered Mankowitz, who snapped a series of dramatic photographs. As they realized what had happened, girls in the audience started screaming, and praying. Two long minutes later, Keith, looking dazed but apparently unharmed, sat up. Three of his guitar strings had been burned apart like fused wire. According to doctors who examined him at hospital, Keith was saved by the thick soles of his Hush Puppy suede boots, which prevented the charge from grounding.

Doctors told Keith that he ought to rest for a few days, but the next day he was back, playing another gig. "As Bob Dylan was doing his first scandalous half-folk, half-rock shows, a few miles south at the Oakland Civic Auditorium, the Rolling Stones were doing their raunchy British version of Chicago blues," wrote the author of *Haight-Ashbury*, Charles Perry. "When the Stones show ended leafleteers appeared out in front distributing hand-lettered sheets reading, 'Can you pass the acid test?' and giving an address. The acid test drew about four hundred people." Keith and Brian attended Ken Kesey and the Merry Pranksters' acid test party that night.

After finishing the tour in L.A. and in between working on *Aftermath*, Keith, Stones aide Ronnie Schneider, and Gered Mankowitz flew to Phoenix, Arizona, and went horseback riding overnight in the McDowell Mountains.

GERED MANKOWITZ: "Keith invited us, and paid all our expenses, which was really sweet of him—frankly, we couldn't have afforded it otherwise. The first thing we did, at Keith's insistence, was to get kitted out from top to bottom in cowboy gear ... ten-gallon hats, chaps, everything. Plus, we were armed to the teeth with side guns, pump-action Winchester rifles—all the genuine article. We went to a well-known dude ranch outside of Phoenix, where we took up with a guide named Sam Earp (a descendant of Wyatt), who took us to a place on the Apache reservation called Green River. The Apaches around there were all shepherds, and it was truly beautiful country. We set up a safe shooting range in a gully and practiced with our Colt. 45 revolvers. We stayed there overnight cooking steaks and baked potatoes on an open fire, drinking beer, telling stories ... we were even woken by gunfire—a bobcat was trying to steal our food, and Sam Earp was shooting at it. Riding back to the ranch the next day we got caught in this fantastic flash flood, and Sam got us to help herd some cattle nearer to the ranch so they wouldn't get isolated—not only did I get to fulfil all of my pop-star fantasies on that tour, being chased by hordes of girls and so on, but I also got to live out every boy's own cowboy fantasy as well! The flight back to L.A. was hysterical. Apart from looking like the James gang, we stank to high heaven, having been in the saddle for forty-eight hours and nowhere near a bath. I assume we must have packed the guns away, otherwise I doubt we would have been let on the plane. Even so, we provoked some truly wonderful, horrified expressions, but once they knew we were the Rolling Stones it was OK."

8

19th Nervous Breakdown
1966

It was getting to the point that we had been playing for years and nobody knew we were playing. You know, on twenty minutes, get off, collect the forty grand, then before the coffee got cold we'd be back on the plane playing poker. It was a drag.

KEITH RICHARDS, *from an interview with John Carpenter, 1969*

At the beginning of 1966, in his first major purchase since becoming a star, Keith bought a house in the country one and a half hours southwest of London for twenty thousand pounds, where he hoped he and Linda might settle down together. Redlands was a Tudor-style house with a thatched roof near the south coast in West Wittering, Sussex. Four upstairs bedrooms were serviced by one bathroom, which Keith had refurbished in a modern, luxurious mode. Eventually he had the whole house completely restored. A five-acre lawn and an eight-hundred-year-old moat supporting a colony of ducks surrounded the house. Keith was particularly proud of his new home's heritage. There were Norman and Saxon arrows in the moat. The foundations had been laid in the twelfth century.

RICHARDS: "They got in touch with me on tour in Hawaii and said, 'We've found this incredibly old bit of wall, what do you want us to do with it?' I said, 'Frame it.' And when I got there it was like one of the most beautiful paintings in the world. It's got glass over it to protect it and it's beautifully framed. It's just these old bricks with cowshit and straw holding them together. A work of art! Redlands is a beautiful joint. I'll always keep that."

Keith also bought a Bentley S Touring Continental, which he christened the Blue Lena (after Lena Horne). It was the same car Ian Fleming's fictitious hero James Bond drove. He had a record player installed and began taking long drives around the country-side, heading southwest through Sussex and Surrey.

Keith's driving habits soon became a mainstay of his legend. The artist Colin Self, to whom he once gave a lift across London, recalled that the car was beautiful and Keith drove it with a lot of confidence. It boasted, he noted, Turkish embassy flags so that Keith would never get pulled over by the police. "On the way," Self recalled, "we stopped at a café and Keith had egg and chips and sort of messed it up a bit and ate like somebody out of a William Burroughs novel, with dead-fish eyes and a sort of semismacking of the lips." Another acquaintance recalled a drive with Keith through Paris: "He was incredible! He'd just bounce off everything. He just didn't care. We'd all be sitting there in the car and everybody would say, 'Oh, I think we've just hit a tree!'"

Just as Richards was beginning to enjoy the spoils of his success, what had become a lifeline relationship with Linda fell apart. She had become heavily involved with drugs, particularly heroin. Richards expected everyone to have his own tolerance and control over drugs. Linda was getting so out of it that she was an impossible companion. She couldn't be there for him when he needed her, and sometimes he couldn't take her anywhere because of her condition. Although he was using speed, pot, coke, and alcohol and had recently dropped acid with Kesey, Linda said Keith still wasn't using heroin or into hard drugs at all.

LINDA KEITH: "I remember that strongly because I used to have to make excuses for the state I was in. And although I didn't want him to start getting into any negative relationship with drugs, when you're using you want other people to. There were loads of drugs around back then and things were getting a bit crazy in general. I mean, I was crazy and I became a bit hard and nasty, probably, and I think I was less likable by then than I had been. I suppose that was part of the problem we had. He wasn't happy with the stoned Linda and it all got a bit awkward. I think Keith maintained his way and I turned, but I think both Keith and I behaved horribly. He did some nasty things, but I just couldn't go on—our relationship was not going anywhere."

*

"Through the beginning of 1965 when the group transcribed the Staple Singers' 'This May Be the Last Time,' Jagger and Richards still had not discovered a satisfactory style of writing their own material," wrote Charlie Gillett in *The Sound of the City: The Rise of Rock and Roll*. "But when Mick Jagger and Keith Richards suddenly escaped from the derivative songs they had been writing before and produced these exciting records with hard, compelling guitar riffs and angry lyrics, they became one of the few groups that pursued the hard sound and joined it to social comment. The Stones made particularly good use of a Dylan-like writing style and posture in successive hits through 1965–1966."

On February 4, 1966, the Stones released another classic Jagger-Richards single, "19th Nervous Breakdown," internationally. Propelled by Keith's guitar and a Jerry Lee Lewis beat, it went to number two in the U.K. and the U.S. "We didn't ask ourselves what is the most commercial," said Keith. "We simply said, 'We like this one the best.' What we have liked over the past few years proved to be what the young people like, so this is how to choose a single. This is probably the way that Mozart wrote. He wrote for himself. So do we. And it is a happy coincidence that what we like is also what the public likes."

The same month, Andrew Oldham's independent Immediate label released an album, *Today's Pop Symphony* by the Aranbee Pop Symphony Orchestra (*Aranbee* stood for *R&B*), which was produced by Richards and featured orchestrated versions of his favorite pop songs. The songs he chose for this revealing anthology were "There's a Place," "Rag Doll," "I Got You Babe," "We Can Work It Out," "Play with Fire," "Mother's Little Helper," "In the Midnight Hour," "Take It or Leave It," "Sitting on a Fence," and "I Don't Want to Go On Without You." Wyman has cast doubt on the album's authenticity, charging that it was "another episode in Andrew's campaign to increase Keith's profile," but this assessment reveals more about Wyman's bitterness than his critical acumen. The record received critical attention. "Anyone who thinks Keith's talents are limited will be forced to think again," stated the *Record Mirror*. "He's taken ten quality pop songs and under his direction the orchestra performs them in near-classical style. His way of blending pop and classical together has worked out well." As early as 1964 Keith had spoken about wanting to produce records, and he was particularly interested in the relations between pop and classical music, as anyone who looked at his record collection at Redlands could have seen. Albums of Tchaikovsky and Segovia music sat next to his Elvis and Beatles collections. Oldham and Richards had collaborated on several projects, producing a single of "Blowing in the Wind" by Marianne Faithfull and even writing a song, "I'd Much Rather Be with the Boys," together. Although Oldham certainly played a role in the project, this was actually Keith's first solo outing. Poor sales may have put him off further solo projects, but the album signaled that his vision went beyond what Ian Stewart called "my little three-chord wonders."

Throughout February and March of 1966 the Stones were back on the road. Their first stop was the U.S.A., where they appeared on *The Ed Sullivan Show*. While in New York, they stayed in separate hotels to avoid being mobbed. After stopping for a show in Hawaii two days later, they flew to Australia for their second Far East tour. In New Zealand, Keith was treated in a hospital for a cut above his eye, inflicted by rioting fans who jumped on him.

On April 15 *Aftermath* was released in the U.K. and went straight to number one.

ROY CARR: "*Aftermath* follows directly in the wake of the Stones' trilogy of songs based on their American Experience: '(I Can't Get No) Satisfaction,' 'Get Off of My Cloud' and '19th Nervous Breakdown,' and it establishes that they had gained sufficient confidence in their own writing prowess to present an album of all-original material. Though perhaps they weren't aware of it then, their initial adrenalin rush (which had sustained them for three years) was just about exhausted. However, the sheer momentum of their struggle for Stateside supremacy enabled them to pull off this *coup de grâce* without showing any signs of artistic fatigue."

It was at this juncture, the writer Hanif Kureishi has pointed out, that pop music began to speak "of ordinary experience with far more precision, real knowledge, and wit than, say, British fiction of the equivalent period." The American writer Camille Paglia, whose idol is Keith Richards, said "In my generation of the sixties, rock musicians read poetry. They thought of themselves as thinking, feeling beings. And out of that, you got great music. I feel the rock musician is an artist." Decca's publicity department announced in a press release, "We look to Shakespeare and Dickens and Chaucer for accounts of other times in our history, and we feel that tomorrow we will on many occasions look to the gramophone records of the Rolling Stones . . . who act as a mirror for today's mind, action and happenings." The Stones began to receive the kind of academic attention that would turn them from pop stars into artists and, in Richards' opinion, put them "in danger of becoming respectable."

An exchange in the *New Left Review* between Alan Beckett and Richard Merton made the following points.

ALAN BECKETT: "The Stones' music is now very much related to social life in the 1960s, and even specifically to London life. Though their music certainly has general reference, it seems probable that their full impact can only be realized by someone who has experience of the metropolitan environment. For instance, consider the archetypal girl who is described in 'Play with Fire,' and subsequently in '19th Nervous Breakdown' and elsewhere—rich, spoiled, confused, weak, using drugs, etc. Anyone who has been around Chelsea or Kensington can put at least one name to this character."

RICHARD MERTON: "The enormous merit—and audacity—of the Stones is to have repeatedly and consistently defied what is a central taboo of the social system: mention of sexual inequality. They have done so in the most radical and unacceptable way possible: by celebrating it. The unmitigated triumph of these records is their rejection of the spurious world of monadic personal relationships. They are concerned with the oppressive matrix that is their general truth.

"The same is true of the second main theme articulated by the Stones—mental illness. Again this is a taboo topic as a normal social experience. These songs are uniquely brutal and truthful, broaching realities which are constantly denied or diluted in the enervating mists of traditional pop music.

"The Stones have refused the given orthodoxy of pop music; their work is a dark and vertical negation of it. It is an astonishing fact that there is virtually not one Jagger-Richards composition which is conventionally about a happy or unhappy personal relationship. Love, jealousy and lament—the substance of 85 percent of traditional pop music—are missing. Sexual exploitation, mental disintegration and physical immersion are their substitutes."

On April 16, 1966, Richards moved into Redlands with a dog, Ratbag, with whom he appeared to identify more than anybody else. Keith decorated the big living room with lion-skin rugs, a wildebeest-skin mat, rabbit- and wolf-skin rugs, Moroccan cushions, tapestries, and a state-of-the-art sound system. A comfortable settee and stone table were the main pieces of furniture. The centerpiece was a baronial fireplace. His library contained *The Great War*, *A Dictionary of Slang*, *Guns*, *Great Sea Battles*, *Rembrandt's Drawings*, and various books on England. Keith had a month off the road to enjoy his new house. However, a further breakdown in his relationship with Linda made the transition traumatic. "Redlands was sensational," she said. "It was a very big turn-on, but it was pretty near the end of our relationship and I don't have good memories of having good times at Redlands."

In May Linda moved to New York. Her abrupt departure could not have come at a worse time. Jagger seemed to be on the verge of a nervous breakdown. Jones had been deteriorating for over a year and was not contributing much to the band. A grueling U.S. tour was scheduled for June. Richards and Jagger were under a lot of pressure to perform and promote *Aftermath*.

Despite his own growing popularity, Richards remained shy among some members of the pop aristocracy. On May 26 the Stones played their next single, "Paint It, Black," on BBC TV's *Top of the Pops*, then went straight to Bob Dylan's electric concert at London's Albert Hall. "Keith wouldn't dare meet Dylan," recalled one friend. "When Keith met Dylan for the first time he was, like, speechless. Brian set the pace. Afterwards it gave Keith the space to come in and be accepted in Dylan's camp." Years later, when he was a junkie, Keith would tell the writer Nick Kent that Dylan had been using heroin that night. "They had to carry him into [the London club] Blaises and then I went over to him and I was pretty frightened of him." "I could write 'Satisfaction,' but you couldn't write 'Mr. Tambourine Man,'" Dylan snarled when the meeting took place. "Everyone was frightened of Dylan because he had a piercing wit," said Kent. "Keith didn't yet have that glimmer that he would shortly acquire, and he was a shy bloke." Richards had had a similar reaction when he had been introduced to Brigitte Bardot a month earlier. According to one observer, when Keith was introduced to Brigitte he seemed totally overcome, "as if he were being introduced to the queen. Brigitte said something to him, he muttered something in return, backed away, and melted into the crowd."

On June 11 "Paint It, Black" reached number one in the U.S.A., where *Aftermath* would go to number two. Two tracks, "Mother's Little Helper" and "Lady Jane," were released as another U.S. single. The A-side went to number eight, the B-side to number twenty-four. By now people were beginning to buy more albums than singles.

When Richards arrived in New York on June 23 to set out on the next American tour and checked into the Holiday Inn, where he would maintain a suite during the tour's Eastern leg, he discovered that Linda had formed an intense relationship with an as yet unknown young black guitar player named Jimmy James, who would shortly change his name to Jimi Hendrix. "Intelligent and cultured, Linda was just as hungry for the real experience of black urban blues as the English musicians," wrote Hendrix biographer David Henderson. "She began to go to Cafe Wha? on MacDougal Street in the Village every night. There, in his long, open-ended sets, she heard Hendrix's incredibly versatile range through everything from blues to young Dylan. It was obvious to her that Hendrix would be a star." Linda began looking after Jimi. She gave him access to Richards's hotel suite, limousine, and a brand-new Stratocaster she "borrowed" from Keith. According to Sheila Oldham, who was now married to Andrew, "Linda was madly in love with Jimi and wanted a committed relationship. She was quite desperate to get something going, but Hendrix was involved with somebody else." "At the point that I met Jimi my involvement with Keith was running out," Linda said. "It was almost out and done. Our relationship was maybe hanging from a thread." Apparently Richards bore Hendrix no ill will. "I had a chick run off with Jimi Hendrix once," he told a friend. "I think he's a nice cat actually."

The Stones were still rolling on the shock-tactic tracks on which Oldham had set them. On the first night of the tour the majority of the band's equipment, including an extremely rare instrument, Jones's electronic dulcimer, was stolen. Their shows lasted little more than half an hour and consisted mostly of frantic renditions of their hits. At every concert the police clubbed the audience, often stopping the show midway to demand calm, or stopping it altogether. At the War Memorial Auditorium in Syracuse, Brian tried to steal an American flag that had been spread out backstage across a chair to dry, and a stagehand snatched it back, creating a scene and a few headlines. The Vietnam War era wasn't the time to kid around with the American flag. The police and management freaked. Keith said, "Fuck you, leave Brian alone." The promoters said, "Fuck you, go back to London and starve."

By now they automatically pushed everything to the edge. Getting off a plane, they might smash a photographer's equipment to assure media coverage in the following day's papers. "Whatever happened," noted Mike Gruber, "Keith would take a stand and stick to it. If seven cops backed me into a corner, Keith would be the only person there swinging."

Rick Derringer opened the shows with the McCoys.

RICK DERRINGER: "The Stones were very much an enclosed unit—no jamming, no private stuff. We got to go to the parties a little bit. They were a very, very close unit, but it was great. We learned a lot from them about crowd control, about how to work an audience, and about promotion and publicity. They were very much in character all the time. And they realized it. They became the bad boys and they used it as much as they could. Keith still uses that kind of character—I mean, he's a really nice guy, he's also got this image that's become him. He might have a fight sometimes, but you don't really get the feeling Keith's going to use the knife."

Reunited by the opposition and hardship and with Gruber's help as road manager, Brian and Keith returned to the us-against-them relationship they had left at Edith Grove.

RICHARDS: "To some extent the hatchets were buried on that '66 tour. It was a big laugh because we got everybody turned on for the first time. We were totally wrecked every day on real good Mexican grass. We knew this was going to be our last American tour for a bit, so this was more of a celebration."

On August 7, the Stones flew to L.A. to record their next single, "Have You Seen Your Mother, Baby, Standing in the Shadow?," at RCA Studios with Dave Hassinger. Despite being temporarily back in Keith's gang, Jones was nearly useless in the studio and Richards had to dub over all his parts. By this method they managed to record a fantastic backing track, but in its haste to release it, the record company substituted a secondary track by mistake. The great track was lost forever. Eight years later Richards would still defend the Stones' original of the song as "a monster." "The difference between our live sound and what we were putting down in the studio was light-years apart," he said. "With 'Have You Seen Your Mother' we were starting to change direction slightly. We just didn't have the physical energy to attempt that. We'd been on the road for four years nonstop." In L.A. that week, in one of his rare attempts to find solace in the arms of a groupie, Keith intercepted a pretty hippie Bill had brought home the night before as she was leaving Wyman's suite. The following day Keith discovered he had acquired a dose of the clap.

The Stones flew to New York to be photographed for the sleeve of the single "Have You Seen Your Mother." Jerry Schatzberg, initiating what would become a theme, shot the first record sleeve of the Rolling Stones in drag, on Park Avenue in daylight. Highly amused by the opportunity to dress up as women, the English boys attached false breasts to their skinny chests, stuck lopsided wigs over their long hair, and pulled together a variety of outfits. Sarah Jagger, Millicent Watts, and Molly Richards, looked like caricatures of working class World War II widows. Worst of all was the mortifying Penelope Wyman, who assumed the role of a crippled maiden aunt sitting in a wheelchair with bony legs crossed grotesquely. Only Brian, whose peaches-and-cream complexion lent itself to his pose as Flossie, an airline stewardess, managed to look attractive. This being New York, the spectacle of these cross-dressers cavorting on Park Avenue in the early A.M. raised not an eyebrow. In fact, after the session Flossie pushed Penelope's wheelchair into a nearby bar and all "the girls" sat around nursing beers undisturbed. A chesty Keith, who one observer thought was "slightly embarrassed by it all," nominated Wyman for "the King of the Queens award for his portrayal of the bird in the wheelchair."

As soon as Keith returned to London that August, he called Linda's parents and painted a horrifying picture of their daughter's plight. "He told my parents that he tried to speak with me in New York and I was cross with him," Linda recalled. "He told them I was living with a bad type called Jimi Hendrix." "Linda's parents were absolutely devastated by the whole thing," said Sheila Oldham. "She comes from a nice Jewish background and it does not fit in at all. Her mother was calling me up quite a lot. They were desperate to get her back and her mother obviously realized that she was out of control. She was completely out of control. You only had to look at her to see that she was right on the edge. And I think, in fact, it was a caring thing for Keith to do. It probably saved her life, actually."

Linda's father made her a ward of the court and flew to New York to bring her back to London. On August 24 Linda returned to her parents' flat in Hampstead, where she would be grounded for the next few months. When she got there, Keith was waiting. "We argued and that was the end of it," Linda recalled. "We couldn't talk to each other. Then it was over. It seemed to go pretty fast. It was all over and done, but then I was pleased. I haven't seen him since that day. I felt very betrayed and I didn't ever really want to see him again.

"After we split up, I got messages from Keith—'Tell Linda she can fuck off!,' stuff like that—for years."

9
Ruby Tuesday
1966–1967

I don't regret nuthin'!

KEITH RICHARDS, *from* The Rolling Stones in Their Own Words,
compiled by David Dalton and Mick Farren, 1980

In the fall of 1966, the Rolling Stones were clearly burned out from three years on the road. Brian was teetering on the edge of a nervous breakdown. Mick was being torn apart by a screaming breakup with Chrissie and had already been treated for nervous exhaustion.

SHEILA OLDHAM: "Andrew was cracking up. He had a lot of drugs prescribed for him and I think he chose the wrong doctor who gave him the wrong drugs, mainly tranquilizers and painkillers. Andrew hurt so much. He was losing control and it frightened him. It just pinpointed all the anxiety he'd instilled in them, that they didn't want to be a one-hit wonder, they wanted to have a long career.

"If you're somebody whose music's being played all around the world, there must be some kind of feedback, and it was very difficult to ground the energy. They were just trying to find ways of getting grounded. And the strain of the work took its toll. They constantly stayed up for days working, and there was so much paranoia it was hard to work out what was real and what wasn't real. You reach a certain stage and then you think this isn't really real and then it suddenly begins to click and disillusion sets in. It was an extremely negative and an extremely positive experience. There was a lot of backlash.

"I think Keith was really hurt by Linda and it took him quite a long time to get over it. It may have made him realize that he needed a strong woman as a lifeline."

*

One of the most extraordinary things about Keith Richards's career was the number of times the perfect person showed up at the perfect time. That fall, as the band came face-to-face with their first burnout, a remarkable woman entered their lives. Anita Pallenberg, nineteen, was a German-Italian actress-model who had fallen in love with Brian Jones and moved into his London flat. At 1 Courtfield Road Anita created a brilliant salon she called "the Grand Central of rock." Anita and Brian's set included, among others, the art dealer Robert Fraser, who represented many pop artists in England. "He ran a gallery and had money and was gay and he was always up for company," recalled the author and UFO authority John Michel. "There were always a lot of openings and he liked a lot of company. He liked rough trade too, of course, but rather kept with rich hippie types." There was the photographer Michael Cooper, who Keith instantly realized was a talent of great promise and originality. Just like Keith, Michael was never without his instrument. "I remember a camera protruding from his chest as if he was some mutant," said Keith, "and he wore pink woolly socks." Michael was the most important connection for Keith in this new scene. He had a strong sense of his own importance as an artist, and this allowed Keith to develop a stronger sense of his own achievements. They spent the majority of their time together and began to take on each other's characteristics. Soon they were dressing, looking, and talking alike. "Michael and Keith were very much alike in their generosity and sense of fun," said Terry Southern. "Michael admired him tremendously. They would hang out, 'grooving on the moors,' as Michael sometimes referred to their sojourns." The development, primarily influenced by Anita Pallenberg, signaled that the Stones had outgrown their old friends. Gered Mankowitz saw the writing on the wall: "I'd gotten in on the latter part of a wide-eyed, slightly naive, this-is-all-fantastic-let's-just-go-for-it period. Michael Cooper was not just a photographer, he was part of a new social experience that they wanted to be part of. He was experimenting in many different aspects of life, and this was attractive to them. Keith became more sophisticated, and that happened quickly. In '66 they'd begun to get more sophisticated, more professional, more aware of their own power. They had moved on and I certainly wasn't moving in that direction so I became of no interest whatsoever. It was very understandable, but rather brutalizing."

An East End petty criminal named Tony Sanchez, described by one visitor as "a tall, chisel-faced Aramis king with immaculate sprayed hair, expensively cut denims, shades, and a *Hawaii Five-o* whiff of neat and silent ruthlessness," became their contact to the underworld and drugs. "Spanish Tony was basically a hustler," recalled another regular, Marianne Faithfull's husband, John Dunbar. "Robert liked him because he fancied him and he loved that frisson of danger." The men's clothes designer Michael Rainey, the film director Donald Cammell (who would make *Performance* with Jagger and Pallenberg), and Stash Klossowski (the son of the painter Balthus) completed the core of the group. Terry Southern, William Burroughs, Brion Gysin, Kenneth Anger, and many others were in and out of the scene. Paul McCartney, George Harrison, Eric Burdon, Peter Noone, the Spencer Davis Group, and other assorted members of the privileged pop world dropped in regularly. There was also a smattering of young aristocrats like the charming, lovable Guinness heir Tara Browne, who often stayed overnight discussing music, mysticism, and all the mind blowing things LSD was doing for them. He became one of Brian's closest friends. Another member of the group was the antique dealer Christopher Gibbs. "He was the key to it," said John Michel. "He was introducing them. He's got a very beautiful, loving eye for everything, he can see the best in everything, and he knows everything about everybody. The art of the time is always brewed up in a homoerotic atmosphere, isn't it? It's where young men and fine-spirited women gather because of the good conversation and sympathy and understanding."

Anita and Brian's cavernous candlelit living room, whose windows filled most of one wall, overlooked the Gloucester Road Underground station. Elegant antique chairs were arranged before a movie projector and television set. German feather beds were scattered across the floor. At one end of the room an elaborate little staircase wound up to a minstrel's gallery over which hung large Moroccan tapestries divided by a pop-art advertisement for Seven-Up. Beyond the tapestries was Anita and Brian's bedroom. At the end of the gallery a rope ladder led to a trapdoor through which a staircase ran to a large attic. Books, magazines, records, and photographs were scattered around in heaps. Messages were scrawled on the wall. Loud music throbbed constantly. Anita and Brian held court like a couple of gypsy monarchs, dressing alike, looking alike, and reigning supreme. "Courtfield Road was the first incredible place in that London scene," remembered Robert Fraser.

RICHARDS: "We were getting stoned and no one else knew what it was about. Instead of just sitting on each other's shoulders in hotel rooms, we were talking to a lot of other people."

LINDA KEITH: "I see Anita as being the forerunner of the Stones' style as it really evolved through Brian, and Brian led the way in style when Brian was with Anita. She was the most wonderful and powerful person. I have huge respect and admiration and love for her. I was in awe of Anita."

CHRISSIE SHRIMPTON: "Anita was very aware of her power but she was very compassionate. Unlike the other girls who were trying to steal my place, I never felt that way about Anita. I knew Mick admired her very much. She could have been evil, perhaps, because she was so very powerful, but what I liked about her was that she didn't use her power in an evil way. She was very weird and freaky and strong, but her feelings were genuine."

For Gered Mankowitz, she was "the epitome of the incredibly beautiful, incredibly stylish sixties woman. But I thought she was evil and manipulative and wicked. I saw her as being rather frightening. There was definitely a clique around those days, of manipulating people into situations. Anita was part of that clique." "It was never very easy, even in the early days, holding a straight conversation with Anita Pallenberg," said Ian Stewart. "She was brilliant; her mind was always racing and she would always be well ahead of you." Keith went to the heart of the matter from the male point of view. "She knew everything and she could say it in five languages," he said. "She scared the pants off me!"

ANITA PALLENBERG: "Loads of people were scared of me. I guess it was all that *savoir-vivre* that I had, and I was from Rome and I had traveled and been in New York and I knew all these people, and I was pretty reckless as well.

"You could see Keith and Mick exchanging looks like, 'Who is this weird bird?' Mick, especially, was very hostile. But he could never make me feel uncomfortable. Even today, I can squash him with just one word. But he was the one most against me seeing Brian and being around the Stones. He told Chrissie Shrimpton she wasn't to have anything to do with me. Mick and I never hit it off. He always put me down, made snide remarks about me, criticized the way I dressed.

"From when I first met them I saw Mick was in love with Keith. It still is that way. It's like they're married, husband and wife, and they'll probably stay that way for the rest of their lives. Keith was the rough-cut, I-don't-care kind of person. Mick admired Keith immensely. In many ways Keith was the man Mick wanted to be. Free and easy in his own skin, not uptight like Mick. Tough when he had to be, never backed down, had a good time, really enjoyed drinking, drugs, and carousing, Mick envied Keith. I felt all the time that Mick would like to be more like Keith."

RICHARDS: "The first time I saw Anita my obvious reaction was 'What the fuck is a chick like that doing with Brian?' Anita's incredibly strong, a much stronger personality than Brian's, more confident, with no reservations, whereas Brian's was full of doubts. I couldn't imagine that she didn't know better."

ANITA PALLENBERG: "When I first met him, Keith was a shy little guy who couldn't come out of himself. When he did say something it would always be very sarcastic and nasty. I was so involved with this beautiful London scene and he had a very resentful attitude toward it and didn't appreciate it."

Richards has said that the time he started hanging out at Court-field Road was one of "my most concentrated periods of pulling chicks." Most friends remember Keith as not having any girlfriends during this period and being rather sensitive about it. "He was alone," recalled John Dunbar, "but at that stage we were all taking so much acid we were all kind of together, we all felt very matey-matey, everything was fine, we were full of optimism. Keith was always good fun." But to Marianne Faithfull, Keith had become the epitome of the romantic hero. She had always understood that Keith was the most important person in the Stones, but Brian's arrogance amazed her. He acted as if he owned the world. Mick was rather bland in day-to-day life, she saw, never as intense as Brian or Keith. They came on in real life the way they did on record and on stage. "If you're a middle-class girl and you've read your Byron, that's Keith Richards," she explained. "He was an injured, tortured, damned youth, dirty, awful, arrogant." After a concert in Bristol on October 8, in the middle of a triumphant British tour with Ike and Tina Turner for "Have You Seen Your Mother," on which Keith and Brian were enjoying themselves and each other's company, Keith roared back to London with Brian in the Blue Lena and spent an evening with Marianne taking LSD and discussing her future. Keith ended up spending the night with her and she began to fall in love with him. But it was a love that would never be allowed to flower because the next day Keith told her that Mick was in love with her and she must never let him know that they slept together.

In October Keith moved into Brian and Anita's flat. Mick was out of the country courting Marianne, so Brian was once again the dominant member of the triangle. Robert Fraser and Michael Cooper joined them on daily explorations as they looned around London or shot up the M1 for weekends on the moors, dropping acid, snorting cocaine, and smoking hash.

RICHARDS: "I moved in slowly. I still have to check myself as to whether I decided to become friends again with Brian because of Anita. I think it was fifty-fifty. Of course I fancied her then—everybody did the minute they saw her—but I wasn't about to fuck up this good relationship with Brian. It was not the point for that. We were just good friends."

At first, Brian was delighted to have Keith back, especially with Jagger out of the picture. For a while Pallenberg and Jones replaced Jagger as Richards's favorite and the three of them became extremely close. As Brian saw it, he and Keith and Anita were the new power axis. "The three of them were living in an incredibly chaste ménage à trois; Keith was very close to Brian at that time but Anita was spinning her spell," revealed one friend. "She was a captivatingly attractive person and she completely bewitched both Brian and Keith."

Robert Fraser, Michael Cooper, Keith, Brian, and Anita met every day and soon became inseparable. Anita was the central figure. She introduced the Stones to the omnisexual art world. The results were both exciting and potent.

"The Rolling Stones were enormous fun," said the Beatles' press officer, Derek Taylor. "They had friends everywhere, quite unrelated to their apparent wealth or undoubted fame. They were also very sweet and aware and open."

In October 1966 the chairman of the New Jersey Drug Study Commission in the United States called LSD "the greatest threat facing the country today—more dangerous than the Vietnam War." That same month the London pop scene was flooded with the best LSD ever made (indirectly courtesy of the CIA, which was experimenting with it as a mind-control and interrogation device). The drug broke down social barriers and helped Richards grasp that he was living in the middle of a modern renaissance. Since London had become the art capital of the world, a rare cross-cultural convergence of outstanding artists from Andy Warhol to Allen Ginsberg passed through the city connecting with the exploding scene. These assorted minds cross-pollinated each other in the seed beds of the clubs and flats, like Brian Jones's Courtfield Road place, that had become the watering holes of this new tribe. Keith felt they were all part of a network of people who were seeking something, attempting to go where no man or woman had gone before.

JOHN MICHEL: "According to Plato, music is the most influential of the arts, and the music began to change minds and there was a big shift in the collective view, which hasn't been acknowledged because the authorities are still trying to hold the line against it. There was a new music, the new drugs and agents of change simply came together to create, or seemed to at the time, a very significant change. You thought the world was really changing in a radical manner and things wouldn't be the same after that. Keith was somebody you got used to seeing there and nice-looking and a Rolling Stone, but he was quiet and didn't put himself forward. But certainly in that particular period it was almost unfashionable to talk. One had to listen, and of course it was not just a matter of fashion because minds were changing very quickly in those days."

In this atmosphere Brian and Keith "were drawn together, jamming better and writing songs," recalled Tony Sanchez. "Suddenly the most fantastic things seemed possible." In November they collaborated on "Ruby Tuesday" at Olympic Studios. Keith came in with the basic track and the words, but he and Brian spent days in the studio layering the delicate music onto the basic track. Brian would tell with relish of how he and Keith "worked and worked on coloring, adding dramatic yet wispy touches here and there, altering the mix between lead voice and background vocal harmonies, while creating an interplay of exotic instruments." The combination proved that Keith and Brian could write songs together. "They drew very close then," wrote Jagger's biographer, Anthony Scaduto, "and Jagger was practically excluded. Brian and Keith worked out 'Ruby Tuesday' together and Marianne was upset because Jagger was not really part of it—he was ignored and forced to work off in the engineer's booth alone."

RICHARDS: "Brian created a vendetta against Mick. Brian couldn't be with Mick and me at the same time. 'Why can't Mick come in?' 'No, no,' he'd say. He was a big whisperer too, Brian. Little giggles."

Brian's abusive, self-destructive temperament also broke down his relationship with Anita.

JOHN DUNBAR: "I remember meeting Brian because it was so dramatic. It was at a party and I was coming up the stairs and he was being hit by this very beautiful woman, quite hard. It was Anita bashing Brian. She knocked him down. It was quite a spectacular kind of thing. I was very impressed. Brian and Anita always had an awful relationship."

Anita and Brian often fought about her career as an actress. As Brian struggled to maintain his starring role in the relationship, their fights became more violent. It soon became obvious that the perfect pop couple were not destined to spend the rest of their lives together, unless their lives were going to be unusually brief.

ANITA PALLENBERG: "By then Brian was very confused. He was very outrageous and very confused. He was jealous of everything I was doing. I remember when I got my first film script he ripped it up."

On December 4, a day before Keith, Anita and Brian left to record and vacation in L.A., a friend of Jones's visiting Courtfield Road was uneasy about the way that Keith and Anita were looking at each other. It was obvious to him that Keith had a crush on her and that Brian did not notice. On December 5–8 the Stones recorded in L.A., then Brian, Keith, and Anita took a holiday, scoring drugs and hanging around in the dangerous Watts section. "We got so much out of it," said Richards, "we wanted to go back and do some more."

"They were both such good-looking young boys when we first saw them in Richmond," said press agent Tony Bromwell. "And then you see these wrecks. Brian was a brilliant musician. But you'd bump into them in town and they'd be totally under the influence of everything. And they'd look like they were sixty—Brian, Keith. They were old men in their twenties." Keith's and Brian's reckless habits also disturbed Jagger. "I don't know where it's all going to end," he complained to Donald Cammell.

On December 18 Brian's close friend Tara Browne was killed in a car accident. Jones was devastated. "At the time," said Richards, "I remember saying to Brian, 'You'll never make thirty, man,' and he said, 'I know.'" The same day, Chrissie Shrimpton tried to commit suicide in Jagger's flat. Jagger took Chrissie's attempt as an exit cue. As soon as he paid condolences at her hospital bed, he revealed that he had been seeing Marianne Faithfull secretly for a month and stopped paying Shrimpton's bills. Richards, who began the season mourning the loss of Linda, ended it that Christmas with friends in Paris on a five-day binge at the deluxe George V hotel. While there, Keith hallucinated that Linda Keith had come to see him, and he realized the relationship was over. Now his way was clear to find himself a new girlfriend.

On January 13, 1967, "Let's Spend the Night Together"/"Ruby Tuesday" was released internationally. That night the Stones were playing *The Ed Sullivan Show* in New York. On the way across the tarmac at Kennedy Airport, one of their limousines was almost run over by a taxiing jet. When they got to the studio they couldn't get into the building. Surrounded by fans and panicking, they rushed the glass doors. Seeing a mob of screaming teenagers coming toward him and having no idea who they were, a terrified old doorman refused to let the Stones in. Keith and Mick smashed their way in, screaming. Keith punched the old man and dumped a can of garbage over his head. When the Stones got into the studio, Ed Sullivan's people informed them that Ed, unwilling to encourage the country's teenagers to fornicate, insisted they change the lyric to "Let's spend some time together." An incredible uproar erupted over this pathetic little attempt at censorship, which ended with Jagger rolling his eyes sardonically at the camera as he mouthed the cleaned-up chorus. At a party afterward Andy Warhol spotted Richards standing in a corner in a pin-striped suit with a drink in each hand, looking at people who approached him with "the blankest stare that anybody could ever give anyone."

A week later the Stones repeated their them-against-us act in London, going on the British TV equivalent of *The Ed Sullivan Show*, Sunday Night at the London Palladium. After being up for two days, Keith and Brian arrived for rehearsal two hours late on LSD. Then, at the end of the show the band refused to honor the tradition of standing with the entire cast on the revolving stage waving good-bye to the television audience.

RICHARDS: "Bollocks to that, we're the Stones. It was Mickey Mouse show biz. Fuck you, just 'cause everybody else is going to go around waving like they're on the end of a children's hour doesn't mean we will. We bothered them because of the way we looked, the way we'd act. Because we never showed any reverence for them whatsoever. That riled 'em somewhere."

Their new album, *Between the Buttons*, was released internationally on January 20. It would go to number three in England and number two in America. Some critics liked it; one went so far as to comment: "The style and content of the Stones' music has been relatively unchanged for some time. *Between the Buttons* is certainly their best album, because, with the effective incorporation of diverse influences, the music avoids the monotony which is perhaps the Stones' worst fault." Others, who felt it was a poor follow-up to *Aftermath*, dismissed it as "sounding more like a bunch of vaudevillian Kinks' outtakes than a bona fide Stones album." "Perhaps the reason was that Jagger and Richards deliberately tried to broaden their range as songwriters, to master a variety of styles as Lennon and McCartney clearly had," wrote one. "Perhaps it was because they were exhausted. What they came up with, basically, was an album of filler material. Saving graces were rare, though 'Connection' [written entirely and sung in part by Keith] was a reasonable track."

At the beginning of 1967 Brian became, for the first time, deeply involved in working on a project outside the Rolling Stones when he began writing and recording the music soundtrack to the German film Anita was starring in, *A Degree of Murder*. Brian's involvement with the project, along with his growing suspicion about his friend's attraction to Anita, served to separate him somewhat from Keith. Richards had recently moved out of Courtfield Road and was spending a lot of time at Redlands, where he was beginning to give weekend house parties, inviting the entourage he had met at Courtfield Road. Keith was still close enough to Brian that he flew with him and Anita to Munich on February 8 to visit the film set so that Brian could work on the score. At the same time, however, he was moving toward a *rapprochement* with Mick, engineered with the help of Marianne, since they had to start writing a new album together. It was time to get back to work.

2000 Light Years From Home
1967

They don't like young kids with a lot of money. But as long as you don't bother them, that's cool. But we bothered them.

KEITH RICHARDS, *from an interview with Robert Greenfield 1971*

The first step toward a new album was to get Jagger to take LSD so he could get in touch with the sounds that Keith and Brian were hearing. Then they could all take the Stones onward musically in a way that *Between the Buttons* had not. The then relatively abstemious Jagger was dragged right into the center of a drug controversy that reached its peak in Britain that January with an article in a tawdry tabloid, the *News of the World*, that misquoted him on taking drugs. Ironically, the reporter had interviewed a stoned, outspoken Jones in a London nightclub and mistaken him for Jagger. That night Jagger announced on a television talk show that he was suing the paper. With this statement he drew the ire of the British press establishment and paradoxically associated himself forever with drugs. Richards would later testify that the day after the article appeared in the *News of the World* he noticed a brown furniture van with white side panels outside a flat where he was staying in London. Later the same day he also noticed this van outside Jagger's flat, and discovered that his phone was tapped.

Just before Keith left for Munich, on January 18, some of his friends helped arrange a party at Redlands for the weekend of February 12 at which Jagger would take LSD with Richards. To make sure the LSD would be of the finest quality, they invited a well-supplied American drug specialist, David Schneiderman (aka the Acid King). Christopher Gibbs can still picture him today. "He was a sort of upmarket flower child. He knew more about drugs than anyone the Stones had ever met. 'What?' he'd say. 'You mean you've never heard of dimethyl tryptomine?'" According to Richards, "The only reason he was there is he had the stuff. Otherwise I never would have put up with him. In my profession there are people who are hangers-on who you have to tolerate."

The weekend party, including Michael Cooper, Robert Fraser (with his Moroccan servant, Ali), George and Patti Harrison, Mick Jagger, and Marianne Faithfull, drove down from London to West Wittering in a convoy, arriving late Friday night. What none of them knew but some would later come to believe was that Schneiderman was apparently a plant by the *News of the World* whose purpose was to get the Rolling Stones arrested for using illegal drugs, thereby both undermining the suit and exposing the scandalous use of drugs among rock stars. The ease with which Schneiderman disappeared two days later, never to be heard from again, indicated that he was well connected.

On Saturday morning the Acid King administered Mick Jagger his dose of White Lightning, a form of LSD that apparently guaranteed a colorful and harmonious trip. The acid test was a success. The party spent a delightful day tripping around the countryside. Richards and Jagger communicated on a new level. Then, that Saturday evening, just as they were all floating down in the living room to Dylan's *Blonde on Blonde*, the police raided.

CHRISTOPHER GIBBS: "There seemed to be a lot of activity going on outside the windows. Suddenly we seemed to be surrounded by all these fascinated cops, who were terribly surprised at the exotic goings-on within."

RICHARDS: "We were in a completely freaked-out state when the police arrived. There's a big knock at the door. Eight o'clock. Strobe lights are flickering. Marianne Faithfull had just had a bath and has wrapped herself up in a rug and is watching the box. The vibes were so funny. I told one of the women they brought with them to search the ladies, 'Would you mind stepping off that Moroccan cushion? Because you're ruining the tapestries . . .' They tried to get us to turn the record player off and we said, 'No, we won't turn it off but we'll turn it down.' We were playin' it like that. The level of drug education at Sussex CID [Criminal Investigation Department] was minimal. I'm sure they worked on instructions to take anything that they didn't recognize as being in their own homes. They left a bag of heroin down the sofa and took the incense sticks."

The police confiscated heroin from Fraser, who was an addict, and four amphetamine tablets from Jagger, but nothing from Richards. Schneiderman, who had the majority of the drugs in the house in a suitcase at his feet, was virtually ignored. Before the police departed, Richards was informed that under British law if anything the police removed from his house was an illegal substance, he would be charged with allowing it on his property and thus be liable for imprisonment. "Oh, I see," he said. "They pin it all on me!"

RICHARDS: "As they started going out the door, somebody put on 'Rainy Day Women' really loud: 'Everybody must get stoned.' And that was it. Originally the only person who got charged was myself, because it was my house. Mick had a few amphetamine pills which you could buy across the counter in Italy but were illegal in England. The prime minister could walk into a chemist's in Milan and say, 'I must stay awake, could you give me a couple of mild NoDoz?' and then find that he could be busted here in England.

"I wrote my father when I got busted, 'cause I didn't want him to just get it all out of the newspapers. But I didn't get an answer, which really pissed me off."

Although Jagger didn't think it was a very serious matter, Fraser understandably wanted the matter dropped, and he persuaded Keith and Mick to join him in arranging to bribe the police. After some negotiation, their go-between, Spanish Tony, reportedly delivered a suitcase containing seven thousand pounds cash to a police official in a London pub, and it looked as if the matter had ended.

RICHARDS: "In the meantime everybody thought the best idea was to get out of England so nothing else could happen. Everybody felt, 'Oh, what a bringdown. Let's all go to Morocco, take a load off, and cheer up.' And this is what everybody did. Me, Brian, Anita, and Deborah Dixon [Donald Cammell's girlfriend] decided to drive down in my Bentley."

Keith wanted to drive to Marrakech in the Blue Lena, and Brian and Anita agreed to accompany him with Brian's driver, Tom Keylock. Mick, Marianne, and Robert Fraser were to meet them there. As they left England on March 4, "Ruby Tuesday" went to number one in the U.S. Brian was ecstatic. However, he and Anita weren't getting along.

RICHARDS: "They had reached an impasse about Anita's movie career. Brian wanted to be the star of the relationship and for Anita to be this chick with a star. It was getting on her."

They picked up Deborah Dixon and headed south. According to Keith, everyone was buzzing on an incredible LSD high as they cruised toward the Pyrenees. Brian wasn't getting along with Anita. Sensing vibrations between her and Keith, he had a bad asthma attack in Toulon. "After he collapsed we stayed a couple of days with him to see how he was getting on," remembered Keith. "Then the doctors said, 'Oh, yes ... he's in a bad way. He'll be here a week.' We said, 'We'd better go.'"

Abandoning Jones to a week's hospital stay, the group continued their journey. The following morning Deborah Dixon, who was no longer needed to balance out the group, returned to Paris, while the Blue Lena headed for Valencia. "Amazing things can happen in the back of a car," Richards recalled, "and they did." In Valencia he spent his first night with Anita.

From Valencia, Keith sent a postcard to his mother, writing: "Dear Mum. Sorry I didn't phone before I left, but my telephones aren't safe to call on. Everything will be alright so don't worry. It's really great here and I'll send you a letter when I get where I'm going. All my love. The fugitive, Keith."

In the morning they realized that their liaison threatened the survival of the band and decided to pull back. "After all," said Anita, "Brian and Keith had to perform together." Keith knew how paranoid Brian could get and how his imagination would run wild once he discovered that Deborah Dixon had split. At the same time the attraction was magnetic, and they were having a wonderful time secretly sharing the first days of a love affair that would become a model for its times. In Tangier they were met by an avalanche of messages from Jones ordering Anita to return immediately to Toulon to pick him up. Ignoring them, they drove on to Marrakech to meet up with Jagger's party, and then Anita and Marianne flew back to retrieve Jones. During the return flight Marianne sensed that the drama was about to reach its climax when Anita kept comparing Brian, unfavorably, to Keith. By the time Brian arrived in Marrakech, stoned on the LSD Anita had given him on the plane, he had realized she already slept with Keith.

The painter and writer Brion Gysin, who lived in Morocco and acted as their host, got a close-up of this delicate moment.

BRION GYSIN: "We take over the top floor of this hotel for a playpen hanging ten stories over the swimming pool. Mick and quietly saturnine Keith Richards with his eye on mini-skirted Anita Pallenberg and Brian Jones with his fringe of frizzy pink hair almost hiding his beady little red rabbit eyes. The action starts almost at once. Brian and I drop acid. Anita sulks and drops a sleeper. Goes off to sleep in the suite she shares with Brian. Keith is plugged in and is sending some great throbbing sounds winging after her and on out into the moonlight over the desert. Robert puts on a great old Elmore James record. Gets Mick doing little magic dances for him. For the first time, I see Mick really is magic. As the acid comes upon me, Brian recedes into big pictures. Looks like a tiny celluloid kewpie doll, banked all around by choirs of identical little girl dolls looking just like him, chanting his hymns. Tom the sinister chauffeur shows up, rolling his eyes, hovering over Brian, whispering in his ear like a procurer.

"The next day dawned late and lazy around the swimming pool. And there I saw something I can only call mythological. At the deep end, Anita is swinging on a canvas seat. Keith is in the pool, dunking up and down in the water, looming up at her. When I go to pass between them, I see that I can't. I can't make it. There is something there, a barrier, I can see it. What I see looks like a glass rod, revolving rapidly. Between Keith's eyes and Anita's eyes, it shoots back and forth at the speed of light. As bad as a laser beam. I don't like the looks of that one bit so I check out of the hotel immediately." (Cecil Beaton, who photographed Keith by the pool that morning, noted in his diary that Richards possessed "a marvelous torso.")

The next day Brian flew into a rage in their hotel suite, attacking Anita because she refused to participate in an orgy with two Moroccan whores. Anita ran to Keith's room crying hysterically.

Keith snapped and, for the first and perhaps only time in his life, put a woman before the well-being of the group. Regardless of the consequences, he decided to take Anita away from Brian.

RICHARDS: "I couldn't sit there and watch the way Brian was treating Anita, although she was capable of looking after herself. It wasn't some Sir Galahad number. I said, 'Fuck this, come on, darling, I'm taking you back to London.' Issuing orders to Tom Keylock to have Gysin waylay Jones by taking him to listen to some Joujouka music, Richards made plans to drive out of Marrakech that night. Jagger and his party also left Morocco, so when Jones returned to the hotel he discovered himself completely and irrevocably alone. "It was a very cold-blooded affair," Keith said. "Just 'Let's go. I'll take you out of this at least, and then you can do what you want.' So we split."

Keith, in his last formal communication to Linda, sent her a postcard from Morocco on which he wrote, "When you gotta go, you gotta go." Keylock drove them to Tangier, where they got the ferry to Málaga. Spanish customs agents scrupulously searched them and the car for drugs but failed to find the piece of hash taped inside the flap of the gas tank. Keith and Anita left Keylock with the car and flew via Madrid to London, where they crashed at a small flat in St. John's Wood. Furnished sparsely with a tape recorder, a mattress, and a roll of toilet paper, it was, Keith said, an expensive piece of shit he maintained as a place to flop out at between gigs. Parading themselves around London, they became the scandal of the week. Meanwhile Jones, now a tragic, broken figure, flew to Paris and threw himself on the mercy of Donald Cammell before returning to London to face his friends. When Brian finally confronted the pair, there was a big, tearful scene.

Richards, who worried that Anita might return to the more attractive and charismatic Jones, was relieved to hear her tell Brian that he was too much of an asshole to live with and she had something going with Keith. At the same time he realised that Brian would never be able to forgive this ultimate betrayal. Comparing Jones's plight to his own when Linda left him for Hendrix he told a friend, "Hell, shit happens."

*

As soon as they got back to London they were hit by another blow. Apparently the seven thousand pounds Spanish Tony said he had passed on to a policeman had gone astray, because suddenly, six weeks after the event, the tabloids published lurid stories about the Redlands raid stating that Keith Richards, Mick Jagger, and Robert Fraser were to be prosecuted.

RICHARDS: "I guess '67 was the explosion of the drug culture, if there is such a thing. It came into the open from the underground, and everybody started talking about it. And through this whole year we were trying to put up with this incredible hassle, this continual confrontation with policemen and judges. I really feel uncomfortable looking at a uniform anyway, and having to deal with those people for a whole year, it did wear us down a bit. In fact, it put us on our back, really, for eighteen months or so. It was a painful year, a year of change for everybody."

Court hearings were scheduled for May and June. Richards and Jagger hired the best lawyers, who assured them that they had nothing to worry about since the charges were largely groundless. In the highly charged climate of the times, when there was a strong, liberal, artistic community in London that showed support for them, they became the focus of a scandalous trial. No case had drawn as much response and created such debate since the Christine Keeler-Stephen Ward trial of 1963. The English, and in particular the English press, like nothing more than the opportunity to pull down the pants of a public figure. They were like vultures hovering over a dying beast.

RICHARDS: "In a matter of a few months, drugs had become a major way of life. Then they went to look for somebody to blame and, of course, we set ourselves up. 'Would you let your daughter marry a Rolling Stone?' We were easy meat. At least they thought we were."

From the perspective of the nineties, it is easy to look back at the Richards-Jagger drug trials of 1967 and cut Keith in the romantic image of a rebel hero waving to the crowd with a languid, lace-encuffed hand from the backseat of his chauffeur-driven Bentley, but the whole thing rattled him. He was bitter about the police taking the bribe and pretending it never happened: "I'd grown up like every English kid, believing in Scotland Yard the way you saw it in the movies. Then they go and ask us for a bribe of seven thousand pounds, they make us think we're OK, then, weeks later, they still go and do us. That's what I feel most bitter about. In America, you pay off the cop as a matter of course. It's business.

"I don't like the way police attitudes have changed. They're getting new power and it's growing at an alarming rate because once something is that big it wants to get bigger. It is becoming a social police, more and more concerned with how you live."

In March and April the Stones were due to play a short tour of Europe. The thought of playing on the same stage with Keith was inconceivable to Brian. According to Jones, Anita pressured him into going on the tour by promising to return to him when it was over. For Keith it was like being back to square one, "except now he resented me for taking his chick."

RICHARDS: "In that last year or so, when Brian was almost totally incapacitated all of the time, he became a joke to the band. It was the only way we could deal with it without gettin' mad at him. So then it became that very cruel, piss-taking thing behind his back all the time. I mean, Brian was so ludicrous in some ways and such a nice guy in some ways. It was like what they used to say about Stan Getz: 'He's a nice bunch of guys.' You just never knew which one you were gonna meet." (Years later, he would say exactly the same thing about Jagger.)

It was one of their roughest tours. Because of the Redlands raid and the temper of the times, they were continually harassed by cops. In Sweden, customs officials strip-searched the whole band, and they were delayed for an hour as officers inspected their sixteen pieces of luggage. In Paris, a customs officer grabbed Richards by the lapels, shook a fist in his face, then punched him. "They seem to think we're working for Che Guevara," Keith said.

The tour was one long riot.

RICHARDS: "We played Warsaw. 'Honski-de-boyski, boyski. Ze Rolling Stones-ki.' The sons and daughters of the hierarchy of the communist party have the best seats in the house right down front. About three numbers and I say, 'Fucking stop playing, Charlie. You fuckin' lot, get out of those bandstands, in back down front.' About four rows just walked out. All mummy's and daddy's boys."

After the tour, in between meeting lawyers, Keith followed Anita around Europe. They had a wonderful time in Rome, where she was auditioning for a part in Roger Vadim's forthcoming film, *Barbarella*. But the conflict with Jones continued to dominate their relationship. *A Degree of Murder* was scheduled to be the German entry at the festival and Brian and Anita had both been invited to attend. The ad for the film featured an image of a beautiful young woman on her knees firing a pistol, above the caption "Men couldn't own her!" Brian flew to Cannes with Anita while Keith drove across Europe for a week, arriving in time for the premiere but staying out of the limelight by hanging out in his hotel room waiting to see what would happen. Once again Brian flew into a rage and sent a bruised and hysterical Anita running back to Keith's suite. That was the last straw for Keith. He started to hate Brian with an at times murderous rage, and concluded that Brian had signed his own death warrant.

From Cannes, Keith and Anita went to Paris.

JOHN DUNBAR: "I was walking down Saint-Germain outside Deux Magots and there was 'John! John!' and it was Keith and Anita in this cab and I got swept up into their lives for a couple of days. They were staying in this great old brothel called Hortense and I used to go there and take drugs. I remember walking down the street with Keith in Paris and he stopped at one of those magazine stands and looked at this magazine. He was reading it and this magaziner goes, in French, 'ARE YOU GONNA BUY IT?' and Keith goes, 'Grrrr,' and rips it in half! There was this terrible scene. No sooner had we escaped from that than it's like one of those cowboy films, somebody bumps into Keith and there's another fight. So I'm kind of going, like, 'Not me, gov, not me, gov.' Those were his aggressive days."

After his holiday in Paris, Keith returned to London to face the drug charges and get to work on the next Rolling Stones album, *Their Satanic Majesties Request*. Anita went to Rome to film *Barbarella*, directed by Roger Vadim with a script by Terry Southern and with Vadim's wife, Jane Fonda, in the lead role. At the beginning of the relationship Anita thought Keith would be cool about her film career, but fifteen years later they would still be bickering about whether or not she had deserted him that summer.

ANITA PALLENBERG: "After *Barbarella* I got to do *Candy* in Rome, so I got to meet Marlon Brando. So Keith heard that Marlon Brando and I had a scene, so he took the first plane and he was out there. Brando was on the set, but I didn't actually work with him, I worked with James Coburn. But Brando whisked me off back to his country house, and he started to do his Brandoish seduction and I got completely intimidated. I remember he was lying in bed reading his poetry and I ran away. So I went and hid and they were playing music and I went and put on '(I Can't Get No) Satisfaction' and it was kind of blasting and he comes in and said, 'It's really a load of shit, it's the drums that count,' and all that Brandoish kind of stuff. And eventually I didn't end up in bed with him but I ran away. He fell asleep and I sneaked out. And then the next morning he was eyeing me and all that. And somehow it got to Keith really quickly, and in the afternoon he came. And while Keith was there Brando was, like, really wicked. He was sitting there putting his arm around me and smiling at Keith and playing all these silly little games. And eventually I thought, 'Well, he fancies Keith.' That's how I solved the whole kind of thing, by thinking Brando was gay and that he actually fancied Keith. But it was the same story [as with Brian], so eventually I tried to time it to work out where Keith was working. But [Keith]'d always stand me up. So eventually I gave up. Being the lady of those kind of guys was always like being set on the side. The girls were always looked down on."

On May 10, the Russell Tribunal in Stockholm found America guilty of war crimes in Vietnam, and Jagger, Richards, and Fraser found themselves in a small Chichester courtroom waiting for their case to be called. Allen Klein had flown in from New York to remain on hand through the trial. "Their problems were mine," Klein said, "and let me tell you, I worked my ass off. Got them the best lawyers, sat in the front row at the trial every day."

Richards and Jagger were released on bail and their trial was set for June 27.

RICHARDS: "We were all squeezed together up on these little benches—the lawyers, the national press, and us. It was a bit like being back at school. I don't think even at that point we expected anything worse than a cuff on the side of the head or a ruler across the knuckles.

"Then, when we were in court waiting to hear if there was going to be bail before the real trial, they busted Brian. They had it timed down to the minute. When we were actually in the fucking courtroom, up in London, an hour and a half drive away, they were going into Brian's house to do him so that the papers would come out with 'Rolling Stones Keith Richards and Mick Jagger on trial for this, meanwhile Brian Jones has just been found with this.' So they could lay that on—'Well, they must be guilty.' I suddenly realized, 'They really want to nail us. They seem to be trying to lock us all in jail where we can't pose a threat to them anymore.'"

In light of the trial, work on the new album, *Satanic Majesties*, was fragmented. Jagger had been so stunned by the brilliance of the Beatles' *Sgt. Pepper* that he insisted the Stones answer it on its own terms, abandoning their R&B roots to make a psychedelic album for which they were poorly prepared and, apart from Brian, who detested the idea anyway, poorly equipped. It was beginning to look as if it hadn't been such a great idea to give Jagger acid. Richards believed that *Satanic Majesties* was the result of the band caving in to trendy pressures. For the first time, his faith in the band's original roots was in conflict with Jagger's tendency to go where the winds of fashion took him.

RICHARDS: "People would say, 'What you playin' that old shit for?' which really screwed me up because that's all I can play. So we heard what the people were saying and we sort of laid back and listened to what they were doin' in Frisco. And we were digging what we were hearin' for what it was. But that other thing was saying, 'Yeah, but where's Chuck Berry? What's he doin'?' So we laid down the album and it didn't connect back. It's got to follow through, it's got to connect. Besides, the album was made under the pressure of the court case and the whole scene that was going on in London at the time."

TONY SANCHEZ: "The album wasn't working out and became the focus of everything that was going wrong among Mick, Keith, and Brian. Brian and I arrived at the studio to find Keith there with

Anita—both making it cruelly obvious that they were enjoying being together. There seemed to be no conscious malice in the attitudes of Keith and Mick. But they were worried."

Bill Wyman's girlfriend Astrid Lundström took this psychological snapshot of the Rolling Stones that year: "These five incredibly strong personalities were definitely guarded, controlling their emotions. They weren't very open with each other, so they certainly wouldn't have appeared relaxed to outsiders. There was rarely any outburst. It was just this tension, moodiness, a sulking. You could never call them hypocrites. They're all very real, whether their nastiness or niceness was showing. But they exercised what I'd describe as controlling silences. They took themselves a bit too seriously sometimes—yet I believe their tension helped in the music. They weren't demonstrative. I've never in my life experienced five such uptight people."

By now the power base within the band had shifted rigidly to Richards and Jagger. They dominated the recording; Brian and the others, even Andrew, were treated like employees or session men. Distressed by his complete loss of control, Brian retreated into drugs and alcohol, and entered the hellish spiral of his descent. "Brian's very tired," Tony warned. "We're all tired, Tony, but if he keeps on getting out of his box like this, we'll have to find a new guitar player," Keith replied. "Can't you find some woman to look after him?"

GLYN JOHNS: "I don't think anyone really liked the fact that Keith and Mick got the stranglehold that they did. Keith never wanted a stranglehold on the Rolling Stones, but as it turned out, because Mick and Keith wrote the material, and because they took an everyday interest in the running of the band and what it should and should not do, they ended up with it. In other words, the others just stood there and let it happen. Keith portrays himself as not really caring about the power in the band, but I would refute that. Let's say he may care less than Mick. Mick's the really active one. But if Mick's in the process of making a decision and Keith disagrees with it, then you'll see how much Keith bloody cares."

Songwriting credits in the Rolling Stones became a problem. Bill Wyman complained that he wrote the crucial riff on "Jumpin' Jack

Flash" but was never credited for it. This gave rise to the charge that Keith and Mick held onto the songwriting credits for the Rolling Stones greedily, weakening the potential of the group. However, the majority of the songs were created by the band in the studio based upon ideas from Richards and Jagger.

The Redlands trial took place June 27–29. Richards was charged under Section 5 (A) of the Dangerous Drugs Act, 1964, which reads: "If a person, being the occupier of any premises, permits those premises to be used for the purpose of smoking cannabis or cannabis resin or of dealing in cannabis or cannabis resin (whether by sale or otherwise) he shall be guilty of an offence against this Act.

"Every person guilty of an offence against this Act shall, in respect to each offence, be liable on conviction on indictment, to a fine not exceeding 1,000 pounds or to imprisonment for a period not exceeding ten years, or both."

On the third day, June 29, Jayne Mansfield was decapitated in a car crash and Richards was the sole witness at his trial.

When he went into the witness box he was still largely unknown to all but Stones fans. When he emerged he had become a spokesman for his generation and among the most famous advocates of drugs in the counterculture. He dressed the part, like a man who knew that what he said would be imprinted on the minds of a generation. In a lace-collared shirt, a navy-blue frock coat, black military-style trousers, and maroon-and-black shoes, he looked like a combination of Maverick and the Scarlet Pimpernel. According to one onlooker: "An almost inaudible shudder greeted this least prepossessing defendant, with his fancy Beau Brummell clothes and his pale, sickly, wolfish face."

The prosecution of Richards was by far the most spurious aspect of the entire case. The government attempted to prove that he had known that people were taking drugs on his property because the place smelled odd and there was a nude woman in the room. Richards made newspapers around the world when he responded to the enraged prosecutor's insistence that he must have recognized something was wrong because of the nude woman with the oft-quoted line "We are not old men. We are not worried about petty morals."

RICHARDS: "My big mouth put me on the spot many times. But I know at times there are things that need to be said, it doesn't matter where it is and who it's said to. Sometimes I can hear myself talking and saying, 'You should keep your mouth shut, boy, and just get an easy ride here,' but meanwhile I can hear my voice booming around the room saying, 'No way!' Half of me is fighting this thing, but it just comes out, you know, this has to be said, and that's all there is to it. Then I'm a victim of whatever it is I've said."

To his surprise, the jury found Keith guilty. The judge berated him for his conduct, intoning that his offense against the Crown carried a sentence of up to ten years in jail. Despite the fact that with the kind of money and legal support they had, both Richards and Jagger must have known that they would be out on bail within twenty-four hours, actually having to go to prison was a stunning blow to them after they had spent their adult lives surrounded by luxury, doing exactly what they wanted. "He said things to me while I was up there that if I'd caught him by myself I'd have wrung his neck," Richards snapped later. "When he gave me the sentence, he called me 'scum' and 'filth' and 'people like this shouldn't be ...'" To screams of "Oh, no," from teenagers in the gallery, Richards was sentenced to a year's imprisonment in Wormwood Scrubs and ordered to pay five hundred pounds in court costs.

Entering the notorious Wormwood Scrubs later that afternoon, Keith was struck by how everything was aimed at making him feel like a "minute turd." As his finery was stripped off him, he was deloused and turned into a number. "First off, neither the accommodations nor the fashion suited me at all," Richards recalled. "I like a little more room, I like the john to be in a separate area, and I hate to be woken up. The food's awful, the wine list is terribly limited, and the library is abysmal." However, any fears he might have had about his reception disappeared when a Stones song came on and the place went wild with yelling and screaming. Everybody was sympathetic. "They've been waiting for you in here for years, mate!" said one voice. "The bastards!" "Don't worry," Keith replied, "I ain't gonna be in here long, baby."

First thing the following morning, Keith found himself falling into the prison routine as it is portrayed in the movies. He dragged his chair to the window and stared dolefully at the "little square of sky, trying to reach it." Then he was taken off to the factory, where he was instructed on how to make miniature Christmas trees to put on cakes. Following that bizarre lesson, he found himself shuffling around the courtyard in line with the other prisoners for their hour-long constitutional. No sooner had he gotten in line than some joker whispered, "Psst, Keith! Want some good hash? Want some acid?" "Wot? You crazy? In 'ere!" he replied. "No talking over there!" barked a big screw. Later that afternoon, lying in his cell, immersed in feeling just like Jimmy Cagney, he was interrupted by an excited voice yelling, "You're out, mate! It's just been on the radio!" Reverting to his role as a Rolling Stone, Keith leapt off the bed and started kicking the door, screaming, "Let me out, you bastards, I got bail!" An hour later, sailing out of the Scrubs in the back of his chauffeur-driven Bentley, he heard the warden's voice echoing, "You'll be back, you bastard!"

ALLEN KLEIN: "I was thrilled when they got off. I can't do this job any other way than to get completely involved with my artists. But I got pissed the day I got them out on bail because when Mick and Keith and Marianne got back to my hotel room she pulled out a hash pipe and lit up. I mean, how goddamn stupid can you get? I grabbed the thing away from her and fucking threw it out the window. She stood there saying the law was unrealistic; well, I don't give a shit if it is. I didn't want them to go to jail. And it's not the money; I don't care only about that. It's just that if I'm involved, then I'm responsible. It becomes my cross to see that they stay out of prison."

In the next week support would flow to them from liberal forces around the world. It was summed up on July 1 by a famous editorial by William Rees-Mogg in *The Times* of London entitled (after Pope) "Who Breaks a Butterfly on a Wheel?," which questioned the verdicts: "In the courts at large it is most uncommon for imprisonment to be imposed on first offenders where the drugs are not major drugs of addiction and there is no question of drug traffic . . . If we are going to make any case a symbol of the conflict between the sound traditional values of Britain and the new hedonism, then we must be sure that the sound traditional values include those of tolerance and equity."

"The Rolling Stones are one of Britain's major cultural assets who should be honored by the kingdom instead of gaoled," wrote Allen Ginsberg in a letter to *The Times* on July 12. And, in an act of solidarity, the Who declared in a press release, "The Who consider Mick Jagger and Keith Richards have been treated as scapegoats for the drug problem and as a protest against the savage sentence imposed on them at Chichester yesterday, the Who are issuing today the first of a series of Jagger-Richards songs to keep their work before the public until they are again free to record themselves." To cash in on the publicity, Decca's U.S. subsidiary, London Records, released another cobbled together album of previously released tracks and outtakes, *Flowers*.

From July 12 to 22, the Stones worked on *Satanic Majesties* at Olympic Studios. On July 22, *Flowers* entered the American charts, where it would remain for thirty-five weeks, peaking at number three and earning them another gold disc.

GERED MANKOWITZ: "To my surprise there was an evening where Mick and Michael Cooper, who was becoming increasingly a part of the Stones camp, came in and told Andrew in the recording studio what they were going to do for the *Satanic Majesties* cover. This was a coup d'état. It was the first time Andrew hadn't been involved in an image-making aspect of the Rolling Stones' career. The recording sessions were pretty ghastly—they were falling apart and they were beginning to move into an entirely different world."

That month Andrew Oldham, who had been horrified by the drug bust and increasingly addled by his own prescription-drug problems, finally broke down. One of the most striking things about the Stones over the years is their lack of verbal communication. Brian wouldn't talk to Keith, and Keith and Mick hardly spoke to anybody, particularly Oldham. "They realized that Andrew's ideas were only ideas he'd got from them in the first place," Ian Stewart said. "We went in and played a lot of blues as badly as we could. Finally, Andrew just walked out."

Richards's and Jagger's appeals were heard by Lord Chief Justice

Parker on July 31. Keith, who had chicken pox, was secluded in a private room during the hearing. The dismissal of all charges against Richards and the suspension of Jagger's sentence sent a positive message to the worldwide counterculture.

RICHARDS: "Even though I was foolish enough to get caught and in doing so advertised the fact that I smoked pot, I feel no responsibility for what anybody else may do with their bodies, or what they may put into them. There were certain aspects of that case, a few that went on behind the scenes, which are very unsavory and which once and for all destroyed for me faith in the fairness and impartiality of the English judicial system. English cops are no better or no worse than anywhere else. I just wish they wouldn't pretend they're something they're not. When we finished all that shit I went to live in Rome with Anita for the rest of the summer."

He had discovered the joys of the finest Afghanistan hash and "that's all I wanted to know about except for Anita." From their suite at the terrific little Hotel Ritz at the top of the Spanish Steps, Anita proceeded to pull together Rome's equivalent of their Chelsea set. Gerard Malanga, in town to screen his movie *In Search of the Miraculous*, was among their new circle of friends.

GERARD MALANGA: "The ambience in Rome was wonderful. I referred to it as a renaissance. A whole slew of very interesting people were hanging out with each other. We were hobnobbing with [the artist] Mario Schifano, and [the filmmaker Pier Paolo] Pasolini, and the Living Theater. One day Anita, Keith and myself rendezvoused at Billy Berger's place. He was an American actor who was very successful in spaghetti westerns. I went into the kitchen and there was Keith at the stove stirring up this syrup in a pot. He was a very jovial person. He threw in some brownie mix and made hash brownies. We hung out for a while, he wrote out the recipe for me, and they left. I proceeded to eat one of the brownies and literally turned green."

Anita's influence on Keith was instant. He started wearing her scarves, blouses, jackets, and jewelry. "There's a photograph of them in '67 after he's with Pallenberg," said the English rock critic Nick Kent. "Brian Jones is out of the picture and Keith Richards has got the look. Keith has got his hair finally together." According to Andy Warhol, that summer lots of the boys in New York suddenly had their hair Keith Richards style—spiky and all different lengths. Anita encouraged Keith to apply black kohl underneath his eyes and wear lipstick and fingernail polish. Despite Lennon and McCartney's ongoing doubt about the relationship between Keith and Mick, there was no more masculine man in rock than Richards, and the makeup only served to accent his grace and elegance. Suddenly, Mick's new girlfriend, Marianne Faithfull, realized that rather than Richards living in Jagger's shadow, Mick actually strived to look as good as, if not better than, Keith.

In 1967 Keith went through a metamorphosis. The strongest agent of change was Anita, who left Brian for Keith that summer. However, the relationship between Keith and Anita was no instant fairy tale.

ANITA PALLENBERG: "We kind of became lovers. And then we started living together. But in those days he was, as I say, very shy, and then there was Mick as well. Keith was not like a womanizer. He was not like what you'd imagine pop stars to be like—chasing after women. In the high heydays of the Rolling Stones he used to wear a pair of jeans that were practically glued to him, like he had some girls to help him try to get them off and they just couldn't. And then he just sprayed himself with patchouli oil so much that they just went, 'Choo, get away!' I mean, he just seemed to be a one-woman guy. He was always very loyal to me. He needs the love and security, I guess."

While Keith was in Italy, Mick rushed off to Wales to join the Beatles at the feet of an Indian guru named Maharishi Mahesh Yogi, who had picked up on how vulnerable young rock stars with nobody to tell them what to do were.

RICHARDS: "Mick was going off to see the Maharishi, and I'm thinking, 'Uhhh, I ain't too sure about this shit.' I'm quite proud I never went and kissed the Maharishi's goddamn feet. If it hadn't been promoted so hard—like, by the Beatles, especially—maybe it wouldn't have reached quite the insane proportions that it got to. The basic drive behind it, I suppose, one had to like. But the amount of people who were suckered into it . . ."

ANITA PALLENBERG: "All that psychedelic stuff in England

then, honestly, it was disgusting. The Maharishi was a dyke from Yorkshire. Brian was fucked up because he didn't want to know what they were doing. In the studio he played all those different instruments. When he was in the studio during that period he was trying to hook up with someone else . . . Brian didn't like the whole London trend in music and so he just got more fucked up. He couldn't play with anyone anymore."

In August the Stones went back into Olympic Studios to record a single thanking their fans for their support. "We Love You," backed by "Dandelion," was released August 18. It was not a big hit, stalling at number eight in the U.K. and reaching an astonishingly low number fifty in the U.S., but they had a lot of fun making it.

PAUL MCCARTNEY: "John and I sang on 'We Love You'— Mick had been stuck for an idea and he asked us to come out. So we went down to Olympic Studios and just made that up."

The "year of changes" ended for the Stones with the release of *Their Satanic Majesties Request* on Friday, December 15. It reached number three in the U.K. and number two in the U.S. London Records dispatched a telegram to Decca's Sir Edward Lewis announcing, "It's not a hit—it's an epidemic."

"*Their Satanic Majesties Request* is an ambivalent production," wrote Alan Beckett in the *New Left Review*. "It reflects all the major developments of 1967—the Mothers of Invention ('On with the Show'); the Byrds' science fiction themes ('2000 Light Years'); and the Human Host and the Heavy Metal Kids (in the long instrumental passages). Particularly, of course, it reflects the influence of *Sgt. Pepper*. In some ways the record constitutes an advance for the Stones. It is more sophisticated than their previous work in terms of orchestration, and there is some development of the composing style (using two tempi within the same piece, etc.)."

Despite a generally negative critical response, Richards received praise for the breadth of his composing and guitar playing. "When you hear the sheer drifting lyricism of things like 'Ruby Tuesday,' 'She's a Rainbow' or the intricately haunting '2000 Light Years' and 'Paint It, Black,' one is amazed that Keith's body of work hasn't received more critical attention," noted one critic. "It is certainly as deserving as Paul McCartney's or that of any contemporary composer."

"Richards' guitar playing on 'Lantern' is the best on the album," wrote another. "Richards has always been my favorite lead guitarist in rock and he is certainly the best hard rock lead around. But after the first three Stones albums I never felt he got into the groove again. On *Buttons* he showed he was moving in some directions, and on this cut he turns in a beautiful performance, crowding into a few small runs a great deal of musical force."

RICHARDS: "I liked a few songs, like '2000 Light Years,' 'Citadel,' and 'She's a Rainbow,' but basically I thought the album was a load of crap. I mean, even with *Satanic Majesties*, I was never hot on psychedelic music."

11

Jumpin' Jack Flash
1967–1968

"Jumpin' Jack Flash" is my fucking favorite of all Stones songs.

KEITH RICHARDS, *from a survey in the*
Rolling Stone *special issue, "The Sixties,"* 1990

In the wake of his highly publicized drug trial and in light of his new relationship with Anita Pallenberg, Keith stepped back to reassess the situation. "We were pretty knackered," he said. "And it was about to be the renaissance of the Stones, the second wind, so to speak—and one of their best winds."

On December 22, Keith and Anita traveled to Tangier. They took a suite at the Minza and regularly dropped by Achmed the hash-maker's, going to his shop in the morning and not coming out until sunset. "He used to grade his hash twelve-denier or eighteen-denier, according to which stocking he'd shaken it through," Keith recalled. "The finest would be eighteen-denier." When they weren't at Achmed's they strolled through the medina buying clothes, scarves, and jewels. "We lay back for a long time, and we just decided what we wanted to do. Everybody was trying to work it out, what was going to go on. First off you go round and visit the fleshpots, and when you get slightly debauched and jaded, you remember, 'Ah, yes, the music!' . . ."

It was a confusing time for pop musicians. The Beatles had changed everything with *Sgt. Pepper*. The British R&B boom was over. The San Francisco sound was pervasive. Many bands just disappeared. The Stones, who always seemed nervous about their longevity in the sixties, were torn about what direction to take. Richards started listening to a lot of blues records from the twenties and thirties, by artists such as Big Joe Williams and Skip James, and gradually realized that he had to teach himself a new way to play the guitar.

RICHARDS: "It took me quite a few years of playing, of taking all the knocks you get on the road, before I started to develop my own style. Of course, you can fall into a rut of getting someone's licks down so well that you are never gonna find yourself. After suddenly becoming a pop star, we worked three or four years and had maybe two weeks off in four years. When we took time off, I became aware that I'd learned how to make records and how to write songs, but with all the years of not hearing myself on stage, I hadn't really progressed that much as a player.

"I caught up on listening to music, which to me is maybe the greatest art. It can keep your sanity. I started looking into some twenties and thirties blues records. Slowly I began to realize that a lot of them were in very strange tunings. These guys would pick up a guitar, and a lot of times it would be tuned in a certain way, and that's how they'd learn to play it. It might be some amazing sort of mode. And that's why for years you could have been trying to figure out how some guy did this lick, and then you realize that this guy has one string that's supposed to be up high and he has tuned it down an octave lower. Actually, it's an old five-string banjo tuning that dates back to when the guitar began to replace the banjo in popularity after the First World War. It's called open tuning, or the Sears Roebuck tuning sometimes, because they started selling guitars then.

"Open tuning was something that had intrigued me for quite a while before I took it up, but I'd never had the opportunity or time to get to do it, and it takes time. It was a case of learning everything from scratch. It involved literally learning the guitar all over again. You had to apply yourself in almost the same way as when you started. I really enjoyed it. I thought, 'I can't go any farther in concert tuning,' so I sat down with open tuning and it stretched out. It's a funny thing, that guitar; it's just this piece of wood and six strings . . . but each day it still surprises me. My favorite phrase about this style of playing is all you need to play is five strings, three notes, two fingers, and one asshole."

As Marianne Faithfull saw it, Richards and Jagger "were in that period when they were really consolidating their work as musicians, and they were very disciplined about everything. I had the feeling that they knew they were about to pass over the threshold of being pop stars to become great rock stars."

In mid-March 1968 the band went into Olympic Studios in London to commence work on their next album, *Beggars Banquet*. It was make-it-or-break-it time. If the new album did not pick them out of the creative doldrums of *Buttons* and *Majesties*, they would be finished as serious contenders for the rock throne.

Andrew Oldham was out of the picture for good. He sold his share of the group to Klein for one million dollars.

SHEILA OLDHAM: "I don't think any one of them ever turned around and said, 'Thanks, Andrew, for what you did.' It was excruciating for Andrew, the feeling how was he going to go on from that point, because of the drug thing getting in the way, and not knowing how to deal with the bust. He spent so much time and trouble trying to make sure what went out to the press was what he wanted to go out. They seemed to be sabotaging themselves or taking it into their own hands. I think Andrew in some interview said he lost his bottle. He was devastated by the whole thing, and I don't think he's recovered."

His place as producer was taken by a twenty-four-year-old New Yorker who had worked successfully with the Spencer Davis Group and Traffic, Jimmy Miller.

RICHARDS: "We were just coming out of *Satanic Majesties*, acid, everything was on the point of dispersal, I had nicked Brian's old lady, it was a mess, and Jimmy pulled *Beggars Banquet* out of all that. It was really a gas to work with him. We tried to do it ourselves, but it's really a drag not having someone to bounce off, someone who knows what you want and what he wants. You get somebody like Jimmy Miller who can turn the whole band on, make a nondescript number into something, which is what happened on *Beggars Banquet*."

Jones's place as the third mind in the band had been taken by Anita Pallenberg. Brian rarely participated in the recording sessions. When he did show up he was so drugged on Mandrax, heroin, and alcohol he would often lie on the floor in a corner with his guitar strapped across his chest, reading magazines, nodding out, and looking pathetic.

GEORGE CHKIANTZ (recording engineer): "Mick and Keith would relegate some minor part to him. Those two work very much in collusion; always have and always will. I did think it was a bit much the way they were going on about him. Somebody like Brian was no longer capable of fulfilling a real function in the group. Of course, he still thought he was. I'm sure Mick and Keith did what they consider their best to try to reach him, but it obviously wasn't good enough."

The tension between Brian and Keith was so strong they hardly spoke. In what some saw as an attempt to get back at Richards, Jones had Linda Keith move into his Cheshire Mews flat in London's West End. Although Linda claims the relationship was based more on their love of drugs than of each other, Jones ended up proposing to her on six different occasions.

Free from having to produce their own albums and from the domination of Brian, Jagger and Richards ascended to new creative heights. For the first time they had the luxury of writing and recording for months without the interruption of a tour. The relative harmony between Anita and Marianne further supported the collaboration. Meeting at Mick's flat in London or at Redlands, Mick and Keith spent days playing old blues numbers until they segued into something of their own. Keith would monotonously strum a refrain over and over again, sometimes wailing incomprehensible sounds that only Jagger could translate, until—often after many hours or days—they were singing "Stray Cat Blues" or "Salt of the Earth."

ANITA PALLENBERG: "Writing together was the strongest thing Keith and Mick had going. Keith didn't know what he was saying but Mick could interpret it."

RICHARDS: "I consider myself to be more a record maker than a guitar player. Guitar happens to be my tool to make records. I think the rest of the band were kind of intrigued—'What's he comin' up with by these tunings?' So they stayed out to give me a little air, you know, 'I want to do eight overdubs here, and over here I want to layer this thing.'" From Jimmy Miller's viewpoint as producer, the record became Keith's showcase as he played every rhythm and lead part, overdubbing acoustics into tape recorders, experimenting every day with new effects.

On May 9, 1968, the *Daily Express* printed a story, "Things Look Bad for the Rolling Stones," noting that they had not had a number one single in the U.K. since "Paint It, Black" in 1966. *Beggars Banquet* was due to be released in July. On May 12, the public got a preview of the album when Jagger accepted an award for the best R&B group of the year from the *New Musical Express* at London's Wembley Arena. The Stones did a surprise performance, playing "Satisfaction" and the new single, "Jumpin' Jack Flash." ("Flower power was just a load of crap, wasn't it?" Jagger later said to Richards. "There was nothing about love, peace, and flowers in 'Jumpin' Jack Flash,' was there?") The single was released on May 24 in Britain and June 1 in the U.S. It went to number one in Britain and number three in the U.S. On the record jacket and on a promotional film accompanying the record the Stones appeared for the first time wearing makeup without being in drag. Keith had painted fingernails. "Such a device might have sunk the careers of some groups," one critic wrote, "but they made it work and this androgynous gesture was seen as the precursor years later of an entire rock era."

RICHARDS: "It was the best thing we ever did with Jimmy Miller. As soon as I pick up the guitar and play that 'Jumpin' Jack Flash' riff, something happens here—in your stomach. It's one of the better feelings in the world. You just jump on the riff and it plays you. Matter of fact, it takes you over. An explosion would be the best way to describe it. It's the one that I would immediately go to if I wanted to approach the state of nirvana. Maybe that's what this entire generation felt. An explosion. A rebellion against boredom, and conformity. That's why it broke out amongst white kids like me. Suddenly something happened: Its first impact was an invasion. Like the barbarians at the gates of Rome."

In June the French avant-garde filmmaker Jean-Luc Godard shot an unrecognized rock masterpiece, *One Plus One*, during the two days they recorded "Sympathy for the Devil." "He worked from one point to another, filming a piece and then deciding what to do next after looking at the result," wrote Bill Wyman. "As Keith pointed out, that was precisely how we shaped our songs and recording sessions." In one scene Richards, Pallenberg, Jones, and

Faithfull sing the backup chorus. Jones and Faithfull stand stock still, as if frozen by the occasion. Richards and particularly Pallenberg are rocking. Suddenly she leans over and, in front of Brian, kisses Keith on the cheek.

RICHARDS: "'Sympathy for the Devil' started as an acoustic folk song and ended up as a mad samba, with me playing bass and overdubbing the guitar later. That's why I don't like to go into the studio with a song worked out beforehand. You can write the songs but you've got to give the band something they can use their imagination on as well. You can write down the notes, but you can't put down 'factor X,' which is important in rock and roll—the feel."

CHARLIE WATTS: "Being a drummer with the Rolling Stones is much more creative than people think. Keith writes a song, then I can turn it into a samba or a waltz or anything. And if he likes it then that's fine. But in some other types of music, if a song is a waltz then you can't do anything about it. The dots are there on paper and you just have to play it as it's written."

The *Beggars Banquet* session owed more than a little to the influence of Marianne Faithfull and Anita Pallenberg. Marianne opened a whole new world to Jagger: she gave him books; suggested songs he cover, such as Robert Johnson's "Love In Vain"; and wrote songs with him, such as "Sister Morphine." Anita had an even more profound effect. In the opinion of a number of people in the Stones entourage, during the *Beggars Banquet* sessions Anita became a Rolling Stone, bringing to the band an influence as unsettling and creative as Jones had. A natural rebel, she followed William Blake's dictum that rules were made to be broken and lit a fire under the naturally lazy Keith's ass.

TONY SANCHEZ: "I once heard Anita listen to a tape of 'Stray Cat Blues' as Jagger proudly waited for her to tell him (as all the other lackeys had done) how brilliant it was. 'Crap,' she said when it was finished. 'The vocals are mixed up too high, and the bass isn't loud enough.' Mick ... was so unused to hearing someone dare to criticize his work that he at once went back to the studio and had the number remixed."

"I'd always tell them, and to my amazement, they would listen,"

Anita recalled. "Nobody else would. They were all yes-men. I call them 'shampoo people'—guys with three-piece suits and curlies." Tony Sanchez says she told him, "I feel rather like I'm the sixth Rolling Stone. Mick and Keith and Brian need me to guide them, to criticize them and give them ideas. I'm certain that any one of them would break up the band for me." Clearly, Anita was a much more dangerous character then Marianne, who used to call her Glenda Hindenburg. Anita was stronger than Keith or Mick, where Marianne was a lot less sure of herself. Marianne gave herself totally to Mick; Anita shared herself with Keith. And Mick would take everything from Marianne and move on by 1970, while Keith would be reliant on Anita for another ten years.

With Jones in decline, the Stones began to import a series of studio musicians who would play a big role in painting their sound during the 1968–1972 period. Ry Cooder played on "Love in Vain" and "Sister Morphine" during the *Beggars Banquet* sessions.

RICHARDS: "I met Ry in 1968, when he was hanging around with Taj Mahal and Jesse Ed Davis. There were people like Clarence White around too, some good guitar players! So we'd all pick up stuff from each other.

"Ry was using open G for slide, I saw him and thought, that's a really nice tuning. It restricts you so much. There's something about being restricted that opens up the possibilities. With a synthesizer you can do anything you like. I don't want to do anything I like! I wanna do something that ties me down, where I can maneuver.

"So I started playing in G without the slide, and also I needed a challenge at the time—suddenly after five years the Stones weren't working 365 days a year. It was the first of the stops and the starts. And I started to find other chords and realized this was a really good vehicle for me. Specially 'cause Brian had ... it was a period where there was no other guitar player and I was trying to figure out what the hell to do next.

"Around the time that Ry Cooder came to play on 'Sister Morphine,' I'd been playing around with the open G [guitar tuning], and he was using it too. I picked up a lot of tips on how to handle it. That's when I realized that you don't really need the bottom string, because the fifth string is the root note. The other one you've got to tune down. I eliminated the sixth string, the fifth string is your root note, and the sixth would start to rumble, and also because you have to tune it down two notches it doesn't stay in tune very well, it's too slack, and it would just get in the way, kind of an unnecessary appendage."

NICK KENT: "There are two basic styles of rock guitar playing. There's one in normal tuning, which is the Chuck Berry stuff, and there's one in open G tuning and that's what Ry Cooder taught Richards about on those *Beggars Banquet* sessions. Keith's style from *Beggars Banquet* onwards is based on open G tuning and it's based around the three very easy riffs on 'Jumpin' Jack Flash,' 'Honky Tonk Women' and 'Gimme Shelter' in that particular G style that Ry Cooder plays all the time. Cooder thinks that Richards ripped it off, but it's the way Keith uses those riffs that makes them his own. He took them off into something else. He did to Cooder's basic style what he did to Chuck Berry's. And he just became obsessed with that basic scheme of playing for years, but he's taken an ounce of what Cooder would have done to it and put it into his pound."

Cooder angrily and publicly charged that Richards plagiarized all his riffs as soon as he turned his back.

RICHARDS: "I heard those things he said and I was amazed. He taught me the tuning and I got behind it. I mean, he was a gas to play with, he was amazing. He played beautifully, but I learned a lot of things off a lot of people. Rock and roll is a matter of borrowing. In a way, all musicians do is pass it on. Guys come up and say, 'This guy is copying you,' so what?"

The second person who began to have an enormous musical influence on Richards that year was the country-rock rhinestone cowboy and pioneer of "cosmic American music," Gram Parsons. Parsons lived in L.A. and had recently joined the Byrds, who were riding the crest of worldwide fame. The Byrds came to London in the summer of 1968, on their way to tour South Africa. Jagger and Richards took them all out to dinner and Keith felt an instant affiliation with the unusually courteous, gentlemanly, Southern Parsons, in whom he saw himself reflected. When Richards and Jagger told him English bands refused to play South Africa because of its apartheid policy, Parsons took his exit cue and told the Byrds the following morning that he would not be continuing with them to Johannesburg. He moved into Redlands with Keith and Anita for the balance of the summer; he and Keith proceeded to get wasted and delve down into the music of the Mississippi delta and the Georgia swamplands.

"Gram was ripe," said Marianne Faithful. "He was like an apple waiting to fall off a tree."

RICHARDS: "He was really intrigued by me and the band. Although [the Stones] came from England, Gram and I shared this instinctive affinity for the real [American] South. The reason Gram and I were together more than other musicians is because I really wanted to learn what Gram had to offer. Gram was special. If he was in a room everyone else became sweet. Anything that Gram was involved in had a touch of magic to it."

Parsons had a largely unrecognized influence during the *Beggars Banquet-Exile on Main St.* period. "He taught me the mechanics of country music," Keith said, "the Nashville style as opposed to the Bakersfield style. Also, he got me into playing piano. I like to write a lot on the piano as opposed to the guitar. He started to turn me on to certain classic tracks and certain styles of playing things— George Jones, Merle Haggard, Jimmie Rodgers. We used to sit around at the piano for ages, trying to figure out little licks. But not all country—that was the overwhelming impression, but also blues; Robert Johnson.

"Around '68 up comes this second Robert Johnson collection that included 'Love in Vain.' 'Love in Vain' was such a beautiful song. Mick and I both loved it, and at the time Gram and I started searching around for a different way to present it, because if we were going to record it there was no point in trying to copy the Robert Johnson style or version. So I sat around playing it in all kinds of different ways and styles. We took a little bit more country, a little bit more formalized, and Mick felt comfortable with that. But in a way it was just like, 'We've got to do this song, one way or another.' Because it was just so beautiful: the title, the lyrics, the ideas, the rhymes, just everything about it."

"When the three of us sang together, it sounded like Gaelic

music," recalled Gram Parsons. "Like the Incredible String Band. On one occasion at the piano, with me and Jagger and Richards, we had Little Richard. 'It's all the same,' that's what Keith said. Two Georgia peaches and two English boys, stinky English kids. Fun, it's really far out. Drunk. *Drunk*."

RICHARDS: "That was the other side of Gram. Did he like to get out of it or what? Which was suiting me fine at the time. That was pretty much what I was doing. Gram was just as knowledgeable about chemical substances as I was when I met him. And he had very good taste. He went for the top of the line. He could get better coke than the Mafia. I don't think I taught him much about drugs; I was still learning myself, much to my detriment. I think we were both basically into the same thing. We liked drugs and we liked the finest quality."

Parsons's change of allegiance from the Byrds to the Stones was seen by some in another light. "The Rolling Stones thing got in the way tremendously because Gram was like a groupie to them," said ex-Byrd Chris Hillman. "'Oh, sorry, guys, but I'm going over to hang out with the Stones now.' The times I picked him up over at Keith Richards's were a little strange. They'd come out skipping like little kids."

On July 7, Keith, Anita, Mick, and Jimmy Miller flew to L.A. to mix *Beggars Banquet*. Keith and Anita saw a lot of Gram, visiting his favorite place, the Joshua Tree National Monument in the California desert. They frequently spent the entire night looking for UFOs, snorting coke, and waiting for the sunrise.

Richards and Jagger realized they were on to something good, that they had found a sound that complemented their viewpoint and seemed perfect for the time. Events were moving fast. By the summer of 1968, 1967's summer of love was an antique. The hard-edged, demonic feel of "Jumpin' Jack Flash" and its follow-up single, "Street Fighting Man," which was released in the U.S. in August to coincide with the demonstrations at the Democratic convention in Chicago, perfectly set the tone for the end of the sixties, even though "Street Fighting Man" stalled at number forty-eight in the U.S. after being banned on many radio stations.

By this time, Keith and Anita had abandoned his flat in St. John's

Wood and were staying at Robert Fraser's rooms in Mayfair in a setting adorned by Tibetan skulls, tantric art, Moroccan tapestries, and incestuous relationships redolent of Cocteau. An art college student named David Courts, who shared an aesthetic outlook with Robert, Keith, and Anita, started seeing a lot of Keith at Fraser's.

DAVID COURTS: "At that time there was a big connection between the art scene and the music scene and I think it had a lot to do with a lot of musicians coming out of art school, and so it was quite easy to jell, and of course the drug connection was big and everybody had the same antiestablishment feeling, that it was them and us. I started making jewelry for Keith through Anita. I made a skull pin, which was this carved skull with a bishop's miter of white-yellow gold with sapphires, rubies, and diamonds set in it. It was rather unusual and she said, 'Great, we'll have it for Keith and engrave on it 'The Bishop of Rock and Roll.' So she was right on the ball."

MARIANNE FAITHFULL: "It is a stunning metamorphosis, when somebody changes from being young and unsure of himself to suddenly becoming a kind of young prince with all the power and privilege of royalty. Mick and Keith made the transition very smoothly, just as if everything that was happening to them, no matter how enormous and quickly, was rather normal."

12

Honky Tonk Women
1968–1969

For a few years then we were just flying. We had everything—money, power, looks, protection. We had the lot.

ANITA PALLENBERG, *From an interview with Perry Richardson, 1991*

"Nineteen sixty-eight was a funny year," Richards reflected. "It had a hole in it somewhere." On May 11, the day before the Stones debuted "Jumpin' Jack Flash" at the *New Musical Express*, it was announced that Mick was going to act as a jaded rock star in a film called *Performance* to be directed by their friend Donald Cammell and the ace British cameraman Nicolas Roeg, who had shot *Lawrence of Arabia*. It had been planned that Marianne would star opposite him, but when she became pregnant she dropped out. Consequently, it came about that Anita would star opposite Jagger. This development clearly put Richards in a difficult position. At first he maintained a cool attitude. But then Decca refused to release *Beggars Banquet* that summer with the cover Anita, Keith, and Mick had chosen, a toilet wall covered with graffiti such as "God rolls his own." The Stones refused to change it, and Keith was left with no record to promote.

RICHARDS: "The job of the record company is to distribute. All they've got to do is put it in the shops, not dictate to people what they should or should not have."

GLYN JOHNS (who worked for Decca Records): "I believe Sir Edward took legal advice and discovered that if Decca had put out the sleeve they would probably be sued for obscenity. From that level on there was a big lack of communication and Allen Klein was in the middle. Klein is a strange man. I think his greatest secret is not telling artists exactly what is going on but letting his artists think they know exactly what is going on, and not telling the people he is dealing with what is going on but letting them feel that they also know. I don't think Decca ever felt that they knew what was going on. Sir Edward was always saying to me, 'I'm not sure what's going on,' and I think one of the great things he wanted me to do was to have direct communication with Jagger on a very informal basis, just so that we could make sure that we knew that everything that we were saying and we were agreeing to was getting back to the Stones."

Despite Johns's attempt to mediate, the release of the album that was to reestablish the Rolling Stones as the premier rock band of their age was delayed for six months, until December 1968. Consequently, Keith had to spend from August through October cut off from Jagger and Pallenberg and at loose ends. He had not wanted Anita to take the part. To complicate matters, Anita claimed she too became pregnant, but since she had already signed the contract she felt forced to have an abortion and went on with the film.

"Whatever you do, don't try to play yourself," Marianne urged Mick. "You're much too together, too straight, too strong. You simply can't play yourself. That would be a disaster. The character must be a combination of Brian and Keith. Mix up and combine Brian with all his torturedness, all his paranoia and his coked-up movements, and Keith with his torturedness but his cool, and put them together to make this character. You've got to imagine you're poor freaked-out, deluded, androgynous, druggie Brian, but you also need a bit of Keith's tough, self-destructive, beautiful lawlessness."

Taking the advice of Faithfull, Jagger cleverly prepared for his role by creating a composite character based on Jones and Richards. Marianne, who was worried that she might miscarry (or perhaps wanting to skip the September 12 premiere of *The Girl on a Motorcycle*, in which she appeared totally nude), went on holiday with her mother, leaving this amalgam of the men Anita loved on the loose.

Donald Cammell quickly saw that Keith was deeply uneasy about Anita's role as Mick's lover, which was as mischievous and alluring as her role with the Stones. Their costar, James Fox, who would be changed irrevocably by his involvement with Jagger, was appalled to discover Mick and Anita fucking in the dressing room three days into the shoot. "Anita was having the time of her life," Cammell said. "She'd go home to Keith, who'd be terribly jealous when he heard she'd been in bed with Mick." Tony Sanchez, who had become Keith's paid companion, saw his boss sinking into a depression reminiscent of Jones's collapse. Keith must have recognized that he could not emotionally afford to have the kind of falling-out with Mick that he had endured with Brian, because he chose a see-no-evil strategy.

IAN STEWART: "Keith refused to go into the Lowndes Square house [where much of the movie was filmed] and often parked outside and sent messages in to Anita. As for Anita and Mick, I always felt there was no love lost there; they always seemed to be a bit wary of each other, but when the big sex scene of the movie was filmed, instead of simulating sex they really got into each other, and although what wound up in the picture was a lot of vague, tumbling bodies in the sheets, nothing explicit, there was a lot of very explicit footage of Mick and Anita really screwing, steamy, lusty stuff, that was edited into a separate X-rated short feature that was shown all around and actually copped an award at some X-rated film festival in Amsterdam.

"Of course, Keith got hold of this and was pissed at what he saw. For a while things were strained between him and Mick, and of course things were pretty rough with Anita."

Anita rented Robert Fraser's flat for the course of the filming, but instead of moving out, he merely gave up his room and hung out with Keith, stoking his paranoia. When she came home after a day of shooting, the two would be waiting for her snarling, "What did you get up to today?" Treachery was an affectionate game with Robert, explained Donald Cammell, who, fearing sabotage, barred Fraser from the film set.

The same malevolent tension that gave *Performance* its strange appeal would be heard on the Stones' next album, *Let It Bleed*, which Keith was writing alone at Robert Fraser's flat. He submerged himself in work, playing guitar and taking drugs. He had begun to use heroin for the first time, mixing it with coke and snorting it speedball fashion. Asked what substances worked best for producing music, Richards replied, "Well, a speedball doesn't go down too bad! Those were the days. Oh, fuck. You've got the answer there."

"In the autumn of 1968, that year of assassinations, riots, and undeclared war, I went to England to meet the Rolling Stones," wrote Stanley Booth. "Keith and I spent an afternoon talking, mostly about the blues. He was heavy lidded and remote. We had, all of our generation, fallen in love with the singing cowboys in westerns; in our boyhood games we had all—including Keith— pretended to be Roy Rogers, but Keith, it seemed, wasn't pretending."

RICHARDS: "Believing in your fame is very, very dangerous. It's not very good for people around you, and even worse for yourself. That's my experience of it. It's one of the reasons I don't regret zooming into the dope thing for so long. It was an experiment that went on too long, but in a way that kept my feet on the street when I could have just become some brat-ass, rich rock-and-roll superstar bullshit, and done myself in in another way. I almost forced myself into that in order to counterbalance this superstar shit that was going on around us. I said, 'No, I want to put my foot in a deep puddle, because I don't want to hang out up there in that stratosphere with the Maharishi and Mick and Paul McCartney.' It was almost a deliberate attempt to get out of it."

In twenty minutes one day, inspired by his convoluted feelings, Richards slapped down on a cassette the words and music to "Gimme Shelter".

A vital part of the film deal had been Jagger's commitment to provide a song for the sound track, but as the film was being edited, Cammell found Jagger becoming elusive about the production of the song. Keith's method of retaliation was to postpone working with him. "Keith just refused to get down to it," Cammell said. "I kept asking Mick, 'Where's the goddamn song?' Mick kept saying, 'It's OK, it'll be ready,' but he knew very well what Keith was doing, and why." Finally, Cammell and Jagger wrote "Memo from Turner," but when the Stones met to record it, Keith's sabotage continued. "With Keith against it in the studio, it sounded just awful—stiff and lifeless," Cammell said. "But without the song, we couldn't end the picture. Keith knew he had the power to sabotage the whole thing." Jagger, who was finally reduced to tears before Cammell over his embarrassment at not being able to produce the song without Richards, got a bunch of studio musicians (including Ry Cooder) together and cut the track, but without Keith it lacked the edge that characterized the Rolling Stones at their best.

The breach among Jagger, Richards, and Jones healed temporarily on September 24 when Keith and Mick attended Jones's London drug trial. "Mr. Havers, Brian's attorney, had just completed his summation when Mick Jagger and Keith Richards walked into the gallery," wrote Stanley Booth. "Everyone—spectators, counsel, jury—turned to look: it was as if the outlaws Cole and Jim Younger had walked into the court where Judge Roy Bean was trying their brother Bob. Keith was dressed in a tan suede jacket, white T-shirt, and brown leather pants with, clearly, no underwear."

"As the foreman announced 'guilty,' Brian, near to collapse, staggered back muttering," recalled Wyman. "Girls in the public gallery gasped. Keith was visibly trembling." To everyone's relief, Jones was let off with a fine of fifty pounds. Booth watched in awe as Mick and Keith posed with him for photographers, then "drove away in a blue Bentley whose hood displayed the flag of the Confederate States of America."

In December, *Beggars Banquet*, with a revised cover, was released to critical acclaim. The record broadened the Stones' audience: the Left seized upon it as a manifesto; hard-core blues fans who had dismissed the Stones' earlier work as derivative were won over. The Beatles were "still searching—and it showed," said *The New York Times*, but the Stones "had found out where they were and were building." Most of the credit went to the high-profile Jagger, but there were those who recognized a Richards creation when they heard it. "The Chuck Berry influence became dusted by hayseed as Keith drenched *Beggars Banquet* with the sound of acoustics," wrote one critic. His guitar playing on "Sympathy for the Devil" was singled out by another as "among the finest rock solos I have heard recently. He only uses about five of the simplest rock lines around but he plays them with such finesse they seem to be oozing out of the guitar. His style is pure eroticism and he seems to linger over each note, making sure it comes out exactly like it's supposed to."

The outstanding year's work climaxed with the filming, on December 11–12, of the ill-fated "Rolling Stones Rock and Roll Circus" television special, which features the Who, Eric Clapton, John Lennon, Yoko Ono, and Marianne Faithfull as well as the Stones, but was never released. Asked to dress as he envisioned himself, Keith wore a black patch over one eye, a top hat accentuated his wolfish profile, and smoke from a cheroot encircled his pockmarked features. Meanwhile, "Street Fighting Man" was released in Europe, went to number one in Germany, and was also a big hit in Denmark, Holland, Sweden, France, Switzerland, Hungary, Poland, and Turkey.

In light of the success of the album and emotional weight of the year, the threatening erotic triangle fizzled out without ever really exploding, though Jagger continued to pursue Anita after the completion of the movie.

ANITA PALLENBERG: "Mick wanted to do another movie with me and for us to be a couple, and other people made offers for us to make films together, but I just didn't want it. Mick just wanted to walk around and show me off like he did with all his women, and I felt Keith needed a more human kind of attention and care and love."

Keith and Anita booked passage on a ship leaving Lisbon for Rio de Janeiro on December 18, Richards's twenty-fifth birthday. Anita had just learned that she was pregnant again and they were taking the safest possible route. Deciding to put the past behind him, Mick joined them with Marianne. "We've become very interested in magic and we're very serious about this trip," Keith joked to the press. "We're hoping to see this magician who practices both white and black magic. He has a long and very difficult name which we cannot pronounce. We call him 'Banana' for short."

RICHARDS: "Every night in the bar we met this very vivacious woman who drank pink gin. When she got drunk all she would ever say was 'Who are you, won't you give us a glimmer?' I just loved the way she said it, so we became the Glimmer Twins."

ANITA PALLENBERG: "Marianne left after a while because she couldn't stand the Brazilian climate and felt sick, so it was Mick, Keith, and me staying on this ranch in the middle of nowhere. It was quite a creative time. That's where they wrote 'You Can't Always Get What You Want' and 'Let It Bleed.' Mick wanted me to split with him after we had done *Performance*. I definitely remember that I didn't want to have anything to do with Mick Jagger. I did not want to be his girlfriend. I never did. But Mick and me still had this kind of secret, or thought we did, so for me it was exciting because I thought I was in the middle of this high drama. And Keith was willing to go along with it. He could have just said, 'No, I don't want to know. You do whatever you want to and that's it.' But Keith was willing to go along with it. Me and Mick would jokingly talk about all those things and it was like, you can't always get what you want. It seems to me that everything was very repetitious in those days. The way Mick and Keith write is they don't actually put the words down. They make a tune and they go 'Aah, ah, ah,' and the words come out afterwards. And I think it was a creative process because of this repetition. Every day that phrase would come up."

While Anita was playing with Mick, Keith was writing "Honky Tonk Women," connecting to his roots as a cowboy guitar player in Dartford. On one occasion, finding themselves in the remote town of Urubamba in Peru, which lacked even a small hotel, they played for the local farmers in the hope of earning a meal. Keith reached all the way back to his fake "Malagueña." "We got them all going and got beds for the night, food and everything," he said. "I have to thank my grandfather for that—he taught me to pick up the essentials of any kind of music."

As soon as they returned from South America, Keith and Anita went down to Dartford to visit Doris. Being a traditional British mum, Doris had always found it hard to appreciate Anita's continental style. When Anita proudly displayed her stomach, joking that her baby had been to Brazil, Mrs. Richards thought, this was no way to tell your mother-in-law you were pregnant! And what had happened to her wonderful Keith? He looked like Jesus Christ, floating around the house in a long white robe as if his feet were three inches above the ground. Doris had no idea that Keith had started his long, deadly relationship with what people who took heroin referred to, ironically, as Jones.

Eric Clapton, who also became a heroin addict, thought that musicians were particularly vulnerable to heroin because they live "on a very intense plane of emotional necessity, and heroin is probably the strongest painkiller you can get." Reflecting on his relationship with the white powder, Richards explained that becoming addicted had been a slow seduction. He had taken heroin for two months, stopped for a month, and had no worse withdrawal symptoms than a bad flu. But when the arranger Jack Nitzsche, who had played a significant role in the early recording sessions, flew into London to join them for *Let It Bleed*, Keith and Anita seemed like different people. Richards offered Nitzsche some heroin, telling him, "For every junkie there's a shining example like myself!"

"Keith told me he considered me as smart as he was so how could I get addicted?" Nitzsche recalled. "So I tried it and it was real good. The next thing I know, the shining example is lying on the floor."

Keith often commented that his friends' approach to drugs had followed in De Quincey's footsteps. They saw their bodies as laboratories and were trying to find out if they could improve themselves or understand the world in a more sophisticated way. At first, they were, he insisted, more intent on experiencing ideas, emotions, and a new physical reality than getting wasted.

To begin with, Keith took to the world of junk and junkies as enthusiastically as he took to the world of music. Indeed, for a man who had been wrapped up in closed societies since his teens this was a step up, for there is no more closed and intensely connected a society than that of junkies. It was a world where nobody arrived on time except by accident. Keith adopted its habits as completely as he had adopted the guitar style of Chuck Berry, becoming in time as archetypal a junkie as he was a guitar player. Since it distanced him from other people, making him, at first, less vulnerable, it suited his character, releasing some of his very best work. Heroin undoubtedly played a vital role in Richards's great cycle from *Beggar's Banquet* to *Exile on Main St.* "In a certain stage of the addictive process you can take dope and you can screw for nine hours straight, you can drink everyone on earth under the table and show no effects of it, you can play guitar better than you ever did, your internal creative vision is profound, and you can have this drive for days and days," said a fellow musician and heroin addict. "Within the opening riff to 'Gimme Shelter' I hear that incredible vista that dope can open up and allow you to get to."

The trouble began when Richards started nodding out at the wheel. Anita would nudge him reprovingly—"Keith!"—and he would snap out of it. One of many car crashes occurred in May 1969. Anita had recently persuaded Keith that his Bentley Touring Continental was not car enough for a man of his caliber and talked him into purchasing a nineteen-foot-long Nazi staff car rumored to have been owned by Göring. Keith had it restored to its original splendor at a cost of several thousand pounds. He had smashed it up the first time he took it for a spin and returned it to the garage for further repair. Unfortunately, the reconstruction was to be short-lived. Soon after, driving around a bend at top speed just a few miles from Redlands, Keith crashed the Mercedes into the curb and ricocheted across the road, rolling down an embankment, and bringing a speedy end to the fantastic remodeled car. When Keith had gotten rid of all his drugs and gone through the requisite police routine, he discovered that Anita, six months pregnant, had fractured her collarbone. Undaunted by this near brush with disaster, he got rid of the Mercedes but continued driving his Bentley with the same careless abandon.

The dual influences of Anita and heroin were heavily seasoned by the people Richards surrounded himself with. Kenneth Anger, who lived with them at Redlands for a couple of months in 1969, was a typical example. Richards often slept on the couch in the living room at Redlands and would occasionally wake to see Anger pottering around the lawn between the house and the moat, building a shrine while entwining himself in psychedelic scarves. But Keith never fell under Kenneth's spells or took them seriously. He never saw Anger as anything other than a seeker, like Michael Cooper or Robert Fraser or himself, all chasing their own demons.

KENNETH ANGER: "The active magical element in the Stones' music is its strong sexual connotations. It's basically music to fuck to. I was going to film a version of *Lucifer Rising* with the Stones. All the roles were to be carefully cast, with Mick being Lucifer and Keith as Beelzebub. Beelzebub is like a henchman for Lucifer ... The occult unit within the Stones was Keith and Anita." However, Richards claims that neither he nor Anita was heavily involved with the occult. For him it was a handy image tool; for her it was just another way in which she could mess around with people's heads.

In March Richards and Jagger made a brief visit to Italy, where they stayed in a friend's lofty old house in Positano and wrote "Monkey Man" and "Midnight Rambler." From May through July 1969 they recorded *Let It Bleed* at Olympic Studios in London. Jimmy Miller was once again on the board. Miller was impressed by Keith's contribution. It became clear to him now that Keith's stamina gave him the strength to maintain the sustained drive that pulled together the music. As far as he was concerned, it was on this record that Keith "took over the musical leadership of the Stones and did brilliantly."

Another musician who worked on the album, Al Kooper, who played on Dylan's first electric albums, remembered the effect of Richards and Jagger's entrance the night they recorded "You Can't Always Get What You Want": "Mick and Keith came exploding in the door. Mick was wearing a gorilla coat, and Keith had on this sort of Tyrolean hat with a real long feather in it. It was gonna be party time, and they were the party from the moment they arrived. Everyone sat around on the floor with either an acoustic guitar or a percussion instrument, and Mick and Keith played the song they wanted to record until everyone had the chord changes and the rhythm accents. There was a conga player there who could play congas and roll huge hash joints without missing a lick. It was decided I would play piano on the basic track and overdub organ later.

"I got into this groove I had heard on an Etta James record of 'I Got You Babe' that really fit their song well. Keith picked up on it right away and played a nice guitar part that meshed right with it. When the proper take was gotten, Keith overdubbed an electric part and I overdubbed the organ."

GRAM PARSONS: "They recorded 'Honky Tonk Women' and didn't think it was a single; I think Keith did. Impish Keith the gypsy. He let them put the horns on it and put the screaming guitars on it to show them it was a really good song, that it could be number one."

RICHARDS: "We fooled around with 'Honky Tonk Women,' trying to make it sound funkier, and hit on the sound we had on the single. We all thought, 'Wow, this has got to be a hit single.' And it was and it did fantastically well, probably because it's the sort of song which transcends all tastes."

" 'Honky Tonk Women' was a dazzling showcase for the rhythmic expertise of both Keith Richards and Charlie Watts," wrote Roy Carr. "Like all truly great stylists, Richards and Watts have realized that it's not what you play, it's what you don't play that heightens the effect."

In June, Richards and Jagger finally ousted Jones from the band, easing him out with a golden handshake of one hundred thousand pounds a year for the rest of his life, and the promise of continued friendship. Keith, Mick, and Charlie drove down to Brian's house in silence. Brian knew why they had come, and they sat down in the kitchen to confront the issue. Keith did most of the talking, explaining that they wanted to tour America in the near future. Brian agreed that he just didn't have the physical stamina to go through all those one-nighters. Keith said they understood, but they needed to make a move and they already had Mick Taylor waiting in the wings.

RICHARDS: "Brian was a very infuriating guy. Firing him was hard for Mick and me, but he could hardly play, hardly stand up, hardly breathe. That was one of the things we'd gone on to Brian about; he'd drink and take barbiturates on top of his respiratory problems; you'd see him choking in a corner many times, pumping his inhaler into his mouth. We'd come to the point where we could not bring the guy around, and the only way was to say, 'Sorry, old cock, you're out.' "

The following week they invited a young jazz-blues guitarist, Mick Taylor, to join the band. Taylor, who had made a name for himself in John Mayall's Bluesbreakers, said of the Stones' decision, "I just assume I was the best guitarist available at the time." As a way of introducing Taylor to their fans while publicizing their new single, "Honky Tonk Women," they decided to give a free concert in London's Hyde Park on July 5. Just past midnight on July 3, while the band was recording Stevie Wonder's "I Don't Know Why," Brian Jones, twenty-seven, drowned in the swimming pool of his country house.

RICHARDS: "We were at a session that night and someone called us up at midnight and said: 'Brian's dead.' Well, what the fuck's going on? I don't know, man, I just don't know what happened to Brian that night. If anybody was going to kill Brian, it was going to be me. There was no one there that'd want to murder him. Someone just didn't take care of him."

ANITA PALLENBERG: "The reason he died when he did was that there was no one around who knew what to do when he was starting to overdose and suffering from his asthmatic condition at the same time. He had been in that condition many times before, but there had always been people around to turn him on his side and take care of him."

Had he wanted to deal one final, devastating blow to the two people he loved and hated most, Jones could not have done anything more effective than dying when he did, two weeks after he was fired and two days before the Stones were to play to the biggest audience of their careers. Keith would spend the next ten years, as he put it, becoming Brian and trying to kill himself with heroin. In her attempt to assuage the pain and guilt incurred by Brian's death, Anita would follow Keith down the path of self-destruction with even more harrowing results.

"Keith came into the office that morning and grabbed hold of me and said, 'Are you all right?' remembered Stones assistant Shirley Arnold. "I don't think anyone knew what was happening, 'cause even if they had all expected Brian to die young, when it happens it's still a shock. Then they started talking about their planned free concert in Hyde Park, and the first thing Mick said was, 'We'll cancel it.'" But Keith and Charlie insisted that they go ahead with the show, making it into a memorial concert and tribute to Jones. Later, when a reporter suggested that it was in bad taste for the Stones to hold such a huge concert before Brian had even been buried, Keith allegedly punched him in the nose and pushed him down a flight of stairs.

RICHARDS: "I wasn't surprised about Brian. I didn't wish him dead and there were a few guys who did, but in all honesty it was no surprise. And it was hard to shed a tear at his demise, quite honestly. It was like, 'Wow, he's gone, thank God.' Cold-blooded as that sounds, he was a passenger for us. We had to cover his ass. We all revere his memory, and nobody deserves to go that young. But if anybody asked for it, he did. But you don't leave the Stones singing, you just get carried out. Brian was already effectively dead when he died; he was already out of the band."

ANITA PALLENBERG: "They didn't leave him, he left them."

After Brian died, Keith had to make a choice to become one with the living or one of the living dead. He had very little to hold onto in his life and needed to make a commitment to something. Disillusioned by Brian's death, Anita's infidelity, and the straight world of oppressive authority figures, Keith decided to make the major commitment to Mick. At first the outcome was extraordinarily successful, as they made their greatest records and gave their greatest performances, but some saw it as a partnership, or marriage, born out of hell and pain.

On July 5, Decca released a double-A-sided single, "Honky Tonk Women"/"You Can't Always Get What You Want," that would go to number one in the U.S. and U.K., and in Germany, Sweden, France, Denmark, Belgium, Holland, Luxembourg, Switzerland, Norway, Finland, Turkey, the Soviet Union, Poland, South Africa, Greece, Spain, Portugal, Canada, Australia, Yugoslavia, Japan, Czechoslovakia, the Philippines, Israel, Lebanon, and Bermuda. "'Honky Tonk Women' was the strongest three minutes of rock and roll released in 1969," wrote Greil Marcus in Rolling Stone. "In spite of Mick's screaming, joyful singing, this time the star of the show is Keith Richards. He combines the cleanest, toughest guitar lines in rock with Charlie Watts' jingling cowbell and steady drum shots for an introduction very similar to and equally as dramatic as that of Marvin Gaye's 'I Heard It Through the Grapevine.' Keith moves off after that, really fronting Mick himself, stretching sex with a smile out of every note, running up to the choruses with the same kind of perfect excitement Mike Bloomfield displayed on 'Like a Rolling Stone.' On the last two choruses Richards sings beautifully behind Mick, bending the words in counterpoint to Mick's straight shouts: 'It's a haaaaawwwwww-aw-aw-aw-ky tonk women! Bam! Gimme, gimme, gimme . . .' It would have been a gas to hear Keith sing a chorus all by himself."

On the day the record was released the Stones played their tribute to Jones to five hundred thousand people in Hyde Park. In their office memo schedule the event was listed as the Battle of the Field of the Cloth of Gold.

RICHARDS: "No one really knew what was going on. It was a hassle, quite honestly. It was fantastic from the point of view of a mass gathering. You'll never see Hyde Park like that—just people and trees. But Brian had died and we were breaking in Mick Taylor. We hadn't played live for quite a while and the organization, the logistical end of it, was flimsy. And we played pretty bad until near the end, 'cause we hadn't played for years. And nobody minded because they just wanted to hear us play again. It was nice they were glad to see us because we were glad to see them. Coming after Brian's death, it was like the thing we had to do. We had that big picture of him on stage and it came out looking like a ghost in some pictures."

The root of the problem was more musical than psychological. The band had not played live for an extended period. Mick Taylor had never played live with them. Under the circumstances, their best bet was to look to Richards to pull them together. However, when Keith arrived at the designated meeting place after being up for several days, he looked like a derelict, and when he climbed onto the stage, as one critic noted, "Every chord he played seemed resolutely drugged up to the eyeballs."

13

Get Yer Ya-Ya's Out
1969

There was no time to sit back and think about what we were doing. Everything was done on impulse and instinct. There was no use in trying to intellectualize and rationalize about it or analyze it. Things just happened.

KEITH RICHARDS, *from an interview with Mandy Aftel, 1974*

Anita was to give birth in August. That summer she and Keith had moved into a beautiful five-story Queen Anne house opposite the Thames he had bought for fifty thousand pounds from a Tory government official, Number 3 Cheyne Walk. The house stood in one of the loveliest parts of London next to a home once inhabited by the novelist George Eliot, several hundred feet up the street from Mick's place at Number 48. In order to acquire the twenty thousand pounds he'd needed for the down payment, Richards had dispatched the gruff Tom Keylock to Allen Klein's office in New York, ordering him not to return without the money. "I just kept walking until I was in Allen Klein's office," Keylock said. "He was so amazed that I'd managed to get to him, he agreed to give me the money for Keith."

According to one witness, Anita transformed what had been classic eighteenth-century wood-paneled salons into "replicas of Moroccan hashish dens." The house was a hippie's dream pad. The second-floor front reception room was dedicated to tripping before a fireplace flanked by two giant candlesticks. A glittering mirrored ball hung from the ceiling, reflecting endless shards of light across the walls. Another room contained a shrine to Jimi Hendrix. Keith and Anita slept in the bed on which Mick had fucked her during the filming of *Performance*. A number of people who stayed there claimed the house was haunted.

On August 10 Anita gave birth to their first son. They named him Marlon after Brando, with whom the couple had remained in touch. On August 18, Keith picked them up at the hospital. "I want lots more babies," bubbled a radiant and childlike Anita. "I'm going to have thousands more. I think having babies is wonderful." "Anita's an amazing lady," Keith expounded. "There are some people who you just know are going to end up all right. That's why we had Marlon, because we just knew it was the right time. We're very instinctive people."

RICHARDS: "Having kids turned me on a lot. It reminds you of so many things that you'd totally forgotten about and you get these double takes, just because there's an incredible difference.

"It changes your life, your thinking; the kid is your little thing, and you think, 'Goddamn, I helped make that.' And it's all full of purity and innocence, and it's just smilin' at you and wants to kiss you and hug you, and all it wants to do is just feel you and touch you, and you've never felt so loved in your life. It's that bit of love you gave your own parents, the bit you don't remember—your kids give that back to you. And you realize, 'I've just been given the first two or three years of my life back.'"

TONY SANCHEZ: "I was astonished the way Keith took to the child. Sometimes Keith would pick him up from his crib and whisper to him about all the things they would do together once he got a little bigger. 'You and me, baby,' he'd say. 'We've got the whole world together. We don't need nobody else.'"

But Anita confided to Tony, "It's beautiful that Keith is so crazy about Marlon. But sometimes, just sometimes, it seems as though he loves him more than me." Anita's intuition was correct. In a male-dominated world, with the entrance of Marlon, Pallenberg began to lose her hold on the band and, to a lesser extent, on Keith. People began criticizing her openly.

ANITA PALLENBERG: "Everybody was slashing me when I had Marlon, saying, 'You must be crazy to have children. How can you have a child on the road?' Keith's mom always saw me as a foreigner. You know those English moms. I remember everything I did was strange—'Isn't that strange?'—even milk bottles I had for the babies. Everything was weird. For me, children are the best thing I ever had. I thought it was better to be with the parents than by himself. Marlon learned to walk on stage."

In September the Stones began laying the groundwork for their first tour of America since 1966, scheduled from November to December. Keith wrote "Wild Horses" because of the bittersweet tension he felt about having to leave Anita and Marlon to go on the tour. "I knew we were going to have to go to America and start work again to get me off my ass," he said, "but I didn't really want to go away. The kid was only two months old. It was a very delicate moment."

During tour preparations in London, Jagger was in Australia making his second film, *Ned Kelly*, so Richards had more to do with planning it than anybody else in the band; this would be the last tour for a decade for which he was clearheaded enough to make such arrangements.

RICHARDS: "That whole film thing in Australia was a bit of a drag. I mean, it sounds dangerous to me. He's had his hand blown off, and he has to get his hair cut short. But Mick thinks he needs to do those things. We've often talked about it, and I've asked him why the hell does he want to be a film star. But he says, 'Well, Keith, you're a musician and that's a complete thing in itself, but I don't play anything.' So I said that anyone that sings and dances the way he does shouldn't need to do anything else. But he doesn't agree so I guess that's cool.

"The trouble is that it has disorganized our plans: It happened just as we got Mick Taylor into the band, and just as we were finishing the album. We had one track to do and we accidentally wiped Mick's voice off when we were messing around with the tape. And there's Mick stuck down in Australia, about three thousand miles from the nearest studio. It's pretty far out. I'm going to go out and meet Mick in California about midway through October and we're going to have to rehearse like hell."

In the summer of 1968 several American radio stations had banned "Street Fighting Man," calling it "subversive." "Subversive? Of course we're subversive," Richards had responded. "But if they really believe you can start a revolution with a record, they are wrong. I wish we could. We're more subversive at live appearances."

While "Honky Tonk Women" stayed on the U.S. charts for sixteen weeks, their second greatest-hits album, *Through the Past Darkly*, dedicated to Brian Jones, went to number two that fall. The '69 winter tour would be a watershed for the group, particularly for Richards.

America had changed since the innocence of the pop years. The murder and mayhem of the Manson era had broken out. Cocaine and heroin and loopy Quaaludes were the drugs of choice. Nobody smoked pot to look at paintings anymore. The rock concert had metamorphosed: Audiences listened now, had a political agenda, and could exert themselves as an incredible, and potentially volatile, force. "America is not a young land: it is old and dirty and evil before the settlers, before the indians. The evil was there waiting," wrote William Burroughs in *Naked Lunch*. When the Stones returned to the American stage for the first time in three years, they would discover what he meant. "I flew with the Stones to their first date, on November seventh," said clothes designer Ossie Clark. "I remember vividly that from the moment I set foot in that plane, before it took off from London, I felt a kind of oppressive fear. There was a negative electrical charge in that atmosphere compared to the tours I had gone on before that. The flight over was a nightmare, truly scary, the way the Stones were towards each other, towards me, an insistent, brooding, uncontrolled intimidation. In Los Angeles we were put up in a big house, and the evil vibes intensified. The Stones were taking all kinds of horrible drugs, primarily a new kind of potent acid that they had gotten hold of."

Gram Parsons was once more much in evidence. Gram and Keith embarked on a series of drug binges that often saw them on the trot for three days running. Many of Gram's friends saw him become a clone of Keith. "He's been so high all the time, I've been calling him Gram Richards," said L.A.'s number-one groupie, Pamela Des Barres. "He'd come out of the house holding hands with Keith, skipping along," Parsons's embarrassed roadie recalled, "with painted nails!" Stanley Booth, who lived with the band throughout the tour and wrote a classic book about them, thought they were all seduced by androgyny.

STANLEY BOOTH: "We all got faggier by the day. We all had to brush our hair out of our eyes every eight seconds. You never saw a more limp-wristed bunch of sissies. The wonder is that by the end of the tour we weren't all wearing dresses."

The intimidating, brooding coven gathered in L.A. in October to rehearse and complete *Let It Bleed*. An astute observer, road manager Sam Cutler, called them "the scaredest band in the world," but he introduced them at each concert with resounding confidence as "the Greatest Rock and Roll Band in the World—the Rolling Stones!"

RICHARDS: "For us it was all like school again, the '69 tour. We'd been off the road for three years. Suddenly we had to deal with a PA system, and there's an audience there that's listening instead of screaming chicks. Suddenly it was back to learning how to play on stage again.

"Some of the highlights of my life are the gigs where no one can remember where they were but as you walk off the stage you look at each other and say that maybe, tonight, we were the best rock and roll band in the world. That marvelous feeling when you go beyond your expectations of perfection. But to call us 'the Greatest Rock and Roll Band in the World' . . . God, my God—you've gotta be joking. Maybe one or two nights, yeah, you could stick them with that. My opinion is that on any given night, it's a different band that's the greatest rock and roll band. It's gotta go up and down. Otherwise, you wouldn't know the difference. It would be just a bland straight line, like lookin' at a heart machine. And when that straight line happens, baby, you're dead."

The four-week tour was as close to perfect as a rock and roll tour could be. The live album *Get Yer Ya-Ya's Out!*, recorded in New York, set the standards. But the Stones' stardom was now making them dangerously isolated. Keith had always kept an eye on American politics by watching television on tour. In 1964 he had sneered at the Goldwater-Johnson presidential campaign. During his 1968 visit he noted the different tone of the Nixon-Humphrey campaign. By the time he took the stage in America in 1969 he was aware that they were facing "a completely different kind of madness," but he wasn't able to see it for what it was. "Our show was interpreted as violent or a 'goddamn riot' when it was just people letting it out," he said. "But in America in '69, one got the feeling they really wanted to suck you out."

To thank America for the great reception accorded them at every appearance across the country and to capitalize on the Woodstock Nation ambience, they decided to give a free concert at the end of the tour on December 6. Things went wrong from the outset. The site had to be moved several times at the last moment. From the initial idea of playing in San Francisco's idyllic Golden Gate Park, they ended up settling for a burned-out auto racing arena in the middle of Nowhere, California, called Altamont. As a result, the three hundred thousand people who descended on Altamont that day were expecting a Richard Brautigan fantasy and found themselves instead in a William Burroughs nightmare, stranded without water, food, or facilities of any sort. "One girl told me solemnly that it would be a heavy day," wrote *Rolling Stone* editor Michael Lydon, "'because the sun, Venus, Mercury, and some other planets were all in [Keith's sign] Sagittarius.'"

A lot of bad acid and cheap wine wired the crowd to the breaking point. The Hell's Angels, who had been recommended by the Grateful Dead as security guards, heightened the tension. The Stones were criticized for hiring the Angels because the bikers had recently beaten up anti-Vietnam War demonstrators, but Allen Ginsberg and Ken Kesey had since parleyed with them, and in the heady atmosphere of the time they were looked upon as "brothers." The juxtaposition of the many chemically deranged members of the audience with even more demented bikers led to a series of accidents, freak-outs, and, finally, murder. According to Wyman, "It quickly became obvious, as we helicoptered in from our San Francisco hotel, that tension was in the air." On the other hand, Keith, who had been on a four-week roll playing to exuberant crowds all across the country and was high on LSD, opium, cocaine, and pot, was unaware that anything was wrong.

RICHARDS: "There were all these rumors flashing around everywhere—'There's a bomb gone off and twenty people been blown to bits, man.' You say, 'I think you got it wrong, man, I'm sure you got it wrong.' 'Cause you been hearing crazy rumors all day, that you're dead, as ridiculous as that. By the time you're in

California and you've gone through the whole tour and you've heard all those rumors that seem to go around and around and around . . . you don't believe anything. I didn't believe anything at the end of an American tour, ever."

By the time the Stones took the stage that night, the audience had sat through a numbing six hours of poorly amplified, hardly visible sets from six groups interrupted continually by charging Angels, and was on the edge of hysteria. Their satanic guards were on the brink of turning on their employers and taking over the stage. "No one knew how to deal with a spectacle that from the moment it began contradicted every assumption on which it had been based, producing violence instead of fraternity, selfishness instead of generosity, ugliness instead of beauty, a bad trip instead of a high," wrote Robert Christgau.

"The violence was incredible," remembered Keith. "I thought the show would have been stopped, but hardly anybody wanted to take any notice." As Jagger sensed his loss of control and made requests for calm, Richards knew that if they hesitated or tried to reason with a rock and roll crowd they were lost. He strode to the microphone, pointed directly at a Hell's Angel in the crowd who was beating an innocent bystander, and shouted, "Either those cats cool it or we don't play. I mean, there's not that many of 'em." As the next song ground to a halt in the face of furious beatings in front of the stage, he shouted, "Keep it cool! Hey, if you don't cool it, you ain't gonna hear no music!" A huge Hell's Angel jumped onto the stage and grabbed Keith's mike, screaming, "Fuck you!"

The Stones tried to contain the chaos by continuing to play, but Jagger had sung only the first line of "Under My Thumb" when a young black man was spotted flashing a gun. Instantly six Angels swooped down on him like vultures and the band crashed to a halt. "OK, man," Richards shouted. "Look, we're splitting, if those cats, if you can't—we're splitting, if those people don't stop beating everybody up in sight. I want 'em out of the way."

RICHARDS: "I realized I'm surrounded by four hundred Hell's Angels. I didn't lose my bottle, but I swallowed. My thoughts went out the window. Actually I don't give a shit about a few guys who ride Harley-Davidsons. Why should I? I'm a guitar player."

As the Stones played on through the hail of violence, the rest of the performers were evacuating the doomed site. Halfway through their set a helicopter pilot rushed onto the stage and told Wyman that he was the last pilot and if they didn't come right now he was going to leave without them.

RICHARDS: "The other memory was the getaway: everyone running up this hill to a hovering helicopter. It was like Vietnam. You had to jump and climb up this rope ladder. Gotta get away. Trying to make sure you got the women on there first. Pushing them up by the arse. Sorry, darling, my finger slipped!"

BILL WYMAN: "It couldn't even lift off, that's how full it was. We piled in there on top of each other and we took off going slantways and when we landed we were going in sideways and couldn't come to a stop properly because it was too heavy. It was terrifying."

Answering a distress call from Jagger, Pamela Des Barres rushed to the Stones' hotel. "It was the most intense room to be in on earth," she said. "Mick kept saying he felt like it was his fault and maybe he would quit rock and roll forever. Everyone was extremely high. Gram was there, leaning against the wall wearing black leather and makeup, nodding out. Keith was wearing cowboy clothes. It looked like they were turning into each other."

"Just when hedonism and wide-open hopes of the sixties began to shut down," wrote Jim Miller in Newsweek, "the Rolling Stones met the times head-on, in a volatile mix of art and violence that transformed them, in the course of one astonishing year, into 'The Greatest Rock and Roll Band in the World.'

"The cultural events were well known; their sheer pace may be harder to recall. In December 1968, the Stones released Beggars Banquet, which opened with the coy savagery of 'Sympathy for the Devil' and climaxed with 'Street Fighting Man,' an anthem for the era. On July 3, 1969, Brian Jones, 27, one of the band's founding members, was found dead in his swimming pool. On July 19, 'Honky Tonk Women,' the Stones' great new party single, stormed into the American charts, headed for number one. In November, the group began a tumultuous American tour that ended on Dec. 6 in Altamont, Calif., where the band helplessly played on while members of the Hell's Angels motorcycle gang beat and stabbed to death a gun-toting fan."

ALBERT GOLDMAN: "What has emerged from their triumphal progress . . . is a public image of sado-homosexual-junkie-diabolic-sarcastic-nigger-evil unprecedented in the annals of pop culture."

"After that bloodstained tour," concluded Miller, "the Stones' music seemed to become a mythic force unto itself—ecstatic, ironic, all-powerful, an erotic exorcism for a doomed decade."

14
Dead Flowers
1969–1970

All these guys running around in long hair talk about being wild and Rolling
Stones. I don't think someone abusing themselves on drugs necessarily
determines how wild they are. It might determine how ignorant they are.

MERLE HAGGARD, *from an interview with Ben Fong-Torres, 1990*

"The day after Altamont they couldn't get out of America quick
enough," said Ian Stewart. After a bracing breakfast of Old Charter
whiskey and cocaine, Richards was the first to leave, but he found
himself flying out of the fire and into the frying pan. News of
Altamont had not yet reached England. At Heathrow Airport in
London, Anita had told the assembled press that she was being
threatened with deportation if Keith didn't marry her. As soon as
he emerged from customs, she held up Marlon and screamed,
"Keith, they're throwing me out of the country." The reporters
asked, "Keith! What are you gonna do about it?"

Weary from the tour, the horror, the flight, the sleepless nights,
Richards replied, "It's a drag that you are forced into marriage by
bureaucracy. I refuse to get married because some bureaucrat says
we must. Rather than do that, I would leave Britain and live
abroad. But if I want to continue to live in England, and that's the
only way Anita can stay, we'll get married. I have nothing against
marriage—I'd just as soon be married as not. We'll get it straight-
ened out sooner or later, but first I've got to get some rest." Later
he confessed, "Anita and I in the sixties, we were never interested in
marriage. It seemed an archaic and dumb thing to do just to have a
child." When they complained about the situation to Kenneth
Anger, he suggested they have a pagan marriage ceremony. At first
they were enthusiastic but Richards backed off when some of
Anger's black-magic preparations frightened him.

As the news of the disaster at Altamont hit the newspapers internationally, an avalanche of criticism came down on Keith and Mick. Their so-called friends in the rock business were quick to blame the Stones for either not consulting the right psychics or not reading the astrological charts correctly. The fact that it had been the California bands who had suggested the Angels work the show was played down. David Crosby, who was at Altamont with Stephen Stills and Graham Nash, took a typically damning stance. "I think the major mistake was taking what was essentially a party and turning it into an ego game and a star trip of the Rolling Stones, who are on a star trip and who qualify in my book as snobs," he snorted. "I think they're on a grotesque, negative ego trip, essentially, especially the two leaders." The establishment viewed the violence as definitive proof of the Stones' destructive, possibly satanic, powers.

In an interview with Ray Connolly at Cheyne Walk the day before a Stones Christmas concert in London, Keith answered the charges as directly as he could. If America was going to blame it on the Stones, he was going to blame America right back: "Do you want to just blame someone, or do you want to learn from it? I don't really think anyone is to blame, in laying it on the Angels. Looking back, I don't think it was a good idea to have the Hell's Angels there. But we had them at the suggestion of the Grateful Dead, who've organized these shows before, and they thought they were the best people to organize the concert. The trouble is, it's a problem for us either way. If you don't have them come to work for you as stewards, they come anyway and cause trouble. In a way those concerts are a complete experiment in social order—everybody has to work out a completely new plan of how to get along. But at Altamont, people were just asking for it. They had those victims' faces. Really, the difference between the open-air show we held here in Hyde Park and the one there is amazing. I think it illustrates the difference between the two countries. In Hyde Park everybody had a good time, and there was no trouble. You can put half a million young English kids together and they won't start killing each other. That's the difference."

While the controversy raged, the Stones' next album, *Let It Bleed*, which had been released on the day of the disastrous concert, began its rapid climb up the charts reaching number one in the U.K. and number three in the U.S. This extraordinary record, which opened with "Gimme Shelter" and closed with "You Can't Always Get What You Want," is considered by many to be the zenith of the Stones' career. "They suddenly shifted from a head music of ideas about other people's ideas to a genuine musical life flow," wrote Albert Goldman. "The rolling, roiling *moto perpetuo* of 'Sympathy' showed that the Stones had a real musical body that answered to the rhythm of Mick Jagger's body, shaking and soliciting from the stage. Now, in *Let It Bleed*, this movement toward musical and sensuous beauty reaches its culmination in a remarkable track that blazes a new trail for English rock.

"The beauty of the new record is not the expanded version of 'You Can't Always Get What You Want,' featuring a sixty-voice boys' choir, or the new country version of 'Honky Tonk Women'— though those are good cuts for everyday consumption. The real Thanksgiving feast is offered on the first track, titled 'Gimme Shelter.' An obsessively lovely specimen of tribal rock, this richly textured chant is rainmaking music. It dissolves the hardness of the Stones and transforms them into spirit voices singing high above the mazey figures on the dancing ground. The music takes no course, assumes no shape, reaches no climax; it simply repeats over an endless drone until it has soaked its way through your soul."

" 'Gimme Shelter' is a song about fear," read a review in *Rolling Stone*; "it probably serves better than anything written this year as a passageway straight into the next few years."

By the time Keith returned to London, Anita was addicted to heroin. "After Marlon was born," she explained, "it was a very heavy period and I suffered for about three months. There were so many creeps in the house. Then when Keith went on the American tour that was very hard for me because this is the time when the father should be with the child and I felt completely forgotten. So I just started taking drugs again, and then I smothered all my feelings with drugs. I spent most of my time with Marianne, just sitting together." After he returned from Altamont, Keith also became, for the first time, a heroin addict, regularly purchasing pharmaceutical heroin from a man who stole it from chemists in the north of England.

Richards, who initially saw his addiction as a by-product of his profession, retreated into the toilet, the room in which he had always felt the safest since he had started playing the guitar.

RICHARDS: "It's only the periods with nothing to do that got me into heroin. It was more of an adrenaline imbalance. You have to be an athlete out there, but when the tour stops, suddenly your body don't know there ain't a show the next night. The body is saying, 'Where's the adrenaline? What am I gonna do, leaping out in the street?' It was a very hard readjustment. I was glad to be home but still hyper. And I found smack made it much easier for me to slow down very smoothly and gradually."

"I felt I had to protect Keith," Anita said. "He was flying so high in the music world. He couldn't recognize a face or anything. He sat for hours and hours on the toilet. He used to play the guitar and write in the bathroom. And then when evening came he just got very nervous and didn't know what to do with himself, basically, because he had this routine of being on stage. It was very hard for him."

"I think it's a drag," Keith said, "when people thumping on the door go 'Are you all right?' 'Yeah, I'm having a fucking crap!' But people do it—I mean, if someone's been in the john for hours and hours I'll do it, and I know how annoying it is when I hear a voice coming out, 'Yeah, I'm all right.'"

Marianne Faithfull had publicly cuckolded Mick during the American tour, leaving him for an old boyfriend of Anita's, the Italian artist Mario Schifano. Dumbfounded, Jagger, who had become rock's greatest sex symbol, summoned a backup girlfriend, the black actress Marsha Hunt, who starred in the smash hit musical *Hair*, to, as she saw it, "help him make the transition."

MARSHA HUNT: "Mick was close to Keith Richards and Anita Pallenberg, who lived on the same road. After one visit to their house, I decided to keep my distance. I didn't find their being into hard drugs cute or adventurous. Mick doted on Keith, and I didn't voice an opinion but I avoided contact."

Tony Sanchez, who was living at Cheyne Walk as Keith's

bodyguard and drug procurer for $250 per week plus room and board, saw how addiction was destroying Keith and Anita: Like all crafty junkies, Keith, who was paying for the drugs, began to hide his own private stash. Richards, who said he had never been a big fucker anyway, had not fucked Anita in months, and Tony often heard them fighting about it.

Ever since he had escaped the isolation of childhood, Keith had collaborated with Mick, Brian, or Anita. Now heroin became his collaborator. Keith and Anita had never had many close friends, but as Anita's salon fell away they spent most of their time holed up at Cheyne Walk, with Tony and their drugs.

According to Dr. Joseph Gross, a New York specialist in, among other things, helping rock stars and other creative artists grapple with the tentacles of drug addiction, drugs can appear to boost creativity for a short time: "They may be used constructively and they may be used destructively, but it's really hard to tease out a consistently clean line between them . . . One would suppose that at first the heroin blotted out all interfering influences so he could be, you might say, 'free to create.'" The womblike atmosphere at Cheyne Walk was also important in supporting both the addiction and the freedom to create. "One might see a real need for all these domestic supports so he could be a pure child musician," explained Dr. Gross. "Musicians are like sheep. They must be literally guided or else they just sort of wander off a cliff. They need someone to take care of all the other business while they're involved in doing their particular musical thing."

Although he denies that heroin had any effect on his work, and claims that he could have written "Honky Tonk Women" or "Tumbling Dice" without heroin, Richards's use of drugs is probably as significant to his actual creative work as it was to William Burroughs's. The years 1970 and 1971, Keith's honeymoon period with addiction, would be his peak as a songwriter. Even Jack Nitzsche, who had felt so uncomfortable when he'd visited Keith and Anita in 1969, agreed that Keith was still "putting reality into the Stones. And junk or no junk, it's the only reality."

While Richards reacted to the horrors of 1969 by withdrawing into the neutral zone of junk, Jagger began to re-create himself on a safer, more empowered plane. But as he took a firm hold on the reins of the Rolling Stones, Jagger lost his three closest friends to heroin. His relationship with Marianne, whom he had quickly won back from Schifano, fell apart again, as she too became a heroin addict. Many in the Stones' entourage thought that his heart was broken by Marianne Faithfull and that that was why he never fell in love again without reservations. Whatever the psychological checks and balances, from 1970 on Jagger increasingly devoted himself to moving away from the satanic and hard-drug images and attaining a power base in the worlds of glamour and influence.

As Richards commenced his long slog through "Dopesville," Jagger, who had flown out of the ash pits of Altamont to Switzerland, where he deposited the $1.2 million in cash the tour had generated, turned his attention to financial matters. The Stones had come to the end of their tether with their record company, which had not only cut a side deal with Oldham and Easton in 1963 that gave them royalties due to the band, but continued to nickel and dime the Stones despite their steady and increasing sales. In addition, by now they all realized just how grievously Allen Klein had misled them.

"There's corruption in just about every business, but I've never seen it anything like the level of the record business," noted the veteran *Wall Street Journal* reporter Fredric Dannen. "I've covered the coal business, insurance, investment banking, the chemical industry, and trucking; and although they all have their roguish elements, they're nothing like the record business, which to my way of thinking is no business at all. I don't know how to describe it except as some sort of cartel."

Richards had become infuriated when he'd discovered that the money they had made from Decca had been invested in devices that aided American bombers in hitting targets in Vietnam.

RICHARDS: "How can you check up on the fucking record company when to get it together in the first place you have to be out on that stage every night? I'd rather the Mafia than Decca.

"I've done my best over the years to sort of change the course of things here and there. Rock and roll and popular music won't exist if it's boring. The only thing that keeps it going is that it's popular and people like it. I know nothing about the state of the industry. I think what helped make the music business so complacent in the last few years was that they knew that they could shlep out an Eagles album and it would sell so much. Circumstances changed and suddenly they're running around like 'Oh, my God, they're going to send me back to the A & P and I'm going to be the manager of a supermarket.' I like nothing better than to watch all these record company executives shit themselves."

They were determined to extricate themselves from both deals. In 1970 they decided to terminate their contracts with Decca and Klein, manage themselves, and form their own record company.

To oversee the complex transition and manage their financial affairs, Jagger hired Prince Rupert Ludwig Ferdinand zu Loewenstein-Wertheim-Freudenberg (a descendant of the Bavarian royal family whose title was a matter of debate since several of his predecessors had been mere counts). Described as a "podgy, camp, but affable, bright fellow with the lightest of accents, whose mother was rumored to have run a button factory," Prince Rupert Loewenstein had "helped Jonathan Guinness set up the merchant bank Leopold Joseph." By the time Jagger was introduced to him, Prince Rupert was grounded in Eurotrash aristocracy and cross-connected to what would become the international hip crowd of the 1970s. These were exactly the kind of people Keith and Anita most despised. However, Loewenstein clearly had two outstanding advantages over Klein: A deft financial manager, he was scrupulously honest; and he was able through his connections to construct for the Stones an international network of lawyers and accountants who would serve to protect both their money and them. As a result, not only would Keith Richards be able to continually elude the police of every country he entered, but between 1970 and 1990 he would move from the edge of bankruptcy to a net worth of approximately fifty million dollars.

Jagger arranged for the Stones' records to be distributed in America by Atlantic Records, whose suave, jet-setting Ahmet Ertegun had a fine résumé as a producer of blues and was well connected beyond the insular world of rock music. Like Loewenstein, Ertegun represented the new international chic that Jagger was trying to substitute for the Stones' satanic image. "Control was what Ahmet and Prince Loewenstein had to offer the Stones," noted George Trow in *The New Yorker*. "Both offered access to productive adult modes—financial and social—that could prolong a career built on non-adult principles."

After ten years in the rock business, Keith didn't trust anybody and was suspicious of the sophisticated, smooth international types. Trow, who spotted him at a party Ertegun gave for the band to celebrate signing the distribution deal, wrote that "Mick's mate, the jaded weasel, wasn't so eager to have his tail cut off, and socialized only with the other guests who still had one to wag: Keith Richards, the other essential Rolling Stone, left the party early. He was looking for his dog. 'I have to find my dog,' he said. 'That's my only friend at the party, man.'"

To run Rolling Stones Records, Jagger appointed Marshall Chess, a scion of Chicago's Chess Records family. His interaction with Keith and Mick gave him an intimate view of them.

MARSHALL CHESS: "Mick is very smart, but to me Keith is the Rolling Stones. I always say that if the Stones finish tomorrow, Keith would still be Keith. He'll always be the way he was; he'll never change. He may have more money, more drugs, more drink, more whatever, but he'll always be Keith and his favorite meal will be bacon and eggs with brown sauce; he is the constant factor."

For the label's logo they chose the famous lapping tongue, often incorrectly said to be based on Jagger's. According to Richards, "It's Kali's tongue. Kali is the Hindu female goddess. Five arms, a row of heads around her, a saber in one hand, flames coming out the other, she stands there with her tongue out. But it's gonna change. That symbol's not going to stay as it is. Sometimes it will take up the whole label. Maybe slowly it will turn into a cock."

On July 30, 1970, another new man on their team, the veteran British publicist Les Perrin, announced that the Stones had formally ended their relationship with Allen Klein and with Decca Records and its subsidiaries. However, in negotiations that were yet to be finalized, Jagger and Richards would lose to Klein the publishing rights to all their compositions from 1963 to 1969. Ironically, Richards had little to do with arrangements that were to have such an impact on him.

RICHARDS: "I'm only forced to become a businessman for short periods of time. Once a year I go through the little folder. This has come in, this has gone out, this is a projection of next year. And then I wonder why I bother to read it anyway, because it hasn't made the slightest bit of difference to my day, or the next day. What's important is that I keep on doing what I do, not how much money it's making. Because all that matters really is that it generates enough money to keep going. That's all that's bothered any of us. Even so you can say, 'You fucking liar, you've got three Rolls-Royces and huge houses all over the place,' but I mean they're like there, see. I might as well not have them—it wouldn't matter that much to me. They're there just because I've had surplus capital. It hasn't affected whether I do what I do. As long as there's enough bread to pay for guitar strings and food and a roof over the head, you can keep going and that's all that's important. I live on the road three or four months a year. I'd like to do more of it. And that's probably the least luxurious way of living I can imagine. Even if the hotels are the best ones, hotel rooms are hotel rooms."

On looking into their accounts, Prince Rupert discovered that despite the fact that they had generated two hundred million dollars during their seven-year run, so much of the money had slipped through their hands that taxes would bankrupt them if they didn't move out of England by April 1971, the start of the tax year. "When they couldn't put us in jail, they put the economic sanctions on us instead," Keith recalled. " 'Oh, we've blown that one, let's try 'em with the big screw: eight million quid.' " Consequently, in the midst of renegotiating their record contracts, launching a lawsuit against Klein for twenty-nine million dollars, putting together Rolling Stones Records, and recording their next album, *Sticky Fingers*, Keith had to contend with leaving his new Cheyne Walk house and Redlands and relocating to some foreign country where the people didn't speak English or serve the English food—like shepherd's pie—that was all he liked to eat.

The *Sticky Fingers* sessions inaugurated the new period in which the rest of the band would be forced to live on "Keith Richards time." "He worked on his own emotional rhythm pattern," said recording engineer Andy Johns, who never saw Keith stop to explain anything. "If Keith thought it was necessary to spend three hours working on a riff, he'd do it while everyone else picked their nose."

The making of *Sticky Fingers* in the summer of 1970 marked a turning point in Richards's career. With the exception of "Brown Sugar" and "I Got the Blues," which were included on *Sticky Fingers*, Richards had by his own account now written all his favorite Stones songs. A list of his top-ten favorite Stones songs, compiled in 1990, read: "Jumpin' Jack Flash," "Street Fighting Man," "Satisfaction," "Honky Tonk Women," "Gimme Shelter," "Sympathy for the Devil," "Midnight Rambler," "Brown Sugar," "Ruby Tuesday," "I Got the Blues."

Keith, who had been so angered by Brian's habit of missing sessions or showing up too stoned to perform, started to do the same thing. By the time the Stones came to record "Moonlight Mile" (which was composed by Jagger and Taylor), Keith was so out of it that he didn't play on the track at all. Also, he started importing session musicians who would increasingly shape the band's sound. At first Keith's position in the band was bolstered by the influence and playing of the like-minded musicians he imported. Gram Parsons made major contributions to "Wild Horses," "Country Honk," "Dead Flowers," "Far Away Eyes," and "Sweet Virginia." Parsons and many others who would travel on Keith's road over the next two decades were replicas of Jones. A second character in the mold was a twenty-seven-year-old Texan sax player, Bobby Keys, who was born on the same day and in the same year as Keith, and had played with Buddy Holly. "A lot of people overlooked the fact that it wasn't just Mick Taylor joining the band that changed our sound in '69—that was the whole period where the horns joined too," Richards pointed out. "Both the horns and Mick Taylor made their debut on *Let It Bleed* on 'Live with Me' at the time." A roly-poly, pasty-faced, rollicking lad whose brand of Southern humor contained a racist vein, Keys became Richards's new drug sidekick as well as brilliantly complementing Keith's guitar playing on numerous Stones classics, like "Brown Sugar." Richards, he said, always reminded him of Buddy Holly.

Keys's entrance into the Stones, something Jagger was always dubious about, served to further enhance Richards's leadership. Keith, who was always trying to connect back to their roots, was fascinated by Bobby's background.

RICHARDS: "It's a gas not to be so insulated and play with some more people, especially people like Bobby, man, who on top of being born at the same time of day and the same everything as me has been playing on the road since '56, '57."

Watts and Wyman—who rarely took drugs, although Watts was at times a heavy drinker, and thus were dubbed the straightest rhythm section in rock and roll—remained passively in the background, going about their tasks with extraordinary efficiency, considering the extreme aggravation caused them by the new Keith. Mick Taylor, who never bonded with anybody in the band although he and Keith enjoyed a mutual admiration as players, insulated himself.

RICHARDS: "He was very reluctant to take any direction. I don't mean from the band, because we don't tell anyone what to play, but from the production end of it. Jimmy Miller used to go through reams of frustration, saying, 'Tell the guy not to play there!' Meanwhile, Mick is over there and he's just going to do what he's going to do. And so he did it."

Jagger was most affected. He was particularly jealous of Keith's relationship with Gram as they began to work on "Wild Horses" together. Mick observed that Gram flattered Keith a lot and doubted Gram's motives, believing that Parsons was just trying to pick up some glimmer from them. "Mick's very, very possessive," Keith said. "His attitude was 'You can't have him.'"

ANITA PALLENBERG: "To a certain extent Mick will bitch about whoever is in Keith's life. He always put down all of Keith's friends. But Mick didn't realize that because he is the one who actually writes the tunes Keith needs his own sources. Gram had an enormous influence on Keith, that's for sure. Keith used to listen to Vivaldi and classical music for inspiration and Gram was definitely a source of inspiration."

Despite what might have appeared to be interruptions, the Glimmer Twins operated as a unit. According to Mick Taylor, they continued to be the creative force within the band and they made all the decisions for the Stones.

*

From September to October 1970, the Stones toured Europe with Bobby Keys; Jim Price, another horn player; and Nicky Hopkins on keyboards. To their fans, everything the Stones did appeared to be perfect. They particularly liked Keith's new look, which reeked of contempt for all the sartorial symbols of the status quo, from the glittering, sequined blouses of a female fashion model, which he borrowed from Anita, to the carapace of shoulder-length black hair that emphasized his nodding head and hooded eyes and set off his wolfish skull and ghoulish face painted the colors of Nosferatu. Despite Mick's desire to pull back from the edge of the devil's pit, once the music started a fervor gripped the crowd. Riots, arson, arrests—entropy—accompanied every show. "They were totally freaked out," recalled John Dunbar, who operated the lights. "They'd see Mick and they were going, 'Mick! Mick!' Guys weeping—it was like the fucking holy virgin. I was on stage with them. I was watching horrible shit, watching all of these people."

Rather than travel with the band, Keith traveled with his own junkie's entourage: Anita, Marlon, a nanny, Bobby Keys. Every time they crossed an international border they were bound to be searched. Scoring heroin in the brief, highly pressured time they had in each city was nigh impossible given their flamboyant appearance and international fame. Being a junkie is not just a way of life, it's a job, and Richards, who believed that a professional always specialized, took a hands-on approach to the problem. First, he acquired several James Bond-type devices in which to carry his stash. There was, for example, the fountain pen that operated normally and would have drawn no suspicion unless dismantled. It could carry two grams of white powder. Then there was the shaving cream container. Keith took great pride in outsmarting customs officials because it emphasized how bad they were at their jobs and how good he was at his. Should any drugs be discovered, as they occasionally were, the increasingly tight safety net that contained the Stones would take care of the situation. So much money was at stake that Keith could demand and get what he needed to perform. It was taken for granted now that without him there would be no show. In some cases promoters found themselves saddled with the dicey task of locating the necessary narcotics at the last minute, and audiences were kept waiting for an hour or two while they scrambled around to find enough heroin or cocaine for a night's show, but Richards never missed a gig, and for the most part he still managed to lead the band on stage night after night. As the British writer Jon Savage has pointed out, "One of the problems of heroin use is that, although the drug offers insulation from the stresses of everyday life, it does so by effectively embalming the user's body and emotions." For the first time on tour, instead of being the social fulcrum of the band, Keith became antisocial and was forever falling asleep or spending hours on end in the bathroom. Ian Stewart, who regarded Richards's disintegration as "a bloody tragedy," reflected on how ironic it was that Keith, who had always been the one most angered by Brian's drug-induced incapacity, had somehow turned into Jones.

The establishment of Keith Richards as a man not so much of wealth and taste as death and waste was completed by the release of the two works that perfectly completed the Stones' sixties oeuvre, the live album of the 1969 U.S. tour, *Get Yer Ya-Ya's Out!*, that September and the tour film *Gimme Shelter* in December, for which the ad read, "The music that thrilled the world . . . and the killing that stunned it!"

"I'm beginning to think *Ya-Ya's* just might be the best album they ever made," wrote the American rock critic Lester Bangs in *Rolling Stone*. "'Little Queenie' as done here is all-time classic Stones. Just strutting along leering and shuffling, the song has all the loose, lip-smacking glee its lyrics ever implied. This kind of gutty, almost offhand, seemingly effortless funk is where the Stones have traditionally left all competitors in the dust, and here they outdo themselves. I even think that this is one of those rare instances (most of the others are on their first album) where they cut Chuck Berry with one of his own songs.

"'Honky Tonk Women' is just a joy, but 'Street Fighting Man' takes the show out on a level of stratospheric intensity that simply rises above the rest of the album and sums it all up. Keith's work here is a special delight, great surging riffs reminiscent of some of the best lines on the first Moby Grape album, or the golden lead on Stevie Wonder's 'I Was Made to Love Her.' I don't think there is a song on *Ya-Ya's* where the Stones didn't exceed their original studio jobs. And this one leaps perhaps farthest ahead of all."

In *Gimme Shelter*, it was Richards who came across as what he really was: the quintessential, bad-ass, immovable Rolling Stone. This was particularly striking in the footage of Altamont when, as Jagger realized he was losing control and fear crept into his voice, Richards spoke his mind. "As a work of art it was exquisite, the culmination of the Stones' oeuvre, not to mention a great movie script," wrote Robert Christgau. "Keith Richards, the stud to Jagger's sybarite, acknowledged its aptness in his own rough way: 'Altamont, it could only happen to the Stones, man. Let's face it. It wouldn't happen to the Bee Gees and it wouldn't happen to Crosby, Stills and Nash.'"

15

Happy
1971–1972

In this season of self-indulgence and conceit, the Stones reached their musical apotheosis. While Mick was busy socializing with Bianca, Keith took over the direction of the group and wrote a series of pared-down classics built around lazy, lethal chord riffs that plunged the songs into the bloodstream almost before Jagger could open his mouth. Their vital energy was tapped from a physique in which the most murderous of all drugs could not dull or smother the instinct to make marvelous sound.

PHILIP NORMAN, *Symphony for the Devil*, 1984

While his fans around the world soaked up Richards' images in *Get Yer Ya-Ya's Out!* and *Gimme Shelter*, Keith found living in London increasingly difficult. On January 4, 1971, he attended the premiere of *Performance*, which was a benefit for the drug program Release. He was spending a lot of time with Michael Cooper, who had become his closest friend, and Tony Sanchez. They were all, Keith later said "busy doing ourselves in." His last adventure with Michael Cooper centered characteristically around a car crash. Shortly before the band was to move to France Anita took a drug cure in a London clinic. After two or three days looning about, Cooper, Sanchez and Richards found themselves bowling out to the clinic to visit her in what had now become the pink Lena. (In order not to lose it Keith had the car painted outrageous colors on several occasions.) Nodding out at the wheel he was startled awake by a resounding wallop as the big car hurtled over a roundabout and smashed into a wall. Instantly realizing that they were sitting ducks with their long hair, fantastic outfits and pockets full of drugs, Keith threw the keys to Tony with brisk instructions to take care of the car as he and Michael leapt out and scarpered up the street, the sounds of police sirens reverberating in their ears. Vaulting over the first wall they came to and hastily digging a hole in which to hide their stash, they were further astonished to discover that they had wound up in the garden of their piano player, Nicky Hopkins, who politely invited them in for a cup of tea. Such was the Alice in Wonderland like world of the rock star in Britain in 1971. It would soon crumble into a harsher reality.

While Keith was busy smashing up his car, Jagger was constructing the machinery of a whole new Stones operation. He had become passionately involved with a Nicaraguan model he had met on the European tour, Bianca Perez Morena de Macias. The direction in which he was taking the group reflected her *haute* Eurotrotting style.

Jagger's takeover did not sit well with Richards. He didn't like Bianca, with whom he had little in common, or her effect on Mick. He thought she threatened their relationship. Above all, he didn't like the fact that he was being told that he had to leave England. He was, however, taking so much cocaine and heroin and drinking so much alcohol on a daily basis that he was hardly in a position to make constructive contributions. Richards simply refused to face the Stones' business responsibilities. Meetings were arranged for him to be informed of this or that, but he failed to attend them. If Jagger had not taken such a firm hold on running the band, their career could not have progressed as it did.

On February 6, 1971, the Rolling Stones announced their decision to exile themselves to France, thus becoming the first in a long line of British rock stars who would banish themselves from the realm.

RICHARDS: "I think the reason we got forced out in '70–'71 was they realized it was pointless. They were showing their own weakness, a country that's been running a thousand years worried about two Herberts with guitars and a singer. Do me a favor! They started to look bad. 'Specially when they hit John Lennon. After they'd given him an MBE, they tried to bust him! That's when you realize how fragile our little society is. But the government allowed that fragility to show. They let us look under their skirts—ooh, just another pussy. To me there was no choice; I'd rather fuck off. Why not? I mean, I love England and it's my country. If you're forced to stay out too long and you go back, you feel like D. H. Lawrence. He said, 'I feel more alien there than anywhere else.'"

High British taxes and paranoia had tipped the scale. It had become almost impossible for Richards and Jagger to set foot outside, or inside, their homes without being harassed by greedy, grinning policemen. In March the band was to do a farewell tour of Britain. When Gram Parsons flew in from L.A. with his wife, Gretchen, to accompany Richards on tour, Gretchen got a glimpse of just how difficult it had become for Richards to live in England. On the evening of their second day at Cheyne Walk, "we went outside, got into Keith's chauffeur-driven Bentley, and we'd only gone a few yards down the street when the police were on us," she recalled. "They searched us and were definitely trying to find something on Keith, but couldn't."

On the four-week tour Richards again operated as a separate entity, traveling with the Parsonses, Bobby Keys, Anita, Marlon, and their dog, Boogie. As they barnstormed around the country, Keith constantly fought with authorities. On a midnight flight from Glasgow to London he locked horns with an official after smuggling his dog onto the plane, summoning the police despite being in possession of a quantity of illegal drugs. He constantly missed trains or planes, and he was so late for one concert that he blamed himself for the consequent poor performance.

By the time the Stones were scheduled to film a TV special at Harold Pendleton's Marquee Club, from which they had been so ignominiously fired in 1962, Richards was in revolt against his own apparatus. According to one observer, Keith was deliberately late, and, repeating history once again, swung his guitar at Pendleton's head. It took Jagger an hour to persuade Keith to return to the stage, and when he did he gave a performance so sullen that the BBC deemed it unreleasable. It was, however, a big hit in Germany.

In preparation for moving to the south of France, Keith took his first heroin cure at Redlands.

RICHARDS: "Dr. Dent who gave Burroughs the apomorphine cure was dead, see, but his assistant whom he trained, this lovely old dear 'oo's like a mother hen called Smitty, still runs the clinic. I 'ad her down to my place for five days and she just sort of comes in and says, "Ere's your shot, dear, there's a good boy.' Or 'You've been a naughty boy, you've taken something, yes you have, I can tell.' But actually it's a fairly medieval cure. You just sort of vomit all the time. You sweat, you scream, you hallucinate. I can remember being sure that behind the wallpaper there was a needle and some smack, if only I could get to it. In seventy-two hours, if you can get through it, you're clean. But that's never the problem. The problem is when you go back to your social circle—who are all drug pushers and junkies. In five minutes you can be on the stuff again."

Ten days later, Sanchez drove down to Redlands to pick up his boss and was glad to see Keith looking battered and pale but with his old enthusiasm restored. However, that same night he realized that, like most junkies, Keith had taken the cure primarily to experience the euphoria of taking the drug all over again. "[That night] Michael [Cooper] pulled out some heroin—he had become firmly addicted—and offered it around," Sanchez remembered. "'I suppose you don't want any, Keith, do you?' he asked."

"'You bet I do,' said Keith, and that was the end of his cure." He had to take a second cure with Smitty at Cheyne Walk. This time Gram shared the agony with him. Shuffling around the house like the Odd Couple, they'd spend days at the piano arguing over chord changes in an attempt to distract each other from their suffering.

On April 16, the new label's first single, "Brown Sugar" (a term for Mexican smack and/or black pussy), was released. It went to number two in the U.K., and number one in the U.S. as well as many other countries. The first Rolling Stones Records album, *Sticky Fingers*, much of which had been recorded in 1969 and 1970, released later in the month with a cover by Andy Warhol, was also an international number one. "*Sticky Fingers* went even further in the direction of the aesthetic image exacerbation than had marked their 1969 tour," pointed out Robert Christgau. "The single, 'Brown Sugar,' was at once a brilliant exposure and a blatant exploitation of the racial and sexual contradictions of their stance, and 'Moonlight Mile' commented definitively on the relationship between sex, love, and distance from self." To criticism that it was a drug album, Richards responded, "I don't think *Sticky Fingers* was a heavy drug album any more than the world is a heavy world."

*

Although he had a traditionally British antagonistic attitude toward the French, when Richards was finally exiled in April 1971 he actually made an easy transition to living on the French Riviera.

To set the stage he rented Nellcôte, one of the most fabulous palaces in the whole glamorous region, an enormous white Roman-style villa that had been built, appropriately, by an eccentric British admiral in the nineteenth century who ended up throwing himself from its roof. Nellcôte's ground floor consisted of a series of spacious and elegant reception rooms with thirty-foot ceilings and enormous fireplaces. Beautiful French windows led onto wide terraces overlooking sumptuous sloping gardens, beyond which lay the sparkling blue diamond bay of Villefranche-sur-Mer and the mountains of Cap Ferrat. It was a setting redolent of F. Scott Fitzgerald, Cocteau, and Errol Flynn—Flynn's yacht, in fact, was still harbored below. Keith coveted it but failed to acquire it, but he did buy another yacht, which, waving a red flag in front of the French police, he promptly named the *Mandrax*. He also acquired a new E-type Jaguar, which he raced along the narrow coastal roads, characteristically oblivious of danger.

No sooner had he moved his family and entourage, including Tony Sanchez, Marlon's nanny, and his dog Boogie, into the luxurious mansion than he started turning it into his very own Graceland. Just as Elvis had gathered a gang to party and play with in his big white house, Keith set about gathering a gang of good old boys to rival even the Memphis Mafia. Anita set about organizing the household, hiring one of the best cooks in the area to concoct extravagant daily repasts served with copious quantities of the finest local wines. Despite his own simple tastes, Keith was not about to spare any expense in throwing the biggest, longest, most lavish party of his life. Between April and November he spent seven thousand dollars per week—one thousand dollars for food, one thousand dollars for alcohol, twenty-five hundred dollars for drugs, and twenty-five hundred dollars for the rent. The total came to just under one third of his weekly income of twenty-five thousand dollars. Just as Keith's hotel room had always been the Stones' home on the road, Nellcôte became their headquarters in France. During that summer as many as thirty people at a time stayed at

Nellcôte, including the most creative and self-destructive people he ever worked with.

After much discussion it was decided that between July and October they would import the new Rolling Stones Mobile Unit, a large truck fitted out with the latest recording equipment, and record their next album in the basement of what was dubbed Keith's Coffee House. Once recording got under way it became inconvenient for each member of the band to return to his own home every day, so the whole group moved into Nellcôte. Soon Keith's mansion began to look like a giant Edith Grove. Records, empty bottles, joints and half-smoked cigarettes, guitars, and clothes littered the floors and furniture. Although some of his junkie friends stayed at Nellcôte for months as his guests, Keith made a point of charging each Rolling Stone 250 pounds a week for room and board. Richards was in seventh heaven. Despite the fact that the band had never gotten along for more than a few days running, for him the ideal conditions for making a record were that the band all live together and record in their living room. This was the only time in the history of the Rolling Stones that he managed to create the perfect setup.

Mick's precipitous marriage to Bianca, who was pregnant with their child, on May 12, 1971, in Saint-Tropez opened the drama that would become the making of *Exile on Main St*. Up until the last moment Keith had begged him not to do it. Apart from Keith, none of the Stones were invited, and Keith had to punch his way past photographers and security guards to get in. "At one point I did heave a rather hefty piece of metal at a policeman," he admitted. "They didn't know me from Adam, I had to get in somehow . . ." Having arrived at the function that would mark such a vital turning point in his relationship with Jagger, Richards promptly passed out and spent the balance of the night supine upon the floor. Not being able to play at Mick's wedding—the only gig he ever missed—was as symbolic a gesture as he could have made. Anita, who was no happier than Keith about the event, snapped, "I just remember there were loads of people there and afterwards they all came to my house to slam shut the door and have a fix."

During the recording of *Exile on Main St.*, Keith and Anita both tried to welcome Bianca to the fold, but the chemistry between them was never good. They distrusted her motives and despised her personality. As for Bianca, she thought Anita was a cow and told Mick she never wanted to see her or Keith again. Bianca moved to Paris and refused to return to Nellcôte. On many afternoons after a great night's work Jimmy Miller would wander into Keith's mansion to find the guitarist out of sorts because his partner had flown off to Paris.

In fact, Keith resented Bianca's hold on Mick with a smoldering, sarcastic vengeance. Referring to them as royalty he spat at the notion that having a baby was more important than making a Rolling Stones album and pointed out that Bianca's influence on Jagger seemed to him to be far more negative than anyone could imagine. Mick, Marianne, Keith and Anita had spent days together in harmonious collaboration. Bianca's presence made it difficult for them to spend any time at all which was not interrupted or unbalanced by her pull on Jagger's attention.

According to several witnesses, Keith tried to keep up appearances. "Bianca's a groovy chick," he announced, adding, "we all dig her." Mick made it clear he didn't want Bianca to fall out with Anita. "Anita is one of the Stones now," he said. "You'll have to sort it out between yourselves. Put up with her as best you can."

ANITA PALLENBERG: "She was really, like, totally self-obsessed, like she'd come to my house and disappear into the bathroom for four hours and do makeup and then have these airs and barely talk to anybody. She was always incredibly aloof and never gave out nothing. And Keith used to slag her off. When she was there Mick wouldn't come down for dinner and she'd hide out in the bathroom and the atmosphere was not good. Mick was changed—he was responsible for her. And then nobody liked her in the group, so I'm sure it was really hard for her to try and fit in and all with that kind of way of life. And then she used to hang out always with much older people, Prince Rupert and that lot, and we used to kind of sneer at those people and make fun of them. There was like this huge gap."

In many ways Richards was well prepared for what he saw as Jagger's desertion. He had assembled a backup support group at

Nellcôte, most prominently Bobby Keys, Gram Parsons, and another good old boy from Texas, Ted Newman Jones, who became his guitar roadie, as well as British piano player Nicky Hopkins. Gram and Gretchen Parsons moved into Nellcôte with Keith and Anita for three months, and Gram and Keith played together when Jagger wasn't there, which was most of the time.

RICHARDS: "Usually, when I'm working with the Stones it's very rare that anybody not involved with the job gets involved. Usually I block off and I work. There's not a lot of guys in the world that you don't mind waking up and they're there, for weeks, and it's a pleasure to have them around. For me, Gram was a way of getting a bit outside of the Stones, which was getting very claustrophobic in those years. It was very nice to have another musician, a writer, just to bounce ideas off, without any sense of intrusion."

Many elements combined to make *Exile* a raw, flawed masterpiece.

MICK JAGGER: "We recorded in Keith's disgusting basement, which looked like a prison. I like really big rooms to record in. The humidity was incredible. I couldn't stand it. As soon as I opened my mouth to sing, my voice was gone. It was so humid that all the guitars were out of tune by the time we got to the end of each number."

RICHARDS: "It was a hundred twenty degrees. Everyone sat around sweating and playing with their pants off. That's when I got into Jack Daniel's, because you're trying to get the backup vocals finished on a track or the lead vocal on 'Happy' and the voice starts to go. This'll give you another half an hour. It's those fumes that do it, man."

Keith particularly liked what the orderly Mick didn't like—circumstances that unbalanced things just enough to make the perfect difference: "There's plenty of times when maybe the guitar's not supposed to be out of tune when I cut a track, but then when I'd hear it back I'd say it'd be lost without it," he explained. "Happy," on which Richards sang the lead vocal, was a good example.

RICHARDS: "The basic track was Bobby Keys on baritone sax, myself on guitar, and Jimmy Miller on drums. 'Happy' was cut one afternoon. We were basically doing the sound check, making sure that everything was being set up for the session, and the track just popped out. It was just because, for a change, people weren't lying down on the beach or at a local bar in Nice. Sometimes I'd be ready to play and some guys would come over early. I had this idea for a song, but it was really like a warm-up."

Despite being a heroin addict for one and a half years, Keith was just peaking. "I did a fucking double album, *Exile on Main St.*, when I was heaviest into heroin. I would definitely not say it affected my ability to play."

Anita, whose drug addiction had by now ended her acting career, had somewhat different memories from Keith's: "It was this marathon of music, it was quite incredible, but it was also a nightmare. I mean, creatively it was really great, and everybody was on the spot, and then Mick would get there and he was singing 'Black Angel' and that went on for like two days—but in all the time we were in that place we were never by ourselves. Day after day it was ten people for lunch, twenty-five for dinner. I don't think anyone slept that whole summer. I was completely responsible for everything that was happening. I was basically the only person who could speak French well. And there were the local cowboys—they kind of moved in on us. They said, 'We're going to come here, we're going to destroy this place, we're going to do this, that, and the other. ' So I thought, 'Well, might as well hire them and make them work for us,' so we had all these kinds of locals working in the kitchens. And eventually we found, outside the door, drug dealers, and they were doing all kinds of things, and that's how it came to a bust. We had opened the gates; the doors were open because basically everybody was coming and going—the musicians, everybody—so it was open house. I mean, one day I walked into the living room and there were these two bad characters and they each had half a kilo of smack in their boots and I just kicked them out. It was mad. There were people like Bobby Keys, who was a complete maniac, and everybody was doing outrageous things there."

Just as the Nellcôte sessions marked a break in the relations between Keith and Mick, they also marked another turning point in Anita's descent into the labyrinth of heroin. Despite being three months pregnant, she continued to shoot up three times a day and encourage others, including, allegedly, the teenage daughter of their French chef, to take heroin. One night Keith and Anita were so stoned that, in an ironic metaphor for their situation, they set the bed on fire. Keith's relations with Anita were also beginning to crack under the stress of drugs, largely, it would seem, around the subject of sex. Anita screamed that Keith hadn't fucked her for months and constantly flirted with the many men who visited. But even this did not appear to faze him. "Anita was always running Keith down for not having fucked her properly," recalled one friend. "But he's a funny guy—he's not really motivated that way. And I kind of admired that in him."

"I never managed to get a reaction," Anita admitted. "I remember one time we had this incredible argument and [Keith] threw his guitar down and I stepped on it. I think I did it expressly just because the guitar is our biggest enemy. And I thought, 'Oh, God, I'll get a big reaction from him, like he's going to hit me or shout at me or something,' and all he did was get right on the phone to Ian Stewart and said, 'I need a spare guitar.'"

TERRY SOUTHERN: "The relationship between Keith and Anita is very complex. Keith is up front in a very natural way, whereas Anita is more complicated. She has a mischievous deviousness which always reminded me of that scene in *The Third Man* where Joseph Cotten asks the girl, 'What is it, comedy or drama?' and she says, 'Comedy, I never play drama.' That's exactly what Anita would say. That's her idea of a very attractive way to be. She's hip enough to remember that it's corny to tell you her problems. But Keith is not into that. He's Mr. Pure Guy. He's not into deception or complexity. Even his music is very straightforward."

The only person Keith continued to be close to, apart from the good old boys with whom he could maintain a surface relationship devoid of any emotional demands, was Marlon, with whom he spent a lot of time. Often in the middle of a recording session Keith would excuse himself to put Marlon to bed, sometimes returning as much as five hours later, having made a pit stop to communicate with his two other closest companions, heroin and his guitar, in the bog.

If the roots of the eventual split between Keith and Anita were planted that summer, they may have grown more than anything else out of their different attitudes toward heroin. Whereas Anita glorified in turning people on and seemed to think it was funny to get them hooked, Keith was adamant in his refusal to introduce others to the drug. Ian Stewart saw Keith stop people from taking heroin on several occasions, and one of Keith and Anita's oldest friends, Stash Klossowski, testified that Keith saved him by discouraging him from taking it at all.

In August 1971, *Rolling Stone* magazine published an epic interview with Keith conducted by Robert Greenfield over ten days at Nellcôte. Its length and scope were rivaled only by the great "Lennon Remembers" interview the magazine carried earlier that year. This was a big step in establishing Richards's seventies image. "I think it was not until the seventies that he really came into his own," noted the English rock critic Michael Watts. "It was all Jagger in the sixties. And before he died, it was all Brian Jones. [Keith] was a rhythm guitarist. The rhythm guitarist is always derided. By the late sixties there was something called rock culture that was observing critical standards and tenets that existed within it, and I don't think that up until then Richards's abilities were properly adjudicated . . ."

On October 1, when Keith's entire collection of eleven guitars was stolen, he must have sensed that the end of his French idyll was drawing near. Although the guitars were fully insured (for a total value of forty-four thousand dollars) and Keith was able to replace the majority of them, he was in tears when he called Ted Newman Jones with a request to replace them. "I said, 'Yeah,'" Jones recalled. "And he told me to come out to L.A., where he was going soon to live, and I said, 'I ain't got no money,' and he said, 'I'll send you a ticket, just come on out to L.A., you can live with me, fix all my guitars, we can set up shop in one of the bedrooms, kitchen table, or wherever.'"

"That was pretty bad," Anita said. "But then again, I mean, the one thing with the Stones, they always have to be so trustworthy and trust everybody until something happens, and then when it's already happened, then it's too late, you know."

By then the recording sessions had ended and Keith was killing time before going to L.A. to mix the album, getting stoned and hanging out with a parade of visitors, including Eric Clapton.

Ever since Keith had moved into Nellcôte the house had been under surveillance. Living with the protective legal security net of the Stones for so long, Keith and Anita had become used to living above the law. However, the French were not impressed by the Rolling Stones and didn't choose to embrace them as national mascots. The French police had interviewed several of Richards's disgruntled ex-employees, who claimed, among other things, that Anita had turned their children on to heroin. The Stones' new team of lawyers and accountants found themselves constantly bailing Richards out of trouble. By September the police had assembled a case, and Richards could feel the heat closing in. "We've got to get out of this place quick," he told Tony. "They're going to sling us inside and throw away the key. It's coming any day now."

When the net fell, Keith and Anita appeared to be caught at last. While the remainder of the band were permitted to leave, the French police insisted that the pair stay in France until the investigations were complete, which would have ensured their eventual incarceration in a French jail. Fortunately for Keith and Anita, the expensive lawyers who came via the Ertegun-Loewenstein connection were influential enough to spring them on the condition that Richards agree to continue renting Nellcôte at twenty-four hundred dollars a week as a sign of good faith.

On November 30, the Stones flew out of Nice. Keith, Mick, and Anita headed for New York, where Jagger changed planes for L.A. while Keith detoured to Nashville to pick up the new guitars he had ordered. Two weeks later, on December 14, French police finally raided Nellcôte, reportedly turning up enough cocaine, heroin, and hashish to hang a long sentence on the Human Riff.

Anita was due to give birth in April 1972. "When I'm five months pregnant, I'll give up heroin," she said. In January and February she tried to kick but couldn't. Her doctor warned her that her baby would suffer if she kept taking drugs, but her fear only made her take more. In March she entered a sympathetic and discreet clinic in

Montreux, Switzerland, where such situations could be managed for a thousand dollars per day. Keith and Marlon moved into a suite at the Montreux Métropole, on Lake Geneva.

On April 4, the first single off *Exile*, "Tumbling Dice"/"Sweet Black Angel," was released on Rolling Stones Records. It would peak at number five in the U.K. and number seven in the U.S. On April 17, Dandelion Richards was born with a harelip. "When my youngest daughter was born," Richards recalled, "the doctor who delivered her came up to me in the dark, right after the birth, and held up five Stones albums for me to sign. It's a crazy world."

Anita became introspective and reclusive, refusing to leave the suite. Keith and Tony would take the children out for walks beside Lake Geneva, leaving her in the dark hotel room.

TONY SANCHEZ: "Anita languished in solitary splendor, smoking joints, jabbing needles into her bottom and musing. . . . After three weeks, the place stank of dirty socks and stale cigarette smoke. There were empty bottles everywhere, cigarette burns on most of the mock Louis XIV furniture and the sheets were an uninviting shade of gray. 'We can't go on living in this pigsty,' Keith announced at last. He buzzed the manager to ask for another suite on a different floor. The maids stuck with the onerous task of cleaning out the abandoned suite insisted on defumigation."

ANITA PALLENBERG: "It should have been a good time, but it was difficult having children and belonging to Keith's world. We were both still on heroin, and then he'd go off to perform and I'd have to stay there by myself still stuck on heroin. I had kids to take care of but I couldn't do a good job of it. I was more interested in getting my supply than I was in looking after them. People started to condemn me as a bad person, neglecting my kids, only interested in feeding my habit. Instead of getting them dinner, I'd go out and wander around and meet some people and spend the night in the park looking for flying saucers."

Keith was not in such great shape himself. In May, shortly before a grueling summer tour of the U.S., he flew to L.A. to put the finishing touches on *Exile*. However, once again due to overindulgence, he was unable to complete the project, and he had to return to Switzerland and enter the Montreux clinic for another heroin withdrawal cure.

By 1972 Jagger, in tandem with Loewenstein and Ertegun, had taken such a firm grip of the band's affairs that he had made the decisions about how the U.S. tour would be run without much attention to his partner's preferences. Keith railed against the businessmen's insistence that they play the largest stadiums rather than smaller venues. He resented the bodyguards and lawyers who now surrounded them, and particularly disliked the no-nonsense public-school-prefect-style tour manager, Peter Rudge. The band's new American publicist, Gary Stromberg, saw the conflict as a schoolmaster-pupil relationship: "You had to be with Keith a lot, baby him. From a managerial standpoint he was probably more of a problem than anyone else." Rudge's assessment of the Glimmer Twins was that "Mick would die for Keith, and I think Keith would die for Mick."

That May rehearsals were conducted in Montreux in such a military atmosphere that Peter Rudge said, "I feel a bit like Montgomery before Alamein—it's not like a rock and roll tour, more like the Normandy landing." On May 12 the Stones' twenty-nine-million-dollar lawsuit against Allen Klein was settled out of court. On May 26, *Exile on Main St.* was released with a cover designed by the photographer and film-maker Robert Frank, whom the band hired to film a documentary of the tour. The album confused both critics and the public, seeming at first, in the words of one critic, "the work of a band surrendering to utter chaos." But, the critic continued, in what would become the consensus of opinion, "this two-record set was tough and unassuming, containing raw blues, FM radio faves and some blistering rock 'n' roll. From Keith's hands, chords became just as expressive, just as soaring as the runs of other more versatile players." That summer it went to number one in both the U.S. and the U.K. as well as many other countries.

The fifty-four-day-long tour opened in Vancouver on June 3 and closed in New York on July 26. The entourage traveled in a private DC-7 jet on whose fuselage Kali's tongue lapped lasciviously. Robert Greenfield, who wrote a book about the tour, *S.T.P.*, which rivaled Stanley Booth's account of the 1969 tour, took a mental snapshot of Keith deplaning on the first day, "wearing a black and white striped suit made out of silvered sailcloth that glowed in the dark. Huge silver shades hid his eyes. Wound around his neck as a scarf was a three and a half foot bright yellow Tibetan prayer flag covered with red ink mantras which used to hang as a window shade somewhere. In his hand he carried a small black doctor's bag."

When the ultraconservative segregationist governor of Alabama, George Wallace, was gunned down in a shopping mall that summer, Richards commented, "I'd dig to meet Wallace. I bet he's a gas, man, behind his game." But fearing that he too might be a target for assassination, in that crazed, violent summer, Keith carried a .38 throughout the tour. "During my hairy wild-West dope period on the road with some nutters, it came in very handy," he recalled.

Although Richards was fixing so much heroin that he was, according to one witness, a shambling wreck, his playing on the tour was outstanding. "His guitar tore through everything, making you feel as though you were seeing the band playing together for the very first time," noted one witness. "As Keith shouted, 'Come on, let's get it, get it,' bouncing as though his Les Paul was discharging electricity right into his body, the guitar notes slid one into another like tightly coiled springs. Keith rocked and stumbled through 'Bye Bye Johnny,' cutting it into rhythms and playing through the breaks like the illegitimate son of Chuck Berry, ripping away at his guitar with his arm fully extended."

"Some nights it was as though they brought Keith to the hall in a cage and his hour and a half on stage was the only freedom he was going to get," wrote Robert Greenfield. "Right from the start Keith was cutting it right on time every time, playing fills and breaks that he'd never rehearsed. The energy he generated when he was absolutely on was scary. Keith was right there all the time, playing for his life. He was always putting out all he was worth, doing the best he knew how at the moment."

"If the 1972 tour is remembered as the one in which the Stones exulted in the pure professionalism of their own style of rock'n'roll," wrote another, "it's because Richards's dirty, dangerous guitar work and stage antics undercut the sheer gloss and size of this new industrial-strength juggernaut." Richards understood that performing every night was the only thing that enabled him to survive the ordeal. The constant mental and physical exercise of pushing himself to the limit every night kept him in shape.

In midtour, "Happy," which featured Keith's solo vocal, was released as a single in the U.S. and went to number twenty-two.

Keith was, as always, surrounded by violence. If he wasn't punching out a woman who attempted to serve Jagger a subpoena for Altamont, he was hammering on the hotel room door of Truman Capote, who was covering the tour for *Rolling Stone*, and screaming, "Wake up, you old queen! Come on, you bitch, fucking wake up! Come up to the party and find out what rock and roll's all about!" Banging next on the door of Capote's companion, Princess Lee Radziwill, he screamed, "Princess Radish! Come on, you old tart! There's a party downstairs." Unsatisfied by the negative response, he grabbed a bottle of tomato ketchup from a room-service tray in the hall and spattered it over Capote's door. When the Stones' opening act, Stevie Wonder, called to say he couldn't make a show because his drummer had quit, Keith erupted, screaming, "That Stevie's a bloody cunt! Fuck that Stevie cunt. He's a cunt!" ("I was never sure where he was coming from," a bemused Wonder later protested.) When the security guards beat up and expelled Richards's private drug supplier from the tour without telling Keith, he exploded again, screaming down hotel corridors. Terry Southern, another writer covering the tour to whom Richards was more simpatico, showed him a political pamphlet criticizing the Stones as sexist. Keith complained, "We're imprisoned by other people's fantasies. It's a drag the way people dig evil. It's their fascination with evil that locks us into this projection of it. I don't think they understand what we're trying to do. Politics is what we're trying to get away from in the first place."

On July 17 in Montreal a bomb, courtesy of French-Canadian separatists, blew up the Stones' equipment truck, destroying their equipment. Richards's anger reached a climax on July 19, when their plane, en route to Boston, was forced to land at Rhode Island's Green Airport and Keith was arrested for hitting a photographer who was harassing Jagger. Two cops slapped cuffs on his wrists and dragged him into a paddy wagon. In jail with Jagger, Bobby Keys, and Marshall Chess, who had rushed to his defense,

Keith screamed that they had to get out, they had a concert to do in Boston. After a plea by Boston's mayor, who feared his restless city might be engulfed by a riot if the Stones did not appear, they were released and driven to the gig at 100 mph in a caravan of screaming police cars, but by the time they hit the stage just after midnight Richards, who had been on the road for six weeks and played forty concerts, was exhausted and depressed.

In New York, Rudge met with Hell's Angels who demanded money for the legal costs of Altamont. When he refused, they made death threats and the Stones moved into a series of different hotels using pseudonyms. Keith Richards was Count Ziggenpuss.

On the last night of the tour the Stones held a celebratory party at the St. Regis Hotel in New York. The tour had grossed an unprecedented three million dollars. While Muddy Waters occupied the bandstand, the men who had worshiped him ten years earlier partied with New York's hip seventies crowd—Andy Warhol, Ahmet Ertegun, Dick Cavett, Zsa Zsa Gabor, and Bob Dylan. "If the Rolling Stones are the newest mind-fuck for the Truman Capote crowd, what does that say about the Stones?" snapped *New York Times* reporter Grace Lichtenstein. "Right now," Keith told a friend, "is when you realize you're a product."

16

Angie
1972–1973

Keith loved Anita. He loved her desperately. You know that song "Angie"? It means "ANITA-I-NEED-YA." There's not many people who know that. ANITA-I-NEED-YA.

NICK KENT, *from an interview with Victor Bockris, 1989*

On August 9, 1972, Keith, Anita, Marlon, and Dandelion moved into a rented chalet in Villars, a small village in the mountains above Montreux, Switzerland, and set about re-creating themselves as Swiss Family Richards. The experienced exiles soon re-established their routine. Keith had the Blue Lena imported from England, acquired a bright yellow Dino Ferrari, and arranged for the weekly delivery of topgrade heroin, cocaine, and hashish.

Asking himself what Errol Flynn would have done in his shoes, Keith came up with the obvious solution: In his thirtieth year, the man who often looked as if he couldn't raise himself from the john after a three-hour session with his guitar and constipation (often the result of heroin addiction) took up the sport of the traditional Swiss playboy, skiing. He boasted, "I even learned to ski when I was a complete junkie. As I've said, I've never had a problem with drugs—I've had problems with police." According to one friend, Keith was an adventurous skier.

Keith and Anita made friends with a number of people and became attached to a couple named Sandro and Charudan Sursock whom they met through Stash Klossowski. Sandro Sursock had a band called the Zero Heroes. Before long they were hanging out almost every day.

SANDRO SURSOCK: "We considered it our mission to protect him and make sure he met some people who would not bring him trouble. Whenever he was in Switzerland he was never photographed or put in any newspaper. It was a place he could really be in peace. It was a solid friendship. He gave me the impression of being somebody who would be my friend for life. Somebody you could trust. We shared his love for the blues and listened to a lot of it, as well as Gram Parsons, reggae—mostly the sound track for *The Harder They Come*—the Elvis Sun sessions, the Everly Brothers, and the music he was writing."

Anita looks back on the three years they were based in Switzerland as among the happiest they shared together, not the least, one suspects, because for once they were not surrounded by every creep in London mooching off Keith's stash and hanging on his every word.

ANITA PALLENBERG: "It was actually quite nice. We had this little chalet and we used to ski to the front door. We had the drugs and a good connection in Geneva, and we had friends in Geneva, and we used to drive around in Ferraris and Bentleys . . . It was fun. We always had people in the house and friends would come and visit us."

A French rock journalist, Hervé Muller, who visited Keith and Anita in Switzerland recalled that their house was not particularly extravagant. Keith seemed relaxed and happy. "The greatest thing was to see him playing with his daughter," Muller said. "I mean, he's really a father. She was a baby then and he was obviously thrilled with her. He was incredibly patient with her. I found him extremely bright, extremely honest, no bullshit and incredibly nice."

Although Keith and Anita have good memories of their Swiss sojourn, many of the people they hung out with in Montreux, Villars, and Geneva are now dead. Friends often became friends, said one witness, because they were smack dealers. If you were a smack dealer, you didn't just come, make a deal, and leave, you stayed for three days snorting back half of what you sold. Money, which is the perennial problem for most junkies, wasn't the problem for Keith. There was always a large quantity of heroin wherever he was. Even Keith's driver, who smashed up his car on more than one occasion in Switzerland, was a junkie.

Friends who survived the Swiss period recalled that they were drawn to Keith not only because of his legend but because "he was really a nice guy." If a visitor had to leave at 4:00 A.M., for example, Keith would often insist on driving the person home himself rather than letting the visitor call a cab. "He had a human quality," said one. "When you're on drugs you're obviously very selfish, but Keith could also show incredible generosity."

Despite enjoying the champagne air of the Alps, Keith was, according to Nick Kent, "getting very, very paranoid about the police," and was worried about the future of the band. He was concerned that staying too long in the sanatorium of the Western world was bound to sap his creative juices.

RICHARDS: "I'm actually quite ignorant of a lot of the things that go on, mainly because I'm forced to live in these wooden huts in the forest for quite a long part of the year, in Switzerland.

"They come up to me on the street and say, 'Hey, you're a Rolling Stone! I'm in a band. How do we get to be really big and earn lots of money? What do you have to do to make a really good group?' And I say, 'Well, look, why don't you try starving?' They can't comprehend that, man, they're so rich. I mean, have you ever heard of a good Swiss musician, a good Swiss painter or writer?"

If one had to pinpoint the moment when the comet that rose with "Jumpin' Jack Flash" in May 1968 and reached its zenith at Madison Square Garden on July 26, 1972, receded, it would be the point when Richards and Jagger stopped living in the same country. They ended up doing the majority of their work on the telephone. This was not the best way to write songs, Keith complained.

RICHARDS: "Up until then Mick and I were inseparable. We made every decision for the group. We loved to get together and kick things around, write all our songs. But once we were split up I started going my way—which was the downhill road to Dopesville—and Mick ascended to Jetland.

"We were dealing with a load of problems that built up from being who we were, what the sixties were. There was the fact that we all had to leave England if we wanted to keep the Stones going, which we did, and then trying to re-deal with each other when suddenly we were scattered halfway around the globe instead of 'See you in half an hour.' Also dealing with a lot of success and a lot of money over a long period. We'd been working nonstop and then suddenly had to deal with a backlog of problems that had built up because nobody'd had time to deal with them."

Richards's partnership with Jagger, the longest-lasting close relationship of his life, was and is the only one that is essentially free of the addict's pattern of using others until they are used up, as Keith had done with Brian. According to Richards, he and Jagger had always fought. If so, theirs must have been subtle fights, for witnesses from Linda Keith to Stanley Booth saw the special harmony between them more than the friction. By the time Jagger came to Montreux to work on songs for the *Goats Head Soup* sessions, the creative spark between them seems to have been ignited only by conflict.

ANITA PALLENBERG: "Keith would sit up in the bath until like five o'clock, like disappear completely from Mick's face, and Mick would go completely crazy and so he'd turn to me and say, 'Christ, what's happening with Keith? You know we're supposed to write songs and there he is, God knows what he's doing, I haven't seen him yet!' I didn't feel there was any creativity going on at all at the time, but now, thinking back, that's how it works for them. They've always got this kind of battle going on.

"They had to have friction. They couldn't just sit there because they're such opposites. Mick believes in going into the studio with a sheet of paper and all the notes written. And Keith, he goes into the studio and it's just childhood play."

RICHARDS: "Mick and I have different attitudes, and throughout most of the seventies I was living in another world from him. I don't blame him—he'd earned the right to do what he wanted. It was just that I couldn't relate to that. And even if I could have related to it, I was too busy being busted—which is equally dumb. It kind of got up my nose a bit, that jet-set shit and like, the flaunting of it. But he's a lonely gun, too. He's got his own problems."

The root problem with the new album, *Goats Head Soup*, was this conflict between Richards and Jagger. Whereas Keith, Mick, Anita, and Marianne used to spend days together, it was hard for Keith to see Mick at all now that he was with Bianca. Rather than strumming away together until they hit on something, according to Jagger, Keith would thrust a song at him and say, for example, "'It goes: "Angieeee!"' And I said, 'Is that all?' He said, 'Yeah,' and I said, 'All right.'"

"You get a fixation on something," Keith explained. "You might say, 'Oh, we don't want to call it "Angie."' You know, 'What a drag, another chick's name. Not again!' But you try and change it, man, and it never sounds right. It's only two syllables, it could be 'bank note,' but you always come back to 'Angie.' Once you've put something together with a musical phrase like that, it's like it's locked in, you never pull it out."

With work on *Goats Head Soup* off to a slow start, the Rolling Stones had to decide where to record. Keith's battles with the law had narrowed the range of possible venues. Necessity and curiosity brought him to Jamaica, an island he would come to adopt as his home. He chose the former British colony for three reasons: He was interested in a new form of island music called reggae; Jamaica offered a haven from international legal tentacles; and Jamaica was one of the few nations willing to welcome him. Richards and family jetted into Kingston on November 25, 1972, and checked into the Terra Nova Hotel to begin four weeks of recording.

In the early 1970s, Jamaica was on the cusp of a cultural and musical revolution. The uniquely Jamaican ska music was giving way to the reggae sound, whose chief proponents, Jimmy Cliff, Bob Marley, and Peter Tosh, would bring the music to world attention. The Rasta culture—their ganga smoking, their peculiar combination of gentleness and violence, and above all their hypnotic, politically charged music—was sending shock waves through the shantytowns of Kingston.

RICHARDS: "Jamaica is the most musically conscious place I've ever been to. It's the only place that's come out with a really different kind of new music which still has that basic simplicity of rock and roll. All they've done is turn the beat around and they seem to have a limitless supply of talent. And the time when I was really touched with any religious impulse was probably with the Rastafarians in Jamaica because at that time it was very pure and structured and it worked. It was a very hand-to-mouth existence and pretty squalid, and they managed to get a pride and a community thing and emotion going."

Reggae, which has its roots in the songs of slaves working in the sugarcane fields and is tinged with a strong Latin influence, galvanized the Rastas politically. Desmond Dekker and the Aces' anticolonial message had already made it into the U.S. top forty in the form of "Israelites," and when Bob Marley's *Catch a Fire* was released in 1973, he became an enormous international musical influence.

Despite the fact that the Stones had little contact with reggae artists on their initial visit to the island, the music was everywhere. Even as they worked with Jimmy Miller in Byron Lee's heavily guarded Dynamic Sound Studios in Kingston, Keith would feel the unique Jamaican approach to recording.

RICHARDS: "They've got this very informal attitude: In the U.S. and in England and in Europe, they've got their own completely idiotic rules about what you can do and can't do with these machines, you know, you can never turn something off, you've gotta touch this and focus that knob and get this light flashing. There's all this sort of etiquette. It's like watching etiquette at the table—that's where the knife should be and the dessert spoon there, and you wonder what the fuck it's all about. But they don't know anything about this in Jamaica and they just say, 'With this machine you can do this? BWAN, TSSH, DOING!' And they just play it like another instrument, so the guy behind the control board is like another musician."

Richards continued to follow in the footsteps of Errol Flynn. Flynn, who also chose Jamaica as a spiritual home, loved, in the words of his biographer, Charles Higham, the "emerald mountains, with unique growths crowding up their sides; the winding dirt roads with their dazzling views of the Caribbean; the sapphire-colored moon which sometimes occurred just before twilight after a burst of rain . . ." To both Richards and Flynn, Jamaica was a paradise. Shortly after arriving, Keith plunked down $147,000 in cash to buy Tommy Steele's estate, Point of View, which sat atop a mountain overlooking Cutlass Bay on the northern shore off Ocho Rios and the beautiful grounds of Shaw Park. There, in his beautiful white villa whose pillared courtyard led to a swimming pool, he could look forward to fulfilling his every fantasy.

However, the Stones' recording sessions were not living up to his expectations. It may have been that the complacent attitude expressed by Jagger—"It's 1972. Fuck it. We've done it"—infected the band's spirit. Perhaps the collapse of Jimmy Miller, their producer, who had worked in such harmony with them, and the illness of their longtime engineer, Andy Johns (both drug casualties), had something to do with the disappointing results. But Keith was too weak to provide the creative impulses needed. His own pulse seemed to be one beat ahead of death. Michael Watts, who spent ten days in Jamaica interviewing Richards and Jagger for *Melody Maker*, was shocked by Keith's condition: "He looked very wasted, very frail. You expected this tough guy and he looked as if you could blow him over, which, of course, emphasized his myth and made him seem all the more interesting." Watts was also struck by Jagger's obvious concern for Keith: "Jagger was being very camp and louche but he was also very protective of Richards. I'll always remember that. Jagger came up and put his arms around him and talked to him and you knew that he was looking after his welfare. I think it became a terrific strain for Jagger to hold this guy up."

RICHARDS: "The reason I made it through was because it was all top-quality shit. When I was into it I was a connoisseur! When you're into it, it's that wonderfully warm, clicky feeling, but very quickly you just need the damn stuff. You'll do anything to get your hands on it, and if you've got to move across international borders, then you better start figuring it out, 'Well, do I take it with me or have someone waiting or what?' More and more energy is spent figuring that out than actually doing what you're supposed to be doing. But I never saw it as glamorous. In guys particularly, junk takes the place of everything. You don't need a chick, you don't need music, you don't need nothing. It doesn't get you anywhere. It's not called junk for nothing."

Jagger did his best to keep the band out of trouble, but it was like plastering cracks in a crumbling dam. As soon as he patched one leak, Richards sprung another. The first serious fissure appeared on December 2. Just as they were getting into the groove of the recording sessions, they were interrupted by the news that the French authorities had put out a warrant for the arrest of Keith and

Anita on charges of using heroin and, more severely, distributing it to minors, at Nellcôte and on their yacht, the *Mandrax*. Sensational stories in the French press implied that all the members of the band were involved and had been released on "provisional liberty." Jagger, who was working with a team of lawyers, accountants, and record executives putting together three 1973 Rolling Stones tours of the Far East, Europe, and America, understood by the potential effect of these rumors on their ability to get visas. He flew to Nice immediately to clear his name and make it known that neither he nor the other members of the band had been involved. Accompanied by Watts, Wyman, and Taylor, he issued a terse statement: "Charlie Watts, Bill Wyman, Mick Taylor, and myself deny categorically that we have been charged by the French police with the buying and use of heroin. It has never been suggested that we bought or used heroin. The four of us were not freed on 'provisional liberty,' because we had never been arrested on any charge . . . at no time did we hold drug parties in our homes."

Keith, who remained in Jamaica to avoid arrest, joked that the first he heard of the warrant was when he read about it in the newspapers. "I was so stoned throughout that whole period that I just accepted getting arrested as part of doing what I was doing," he said. The warrants for their arrests made Keith and Anita, who appeared in every tabloid photograph right alongside him, big stars in France.

In an interview in Hawaii five months later, Jagger aired his feelings. "They completely jumped the gun," he said. "They'd like to arrest Keith and put him in prison. But they can't, in my mind, because they're full of shit. Disgusting people. Fascist pigs!"

To Jagger's relief, the French absolved the other band members after interviewing them. "We have been investigating the case in secret for the past thirteen months and three arrests have been made in connection with drugs," Sergeant Maurey of the French police announced. "No other members of the group have been involved—they were given a thorough going-over in Nice and are clean."

In 1973, Keith was at loose ends. On returning to Jamaica after the Far Eastern tour in late February, he was shocked to discover that Anita had surrounded herself with a bodyguard of Rastafarians and rude boys for whom she publicly displayed a dangerous affection. Keith was warned by one member of the white community that if he did not do something to curb his wife's behavior, they would have to take matters into their own hands, but he had little influence over the Rastas or Anita.

ANITA PALLENBERG: "Keith can be in a room with fifty other people and he won't notice anything but the guitar. To live with a rock star, a woman must find her ways of independence."

Just as Keith finally found a real spiritual and legal shelter, Anita humiliated him so much he left the island. In March, he flew back to London alone, leaving Anita, Marlon, and Dandelion with a bodyguard of locals whose manners were, according to Pallenberg's later assessment, on a par with those of the Hell's Angels.

For the first time in years, Richards was unaccompanied by the band and undergrounded by a girlfriend. Calling upon the services of his bodyguard, dealer, and true friend Spanish Tony Sanchez, Keith embarked on a marathon social binge. Each night the two inhaled quantities of fine cocaine at Cheyne Walk, then leapt into the Ferrari and roared over to Tramp, London's top rock club. There, Richards held court at a central table, throwing his weight around like a hip, young mobster in a Jimmy Cagney movie. "Keith hung out with this really fast crowd and they were frightening," recalled Nick Kent. "Tony and Keith looked like Murder, Incorporated together." Tony, however, who had always enjoyed their escapades in the past, was disturbed to see Keith picking fights with people out of his league. Things reached a head one night when a group of Sicilians waited for Sanchez to go to the men's room, then marched up to Richards's table and brazenly flirted with his female companions. When Keith launched himself at the offenders like a teenager in a gang fight, he immediately found himself writhing on the floor from a kick to his balls. As Tony came rushing out of the toilet, Richards was staggering to his feet and waving off the club owner's offer to call the police. But then he icily ordered Sanchez to have the Sicilians beaten to within an inch of their lives. Tony, who had never seen Keith in such a violent state, mumbled something like "I'll take care of it," then quietly paid the men to stay away from Tramp for a while. The next night he was further dismayed to overhear Keith boasting, "See, anybody who messes with me is dead."

Meanwhile, in Ocho Rios certain elements of the white community had finally lost patience with Anita's flagrant flouting of their moral code. The police raided Point of View and found a kilo of marijuana. Without the protection of the Stones' security network, Anita found herself brutally hustled into a jail cell with no legal protection. While Marlon and Dandelion were left in the care of her maids, Anita discovered that her cell was already occupied. According to Tony Sanchez, over the next few days she was repeatedly raped and beaten by prisoners and guards alike.

When Keith received the news of her incarceration over the phone in London, he "flipped out." At first, he planned to take the first plane out to Kingston and rescue her himself, just like Billy the Kid or Gyp the Blood, but wiser counsel prevailed when it was pointed out that since the drugs had been found on his property, he was liable to be arrested. An aristocratic acquaintance on the island advised Richards to let him handle the business, claiming he knew of an international businessman who could help. For twelve thousand dollars in cash Anita would be immediately returned to London. Keith agreed. On the day of her return, Keith and Tony charged out to Heathrow Airport to pick her, Marlon, and Dandelion up. The sight of the woman who emerged from the first-class British Airways lounge was one that would sear his mind as badly as former images of a dying Brian Jones. Tony was shocked too. She looked to him as if she had been beaten to within an inch of her life. When she saw Keith, "she ran into his arms," Sanchez remembered, "sobbing like a lost little girl."

After a doctor verified that there were signs of multiple rape, Richards investigated further and discovered that the man who had arranged for the twelve-thousand-dollar bribe was the very same one who had turned her in in the first place.

When the businessman arrived in London to collect his fee, he called Keith on the phone to make the arrangements. Keith was furious and set up a meeting at the Dorchester Hotel. In his rage he asked Sanchez to use the twelve thousand dollars to have the man killed.

TONY SANCHEZ: "I agreed to everything, but of course, Keith wasn't seriously considering murder. Homicide wasn't our scene. I did toy, however, with the idea of arranging for the man to be beaten up. It was the very least he deserved for the inhuman nightmare he had cold-bloodedly inflicted on Anita. Finally, though, I just paid over the cash to him, and that was the end of it."

Keith and Anita resumed life at Cheyne Walk, where Richards was now maintaining a houseful of addicts and hangers-on. Anita, deeply depressed and heavily addicted, spent most of her time sprawled on her big bed in a fetid trance, while Keith consorted with his cadre of lowlifes.

ANITA PALLENBERG: "By then we were both pretty heavy into drugs and our communication was pretty low, really—I mean, we hardly even talked to each other if it wasn't about drugs or 'Have you got anything?' or 'Let's go get something.' So it was very sad.

"I think Brian died because he was surrounded by creeps. I'm sure the reason Jimi Hendrix died is because he was surrounded by so many creeps too. I was always afraid that Keith also attracted these kinds of people. When our relationship started to deteriorate it was because of all these people. We could never be alone. I couldn't stand it, because I was aware of them, but he was completely unaware. He was living in this other world."

According to Nick Kent, "Cheyne Walk was always vulnerable. It was literally a case of the police saying, 'Well, old Sergeant Jim and his wife need a new three-piece suite. We'll go down to Keith Richards's place, you know, and intimidate him, 'cause you know, I mean, are there going to be drugs there? Of course there are going to be drugs there. Is there going to be something illegal there? Of course there is.' This was happening again and again and there are a lot more—this is what I've been told—a lot more busts and a lot more intimidations than have gone on the record."

On June 26, 1973, Keith and Anita were awakened in their Cheyne Walk house by a group of grinning policemen. "The English police are politely sarky," Richards recalled. "Like, ''Ello, Keithy my boy, old lad, old chum, you know the rules of the game!' Very buddy-buddy, but we're still gonna do you. They always overact, always overdo things. But to actually wake up and find the drug squad in your bedroom, that's something that's indelibly printed on your brain." While the police searched the premises, Anita dropped her cocaine on the floor and massaged it into the rug with her foot, Keith tried every trick in the book to visit the bathroom alone to take a shot of dope, but the police insisted that he keep the door open, so his plan was foiled. Keith, Anita, and a friend were taken to court and charged with possession of drugs and guns: :"ROLLING STONE RICHARD—GUN, DRUGS CHARGES," screamed the headlines once again. The tabloids printed photographs of a couple who stared back at the reader with amused hauteur, but, particularly in Anita's case, their hollow eyes showed signs of alarm.

RICHARDS: "When you're a junkie, it's every man for himself. The 'junkie grind' took me totally out of the world of 'Isn't it hip?' and 'Great turn-on, man, there's them and us'—that usual clannish, stupid inmanship. It cured me of that right away. It took me out of the world of being some pop star, above everything and everyone else. In the junkie world, that don't mean shit; it's 'Where's the dope; where's the bread; who's gonna screw who?' I got my street smarts back together in a jolt."

ANITA PALLENBERG: "With all this weight over our heads and all this pressure, we just got even more into drugs, basically. We were completely embittered. Just out of defiance we got into drugs even more. My attitude was so antipolice as well—you know, fuck them. These nasty things started to happen and so we grew like more subdued, but by then I didn't even have the courage to face Keith or the Rolling Stones anymore. In a way I felt responsible for Keith as well. I felt I had gotten him into that and I was a bad influence on him and it was all a mistake."

By the end of August 1973, the Stones' plans for a European tour to publicize the release of *Goats Head Soup* were complete and the album's first single, "Angie," was released. The album "was so uncharacteristic in terms of what one had come to expect of the Stones," wrote Roy Carr, "that it threw most people and alienated others. Reviews were lukewarm, and some downright insulting. Regarded by many as the Stones' concession to 'Glam Rock,' it opened up a whole new market and in doing so embraced a legion of record buyers who'd previously never shelled out for the Stones."

The British rock critic Martin Elliott wrote, "'Angie' was the first ballad to be released as [the A-side of] a single in Britain, and the public, although at first shocked by the incongruous nature of the song, launched it to number five in the U.K.; in the States and other countries it became a mighty number one. It must be remembered that at this time the Stones were contending for chart positions in Britain with a record-buying public purchasing Donny Osmond, the Carpenters, and Gary Glitter. In America, at least, they were still dealing with contemporary artists Cher (whom they knocked off the top position) and Eddie Kendricks (formerly of the Temptations). [According to the copy editor of this book, however, the argument that the Stones weren't competing with younger artists for American chart positions doesn't hold up. He adds, 'By 1973 the Osmonds and Carpenters had had many U.S. hits, and even Gary Glitter had charted in the U.S. Cher, Eddie Kendricks, Diana Ross, and Marvin Gaye had U.S. number ones in 1973—but so did such quintessential seventies acts as Dawn, Jim Croce, Grand Funk, and Helen Reddy.'] A Michael Lindsay-Hogg promotional film accompanied the release of 'Angie.' The band were shown sitting on the stage edge resplendent in flared suits as they performed the song. Rose petals fluttered down, creating a languid, inert atmosphere."

Before departing for the European tour, Keith had realized that he had to get off heroin again, if only to regain the strength needed to fulfill the demanding schedule. He had discovered that there was a clinic in Switzerland that specialized in an expensive but effective and painless three-day blood-cleansing cure. In between playing Innsbruck, Austria, on September 23 and Bern, Switzerland, on September 26, Keith and Marshall Chess, who had become addicted under Richards's influence, checked in to get their blood cleaned. The treatment involved a hemodialysis process in which the patient's blood was passed through a pump, where it was separated from sterile dialysis fluid by a semipermeable membrane. This allowed any toxic substances that had built up in the bloodstream, which would normally have been secreted by the kidneys, to diffuse out of the blood into the dialysis fluid.

From this cure sprang the myth that Keith regularly had the blood emptied out of his body and replaced with a fresh supply.

This Draculan notion is one of the few elements of his image that Richards has gone to some pains to correct, but to no avail: "Someone asked me how I cleaned up, so I told them I went to Switzerland and had my blood completely changed. I was just fooling around. I opened my jacket and said, 'How do you like my blood change?' That's all it was, a joke. I was fucking sick of answering that question. So I gave them a story."

According to Nick Kent, Richards was frightened by the process because it required being put to sleep for three days. He had heard that not only did this induce terrifying nightmares, but waking from the deep sleep was extremely unpleasant. He tried to encourage Sanchez to do it with him, but the latter refused.

"It's quite simple, really," Keith explained afterwards, trying to down-play the event. "He just changed our blood little by little so that there was no heroin in our bodies after forty-eight hours. There was no pain at all, and we spent the rest of the week just resting and building up our strength."

According to Sanchez, the night Keith left the clinic, "I saw him accept a snort of coke from Bobby Keys and reproached him for his foolishness. 'Yeah, well,' said Keith. 'It doesn't matter if I get hooked again now. I can give it up any time I like without any bother.'" Keith was so wrapped up in denial that he told Anita he believed that if he took heroin on the road he wouldn't become addicted because when he went on stage he sweated out the poison.

On September 1, the Stones—with Keith Richards sort of at the helm—launched a triumphal procession through Europe that began in Vienna and marched through West Germany, England, Switzerland, Sweden, Denmark, Holland, and Belgium, playing two shows a day at twenty-three theaters in seven weeks. The set mixed classics such as "Brown Sugar" with material from the new album. Keith sang lead on one song, "Happy." The lyrics "Never want to be like Papa Working for the boss every night and day" had become ironic in light of the hectic Stones schedule. In between working, Keith partied, gave interviews, did photo sessions, wrote songs, and stayed up for three to five days at a stretch. On the days he went to sleep, he awoke around 5:00 P.M., had breakfast, then took a variety of drugs so that he was pumped up to go on stage by

8:oo P.M. "With all those drugs and partying through the night and seeing people," reported one friend, "he was in such a daze I don't think he had much time to think or worry about anything." All that really mattered was hammering out those twenty-odd songs night after night after night.

The English rock critic Nick Kent, who built his career in the seventies on an enlightened assessment of Richards, accompanied the group on this tour as their official biographer, writing a book that would never get published.

NICK KENT: "In the seventies it was really Keith and the danger around Keith. He lived, and continues to live, an incredibly dangerous life and he doesn't give a fuck. He lives his life like it's a movie. Keith Richards was the Godfather. Everyone wanted to go be like Keith Richards. He was the big Lord Byron figure. He was mad, bad, and dangerous to know. It was a nonverbal thing and it was the seventies and Richards wore it so well. He had immense personal charisma. When he plays guitar in a room he really feels something. He just sits there and he is the center of attention in that room and Jagger is like a little boy running around doing silly things to get attention, but the power base of the Rolling Stones emotionally is there, and there's always been and there always will be this thing about Keith.

"It was a very stupid tour for someone like me to get on, because it was a drug tour. Mick Taylor was becoming seriously lost in a drug fog. Between '73 and '74 a lot of people in the music business got into heroin. It went from being a thing they did every weekend to something they did every day and they sorta didn't know what happened. Taylor became like that."

The real test of endurance for Keith, though, was how well he could play his music. Keith always prided himself on his ability to play, no matter how screwed up he was. "I don't really give a damn what the media writes about me," he told Nick Kent. "I'd just like to see all those cocksuckers spending an hour on stage doing what I do, and see how they stand up to it."

However, much as he might protest, Keith's music did suffer during this period. As Kent pointed out, "People said, 'Oh, yeah, Keith, you were still on top of it,' and I'm sure everyone's going to say, 'He rode it out.' He didn't ride it out. All his guitars had capos on them so he didn't have to play bar chords. There was a different guitar for every song because he was too fucked up to make the effort. He was on automatic most of '73. Certain nights were good, but he was on automatic. He was numb. He wasn't even there."

Later, Keith admitted as much. "I did get to a point where the music was secondary. I was devoting most of my time to scoring and taking dope. I was completely out of it, and Mick had to cover for me. He took over completely. I managed to make gigs and write some songs, but Mick took care of everything through most of the seventies. The cat worked his butt off. He covered my ass. I feel I owe Mick. I've always admired him very much for that. He did exactly what a friend should do.

"The drugs thing was just an extra side of the image that was forced upon us by political circumstances. You've got a particular image and people kinda expect you to live up to it. To a certain extent I suppose I did try and live up to that image, because I continued getting very wasted. I know I was an odds-on favorite as rock and roll's next celebrity casualty. But those presumptions were not correct because, despite everything, I'm a survivor."

MICK JAGGER: "Eventually, of course, I do think the image stuff contributed to Keith becoming a junkie. The pressure obviously got to him. He didn't like it, couldn't live with it, and it just became very sad. I think eventually Keith suffered that way."

The European jaunt marked the first time the heady intoxication of performing together in front of thousands of screaming fans didn't bring Jagger and Richards close.

RICHARDS: "It's hard going for that front-man gig Mick does. It's hard being out front. You gotta be able to make it work: You gotta actually believe that you're semidivine when you're out there, then come off stage and know you ain't. And that's the problem: Eventually the reaction time gets slower. You still think you're semidivine when you're in the limo and semidivine at the hotel, until you're semidivine for the whole goddamn tour."

MICK JAGGER: "When I go on the road I just go crazy. I become a total monster. I don't recognize anybody—I don't even see them. I feel guilty about it afterwards, then I laugh, because the whole thing is a joke. But Keith is worse than I am. Is he a prima donna? Oh, yeah!"

The release of *Goats Head Soup* in the middle of the European tour signaled to fans who had not seen the band play in 1973 that all was not well. Except for a media song-and-dance routine over a song called "Starfucker," which, for propriety's sake, was billed as "Star Star" on the album, and the smash pop hit "Angie," the critics thought it was a "weak album that lacked depth and focus." Roy Carr defended the beleaguered record: "In many ways *Goats Head Soup* was a victim of circumstance. The problem is too many people continue to use what the Rolling Stones recorded ten years ago as a yardstick. By doing so they sometimes miss some good music."

It also suffered in comparison to the particularly vibrant crop of albums that heralded the arrival that year of "cock rock": Lou Reed's *Berlin*, Iggy Pop's *Raw Power*, and David Bowie's *Alladin Sane*. The album cover, photographed by David Bailey, sent its own strange message. For the first time only Jagger and Richards appeared on it. On the front, Jagger's face was covered by a stocking mask that made him like a ghost. On the back Richards matched him, looking, in his own words, "pretty grotesque. I think most people used the word *charred*."

If the critics panned *Goats Head Soup*, the new fans roped in by "Angie" loved it, and it went to number one on the U.S. charts. For the first time, their career took a traditionally commercial turn, and Keith started to wonder how the public's mainstream tastes would affect his sense of independence. The album's popularity did not fool the Stones into believing it was a good record. Both Jagger and Richards expressed their disappointment with it. *Goats Head Soup, It's Only Rock 'n Roll*, and *Black and Blue* are generally considered to represent the nadir of Keith's musical career. Between 1972, when he began to record *Goats Head Soup*, and 1976, when he finished recording *Black and Blue*, Richards made a lot of what he would call "junkie music." Still, Keith was annoyed at having to live up to Rolling Stones standards set the previous year or decade.

RICHARDS: "You put a record out and then you get the feeling everybody's disappointed with it. Then two years later you bring another record out and you suddenly realize that they're all holding this other record up and saying, 'If only it was as good as this one.' And I know it's not because we're ahead of our time, because that's not ever what we're trying to do. It's not avant-garde, no, that's not it, it's just that when you've been around as long as we have, people have got their own fixed idea of what they want from the Stones and it's never anything new. A lot of the time with records it's the experiences that people have been through while that record's been playing that make it special to them. Although they're interested and they'll buy the new record, it doesn't mean as much to them as the one they heard that magical night when they screwed fifteen chicks."

Richards was also disconcerted to see some of the album's better songs, like his own "Coming Down Again," getting buried by "Angie." "'Angie' just took everything that album had to give," he said. "It was huge in Europe. And it was bought by people who normally wouldn't go near us with a barge pole."

As the European tour neared its end, Richards's court cases in England and France came to trial. On October 17 he was given a one-year suspended sentence, fined one thousand dollars, and banned from France for two years for using drugs at Nellcôte. "Thank Christ that's over," he told Tony. "Now, at last, I can stop paying that grand-a-week rent for that bloody house. It cost me more than a hundred grand already [£250,000] just to keep it going so the cops wouldn't try to extradite me." When Richards returned to London, where he and Anita were to be tried at Marlborough Street Magistrate's Court for the Cheyne Walk bust, his new "charred" look featured black teeth, a skull-like visage, empty eyes surrounded by kohl-black smudges, and a sickly deathlike pallor, all of which was considered echt cool among his followers. "He's a wild motherfucking guy and to me he was one of the best-looking guys ever to walk the face of the planet," Nick Kent recalled of this period in Keith's life. "He looked really poisoned that year."

On October 24, Andy Johns and Mick Jagger attended Keith and Anita's trial. Keith admitted possession at his Chelsea home of cannabis, Chinese heroin, and Mandrax tablets, plus a revolver, a shotgun, and ammunition. After hearing the list of charges, Richards's lawyer claimed the drugs had been left by guests who had stayed at his house while he was abroad. Anita was given a one-year conditional discharge for possession of the Mandrax and Keith was merely fined £205.

RICHARDS: "A very sensible magistrate saw that I'd walked into my house, which I'd rented to a lot of people who'd been very clumsy and not cleaned up after themselves. The cops even tried to string in this old Belgian shotgun that was built in—ah—1899 or somethin'. The police tried their damnedest to tell this 'ere magistrate that this weapon was a sawn-off shotgun. From that moment the magistrate saw what was 'appenin'."

After the decision, Keith and friends went to the Londonderry Hotel to celebrate. As people dropped in to offer congratulations, Richards's children and Johns's son played in the bedroom. As music blared through the rooms and people toasted Richards's charmed life with curses and laughter, Keith nodded out and set a bed on which several children were playing on fire. As the celebration turned into yet another charred nightmare with people screaming in the halls and the children, who were luckily unhurt, shrieking in shock, Andy Johns, who had been the Stones' recording engineer since 1968, ruefully told himself, "I'm getting out of here, man."

Keith's second most hazardous habit after nodding out at the wheel had become falling asleep with a lit cigarette. After being arrested in June, he had taken his family down to Redlands to contemplate their fate in the tranquillity of the country. Four weeks later, on July 31, the main house caught fire, and they barely escaped with a few valuable possessions. In a widely distributed photograph of the incident, a soaking wet Anita points at the burning house like Brünnhilde screaming at Keith to rescue their Charles II chairs, while a wet, crestfallen Richards appears to be playing air guitar. Though he lost many possessions in fires and robberies over the years, he managed to maintain his sense of humor. Referring later to a Nick Munro sculpture that was damaged in the blaze, he cackled, "All we have left is her bum!" Asked why Redlands caught fire, he replied, "It's a combustible bastard! It's not the most pleasant experience—sitting in your joint and the fucker combusts."

*

Once the smoke from the '73 tour had cleared, the bodies could be counted. "The Rolling Stones destroy people at an alarming rate," Richards said. "Something about us makes them come face-to-face eventually with themselves, sometimes for the better, sometimes in the worst possible way. Maybe that ultimately is the most important thing about the Stones. For some unknown reason, they strike at a person at a point and in a position that they don't even know exists."

The first to go was producer Jimmy Miller, who, after five years with the Stones, had reached the breaking point on *Goats Head Soup*.

RICHARDS: "There isn't one producer who can handle the whole thing. You run through them like you run through gas in your car. You burn them out. It's a ruthless circle. Jimmy went in a lion and came out a lamb. We wore him out completely. Jimmy was great, but the more successful he became the more he got like Brian. Jimmy ended up carving swastikas into the wooden console at the studio. It took him three months to carve a swastika. Meanwhile Mick and I had to finish up *Goats Head Soup*."

Keith, however, seemed to take it in stride. He never tired of pointing out that most of the victims were the sort—like Brian—who were going to die anyway, one way or the other. During the European tour Gram Parsons had succumbed to an overdose of drugs at the Joshua Tree Inn in California. According to Parsons's biographer, Ben Fong-Torres, "Keith Richards was halfway around the world . . . when he got the news a few days later. He was in the bathroom backstage at a stadium in Innsbruck, Austria, when horn player Bobby Keys approached.

"'Hey man, I got something bad to tell you,' said Bobby . . . 'Gram just croaked out in Joshua Tree.'

"Keith was shocked. 'I said, "*What*?" Because I always had a feeling—it was like with Otis Redding—you would think there were many many more years, that it was only a beginning. And then the hard bit comes in. You say, "Well, he was just too good to get old." Just to soften the shock on yourself.'

"But there was no getting around it. 'I was shattered for ages.'"

Although Keith told Roy Carr that Gram's death was a great

shock, "because Gram was one of my closest friends, and just when it seemed he was really gonna get it together, he popped it," he blamed Parsons's demise on having left Keith's constant care! "Unfortunately, many of my closest friends have died suddenly. Brian Jones always used to say, 'I'll not make it much beyond thirty,' and Gram Parsons also had that kind of thing about him. While they were with me, I could always hold them down . . . I could take care of Gram. But once he moved back to L.A. to form his own band, I started hearing stories. People are often driven by certain forces within themselves. They well may be highly intelligent and fully aware of the inevitable results, but nevertheless they succumb to their own weaknesses."

Nick Kent thought that Gram's death made Keith even more defiant about his life-style: "Bobby Keys and Keith were the pirates on that tour. They were bad-ass guys. They didn't verbalize it, but their attitude was, 'OK, we've lost a buddy but we're gonna go on and we're gonna take drugs to the max.' They were very morose that evening but it was the moroseness of people who thought, 'Oh, fuck, this guy is dead, but we're gonna keep doing it.'"

Richards had a similar reaction to Michael Cooper's suicide by self-administered overdose that same year: Keith was convinced that Michael, who, like Keith, was a great romantic idealist and somewhat susceptible to strong women, had killed himself in despair over the recent loss of his girlfriend. "People were dropping like flies then," Keith said. "It was nothing to wake up once a week and hear so-and-so's gone—'What, the usual?' 'Yeah, the usual.' Nobody seemed to die of anything but ODs in those days. The amazing thing about Michael is that I don't really remember meeting him. I think I just ended up once with Brian at Michael's studio—we just dropped in. He slipped into my life and then slipped out."

"At each death people said much the same thing: 'That's what comes of living too close to the Stones,'" recalled Tony Sanchez. "In the end you try and live just like them. The Stones use people up." But Richards defended the Stones: "The thing about my life and the Stones' life is that there was nothing phony about it. If anybody was going to take knocks, we were going to take the knocks along with everybody else. It isn't that we're sitting up on some comfortable faraway paradise and putting out this stuff and saying, 'Well, fuck yourselves up.' We got beat up more than anybody.

"I've always just tried to avoid doing anything that would make me cringe. Anything I do, I like to be able to live with. I'm aware of those rumblings—'Oh, Gram would still be around if it wasn't for Keith Richards.' But I would honestly say that his attitude toward those things reminded me of what was going on everywhere."

Two weeks after Parsons died, Bobby Keys collapsed. "Bobby Keys walked out on the last tour," said Keith. "Not walked out, just collapsed." Like Brian Jones, he had begun making drugs, drink, and groupies his priorities. Keys was slowly shut out of the Stones' inner circle. The band had no time or patience for anyone who broke down on them. If you couldn't make the gig, you were off the tour. He had made the mistake, one aide pointed out, of believing that he was a Rolling Stone and not a session musician, winding up "broke in mind, body, and pocket."

"The Stones didn't fuck around," recalled Kent. "They just dumped him in a taxi. It really fucked Bobby up for a long time."

Closer to home, Keith's grandfather, Gus Dupree, who had been his inspiration as a child, died of old age in England.

The one force that kept Keith off the casualty list in the early 1970s was a twenty-two-year-old German actress and model, Uschi Obermeier, whom he fell in love with in the middle of the European tour. Uschi was talented, strong-willed, smart, and incredibly sexy. Her big lips and whispery, humming voice magnified her allure. She was already something of a celebrity in her own right in Europe, and had spent some time with Mick during the 1970 European tour. Though she had seen Keith then, they had never spent any time together.

USCHI OBERMEIER: "I was in Paris on a photo job and some time in the middle of the night the phone rang. At the time I didn't speak that well English and I thought it was Mick, but then it was Keith and he wanted to meet me, he said. The real reason, I found out later, is that he and Mick have a little rivalry thing, especially about women. He only wanted to give Mick a little stab. We settled that we would meet in Munich, where I lived. Actually, they both called me and said they were coming to Munich that night in the car, so they both wanted to see me at the same time. It was really like a teenage dream come true, because for me the Rolling Stones were the group. They were wild and they exactly expressed what you were feeling.

"They both came up to my place and I couldn't decide, really, who I wanted, and they said to me, 'Hey, you make up your mind.' I said, 'I can't, because I like both of you guys.' They played music and smoked and nobody would leave. Keith said, 'Jagger, you cunt, leave!' Finally Keith left because Mick really insisted on it. Bianca was coming the next day and he really wanted to see me before. The next day I saw Keith. It was really kind of strange because I liked how sick he looked because he took all the drugs and I really was fascinated by his aura, but he was such a sweet person."

Uschi went to travel with sweet, sick Keith on part of the tour. Two things struck her: Keith could take more drugs and stay up longer than anybody else, and the drugs did not affect his ability to perform sexually with her. But what she liked most about him was how open and unaffected he was. "He could have been such a prick," she recalled, "and he wasn't. He had a very good sense of humor. And he was such an interesting person. It didn't matter where he was or who he was around, he was always himself, contrary to Mick, who changed like a chameleon." Even better than this for her was his absolute loyalty to whichever woman he was with. "And he really stood by me. I mean, I knew he was with Anita, but when I was with Keith there couldn't be any other girl." Anita, meanwhile, was in a Swiss clinic having a physical and nervous breakdown.

"I felt like a queen," Uschi remembered. "He made me feel really good. The fans would tear their clothes off right in front of him, but he just wouldn't even look, he just took me by the arm going from the hotel to the concert with our ghetto blaster playing Jimmy Cliffs's 'The Harder They Come' as loud as he could all the time. That was our theme song."

Richards took "The Harder They Come" as his watchword in the mid-seventies, playing it day and night wherever he went. Its lyrics seemed to directly reflect his life and mission as rock and roll's number-one outlaw: The police, he noted, might try to control his actions, but he would ask God to forgive them because they did not know what they were doing. Ironically, they also mirrored his arrest-plagued Jamaican experience.

The uncertainty of being Keith's girlfriend, however, was as extreme as the exhilaration. Since they hardly ever spoke, Uschi had no idea of how strong Keith's feelings for her were. "We really loved each other more than we intended. We really fell in love. But I myself never knew how much he really loved me because I took it more as a kind of game. I had too much respect for Anita that I wasn't really even thinking that I could take her place. And I never really thought it could have been anything serious because he never really said too much and he actually never showed too much." She was keenly aware of Richards's priorities. "Also then, for me, it was difficult, because with them music is the first love, second place comes music and also third place, and then in fourth place you come."

"Uschi was a big force, and he almost left Anita for her," recalled Nick Kent. "On the last night of the '73 tour Keith had his photograph taken with Uschi, and they were going off and kissing and I mean this looked like love. She was an incredibly sexual, very, very attractive girl, like the model of the year, and they enjoyed a very good relationship together."

While Keith was on tour, Anita continued to disintegrate in London. Their relationship was on its last legs. Signs of the rift had become apparent as far back as March, when the couple were holed up in their Swiss chalet. Just as Anita was trying to get off heroin, Keith came home with a heavy habit and a load of hangers-on. Anita described the difficult scene: "While Keith was away I'd be starting to get off heroin, really trying, but then he'd return and he'd get me on it just as bad as before. People who used to be friends began to get very bitchy toward me. Keith had this entourage of hangers-on who were always around the house, came for a weekend, stayed on for weeks and months, always a house full of freeloading sycophants, 'Yes, Keith, yes, anything you say, Keith,' no private life, no time to talk, the suppliers bringing us the heroin, but that's all we had in common. Then Keith started to have girlfriends that I found out about, and I started to see other men." When the Stones flew back to London for a September 6 publicity party at Sir Winston Churchill's birthplace, Blenheim Palace, she refused to get out of the car, then stormed in looking so wrecked Keith had to drag her out and take her home. During the ride back to London in the limousine, Marlon pressed his anxious face against the window, trying not to see what his parents were doing as Keith methodically punched Anita in the face.

Meanwhile, the poignant lines from "Angie" noting that Keith's and Anita's dreams were burnt to a crisp and how he hated the haunted look in her eyes played around the world.

17

Coming Down Again
1973–1975

The things that would kill other people don't kill me. Despite everything, I'm a survivor. I can only suppose that I possess the kind of mentality and psychological makeup that could handle it. I come from very tough stock.

KEITH RICHARDS, *from an interview with Stanley Booth, 1989*

On November 13, 1973, the Stones went into Musicland Studios in Munich, Uschi Obermeier's hometown, to start work on their next album, *It's Only Rock'n Roll*. Planting their standard at the Munich Hilton, they summoned the personnel required to create a Rolling Stones record. Jimmy Miller was out, another victim left by the wayside to find his way back to reality alone. Richards and Jagger would produce the record as the Glimmer Twins.

Jagger recalled the sessions dourly. They got up around five in the afternoon, went for a walk in the Englischer Garten, had something to eat, and worked through the night. "The Stones are men of few words," he said in New York before embarking for Munich. "We don't so much say anythin' to each other as grunt. I'll say, "Allo, Chawlie, 'ow are ya, where've you been, then?' He'll say, 'I've been on 'oliday, 'aven't I?' And that's about it."

NICK KENT: "I spent about three days with them snowbound. It was just horrific. Richards was holed up taking loads of drugs. Jagger was doing business and the others were just 'We gotta record, oh dear, let's go to a club, we're bored.' There's this working-class thing that becomes very oppressive. They almost talk to each other in grunts, because there are so many different personalities that don't get on naturally when they're together. It's 'We're the Rolling Stones so we gotta put this act on,' and they literally become more than the sum of their parts. I said to Jagger, 'I just can't handle it when you guys are all together. It's just depressing.' He said, 'I know, you're right.'"

Richards saw things in a more upbeat manner. When not nodding out, Keith approached the Munich sessions with singular, hard-driving focus. "Keith is a Sagittarius," Anita once observed about Keith's drive. "He's like an arrow that goes straight to its target without deviating from its flight path." He loved to record just after the band had come off the road. "We were really hot and ready to play some new material," he enthused. "We booked a couple of weeks, went in, and cut about half the album with Billy Preston on keyboards." Keith thought the others felt as attuned to him as he was to them, but as he disappeared into a drug fog, it became harder for them to work with him. This was particularly difficult for Wyman, who was not taking cocaine and found his endurance lagging behind Keith's. After a while, tired and dispirited, he would start to play sloppily. Taylor didn't even show up for these sessions, citing a "mysterious illness."

Glyn Johns, who came back to work with the band briefly, soon quit again.

GLYN JOHNS: "There's no doubt they're an incredible group, but I didn't understand why they had to sit and play the same number over and over again for nine hours or two days in order to get it right. It was Keith Richards more than anybody else, the way he formulated for getting the feel he wanted. He didn't communicate tremendously with the others. I mean, they just went along with it. I never really figured it out. It seemed to have got worse over the years. If they recorded two tracks in one night history was made."

They finished the first Munich sessions on November 24, broke for Christmas, then returned on January 14, 1974, for another two weeks.

RICHARDS: "Even when we're not actually in the studios, nobody has actually forgotten about it . . . You're thinking about it all the time. You're at home listening to a rough cassette mix of it, thinking how you want to put the whole song together because maybe you've got it on this very thin thread, just a hook line, and you've got to expand the song in a particular way, both in the way you want it to go and in what you want to say. When you've got a certain kind of track, only certain kinds of lyrics are going to fit that feel, that sound, so you've got to put it together. A lot of times it's really painstaking work. By the end of those sessions we'd cut enough tracks for the album plus half again. Then we had to choose which ones we were going to work on vocalwise. So we made a short list of about twelve or thirteen tracks."

In April, Keith flew to England to join Mick in finishing the album's vocals.

RICHARDS: "We finished off writing the songs that hadn't been completed lyricwise, because a lot of them had been written in a very loose framework to start with—maybe just a chorus, a hook line, or something. Then we got on and did the vocals and I left Mick for a couple of weeks to do his solo vocals, because he often comes up with his best stuff alone in the studio with just an engineer. Then he doesn't feel like he's hanging anybody up. While Mick was doing this I got a call from Ronnie Wood . . ."

Keith had become friendly with Ron Wood one night in the spring of 1973 when Ron's wife, Chrissie, had taken Keith to their home, the Wick, in Richmond, where Jagger and Wood were jamming in the basement studio. The relationship got off to as rocky a start as Keith and Mick's relationship with Brian Jones when Jagger wrote the next Stones single, "It's Only Rock 'n Roll," with Wood, and asked him if he would be available to replace Keith on tour should Richards be unable to get a U.S. visa. Jagger's invitation became an international rock rumor and he, Richards, and Wood each had to vigorously deny it in the press. However, when Ron asked Keith down to the Wick in April of 1974 to help him finish his solo album, Richards leapt at the opportunity and ended up staying there for several weeks, contributing two songs, "Cancel Everything" and "Sure the One You Need" (both credited to Richards and Jagger).

RICHARDS: "I've never thought of doing anything on my own. As far as I'm concerned, it's no fun if you're there by yourself, just you and your ego, and of course your ego comes out on top every time. You need somebody to bounce ideas off, to have a laugh with. Two people can deflate each other nicely—that's how it works with Mick, and it's happening at the moment with Ronnie."

But his involvement with Wood clashed with his collaboration with Jagger: "I really got involved and Mick was calling up saying,

MICK JAGGER: 'KEITH SAID HE WANTED TO
BE LIKE ROY ROGERS AND PLAY GUITAR'

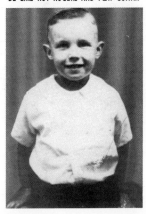

DICK TAYLOR: 'KEITH WAS <u>OBSESSED</u> WITH CHUCK BERRY'

KEITH RICHARDS: 'HITLER HAD ME MARKED'

'NOT AN ACADEMIC BAND'

THEY WERE LIKE SIAMESE TWINS —
ONE PERSON WITH FOUR ARMS

1965: KEITH FULFILLED HIS BOYHOOD FANTASIES WHEN HE VISITED A DUDE RANCH IN ARIZONA AND RODE WITH SAM EARP (A DESCENDANT OF WYATT)

EXHAUSTED AND ABOUT TO BECOME BITTER ENEMIES,
BRIAN AND KEITH MAKE ONE LAST LOOK-A-LIKE
APPEARANCE, 1967

1967: KEITH OUTSIDE REDLANDS WITH JAMES BOND-INSPIRED
BLUE LENA (NAMED AFTER LENA HORNE)

ANITA AND KEITH IN ROME, 1967. PALLENBERG:
'FOR A FEW YEARS WE WERE FLYING.
▼ WE HAD THE LOT'

1969. RICHARDS: 'WE HAD MARLON BECAUSE ▶
WE KNEW IT WAS THE RIGHT TIME.
WE'RE VERY INSTINCTIVE PEOPLE'

1968: THE REAL JUMPING JACK FLASH

'I HAD A LOT OF GOOD TIMES WITH ANDREW (OLDHAM), AND I DUG IT. HE'D SAY THE SAME – HE LEARNED FROM US TOO'

GERMANY 1970 ▶

▼ 'MOST PEOPLE DON'T KNOW WHAT A BAND IS. YOU HAVE TO FIND IT. THOSE ARE THE MAGIC MOMENTS.' (US TOUR, 1969)

WEATHER:
Thundery rain
Lighting-up time
9.51 p.m.
Details—Back page

46,330

Evening Standard

London: Tuesday June 26 1973

7RR

3p

Girl friend also arrested in Cheyne Walk ra

ROLLING STON RICHARD—GUN, DRUGS CHARGE

By JOHN STEVENS

EITH RICHARD, -year-old lead itarist of the Rolli- Stones, was rested by Drugs und officers in a d on a house in eyne Walk, Chel- today.

so arrested were ard's friend Anita Pal- rg, 30, and actor e Jean Stanislas Klos- i, also 30.

er, the trio were ed at Chelsea police n with being in ssion of cannabis. Richard was addition- charged with possess- revolver and ammu- without a certifi

were bailed to in court at Marl- h Street tomorrow. detectives who raided ouse armed with a warrant took posses- firearm and ammu- hey found during the

d and Miss Pallenberg hre-year-old son, Mar-

birth to another baby n a Geneva nursing April last year.

KEITH RICHARD and Anita Pallenberg—they appear in court tomorrow.

Evening Standard: Ray Jones

al clash r over e loans

clash between the nt and the building ver the home-loan 's long-term future s nearer today. d Boyle, the Building ssociation chairman, definite than ever in the Government's oan for building ons—a stabilisation

sources confirmed y that the idea of s—to iron out the peaks in the flow funds—was still the ement their present pro-

Mr Boyle said in a Financial Times on Pro- Finance. "It seems stabilisation fund

Assassins kill top Ulster man and woman

BELFAST Tuesday.— SENATOR Paddy Wilson, a leading member of the Social Democratic and and Labour Party in Nor- thern Ireland, was found shot dead on the outskirts of Belfast early today.

Beside him was the body of 29-year-old Miss Irene Andrews. It is believed he had offered her a life home after leaving a city centre public house.

They were found after an anonymous call to a Belfast newspaper from the newly formed terrorist group, the Ul- ster Freedom Fighters.

Shot

Senator Wilson was election agent for the leader of the S.D.L.P. Mr Gerry Fitt, for assembly elections in two days time.

And in another incident today a shot was fired through a win- dow narrowly missing a Unionist Party candidate for the election. Mr Cecil Walker was talking when the bullet passed between them as they sat in Mr Walker's bungalow at Carnmoney outside the city.

A Pakistani man was shot dead in the New Road Mews area of Londonderry this afternoon.

First reports said the man, understood to be a civilian who worked at an Army case in the city was shot dead in a van ambushed as it drove along the road.

Senator Wilson and the woman, a Protestant clerical official, had left the public house at about 11 p.m.

It was some two hours later when a caller describing himself as Captain Black of the Ulster Freedom Fighters telephoned the Belfast Newsletter.

First he told a reporter that the organisation had been re- sponsible for a killing at the weekend, then he said: "Tonight

we got Senator Wilson." Then he gave details as to where the bodies could be found.

Police and troops rushed to a quarry near the Horseshoe Bend on the main road between Bel- fast and Aldergrove airport and found Senator Wilson and the young woman dead beside the Senator's mini-car.

They believe that the Senator's car was followed from the city by terrorists who overtook it and

Contd. Back Page, Col. 2

Crisis hou for the kidnap ba

'Impeach Nixo bid for inquiry

Dean quizzed

So. easy for Billie Jean

England survivi then wickets fa

John Thicknesse—P

Diamond man robbed at gunpo

News on Camera—

£27½m. property takeover bid

TV/radio

Entertainment

FOUND

the answer to hair loss.

Svenson is a unique process that actually adds hair to your own. You can regain a whole new head of hair, or just thicken what you have. Come in and discuss it with us. Our Consultations are free.

HARVARD HAIR CLINIC

4 Mandeville Place, London W.1. 01-935 1671
(off Wigmore St., five minutes from Bond St. Tube)

▲ WE COVER EACH OTHER'S
ARSES.' (US TOUR, 1975)

ON A SLIDING SCALE OF HOMO-
EROTIC DUOS PUNCH PLACED
JAGGER AND RICHARDS AHEAD
OF GILBERT AND GEORGE
AND BEHIND LAUREL
AND HARDY

KEITH ACTUALLY FELL ASLEEP ON STAGE
DURING THE 1976 TOUR OF EUROPE

1977: AT ANDY WARHOL'S FACTORY
THE DAY BEFORE FLYING TO PARIS TO
START WORK ON 'SOME GIRLS'

1977: KEITH EXPLAINS TO THE AUTHOR
HOW THE BLACK BOX WORKS

1979: AT THE NEW YORK PARTY
FOR 'EMOTIONAL RESCUE'

◀ 'PATRICIA IS A REMARKABLE GIRL.
SHE TURNED ME ROUND JUST WHEN I
NEEDED TURNING'

US TOUR, 1981. STANLEY BOOTH: 'KEITH IS A GUITAR PLAYER.
HE'S DEDICATED. HE LOVES WHAT HE DOES AND HE
DOES IT ALL THE TIME. I'VE NEVER KNOWN
ANYONE WHO WORKS HARDER'

PATTI, KEITH, RONNIE AND JO, THE EMOTIONAL CENTRE OF THE STONES IN THE MID 80s

MICK JAGGER TELLS WILLIAM BURROUGHS, VICTOR BOCKRIS AND ANDY WARHOL THAT THERE MIGHT NOT BE A ROLLING STONES IN 1982

'THIS IS A VERY ROOTLESS LIFE. THE ONLY THING YOU HAVE TO HOLD ONTO IS FAMILY.' KEITH WITH HIS FATHER AND HIS SON IN THE MID 80s

1987: WITH CHUCK BERRY IN 'HAIL! HAIL! ROCK 'N' ROLL'

'WHEN YOU LOOK KEITH IN THE EYE, YOU KNOW YOU'RE NOT GOING TO BULLSHIT HIM,' SAYS X-PENSIVE WINOS' DRUMMER, STEVE JORDAN. 'AND WHEN YOU ARE GOING TO BULLSHIT HIM, DON'T LOOK HIM IN THE EYE'

CHARLIE SHOWS KEITH HOW IT'S DONE (US TOUR, 1989)

WITH VACLAV HAVEL, PRAGUE, 1990. RICHARDS: 'THE REASON YOU'VE GOT MAJOR SHIFTS IN SUPERPOWER SITUATIONS IN THE PAST FEW YEARS HAS TO DO WITH THE PAST TWENTY YEARS OF MUSIC'

'I've finished my vocals. Come and help me out … do some harmonies and do some vocals.' I had to say, 'Hang on, I've just written a couple of songs down here for Woody and I want to get 'em down!'—which I did, pretty quickly." Keith was the member of the band most insistent that the Rolling Stones were the number-one priority in his life. He set standards of allegiance. It was Keith who had been most annoyed when Brian showed up to sessions or concerts wasted, Keith who flipped out when Bill Wyman released a solo album in 1974. And yet in Keith's work on Ronnie's album lay the seeds of their solo careers.

By the midseventies, performing had become a life-or-death necessity for Richards. He believed that the cleanup and preparations required of him before he embarked on a tour provided the only way for him to get off heroin periodically and pull himself together. However, that July when the Stones released the single "It's Only Rock 'n Roll," Keith's detachment from the band was evident.

"It's Only Rock 'n Roll" stands as a crossroad in the Stones' career and an anomaly in their oeuvre. Neither Charlie Watts nor Keith Richards had anything to do with its creation. Kenny Jones played drums on the track and, despite rumors that Richards wiped it from the original tape, Ron Wood's sinewy guitar lines supplied the hook riff. For a minute there it looked as if "old bum's rush Jagger," as Ronnie would come to call him, might actually be running away from the slowly dying Keith (whose doctor told him he had only six months to live if he didn't stop treating his body as a laboratory) and pulling together another version of the Stones that just might be a success. It was the last of their anthems and represented the point at which Richards and Jagger began to pull strongly in opposite directions. "It's Only Rock 'n Roll" was a huge international hit, but it didn't have the kind of biting riff Keith had brought to their best work. Taylor sniped that it was an attempt to write something in the classic Stones style, but the song had come out like a parody.

When Keith wanted to do a summer tour, the band refused. Keith, though, could not see their abandonment for what it was. "I would like to work on the road a lot more," he said when asked about the rumored summer tour. "I like playing live, because for me it helps everything else. It helps me write songs, it helps me improve my playing, it gives me ideas, and it stimulates me. But I have to respect the fact that there are other members of the band, say, Bill and Charlie, who have a need for a really stable home life in one place. They need that anchor, whereas my old lady and myself are very nomadic sort of people."

Circumstances forced him to find somebody to play with. When Keith complained about being constantly under surveillance at Cheyne Walk, Ron invited him to move into the gardener's cottage of his estate. Nothing could have pleased Keith more than the opportunity to start all over again. That summer he lived with Ronnie and helped him put together a band and make a record. By turning away from the Stones and picking up with Ron Wood, Richards opened a whole new chapter in his and the band's life.

Living at the Wick was perfect for Keith. Not only could he play uninterruptedly with the man who would soon become his new twin, but he could escape for a while from Anita, who was becoming impossible to live with. In between modeling assignments that summer, Uschi, who had no trouble exciting Keith sexually, spent ten days with him at the Wick—in bed.

On July 13 and 14, Keith and Ron played the new materials at the Kilburn State Cinema in northwest London. "It was a great night," Nick Kent recalled. "A grand meshing together of sublime musicianship and the archetypal dishevelled get-down. When Messrs Wood and Richards step to the mike for the harmonies on 'Cancel Everything,' it's difficult to tell them apart; the effect is not unlike a degenerate Everly Brothers."

"The Richards influence is well stamped throughout Wood's solo album, *I've Got My Own Album to Do*," Kent wrote when it was released that September. "Richards' presence has given what so easily could have been thought of as yet another aimless supersession masquerading as a solo album the edge of notoriety it's currently gaining for itself."

On July 27, Nick Kent in the *New Musical Express* labeled Keith Richards "The World's Most Elegantly Wasted Human Being." By now Kent had become such a public clone of Richards he feared Keith might resent him. Instead, Richards was clearly flattered by

Kent's adulation and embraced him as a friend, spending days at a time with him at the Wick.

NICK KENT: "As I got into heroin, I was buying it from these guys Tony and Marty at Granny Takes a Trip, which is where Keith and Ronnie also used to buy their clothes, so I was seeing Rose Taylor [Mick Taylor's wife] going down there to score and Jimmy Page and Keith Richards. That's how I really got to know them, not as a journalist, but as a person scoring heroin from their local connection. One night after I did an interview with him Keith said, 'Let's hang out together, man. Let's be pals.' I said, 'All right! You fucking said it, boy! OK.' And it was like, 'Let's do some drugs, man!' He put a pile of heroin on the table that was easily half a gram and then he put down another half of cocaine and he said, 'OK, you're with me.' I thought this was going to kill me, but I'm with Keith! Sniff! Oh, Jesus Christ, I was holding on to my chair but he was just getting started. This is what really frightened me. These drugs affected him physically in a very strange way. He'd taken an amount that you'd think would really do it and it wouldn't have any effect. He was staying up for nights and nights now, his engines were running, but then what would happen is he'd fall asleep in midsentence for like a minute and then he'd wake up and continue the sentence. It was a bit disturbing because he was living on this weird time. Anyway, he had to do a television interview and we went off together and Richards nodded out and it was a live TV program. His eyes went up in his head and it was pretty obvious, but it was incredible, he just didn't give a shit, really wanted people to know.

"I almost killed myself taking drugs with Keith Richards, but driving with him is even worse. He's driving out to Ronnie Wood's place, it's pitch black and he's going at ninety miles an hour in a Dino Ferrari. I was pretty shaken up when we got to Ronnie's. Ronnie wasn't there. He phoned from Germany complaining that he couldn't relate to his amplifier. It's like, 'I'm in Germany, man, and I can't relate to the amplifier they gave me for the gig!' And Keith was being fatherly about this. Then he wanted to play me some tapes, but the thing was, this was Keith Richardsville. Nothing worked! Nothing worked but he had all this expensive audio stuff, and he was on his knees shaking things, going, 'Oh, shit!' He had this guy named Frank, who seemed a bit of an asshole, who was his driver, and so Frank goes off to try to get it fixed and me and Keith sit down and have this great conversation in which he tells me what a cunt Mick Jagger is and how Jagger can't handle women. I told him some stories about all the people who were dying around him. I said, 'You know that you've got a heavy rap. People say that you killed some guy.' You could see it kind of flattered him. I think he's really into being bad without actually being bad. He's actually a moral guy.

"After this talk, Keith goes upstairs for fifteen minutes with a box of tissues. He told me, 'I'm not a junkie because I don't use syringes,' and then he dropped the box of tissues on the floor and all these syringes rolled out and he said, 'Oh, man, I've got a cold. Sorry, man, I've got a cold.' Fair enough, fair enough. Then he came and sat down and suddenly slumped forward and his skin started to turn colors. He just went. It looked as if he'd OD'd, and I went over to him and I had to slap the guy several times. Keith Richards, my hero! There was no reaction. I'm thinking, 'Oh, fuck, what do I do if this guy is fucking OD'd?' I'm in his fucking flat, this guy Frank ain't gonna come back for another hour. Do I call the cops? There are drugs all over this place. I'm shaking him for five minutes thinking, 'What the fuck do I do?,' and suddenly he came out of it, but Tony [Sanchez] used to tell me it was happening a lot.

"We crashed out on pillows for about six hours. The next day I felt horrific. I was trying to get out the front door and the first thing I did was throw up on the welcome mat. He came over to have a look. He wasn't particularly amused. He was like, 'Oh, well, you're one of us.' Then he pointed over to this field and he said, 'Listen, man, it breaks my heart to look out into those fields because me and Tony Sanchez hid a kilo of raw morphine in a barn out there and we can't find it and I just look at the crows and they're probably more stoned than I am.' We were just standing there looking at these crows and I thought that really summed up his life at that point."

On October 15 Richards announced, "I'm changing my image.

I've arranged for a whole series of dental appointments in Switzerland... A young journalist-fan in the Nick Kent mode, Peter Erskine, asked Keith about his deteriorating visage. "The thing is," Richards said, "I'm terrified of dentists. You've only got to 'ave one broken tooth for everyone to think you're a villain—but I'll surprise you all next year. I promise you. I'm just waiting for this new technique to come out—there was a point where I could groove on it but—ah—last month another chunk fell off and since then it's fallen out of favor with me."

In October 1974 the album *It's Only Rock 'n Roll* was released. Its second single, a remake of the Temptations' "Ain't Too Proud to Beg" backed with the Richards-inspired rocker "Dance Little Sister," represented the high point of Keith's raw contribution. The LP competed on the charts with albums such as Stevie Wonder's *Fulfillingness' First Finale*, Wings' *Band on the Run*, Clapton's *461 Ocean Boulevard*, and Lennon's *Walls and Bridges*. Among critics and long-term fans the album was seen as another disappointment. But the Stones' steadily growing international audience loved it, and the album and its singles were enormous hits all over the world. In January 1975, *Creem* magazine voted it the best album of 1974, the Rolling Stones the best band, and their 1972 tour movie, *Ladies and Gentlemen, the Rolling Stones*, best rock film.

RICHARDS: "Rock and roll can't be planned or prepared. *Goats Head Soup* to me was a marking-time album. I like it in many ways, but I don't think it has the freshness that this one has."

In December, as the Stones were gearing up to record their next album, Mick Taylor suddenly resigned. "Mick Taylor was a great guitarist, but he had a very stupid wife," said Nick Kent. "They broke up since, but she was always pushing Taylor. He felt he should get songwriting credit because Keith hadn't turned up to a few sessions and he'd done a few riffs with Jagger."

"It was a shock announcement, especially since on *It's Only Rock 'n Roll* he finally seemed to have meshed perfectly into the group's overall sound," wrote Roy Carr. "But in personality terms he was shy, and had never become a natural group member. A contributory cause was certainly the songwriting upsets, but more importantly there was a desire by Taylor to broaden horizons. He joined the Jack Bruce Band."

According to the rock critic Robert Palmer, "Taylor was the most accomplished technician who ever served as a Stone. A blues guitarist with a jazzman's flair for melodic invention, Taylor was never a rock and roller and never a showman. The day after he quit, Keith sent him a telegram whose very brevity tells the story of the Stones II: 'Really enjoyed playing with you for the last five years. Thanks for all the turn-ons. Best wishes and love.'" According to his wife, Rose, "Mick just read it and started crying."

On December 12, the day the Stones returned to Musicland Studios in Munich, an official press release announced Taylor's departure. Nick Kent was with the band for the sessions.

NICK KENT: "Keith was very on edge. He was very pissed off about Mick Taylor. His attitude was 'We've got these sessions to do, we're the Rolling Stones. Fuck him.' Keith was very wired at that point. On certain days, because of the amount of drugs he was taking, he couldn't talk. It wasn't anything personal—he was pissed off at everybody. You never knew what you were going to face with Keith Richards. Most of the time it was OK, but I always walked on eggshells around him.

"Jagger came in and showed his chord progressions to Richards. Richards worked on it for half an hour. His drugs were on the amplifier. He didn't even bother to close them up. They were bouncing on his amplifier and it was 'Keep away from my amp. I'm a musician!' Wyman and Watts were like, 'Oh, fuck, give Keith a half an hour to get his riff right.' Bill Wyman would be sitting there with Charlie Watts eating fish and chips. He was the downside to hanging out with the Rolling Stones. They can't stand his dirty old man thing, even Charlie. Charlie has to sit with him because he's such a nice guy, but Uschi Obermeier was there in the studio and Bill Wyman was just muttering obscenities. He was just a filthy old man."

When Taylor boasted about being "the only guitarist to leave the Stones alive," Richards riposted, "The Stones aren't gonna end just because a guitar player dies or leaves. He never really wrote things, in spite of what he said. It's basically imagination. Mick hasn't done anything since he left the Stones that he couldn't have done in his spare time with the band. He just said he wanted to do his own thing. Mick Taylor is an admirable gentleman and a beautiful guitar player, but I don't think he knew what he was good at and what he wasn't." Asked why he left, Taylor had oscillated between "I don't know" and "They couldn't afford me." Actually, the mystery of Mick Taylor's defection from the Stones was transparently simple: He was convinced that the band wouldn't last for more than another year and thought it was better to leave them while they were still hot rather than wait until they fizzled out.

The Great Guitarist Hunt began in January 1975, and it took Richards until early April to find the appropriate replacement. He knew it was going to be a lot more difficult to replace Taylor than it had been to replace Jones. But he was confident about what he could do. He told the American rock journalist Barbara Charone: "It doesn't matter about the B.B. Kings, Eric Claptons, and Mick Taylors, 'cause they do what they do—but I know they can't do what I do. They can play as many notes under the sun, but they can't hold that rhythm down, baby. Everything I do is strongly based on rhythm 'cause that's what I'm best at. I've tried being a great guitar player and, like Chuck Berry, I have failed."

His shopping list included: the sixties veteran Jeff Beck; Mick Ronson, newly unemployed since the breakup of Mott the Hoople; Peter Frampton; his old nemesis Ry Cooder; Rory Gallagher; and the proto-Rolling Stone Geoff Bradford.

The guitarists were put up at the Munich Hilton, where Ron Wood joined them as an "observer." The competition was tense. An American guitarist named Nils Lofgren, who would release an unfortunate but well-meaning song that same year called "Keith Don't Go," wanted to try out for the band. According to Wood, Richards answered his request by saying, "Oh, yeah? How much you gonna pay me for an audition?"

"I was stuck between a rock and a hard place really," Ron Wood recalled. "I didn't want to dump the Faces and I didn't want to leave the Stones in the lurch, but the Stones said, 'Well, it's a shame we can't have you, Woody, but put your thinking cap on and see if you can come up with anybody who would be right for the band.' I was thinking, 'Me! It's me!'"

After listening to this steady parade of auditioners, Keith hit upon the American sessions musician who had played on albums by such noted artists as Bob Marley, Wayne Perkins. "Nothing clicked until the last day, when Wayne Perkins walked in, and he was a fantastic guitar player. I sort of cultivated him." From February 16 until the end of the month Richards rehearsed with Perkins at the Wick.

On March 22, Keith flew to Munich, having pretty much made up his mind to choose Perkins, but Wayne had two drawbacks: He was an American and Keith saw the Rolling Stones as a London rock band, and he played too much like Mick Taylor. "There's a couple of tracks on *Black and Blue* with Wayne Perkins, who plays very similar to Mick Taylor in that the way we play together, one played rhythm, the other lead," he said. "That's cut and dried, there's no mixing."

On March 30, Ron Wood flew to Munich to help out with the sessions. "I had Perkins living with me for over a month," Richards remembered. "He came to Munich as the Stones' guitar player. But Mick felt that we should try out somebody else—Harvey Mandel. Then Ronnie Wood walked in, and any other consideration just collapsed. We just had to own up that we were an English rock and roll band, and not just English, but London. That's why Ronnie and I burst into gales of laughter at a certain word. Those little things become such a big advantage on the road.

"It was so obvious to me that Ronnie should be in the Stones. The only reason he didn't join earlier is that nobody wanted to be the reason for the Faces breaking up. After playing with Mick Taylor for four years, I had almost gotten used to the Stones sound being myself and Mick Taylor's style. Woody and I can start playing together until we don't know who played the last lick. It's as close as that. We both become one instrument. You're in the other player's head and he's in yours, and you two are on this little mental plane where no one else is, trying to predict and guide and follow, all at the same time."

Not only did Ron fit into the band's image, but he already had a more dynamic relationship with Keith than Mick Taylor ever had. Keith and Ronnie played the same way Keith had played with

Brian, and their connection was similar, except that Richards was the senior partner, with Wood playing the frisky younger brother. In the spring of 1975, a whole new emotional engine began to run.

"Ronnie's very stupid but nice," Nick Kent concluded. "When Ronnie came in, Keith Richards had a real buddy, a guy that was like him and was a lesser version of him, but it was like he had a little buddy personality. And he was also, I hope you understand, exactly what Jagger wanted. Jagger was worried about Keith. Ron Wood was brought in as much as a mediator between Keith and Mick as he was a guitar partner for Keith."

18

Doo Doo Doo Doo Doo [Heartbreaker]
1975–1977

"White Powder" was a great story. That's where a guy has a friend who changes slowly as he takes this white powder. From a happy-go-lucky fellow, he becomes morose and, you know, *withdrawn*. Nobody sees him, until one day there's this foul black liquid starts dripping through the ceiling of his friend who lives below. They go up there and he's not to be found, you know. That's him. This black drip.

KEITH RICHARDS, *from an interview with Victor Bockris, 1977*

Richards's repeated convictions for heroin possession appeared to rule out any chance of his getting a visa to tour the U.S. Keith's attitude was simple: If you stick to the etiquette of drug taking and don't create a scene, what's the problem? "I've never turned blue in someone else's bathroom," he told a reporter proudly. "I mean, I consider that the height of bad manners."

Luckily for Keith, Mick Jagger had picked up more than just social graces from his privileged friends. He went to the United States ambassador to Britain, Walter Annenberg, whom he knew socially, to ask for his intercession. Not unmoved by the band's 1973 contribution to the U.S.-sponsored Pan American Development Fund as a result of a benefit concert they had played for earthquake victims in Managua, Nicaragua, Bianca's home city (and not indifferent to the millions of dollars a U.S. tour would generate), Annenberg helped arrange for Keith to get a visa so long as the U.S. embassy doctor in London could certify that there were no drugs in his bloodstream. The Stones were also helped by a new American lawyer, Bill Carter, who had been a Secret Service agent during the Kennedy and Johnson administrations, and by the changeover from Nixon's DEA-obsessed administration to the more relaxed era of Gerald Ford. Meanwhile, Keith flew to Switzerland to have his blood cleansed once again. As soon as the cure was over, he flew back to London to be examined at the American embassy, where it was determined that his blood was pure. He was granted a visa.

While Keith was looking for their new guitar player, Mick flew to America to make preparations for the tour, which was scheduled to take place June 1–August 8, 1975. America's music scene was in the doldrums. The punk explosion was still two years away from gaining national attention, and most other pop acts of the day were working in glitter rock or bubblegum modes. In the summer of 1975, John Denver, the Bee Gees, and the Captain and Tennille dominated the charts. Led Zeppelin, Aerosmith, and the Faces were the dominant touring bands. But even these legendary groups were overshadowed by the enormity of the Stones' influence. "I love the fucking Rolling Stones," said Aerosmith's singer, Steven Tyler. "Mick and Keith were the baddest boys on the block. Theirs was the hole I crawled out of." With the field wide open for a major player, the time was right for the Stones to storm the Western world's biggest market. Ron Wood, who officially remained a member of the Faces, signed on the tour for the bargain price of $250,000 (each founding Stone got $450,000).

Embarking on such a long, ambitious tour without putting out a new album, or at least a single, indicated a breakdown in the Jagger-Richards collaboration. The two were unwilling to release any of the tapes recorded for *Black and Blue* or left from earlier sessions. In the meanwhile, Allen Klein's Abkco Records was preparing to release an album of rejects, outtakes, and dubs, *Metamorphosis* (aka "Klein's Revenge"). As a result, the Stones put out a slapdash greatest-hits package, *Made in the Shade*, which reeked of rip-off. These albums represented an all-time low in Stones product. Ron Wood, whose second solo album, *Now Look* (also featuring Keith Richards), was released in June 1975, seemed to be the sole beneficiary of the tour publicity.

The '75 tour would make the poorly lit stages and unadorned performances of the sixties look like amateur night at the Apollo. Not to be outdone by Led Zeppelin or Elvis, Jagger and Charlie Watts designed a lotus-shaped stage. It would unfold to the strains of Aaron Copland's "Fanfare for the Common Man," revealing one Stone in each of its five petals, plus the successful session musician Billy Preston, wearing an enormous Afro wig, on keyboards, launching into the raunchy chords of "Honky Tonk Women." During the show Jagger would soar over the heads of his fans on a rope like Tarzan of the Apes. At the show's climax a twenty-foot-long inflatable cock would erupt from the floorboards.

For transportation, the Stones hired the luxurious *Starship*, a Boeing 707 fitted out with a bar, telephones, a television, and enough room to carry the key members of their entourage as well as any important guests. Their days of wrecking hotel rooms and throwing TV sets out windows over, the Stones simply acquired rooms in which they could most efficiently continue to work in between concerts on honing down the shows, composing new material, keeping in touch with their many contacts, and recharging their batteries. For this they required tight security, twenty-four-hour-a-day room service, and insulation from noise-weary guests. In most cases they rented entire floors of hotels, sealing them off by stationing security men at the elevators, at exits, and, in many cases, outside the suites of Richards and Jagger.

Richards fought with Jagger and road manager Peter Rudge over the theatricals. He wanted to keep the show stark and simple. Jagger, Rudge thought, felt naked next to Keith and so he needed a lot of props. Keith would say, "Let's go on stage with a couple of lights."

Despite Jagger and Rudge's precautions, when the band arrived in New York in late May rumors abounded that the police of several cities were preparing to hassle Richards. It was not an easy thing to be in hostile territory while you were hooked on junk. For this reason alone Richards needed extra-heavy security. Paranoid about legal authorities, Keith feared the worst when, on the night of his arrival, two large men banged on the door of his New York hotel suite. Keith told Tony Sanchez that the men "identified themselves as FBI agents and flashed their cards. Keith expected them to rip his belongings apart—'pray God they won't try to unscrew the shaving foam or the pen,' he thought—but they settled down in easy chairs."

According to Richards, the men told him that the car manufacturer sponsoring the tour knew he was a heroin addict and feared that if he was arrested the company would lose its investment. Consequently, they explained that they would be supplying him with pharmaceutical heroin throughout the tour so that he wouldn't have to buy from anyone else. Apparently they were as good as their word and throughout the three-month tour Richards never had to worry about where his drugs were coming from.

The Stones extravaganza kicked off on June 1 in the heart of the Deep South, Baton Rouge, Louisiana. Before the show, birthday boy Ron Wood, who was twenty-eight that day and no stranger to the concert stage, was incredibly nervous. Keith and Ronnie ducked into a small side room designated for tuning their guitars. "The tune-up room is the psychotherapy area for the guitarists to get their shit together and loosen up," Ron explained. "It can get pretty funny in there. Keith and I always take the attitude that when we unplug ourselves in that tuning room and we go out there, we should try to keep the same private laugh, but with fifty thousand people watching." Then they gathered for the walk from the dressing room to the stage, during which the band merged like a football team stepping onto the field.

As the house lights went down and the keening notes of "Fanfare for the Common Man" filled the hall, an army of fans erupted into a cacophony of screams and stormed the stage. "As the first notes of 'Honky Tonk Women' cut through the haze, looking as if he didn't need make-up to look bizarre or sinister, Keith ground into the down-and-dirty opening chords," wrote *Rolling Stone* magazine's Chet Flippo. "The next song, 'All Down the Line,' led by Keith's savage metal attack, redeemed the Stones."

RON WOOD: "After the first couple of songs were out of the way we all breathed a sigh of relief. We winked at each other, shook hands, raised our glasses. Mick said, 'Great. Woody,' with a tinge of surprise in his voice."

IAN STEWART: "Keith was the best rock and roll guitar player there was, yet people didn't realize it because he didn't do a lot of solos. He always left gaps and he was great at tempos. When it came down to playing on stage, he was unbeatable. Keith always flogged himself to death on stage. He never coasted. You had to admire Keith in many ways on the '75 tour because he was so single-minded. He was really the pulse of the Stones, and he led the band and he'd never displayed any flashy guitar techniques or anything."

There was undoubtedly fresh energy in the new dynamics of what Richards called the Rolling Stones Mach III. "Ronnie began to make an important contribution to the Stones as soon he joined the 1975 tour," wrote Robert Palmer. "He brought energy and high spirits, a perpetual cockeyed grin, jokes and pranks—in short, a boyish, Faces-style sense of fun, something that had been in short supply among the Stones for some time. He was a sometimes inconsistent player; he was anything but slick. But like Keith, he was versatile, equally adept at simple, biting leads and slash-and-burn rhythm. And instead of assigning him lead or rhythm chores on each tune, Keith worked with him in the way he'd worked with Brian, practicing and experimenting, adding and discarding, figuring out two guitar parts that would complement each other by a time-consuming process of trial and error. Keith had to keep his eyes open to shape Ronnie's playing and cue him into chording or soloing, embellishing or laying back. Mick, who had unchallenged run of the stage since the midsixties, would suddenly find Woody outflanking him with a mad charge at the audience or sneaking up behind him and mugging. Bill Wyman couldn't even stand safely in his sacrosanct 'Ol' Stoneface' corner without Woody baiting him like a tourist teasing a beefeater. And Charlie found he had more leeway to create more rhythm patterns with Ronnie and Keith bouncing syncopated cross-rhythms off him from opposite ends of the stage. The Stones were having a good time on stage again."

"When I get to the mike and push and shove with Mick, I can see Keith in back laughing and going, 'What the fuck?'" Wood said. "But Keith knows it's gotta be done. If I didn't do all that goofing around he'd have to. And he hates that."

"This band is less slick and sophisticated-sounding than the other one at its best when everybody was in tune and could hear each other," said Richards. "This is a lot funkier, dirtier, and rougher and a lot more exciting."

BILL WYMAN: "Woody had a tough baptism when we began the three-month American tour two weeks after he joined. He became an in-between for Keith to relate to everyone else in the band, and a bridge between Mick and Keith. He kept everybody cheerful."

Typical of Wood's attitude was the night he swaggered up to the microphone at an L.A. show and blurted out, "They're a great rock and roll band, aren't they? I wish I was playing with them," but when he was on the ball enough to realize he was part of the band, he was genuinely in love with the idea.

RON WOOD: "The Stones bring out the best in me. I am something of a mediator with the Stones. I guess that I am able to be objective, and to complement each member. Sort of play the Henry Kissinger role. I do take a lot of credit for the Stones' survival. I know I gave those guys a kick in the pants. I became someone Mick could bounce off on stage—figuratively and literally! And I gave the whole unit an objective ear to sound ideas off."

Wood also threw another twist into the Richards-Jagger collaboration. Jagger may have welcomed him as a bridge to Richards, but elements of jealousy remained. The photographer Annie Leibovitz, who covered the tour for *Rolling Stone* magazine, reflected that the love-hate relationship between Mick and Keith was what created their music: "Mick Jagger became very feminine. He seemed like the girl on the tour. It seemed romantic at the time, but in the long run it got sort of ugly . . ." Another observer, movie producer Julia Phillips, came upon Keith and Mick at a party in their hotel sitting on the floor between two beds strumming guitars. "They hung pretty tight, forming a freaky little unit, but there was something peaceful about the scene. They spoke to each other through their instruments."

As Richards passed through the season in which his image as the outlaw junkie prince reached its apotheosis, his fans watched him with the fascination of a circus crowd waiting for the tightrope walker to fall—and miss the net. Many fans admired "Keef Riffhard" because he represented the "fuck you" outlaw they fantasized about being. Asked about his health by one journalist who echoed the concerns of his followers, Keith replied, "I couldn't possibly do what I do on stage if I didn't take care of myself ... I'm very grateful for people that worry about me and all, but it's really a waste of time. I've got it under control. Anybody who worries about me really shouldn't. They should worry about themselves."

Each member of the band had a full-time roadie who was on stage behind the amps to make sure each musician's instrument was perfectly maintained and available—Keith traveled with sixteen guitars—and to provide whatever substances might be necessary during the show. Great lines of powder were laid out on top of the speakers that lined the back of the stage. Since the members of the audience sat below stage level, they couldn't see them. Because of Keith's varied menu, some of the lines contained cocaine, others heroin.

Yet to some people in the audience Keith did not appear to be in very good shape at all. In one show, during "Happy," his voice was very subdued as he sang, and Mick's backing vocal drowned out Keith as he screamed "Happy, happy." When Mick put his hand on Keith's shoulder, Richards nearly collapsed. Jonathan Cott, previously a critical champion of the band, derided the shows: "What all this ceremonious cakewalk finally disclosed was simply that behind the incantation, the gesture, the charm, lay ... nothing. The spirits did not rise. The final mystery was there was no mystery."

The consensus of critical opinion was expressed by Jim Miller in *Newsweek*: "The Stones became the seventies' most glamorous gladiators ... but the shows grew slick, the music slack. Here was rock royalty gone cynical, perhaps because they sensed they could coast on their past and titillate new fans by flaunting their celebrity—fabulously moneyed superstars with enough nasty habits and jet-set sidekicks to keep the gossip juicy."

The inflatable cock constantly drew the attention of the authorities, exasperating Keith. "It was a millstone around our neck. Police chiefs were waiting for it all over America. 'You blow that balloon up and we're gonna throw the whole damn bunch in jail.' It was like a dare."

"I absolutely draw the line at elephants," he declared when Rudge suggested they bring some on stage. "Even with trousers on! I am not working with animals; it's not in the bleeding contract and it's not going to be in the gig either. Go on stage with a bloody elephant? Are you mad? I've paid my dues. I'm not working with no animal act. I worked with Elton and that was enough!"

Keith had an exclusive buddy along on most of the tour. Freddie Sessler, a Pole who had escaped from the Nazis in 1940 and made his way to England, was some twenty years older than Keith. Sessler was, according to many people who knew him, a brilliant, creative entrepreneur who was always involved in something, whether it be hair weaving, flashing light bulbs, an unorthodox cure for muscular dystrophy, or building a hospital in Jamaica. Sessler at one time worked for Merck & Co. (which specialized in manufacturing pharmaceutical drugs such as methaqualone and cocaine for medical purposes). According to acquaintances, Sessler was known for his ability to procure high-grade drugs, although he claims never to have dabbled in smack and to have always been confident that, in time, Keith would kick it. ("Keith was always a man," he said.) A former associate of Billie Holiday, the well-off, well-read, and reportedly well-supplied Sessler was also well versed in Richards's favorite topics: the Second World War and music. On the American tour, Sessler shadowed Keith, flying from city to city at his own expense. "People associate me with drugs, which is a lot of bullshit," said Sessler, "because I was never into smack and I'm the only person he never asked to cop smack for him and he knows how much I suffered while he was doing smack." Speaking with a highly personalized syntax and a thick accent, he was the sort of wise prankster one often finds orbiting rock stars. Sessler played Falstaff to Keith's Prince Henry, the father figure Keith had long been without. Terry Hood, a woman who became close to Sessler in the late seventies, recalled that "Freddie played a very important role in Keith's life, and I knew that Keith knew Freddie loved him, he knows that he idolized him."

As the tour hit its midpoint in July, Keith started looking for adventure. Frustrated by his isolation in the Stones' cocoon as they traveled across the U.S., he determined to break out. On July 5, just as the *Starship* was about to fly out of Memphis en route to Dallas, Keith announced that he was going to drive to their next stop. On hearing the news, Peter Rudge threw a tantrum. "Everybody tried to talk Keith out of driving, saying there might be an accident or trouble," recalled Freddie Sessler. "But as anyone knows, it was very difficult to talk Keith out of anything."

Accompanied by Sessler, Ron Wood, and their British chief of security, Big Jim Callaghan, Richards rolled out of Memphis in a long black limousine with a cargo of Rebel Yell bourbon and headed for the hinterlands. Halfway through his journey, he pulled over at a hamburger joint in the tiny, ultraconservative town of Fordyce, Arkansas. Fifteen minutes later, they discovered that their car was surrounded by a crowd of teenagers. A local cop pulled up. Richards and Co. decided to hightail it, but as soon as their limo spun out of the gravel driveway onto the main road with smoke billowing out its windows, the cop pulled them over. Keith said he "bent down to change the wave band on the radio and the car swerved slightly. A police patrol vehicle then pulled out from a lay-by and stopped us. I was questioned about having a 'concealed weapon,' a penknife complete with tin opener and a device for removing stones from horses' hooves." Richards was arrested for possession of the "concealed weapon" and the police pried open the trunk of the car, where they allegedly discovered, among other things, cocaine. The entire party was escorted to the Fordyce jail.

The Stones' new, well-connected, Southern attorney, Bill Carter, sped to their rescue on a private plane with a briefcase containing fifty thousand dollars in cash (in case things got sticky). Outside the Fordyce jail the crowd grew to such proportions that the state police were called in. Within minutes of Carter's arrival in Fordyce, Richards and his men, having posted minimal bail, were escorted to the airstrip by the local police. (The charges were later dropped on a technicality.) A Stones aide welcomed them aboard their private plane with a bottle of whiskey. They arrived in Dallas having had a bracing day's fun. News services around the world carried the story that Keith Richards had once again eluded the law.

Keith's restlessness may have had something to do with the fact that he was without a woman. He couldn't take Anita on the tour—she caused too much trouble. He had wanted Uschi to come on the tour, but she had remained with her boyfriend Dieter in Munich. Uschi was still torn between the excitement around Keith and the more personally fulfilling relationship she had with Dieter. But halfway through she changed her mind. On July 15, Freddie Sessler arranged to fly her into San Francisco. However, being back on the road quickly reminded Uschi of the drawback of being a woman in what Bianca now called "the Nazi state." Just like Anita, Uschi complained that she and Keith were never alone. "It was very difficult to have a relationship with somebody who is hardly ever alone. There were all these hangers-on and so-called friends around and it really got on my nerves very much. One time in San Francisco we drifted to sleep and when I woke up there was a guy lying like a dog across our feet. And Keith would never throw these people out."

Uschi, who enjoyed taking drugs, also feared that she too would become victim to the touring life-style as a long line of women had done before her. Consequently, when Dieter called a week later, said he was leaving for Asia in two days, and asked her to join him, she decided to go. She made her swift departure while she and Keith were in a Chicago hotel room. Having been up for days, he was crashed out. "I wanted to tell him I was leaving," she remembered, "but I couldn't wake him up. So I just left a note."

By the time the Stones concluded the tour, on August 8 in Buffalo in front of eighty thousand people, they had played forty-five shows in twenty-seven cities in ten weeks, netted thirteen million dollars, and generated about twenty-seven million dollars in receipts, which translated into a net profit of about three million dollars for the Stones. And Keith wanted to keep playing.

RICHARDS: "I haven't been on a tour yet where I was bored. At the end of that tour we began to look around for dates, because for us it's just starting to get good. Because this is a brand-new band for us. It's got a lot more fire. The last band was too intellectual. There ain't a band in the world that can survive without going on the road. If a band doesn't play in front of people and turn them on at least as much as we do, and I don't think we do it enough, then they're not a band. You rehearse for a month, get the tour going, crank it up, and just as you're hitting top gear the last gig comes and it drops for nine months."

*

Richards was at an emotional crossroads. Although he was to pursue Uschi for the next six months, he would neither see nor hear from her again for eight years. His relationship with Anita seemed to have reached an impasse. During the tour she had been deported from Jamaica for a second time, so it was almost impossible for him to live on the island unless he spent his time without her. However, that August he met her in L.A., where, in a final attempt to pull their relationship back together, she became pregnant.

In January 1976, Keith and Anita were in Geneva awaiting the birth of their third child. Anita couldn't stop using cocaine and heroin, and Keith moved her into the Geneva clinic where the doctors were understanding for a thousand dollars a day. The child was born on March 26. They called him Tara (after Brian Jones's friend Tara Browne, who had died in 1966) Jo Jo Gunne (after a song about a meddlesome monkey by Chuck Berry).

According to Anita, Keith was so euphoric over the birth that he decided they should get married. Soon he was making elaborate plans to have a rock wedding that would put Mick's nuptials to Bianca to shame. It was even rumored that, just like Hank Williams, he would get married on stage. So enamored was Keith of Anita and the new baby that when the Rolling Stones met in the south of France to rehearse for the April–June 1976 European tour, Keith delayed his departure from Switzerland. "He was always somebody who welcomed another kid," remembered Sandro Sursock. "When he was there he took care of the baby a lot."

On April 20, one and a half years after *It's Only Rock 'n Roll*, the album *Black and Blue* was finally released to an expectant public. It was measured against David Bowie's *Station to Station*, Dylan's *Desire*, and the Ramones' first album, and would go to number one in the U.S. and number two in the U.K. In the true spirit of Andrew Oldham, the United States release of *Black and Blue* got more attention for its publicity campaign than its music. A giant billboard on the Sunset Strip in Hollywood featured a bruised woman in ripped silk underwear with her wrists bound above her head, under the caption "I'm black and blue from the Rolling Stones and I love it." (S & M was popular in the U.S. in 1976.) In response a group of American women formed an organization called Women Against

Violence Against Women, which tried to persuade record companies and rock groups to tone down their biggest selling point, misogyny. Keith, who saw himself as a great protector of women, defended the ad. "Goddamn it, a large percentage of American women wouldn't be half as liberated if it wasn't for the Rolling Stones in the first place, and people like us. They'd still be believing in dating, rings, and wondering whether it was right to be kissed on the first date or not. I thought it was quite funny. Trouble is, not many people have the same sense of humor—especially institutions. Individually, some people may have a sense of humor, but as part of an institution they have difficulty translating it into the proper perspective. So they just end up like another load of protest marchers with bees in their bonnets and don't realize how funny they look." The ensuing furor generated more interest than the music, but it made the Stones appear relevant once again.

Musically the album was an even bigger disappointment than *Goats Head Soup* and *It's Only Rock 'n Roll*. Lester Bangs summed up the critical reaction: "There are two things to be said about the new Stones album before closing time. One is that they are still perfectly in tune with the times (ahead sometimes, trendies) and the other is that the heat's off, because it's all over, they don't really matter anymore or stand for anything, which is certainly lucky for both them and us. I mean, it was a heavy weight to carry for all concerned. This is the first meaningless Stones album, and thank God." With *Black and Blue* the Stones finally lost touch with a large part of their audience, which had been with them since the beginning. At the same time, as had been customary in the 1970s, they gained a larger new segment via the top ten single "Fool to Cry." At the time Keith told everyone he loved the record. Later he realized that the talented session musicians, such as Billy Preston, whom the Stones relied on throughout the midseventies, had taken over the direction of the band, resulting in what Keith referred to as a lot of "compromised tracks."

RICHARD LLOYD (guitarist for the group Television): "First heroin takes you inward. It opens up this incredible vista, and then it completely fucking rots you inside until all that's left is the shell. And you find that you're no longer creative. There's a hollowness to your attempts to recapture that glory. In my personal view those midseventies albums, from *Goats Head Soup* to *Black and Blue*, they have that hollowness in a way that's painful for me to hear. Because you hear the yearningness, you hear the honest attempt, but you also hear the flat falling. You hear the parameters within which you're now trapped."

With his skeletal frame and pasty, gaunt skull offset by charred black eyes beneath a helicopter-blade haircut, Keith looked as if he might fall over at any minute throughout the April–June European tour. But when he skidded across the stage and fell flat on his ass ("laughed my bollocks off!") on opening night in Frankfurt, he kept on playing. And on another night in Germany when he fell asleep on stage during one of his least favorite songs, "Fool to Cry," he woke himself up with his foot, which was on the volume pedal. In the audience, Nick Kent flashed, "There was just nobody home." Ian Stewart added that as Keith lost it, so did the band. "When things didn't go so well, Mick had a sour expression on his face," said Ron Wood, "and Keith would give you a look that said, 'Your life has been a complete waste of sperm and egg.'" Technically these were among the worst shows of the Stones' career.

NICK KENT: "After the gig they'd go off to these fancy Jaggeresque restaurants and Richards's dealers would come in like headbangers in fur coats. They might as well have had 'I am a dealer' written on their backs. Keith would open the drugs on a plate while waiters would hover around him, and snort cocaine. He would just brandish this stuff. 'OK, I'm a drug user, fuck you! What are you going to do about it?' That was always his thing. Rudge was going haywire. Eventually he just gave up. I was supposed to write something, but I got so fucked up on heroin because it was everywhere. I was an addict but I didn't even buy any. I just went backstage. There was this whole room with six or seven dealers in it. At one point Rudge even delegated me. He said, 'Can you keep these people in that room?' That was what '76 was like, every fucking night."

Apart from their making less money, what made playing Europe so different from playing America was the constant crossing of the borders.

RICHARDS: "Just to move from A to B was a major thing. I knew I was going to be dragged off into a room and given the third degree. The going to court in a tie and trying to explain to your own solicitors and barristers—this total noncommunication about why you're doing this in the first place. Also, the total duplicity of the authorities. The setups, the frame-ups, the goddamned grasses [informers], the snitches. That's an education in itself.

"You're being harassed from every quarter and it becomes a war. Wherever you went, you were subject to the same controls, the same body searches, and you took it as a matter of a grind, and eventually when you got cocky enough you'd still walk out carrying, because they're so bad at their job, and you'd get off on that. But it's a minor victory. Because eventually, of course, they're going to get you. You can't fight authority on a worldwide level. Because all they want to do is slap little Johnny behind the ears to show him he ain't so great, and diminish whatever phony power you had. Biff! The prefect comes along . . . 'Take that, you swine!' All that crap.

"Of course, what I had has a certain appeal to people—everybody would have liked to have lived like that once in a while if they could, to be able to do that 'Fuck you!' thing. But the romantic myth that applied was not very romantic to me. I had to go through it."

Ahmet Ertegun's godson, Julio Santo Domingo, spent some time on the '76 tour:

JULIO SANTO DOMINGO: "Everybody was concerned that because of the heroin Keith might not be able to play—and at the same time it was the heroin that allowed it. Keith without heroin was an impossibility, it wasn't considered. It was assumed that the smack focused his creativity in the way it expressed itself. Mick was really very cool with Keith at the time, and they were much closer, sitting side by side and snorting lines. It was very animal-like. That was when Keith was most like his image, the drugged-out junkie. Promoters had horrible times finding a doctor or the right smack. Keith would say, 'If I don't get this I'm not going on.' The whole show would be delayed an hour and everybody would be pissed off. Bill was always pissed off and Charlie would be pissed off. And with Keith in one of his moods, you didn't want to get in the way.

Marlon was just a little kid running around with a water gun. He was very wild about everything and he apparently ruled Keith. If Marlon would say, 'Let's go to the movies,' then they would go to the movies. But he never shot the water gun at the coke or the smack. It was a really heavy time for everything and everybody. In back of all this is Bianca, which meant there was also a very social connection."

On the night of May 19, after an appalling concert in Stafford, England, Richards decided to drive back to London in the middle of a raging storm rather than stay in a hotel with the rest of the band. Roaring down the M1 in the Blue Lena at his customary 100 mph with six-year-old Marlon and several friends aboard, he nodded out, missed a turn, and veered off the highway through a barrier into a field. After checking that nobody was hurt, he got rid of his drugs. In a daze, he forgot to throw out a silver necklace with a small snorting tube and coke spoon on it. He was also carrying, perhaps without knowing it, some LSD. The police put him through a strip search and held him overnight before letting him go. By the time Keith returned to London on the evening of May 20, he was seriously in need of heroin and a needle. But the real problem was that he had no time to stop and take stock. He was playing Earls Court in London that night. The tour continued, if anything bolstered by the outlaw publicity that attended Richards's every brush with the authorities.

By the time the band arrived in Paris for three nights at Les Abattoirs, June 4–6, it looked as if everybody had gone mad.

JULIO SANTO DOMINGO: "The guy who was organizing everything in France was Freddie Hauser [a cameraman and friend of Keith's]. The typical evening would be to go to the show and then there was some party somewhere and then back to the Royal hotel, where there would always be another party going, and then around six or seven in the morning they'd all watch a video of the night's performance. Keith was so strong he just went on and on, and the people would nod out in shifts.

"Everything was so well taken care of with the police. Their lawyer, who is dead now, was Michael Fellicier, one of the blue-chip lawyers, very influential. They always managed to have incredibly good people. The net was there but they had so much overflow, and it was the overflow that got them into trouble."

NICK KENT: "It was very weird. Jagger, Wood, and Richards were all going off and doing vast amounts of drugs. By that time the heroin abuse had got so bad even the roadies would come in and score. I mean, it was really just incredible, it was heroin city. A jealous boyfriend tried to pull a gun on Jagger backstage. Everything was on edge. You just thought, 'Well, these guys don't give a fuck.' Even I wondered what the fuck they were doing. It seemed obvious that someone was going to get really fucked over because of the drug chaos, it was so open and overt. Richards had this reputation and he knew what he was playing with. He was just lost in a drug fog and he needed to be recalled and if it took the stakes getting up to his freedom, then so be it. At the same time I thought that Keith's subconscious was saying to him, 'OK, I need a big situation to stop 'cause I like this stuff too much.' He always faced things pretty head-on." Jagger continually refused to touch heroin and remained free of addiction, until he gave up drugs completely.

And then, as if on cue, the worst of all tragedies struck Anita and Keith. While Keith had been looning about Europe, Anita had moved back into their house in Geneva with Tara. On the morning of June 6, when the baby was only ten weeks old, Anita discovered that he had choked to death in his crib. In a panic she called Sandro Sursock, who rushed over to her house, but by the time he got there it was obvious that the baby was dead. Sandro called Keith in Paris. Four hours later Keith called Sandro back, pumped up on drugs, and started raving that they were all going to fly back and Billy Preston was going to play the organ at the funeral. "Are you crazy?" Sandro replied. "No, no, no, no, please don't come back, don't do anything."

"It was a big tragedy," he said, "and a difficult time. Nobody knew what to do. Anita was devastated and so was Keith and I figured it would be better if they could be together." As Anita, Dandelion, and her nanny headed for Paris, Sandro and another friend, Claude Nobbs, arranged the burial procedures, while in Paris, Marlon expressed concern over what was going to happen to the two hamsters he had left in the Geneva house.

RICHARDS: "I felt guilty for not being there. Little chap in his cot—'Daddy'll be back in a couple of months, he's going on the road, soon you'll find out what it's all about' All of that to be born for eight weeks. Well, eight weeks is a lifetime. You actually block it out. He comes to my mind in the weirdest places. I just remember his chuckling . . ."

Despite Keith's grief, the band still played their third Paris concert that night. He was particularly smacked out, but since he customarily used his guitar playing as an emotional outlet that June 6 show was really something. In fact, it was so good that all the tracks on the live album of the tour, *Love You Live*, were taken from this single show. His playing, particularly on "Midnight Rambler," was unusually intense.

NICK KENT: "I really thought Keith and Anita were going to die. I'd seen him in bad states but they were crying and literally carrying each other out after the gig that night . . . I mean, Keith is a bright guy and a sensitive guy, but he was taking such large amounts of that drug that they killed his conscience. I think that Tara's death made him understand it morally. 'We're going to shit. My family's fallin' apart. I'm goin' to jail.' When you're a drug addict you know you're going to hell in certain ways, but you know you can't really stop it. There's this terrible feeling of impotence."

After twenty-four hours mourning in seclusion, Richards had to return to the fray. On June 9 the British police confirmed that they had discovered the residue of cocaine in the snorting tube they had confiscated from him on May 19, and they pressed charges of unlawful possession. A trial was scheduled. There were still concerts to be played in France, Spain, Switzerland, and Germany. On June 18 the news of his son's death was finally released to the press.

"He was anguished, of course, but there was a deeper desperation about him these days—a feeling that the drugs that had blackened and rotted his teeth were blackening and rotting his skeleton, burning him out inside as Brian had been burned out," wrote Tony Sanchez. "Death seemed to be shuffling out of the mist toward Keith, coming into sharper perspective. He was passionate to spend every moment that was left to him with Marlon . . . Very like Brian to look at, [Marlon] shared Keith's every hotel suite, barstool and dressing room. There was something curiously knowing in the child's . . . eyes. He had seen too much of the groupies, the junkies, the drunks. At an early age he had to learn to recognize the false flatterers who tried to use him to charm their way into his father's life."

Keith and Anita never returned to Switzerland. Claude Nobbs, who was in charge of moving all of their stuff back to London, asked a mutual friend to clean up before the movers came. He found more than fifty grams of cocaine, fifty grams of heroin, and hashish in industrial quantities, as well as some five hundred used syringes, scattered about the premises. "After Tara's death," Sandro Sursock recalled, "I didn't see Keith again for nine years."

NICK KENT: "I had stayed away from the relationship between Keith and Anita because Anita made me uncomfortable. She was an incredible woman but there was something disturbing about her. She liked to mess with people. Her attitude was 'Come into my web and we'll play a little game,' and Keith wasn't into that. Keith loved Anita, but then he reached a point where I really feel he realized, 'Baby, I can't carry you anymore, you've gone crazy.'"

ANITA PALLENBERG: "Keith was very calm and very protective and very normal and loving. He just said, 'Forget it.' And everybody else told me the same thing. They all said, 'Forget it. Look after your other children.' I am sure that the drugs had something to do with it. And I always felt very, very bad about the whole thing."

19
Sing Me Back Home
1977

I'm just a bloody embarrassment to them now, all because some poxy Mountie from the airport decides he wants to make a name for himself. I don't know what the scam was. There were so many irregularities in what happened that it really is just so impossible to talk about. It's nothing to do with justice or legalities, you know what I mean? It's just pure politics.

KEITH RICHARDS, *from an interview with Victor Bockris, 1977*

Tara wasn't the only victim of Anita and Keith's life-style. Marlon didn't appear to be in great shape either. Aside from missing school, he showed a real streak of violence. "Marlon used to be a little sadist," Nick Kent remembered. "I mean, he'd become like a little psychopath. Everyone was thinking Marlon would go bad." Keith, however, had a different view of his son, whom he had come to rely on almost exclusively for emotional support.

RICHARDS: "He took care of me while I was doing heroin on the road. He used to be my roadie when he was five and six and seven. He's seen everything. To him it's not a big deal. It's just something Dad did. But we keep together and we love each other."

When Marlon wasn't taking care of Keith, he was kept at bay with wads of money that only served to surround him with mounds of lifeless toys. But even if Marlon thrived on the excitement of life on the road, Dandelion did not. Anita recalled how much Dandelion suffered. "On the road she used to go off by herself, pick up guys, bring them back—'Mommy, here!' Big guys. And I'd really get scared. And she'd go out of the hotel room and I'd find her sitting on the lap of somebody. That's why I decided not to have her on the road anymore."

Back in London both Keith and Anita hit rock bottom. Keith was spending hours alone in the bathroom taking heroin and strumming his guitar. "I suffered a bad bout of depression after the baby died and I wasn't able to cope with Dandelion," Anita recalled about that painful time. "I couldn't handle her." Dandelion was shipped off to Doris in Dartford, where she would be brought up just like Keith. She would never live with her father again. "I couldn't put a four-year-old through that. It wasn't fair," Keith said. "Her mother and I were going to court every day and it looked like we might get sealed away. So she went to live with my mum."

While Richards was fermenting, a series of fresh young bands was forming, fueled by a burning, focused nihilism; they would be united under the banner of punk rock in the second half of the decade. The bridge between old and new rock was a visual replica of the Stones called the New York Dolls, who flourished between 1971 and 1975. Their lead singer, David Johansen, bore a remarkable resemblance to Jagger, and their lead guitarist, Johnny Thunders, was a camp cartoon version of Richards, whom he worshiped. Another transitional figure, Iggy Pop, declared that Keith Richards was his "all-time idol," and would dedicate his autobiography to him. The new movement exploded onto the scene between 1976 and 1978, spearheaded by the Sex Pistols, the Clash, and the Damned in the U.K. and the Ramones, Blondie, Television, and Talking Heads in the U.S. The movement nurtured the seeds of working-class rebellion, with a punk philosophy that was antisuperstar and antiestablishment. Many of them wore spiked hair, Nazi paraphernalia, and emblems of self-mutilation, such as safety pins stuck through flesh. Their theatrical method and symbols assaulted conventional notions of morality and sentimentality. They also sought to destroy the barriers between performer and audience. Often deliberately off-key and unpolished, their songs were fast, short, loud, and, in the case of the best of them, as good and invigorating as the Stones had been in their early days.

In an interview in New York, Jagger revealed his fears that the Stones had, in the haze and glitter of stardom, lost touch with the garage sound that had brought them fame.

MICK JAGGER: "Rock and roll is this child of sawdust, so to speak, in the horrible clubs where people are being sick, and this great blue jeans and leather jackets and stuff. So when you take it out of that element, which is very vital and still exists, you're in danger of losing a lot of it. So you come on, you change it around, and it becomes like a faggot, it loses its thing. Not that I have anything against faggots, I don't mean faggots, I mean it loses all its butchness and simplicity, which is the main vital force. And there's very little else in it."

As if predicting the birth of punk rock, Jagger continued, "Whatever [the next big thing in music] is, it will come from nowhere and take everything by storm. It will be as new, as unexpected, and as shocking as we were."

The Sex Pistols signed a lucrative contract with EMI and were immediately recognized as an important phenomenon within the music industry. "The Sex Pistols are the new people knocking at the door," wrote Nick Mobbs in *Melody Maker*. "They're knocking the Stones: the Stones are establishment to them. I think this particular group have a wider significance in that they are the start of a wave."

This blank generation, as Richard Hell labeled it, was particularly pissed off at the Rolling Stones. The Sex Pistols, whose methodology was transparently similar to that of the Stones (particularly in the Andrew Oldham-like figure of their manager, Malcolm McLaren), led the attack "Groups like the Stones are revolting," spat lead singer Johnny Rotten. "They have nothing to offer the kids anymore." Bassist Sid Vicious put the boot in, snapping, "I wouldn't piss on Keith Richards if he was on fire." However, according to the Pistols' songwriter, Glen Matlock, in their early days they "were so into the Faces, they'd go down to Richmond, to Sir John Mills's old house, which Ron Wood had just bought. Keith Richards used to stay in the little cottage at the bottom of Ron's garden. Steve [Jones, the Pistols' guitarist] and others would get in there, rifle around it, have a go on one of Keith's guitars, nick a shirt, and leave a note saying, 'Steve was here.'"

But Richards wasn't as removed from punk as some bands liked to think. Musically, he was written into the fabric of every major punk song. "If you actually follow the guitar sound through modern rock music, the sound you'll always hear is Keith," attested the rock historian Clinton Heylin. "You would expect it to influence the late-sixties American mainstream bands, or to influence T. Rex and glitter and glam in the early seventies, but at exactly the same point in time it influenced the whole underground. The Velvet Underground were doing an American version of the Rolling Stones. The Sex Pistols were totally anti-Stones but by being that they were, of course, the negative reflection of the Stones. They played like the Stones and had the Stones image. The Clash said, 'No more Rolling Stones in 1977,' and yet Mick Jones was fixated on Keith. And then when rock merged during the new wave and all came back together again, it's actually that Keith Richards sound you hear."

"I played with the Sex Pistols six months before Lydon, and all of them were totally obsessed with Richards," recalled Nick Kent. "Malcolm McLaren took us all when Keith Richards did that gig in London with Ronnie Wood on the *I've Got My Own Album to Do* tour in 1974. Keith Richards's influence on these guys was incredible. All those punk bands loved Keith Richards, they fucking idolized him. People would get down and kiss his ring."

Over in New York, where Keith was spending more time than he was in London, the feeling was much different. "I never put much stock in anything anybody in the English music scene said," recalled Richard Lloyd. "The Rolling Stones were the original world people. How can you say they're boring old farts? But Keith does get criticized. He gets criticized, for instance, for being sloppy. He's not sloppy, he's incredibly elegant, and at times he's rugged like a cliff. He's one of the first people using the electric guitar who understood that rhythm guitar is like sex—it's sustained drive.

"The criticism of Keith with respect to the punk scene is just misaligned. He was totally encouraging. He also has a certain sense of competitiveness. It was funny. He would say, 'Well, you may find success and I wish you all the best. You're going to be large . . . but you'll never be as big . . . as huge as we are.' One day his mother, who was wonderful, was there. She's a smallish woman but she also struck me as that kind of English rock. She said, 'I hear you're a musician. Well, you'll never achieve the kind of success my brilliant Keith has.'"

RICHARDS: "In punk rock there was a certain spirit, but I don't think there was anything there new musically, or even from the PR point of view, imagewise. There was too much image and none of the bands were given enough time to put their music together, if they had any. It seemed to me the least important thing. It was more important if you puked over somebody, you know? But that's a legacy from us also. After all, we're still the only rock and roll band arrested for peeing on a wall [as they had been in a highly publicized 1964 bust]. They really seemed to hate bands like the Stones. That's what we used to say about everything that went before us. But you need a bit more than just putting down people to keep things together. There's always somebody better at putting you down. So don't put me down, just do what I did, you know? Do me something better, turn me on."

In retrospect, the challenge of the punks catalyzed a rebirth in the Stones. At the same time the Sex Pistols were getting their record deal, the Stones' record contract was on the auction block and, despite the band being under attack from the punks for being "boring old farts" and "irrelevant dinosaurs," it was potentially worth something in the area of a fifteen-million-dollar advance. To ensure the figure, and possibly kick it up a notch, Jagger had come up with the idea of putting together a double live album highlighted by a side of R&B and reggae classics performed in a small club like the ones they used to play when music was the only thing they all cared about. Three sides of the album would be taken from the Paris concert the night Tara died. The club side was to be recorded over five nights in a dive called the El Mocambo in Toronto.

Jagger had chosen to record in Toronto because it was near New York, from which he could continue to negotiate the new contract; because it presented no visa problems, since Canada was a member of the British Commonwealth; and because it was far enough from the mainstream for the Stones to avoid mass hysteria. The whole idea depended on the Stones coming in quietly, having a week of rehearsals, pulling off the surprise club recording dates, and then splitting before news of the engagement brought on the deluge of media attention.

But when the Rolling Stones assembled in the Harbour Castle Hilton in downtown Toronto on February 20, 1977, they discovered that Mr. Redlands, as Richards was listed on his reservation, was not there. When phone calls were placed to England, it was ascertained that Keith was bunkered down at Redlands with Anita and Marlon.

Inside Redlands, Barbara Charone, who was writing Richards's authorized biography, was visiting, and she recorded the way Anita tore into him. "'I haven't been fucked in months!' she screamed. 'Is television more important than me?'

"'You think you're Superman, don't you? Well, you're only Superman when you play the guitar. You think you can handle drugs but you can't. I know what I am and I've been that way for seven years.' She continued, 'You pretend you don't have a drug habit. You simply go upstairs to the bathroom. You think people don't know. You're no different than anyone else. You can't handle drugs either.' Silently Richards continued to stare at the television. If you looked closely, you could see his eyes filled with water."

The Stones' machinery was standing by—vans to carry equipment and luggage, cars to ferry Keith to the airport, around-the-clock assistants and drug suppliers—but nobody could get through to him. Finally, the Stones sent him a telegram: WE WANT TO PLAY. YOU WANT TO PLAY. WHERE ARE YOU?

Four days later, on February 24, Keith, Anita, Marlon, and twenty-eight pieces of luggage departed on a British Airways flight from London to Toronto. Halfway through the flight, Keith got up, went to the toilet to take another shot, and remained in there for three hours. When he returned to his seat and chucked the burnt spoon he'd used to cook the heroin into her bag, he neglected to mention it. Anita thought the flight attendant looked alarmed but didn't tell Keith. "I don't know why he did it. Sometimes I wonder if he did it expressly, but we never talked about that. Our communication level was so completely disrupted that my fears and all those things, I didn't speak them out." Between them they were carrying two grams of heroin and cocaine.

Considering how tightly organized the Stones' operation usually was, Richards might have realized something was wrong when there were no official Stones representatives at Toronto International Airport to ease his way through customs, but he was so lost in a fog he thought the men swarming over his suitcases *were* Stones security people. As it turned out, they were customs men. The inspection turned up a small piece of hashish, which Anita had forgotten about, mixed in with some yeast pills, and the blackened spoon. The heroin and cocaine were not discovered. The spoon was held for analysis and the party was allowed to proceed.

Within twenty-four hours of arriving, Richards had acquired an ounce of heroin and five grams of cocaine. Anita thought that Keith arranged to have it mailed to him. That was his standard practice if he didn't have a reliable dealer wherever he was going. "I've never actually spoken about this, but that's what I heard," she said later, "that Keith had actually mailed some stuff and they'd found it. They actually were waiting for us, basically, you know. Now I don't know if Keith was aware of it, because we had done this in the past—I mean, we had sent parcels to different places . . . It's just one of those things you hope works out, you know . . ." Drugs in hand, Keith retired for one of his long, hibernationlike sleeps.

By February 28, relations among Keith, Anita, and the Rolling Stones had not pulled together. At one point during that day Anita was told that there were some men in the hotel looking for Keith, but she failed to alert either Keith or the Stones' security people. The Stones in turn failed to protect Keith. They knew he was under surveillance because of the airport search and yet, though it was by now common practice to have a Stones' security man outside the door of Richards's suite twenty-four hours a day, there was nobody guarding the suite that morning. It seemed as if someone had set a trap.

NICK KENT: "Someone had phoned down and said, 'We don't need you,' which considering the context of the situation didn't make sense. Richards was in a paranoid state of mind when he was busted, and because the actual bodyguards posted at the door were told, 'Don't be there,' he came to believe that someone in the Rolling Stones' organization had set him up."

When the police knocked on the door, Anita "thought it was Marlon, so I just opened it and the inevitable foot came in, and that was it. I kept on saying, 'I don't know nothing,' but they had the stuff there."

The fifteen members of the Royal Canadian Mounted Police found what they were looking for within minutes of entering the suite. The hard part was not finding the drugs, but waking Keith up. (Once in the late sixties he had been moved from New York to London while sound asleep!) They spent so much time slapping his cheeks to dredge him up, his cheeks, as he recalled, were "rosy."

RICHARDS: "I was awake. They said, 'You're under arrest.' Oh, great!

"What disappointed me was that none of them was wearing a proper Mounties uniform when they burst into my hotel room. They were all in anoraks with droopy mustaches and bald heads. Real weeds, the whole lot of them, all just after their picture in the paper. Fifteen of 'em round my bed, trying to wake me up. I'd have woken up a lot quicker if I'd seen the red tunic and Smokey Bear hat."

After interrogating Keith and Anita in separate rooms, the Mounties got the story out of Richards, who was in need of a shot and didn't want to mess about. The cops took him downtown and booked him on trafficking charges, which carried a sentence of seven years to life. No one in recent years had beaten that charge in Canada. They let him return to the hotel on nominal bail, but were not amused when he requested a couple of grams back until he could make other arrangements.

The Rolling Stones and the whole Rolling Stones organization were now incensed with Richards. Only six weeks earlier he had escaped a prison sentence in England with a stern warning that the next time he would be incarcerated in what he called "the big house." When he returned to the Harbour Castle Hilton, he found himself writhing on the floor of the bathroom, gagging and vomiting in agony, as he went through acute withdrawal.

As usual, celebrities flocked to the Stones camp, but in Toronto this had particularly dramatic repercussions. Prime Minister Pierre Trudeau and his wife, Margaret, were Canada's answer to the Kennedys. Trudeau had won the hearts of a generation when he met with John Lennon in 1971 and "Madcap Margaret" was cultivating a reputation in the press for disregarding executive protocol by smoking pot and eluding her Mountie escort whenever she could.

When Margaret heard the Rolling Stones were in town she attached herself to them like a limpet mine, taking up quarters in their hotel and partying with them flagrantly in the halls, drawing ten times more attention to Keith than he had already been attracting. A pampered, jet-set partygoer, she was just the sort of woman he despised.

Margaret Trudeau was about to check out of her room when she heard a "timid rattling on my door handle. Outside stood a skinny, pale little boy wearing a jogging suit. He was in tears. It was Marlon, Keith Richards' seven-year-old son. 'Where is everybody? Where are they?' he sobbed. 'Dad's lying on the floor crying. What shall I do?'

"I went with him up to the Stones' suite and found that Anita Pallenberg, Marlon's mother, was out shopping, and that Keith was indeed curled up on the floor in a fetus position, moaning. His case, for possession of heroin for trafficking, was due to come up the next day in court. Marlon and I dragged him off the floor, laid him as best we could on his bed, and I covered him with a blanket. I couldn't just abandon the child, so, clearing a space among the dirty plates, empty bottles and garbage that littered the room, I settled down on the floor to help him glue together a model airplane. He had a lot of very expensive toys he couldn't understand, intended for far older children."

When Ronnie Wood and Bill Wyman dropped by to check on his well-being, they found him in such poor condition that Bill feared he might die, and they rushed out to get him some heroin—a courageous thing to do, considering the hotel was jammed with undercover cops.

MARGARET TRUDEAU: "When Mick and the others came back we discussed what could be done for Keith. I was loath to get involved, but since I had good contacts with the various Canadian mental health associations I offered to find a psychiatrist who could at least give evidence for Keith at the trial. They were delighted, and, having phoned an acquaintance at the H.M.A., Penny and I went to Ward Island, the hippy community across the water from the hotel, to talk to friends who might be prepared to take in Marlon if both Keith and Anita had to go through a period of rehabilitation."

When she attempted to befriend him and Anita with some vague promise that he wouldn't have to go to jail, and an offer to take care of Marlon if he did, the little tyke snapped, "Fuck off!," the sign-off line he had become accustomed to using on all the creeps who tried to get to Keith through him.

The following day the world press featured the arrest in bold headlines. This time it looked almost certain that Keith would go to jail. The press, which had been baying at the heels of the Rolling Stones for fifteen years, closed in for the kill. Jagger's plan for a quiet, well-organized gig had once again been ruined by Richards's preference for "accidents."

Chet Flippo went to Toronto to interview Richards for *Rolling Stone*. "I had heard that Keith was slowly dying from his drug addiction and the Stones were desperate and depressed and they weren't happy with Keith," he wrote. Richards told him, "They are out to make rock and roll illegal. That's the basic drive behind the whole thing. They are just scared of that rhythm. Every sound has an effect on the body and the effects of a good backbeat makes these people shiver in their boots. So you are fighting some primeval fear that you can't rationalize."

"They've made me a much bigger media thing by pouncing on me all over the place," he told the American television interviewer Geraldo Rivera. "Who would know anything about me if it wasn't for all the publicity they get for themselves through me? It makes me wonder about the people they choose to go for. The reason they do it so much is because it's more interesting than busting Joe Bloggs of Number 43 Railway Cuttings. It's a turn-on for them, but for me it's like another gig."

On March 2, Jagger threw up his hands in dismay and flew to New York, pretending that his daughter, Jade, needed him. When he returned, the Stones pulled themselves together, kicked everybody else out of the room, and threw themselves into intense rehearsals for a stripped-down two nights at the El Mocambo. They were suddenly very nervous about how people were going to react.

"Keith looked as if he belonged in the St. Michael's Hospital emergency room," Flippo wrote of the first show. "He was hollow-cheeked and unshaven, gaunt, and he was so almost translucently pale that you automatically wondered how many years it had been since Mr. Sun had shined down on him. He smiled beatifically, though—almost as if he had just gotten out of jail—as he hit the first dead note licks on his black Gibson guitar (with the design of the human skull on it) of the tortured introduction of 'Honky Tonk Women.' It may have been rooted in desperation, but nonetheless, the Stones pulled out all the stops. And Keith, whose soul had been stained blacker than black many years before by the spirit that anointed the legendary Robert Johnson, glowed with internal combustion that no scientist in the western world would want to identify."

John Rockwell of *The New York Times* declared that "the Stones went back to their roots, knocking out raunchy British rhythm and blues in a smoky club. The only nagging fear was that it might have been the completion of a circle, coming back to the beginning at the end. The Rolling Stones would be inconceivable without Mr. Richards. Should he wind up in jail, it might mean the end of the band. But last night was more of an affirmation than a denial. Given the energy, conviction and sheer joy here, it is almost impossible to believe that this could be the end of anything."

"It was one of those weird things in Toronto," Keith recalled. "Everybody's going around talking doom and disaster, and we're up on stage at the El Mocambo and we never felt better. I mean, we sounded great. People were down, asking, 'Is this the end of the Rolling Stones?' In actual fact, it was a real period of productivity for us, and everybody in the band was confident."

Richards made court appearances on March 7 and 8. On March 7 he marched into court cheered by fans with his head up, wearing a white scarf and black velvet suit. As he reached the courthouse doors, a photographer tried to wrestle him to the ground by his hair, amid screams of "Deport the limey!" and "Junkie bastard!" A blond woman shrieked, "Evil cocksucker!" Inside the courtroom the prosecuting attorney revealed that an additional charge of cocaine possession would be brought the next day, and Keith's bail would be revoked. The Stones' lawyers panicked, while Anita noted dryly that she was never afraid Keith was going to go to jail because "we had pretty powerful allies, Mafia alliance from New York." However, when Richards returned to court on March 8, he looked, according to Flippo, "as if he had shrunk. He was plainly nervous and had lost whatever self-confidence he had impressed the crowd with a scant twenty-four hours earlier. In the prisoners' box Keith hung his head like a poleaxed bull, his hands folded before him, and looked pathetic, vulnerable and appeared defeated." But thanks to a minor legal trick the prosecution had overlooked (under Canadian law, the presence of Flippo, an American journalist, invalidated the proceedings), Richards's attorney, Clayton Powell, got him bail of twenty-five thousand dollars, and he was given back his passport. As he left the courthouse he was cheered by hundreds of fans.

But this time when he returned to the Harbour Castle, the Stones broke camp and made for the border. One of the things that concerned them most was that Keith had once again—of necessity—acquired enough dope to put him behind bars for the rest of his life. They had good reason to believe that the Mounties might again come charging into his suite, or theirs, at any moment. When that happened, Mick Jagger wanted to be far away. "Did I know it was going to happen sooner or later?" Jagger remarked. "Of course. It was irresponsible and what happened was totally inevitable. Christ, Keith fuckin' gets busted every year."

Mick didn't bother to come to Keith's suite to say good-bye but phoned instead. Keith could tell he was afraid. A heavier blow was Ron Wood's departure. Keith, as usual, pretended to be unconcerned by the defection of his two closest friends, but bolted down a bottle of wine. Anita was not so sanguine. "Everybody vanished," she remembered. "They all flew. They all disappeared. And that was when Keith made this wonderful recording with Ian Stewart. It seems that Keith always responded best under the greatest pressure."

On March 12, the night before he was to go to court to find out whether the Canadians were going to incarcerate him, Richards went into Interchange Studios, where they had been mixing their El

Mocambo tapes, with Ian Stewart, who had stayed behind to keep him company, Anita, and Marlon, and recorded five songs Gram Parsons had taught him back at Nellcôte: "Worried Life Blues" (the lament of a poor man who works for his weekly pay), "Say It's Not You" (the lament of a man who begs his girlfriend to deny that she has been sleeping with everybody in town), "Apartment No. 9" (the lament of a man who has been left by his girlfriend), "She Still Comes Around" (the lament of a man who pines for his girlfriend), and "Sing Me Back Home" (the lament of a man on his way to the electric chair).

The most remarkable aspect of these recordings was Keith's rusty, high-pitched voice, which had never been heard sounding like this on record. To some extent the change was caused by the false teeth he had implanted in the midseventies and the damaging effect of many pounds of white powder on his nasal passages. The years of smoking, drinking, and staying up for days singing and talking had added layers too—his defensive, noncommittal, negative adolescent voice had given way to the keenly expressive, edge-of-tears sound of a man straining to give vent to his emotions.

Listening to him sing "Loneliness surrounds me/Without your arms around me" in "Apartment No. 9," one got the feeling that Keith had thrown his whole being into the sessions and was finally unleashing emotions he had never expressed verbally. This was the closest he had come to expressing how fragile and tortured he often felt. At the same time, in all five songs Keith came across as a man who was coming to terms with himself. This was the voice of the "tortured creative person," Keith's lawyer would describe him as when the case went to trial in 1978. Another friend said, "The problem with Keith is he thinks rock and roll's real life. He's the most naive person I know!"

"Are you gonna give up music or are you gonna give up drugs?" asked Rolling Stones aide (and eventual Richards personal manager) Jane Rose, who had taken to checking the newspapers each morning to see if he was still alive. "This was his ninth life and there was a choice to be made."

Keith was thirty-three, the age, he pointed out, at which Christ was crucified, and he realized that it was time to take control of his life. In an interesting development, due to the fact that his name had never been legally changed, the hereditary Richards was used in court rather than his adopted stage name of Richard, and the press perpetuated the switch. As if the previous fourteen years had suddenly been attributed to someone else, Keith embraced this return to his roots and would once again be known in his public and private lives as Keith Richards. He finally faced the fact that he couldn't get away with being the most notorious junkie in the world anymore.

RICHARDS: "I never considered myself a junkie because my particular situation was so different and removed from ninety percent of the people hung up on the stuff. Nothing on earth will make you go through coming off it, short of a lightning bolt of logic. I had reached the point of no return. I realized I was endangering everything I wanted to do and what people around me wanted to do.

"I just knew I had to finish with dope. It was a traumatic event that reshaped the rest of my life. You get to the point where you've been doing stuff for ten years like I was, and, hey, it's boring, and also I just couldn't afford to do it anymore. It was either put the lid on it or you're going to live in the big house quite a while."

For Anita also, the Toronto bust was a "lightning bolt of logic." "The bust was reality," she admitted. "I had already lost a baby. I am sure that the drugs had something to do with it. I had lost my daughter. But I couldn't stop, basically. But now we had to do something about it, because otherwise we could go to jail. That was made clear to us."

Meanwhile, six years after joining them to run Rolling Stones Records, Marshall Chess, who had been particularly influenced by Keith, shuffled off stage to once again put back together his own shattered life.

MARSHALL CHESS: "It was very difficult for me to kick drugs. I stopped with the Stones in '77, and I was off drugs in '78. I had been strung out on heroin, coke, Quaaludes. Spent a half million on drugs, took nineteen drug cures. Every time the Stones had another project, I would wind up in some other drug clinic trying to get well."

Richards came up with the suggestion that Bill Carter try contacting a British doctor, Margaret (Meg) Paterson, who in the early seventies had developed a painless withdrawal process called the black box cure, which he knew had worked for Eric Clapton and Pete Townshend. Keith's idea was to rendezvous with Paterson in a setting such as the Bahamas to make the experience more pleasant than grueling.

Richards didn't really want to get off heroin and resented being forced to by the authorities, but the only other route that had been offered him was a methadone cure in the U.S. He preferred the black box cure to the methadone treatment.

RICHARDS: "Methadone should be thrown off the books altogether, and they should just dump it into the sea. It's no good. You don't even get high from it. The only reason it goes on like it does is because there's incredible amounts of money being made off these clinics. I mean, they're just a rip-off."

On March 20, Carter made contact with Dr. Paterson, who was working on another cure in the States. He informed her that Keith was facing up to three months in the penitentiary. She said she could be available to commence Richards's cure in ten days, but she stipulated that Anita submit to therapy also, explaining that she never treated just one addict in a partnership of addicts because the pullback was inevitable and usually, immediate.

Once Paterson agreed to take the case, things moved with the rapidity that is possible only for people with a lot of money and top-of-the-line connections.

The first question was where to administer the cure. Dr. Paterson's husband, George, with whom she worked, recalled that their friend, Shorty Yeaworth, the director of the classic 1950s movie *The Blob*, had said that if they ever wanted to make use of his large seventeenth-century farmhouse in Paoli, Pennsylvania, they would always be welcome. Dr. Paterson arranged to work under the auspices of Dr. Bill Corbett of the Camden Drug Clinic's Turning Point Program in New Jersey. On March 24, Corbett formally requested that the Immigration Department of the United States extend Keith and Anita Richards [sic] one-month medical visas for a rapid drug cure. Permission was granted, providing Richards did not move outside a twenty-five-mile radius of Paoli, that no press be alerted, and that he be under the surveillance of security guards.

Despite his public gratitude, Keith was privately reluctant to put himself in the hands of a medical team, and being uncertain whether the arrangement was on the level or a scam to get him out of Toronto, made alternative plans.

On April 1, as Keith, Anita, and Marlon were scheduled to fly by Lear Jet from Toronto to Philadelphia International Airport, where they were to be met by Paterson's medical team and transported to Shorty Yeaworth's Pennsylvania farmhouse for the three-week cure, Keith made private arrangements to have friends simply pick him up in Philadelphia and whisk him to New York instead. Bill Carter, who was understandably concerned that the transfer go off without a hitch, badgered Richards to be on time for once, but Keith continued to operate on his own schedule. In case the Paterson cure was on the level, Keith and Anita gave themselves big farewell shots of heroin and cocaine before getting on the plane.

A welcoming party of seven, which included Jane Rose, Joe and Arleta Winston and their eight-year-old son, Sammy (the Winstons would take care of Marlon during the cure), Dr. Corbett, and the Patersons, was kept waiting in Philadelphia for three hours. Richards's Lear Jet touched down on the tarmac at 7:00 P.M.

As soon as Keith, dressed in a white hat, blue silk suit, and gray blouse, emerged from the plane and saw Jane Rose with a caravan of limousines, he knew escape was out of the question. Keith and Anita got into one limousine with the Patersons; Marlon rode with the Winstons. The Winstons' son, Sammy, offered Marlon a doughnut. Marlon stuffed it in his pocket, extracting in turn a toy airplane from his bag of goodies and handing it over in mute exchange. The remainder of the group took a third vehicle. As the caravan sped out of the airport and headed toward Camden, where they were to be officially checked in at Corbett's drug clinic, Keith and Anita seemed unreceptive, skeptical, and scared. The no-nonsense Dr. Paterson came across like a schoolmarm with her neat, pulled-back hair and strong Scottish accent, while her gruff, blunt, born-again Christian husband resembled the purveyor of America's favorite fried-chicken franchise, Colonel Sanders. Furthermore, although Meg Paterson was a gentle, considerate woman with infinite reserves of patience, George was the opposite, arrogant and aggressive. A clash seemed inevitable.

Paterson's withdrawal cure was based on a "black box" electronic device about the size of a large matchbox with receptors on each end that were connected to the subject's ears. Through these electrodes the box transmitted a weak electrical signal that caused the patient's brain to release endorphins, natural heroinlike molecules produced deep inside the brain that canceled the pain of withdrawal. The treatment was to be administered twenty-four hours a day for five days, and at decreasing intervals for the remainder of the cure.

At first the method turned out to be as remarkable as Dr. Paterson had promised. However, it soon became evident that the experience would not be smooth. Keith and Anita, long used to living without a thought for another human being, dropped cigarettes wherever they felt like dropping them and had soon burned their way through the carpets and mattress and scorched the rim of the bathtub. Shorty's daughter, whose job it was to make their beds, was further astonished to discover Keith's boots under the bedcovers each day. Although the black box worked and Richards was later vociferous in his praise of it, both he and Anita had some practical problems.

"They didn't trust us with the black box," Anita recounted, "and in my case I was allergic to it. You get a constant shock in your ear, and my ear was completely out of commission. And in Keith's case, the battery on his box ran out and he went into a deep withdrawal in the bathroom one night and that was pretty bad. It does actually work, but you just don't trust it. And we didn't get along with the Patersons. No, no, no. Her husband is that total maniac . . . They tried to control us. She's got this idea—pop star save me—and I remember on the third day she asked us if we wanted to go score. I mean, it was the last thing we wanted to do. We're sick and we can't even get up and she says, 'Do you want some drugs?' That's just her way of doing it."

The Patersons' intentions went beyond effecting a mere physical withdrawal from heroin—they wanted to prepare the patient for life without heroin. To this end, they engaged Keith and Anita in a series of daily conversations about their lives. Keith found himself being questioned in a way he hadn't experienced since he had slammed the door on his parents back in 1962. Nothing could have been more threatening to a man who hardly ever expressed himself verbally to anybody, let alone an authority figure. In dealing with addicts, Meg Paterson noted, "you're dealing with the underlying resentments and bitterness and hatred. You have to pick your way through a minefield of insecurities."

The conflict was apparent in the contrast between the couples. The undead King and Queen of Rock resembled nothing so much as a pair of diseased vultures, with their dark-circled, restless eyes and gently lolling heads that nodded like the toy dogs seen staring out the backs of cars. "I was really rebellious," recalled Anita. "I didn't like the people. They were too remote, too controlling. Every night I would sneak downstairs into the kitchen to swig some sherry. Keith was aware of what I was doing, but he was taking care of himself. He had Toronto waiting for him, so he was more concerned about the outcome."

Dr. Joseph Winston, the American physician who worked with Paterson in the treatment of Richards, said that Keith "came to us terribly ill. He was literally green . . . Ten days later he was playing tennis, and the Stones said he hadn't looked so good in years."

As the cure entered its third week, the conflict between George Paterson and Keith Richards, which focused primarily on the up-bringing of Marlon, came to a head. When George insisted that a child should be disciplined, Keith was vehement about kids not being tampered with.

RICHARDS: "One of the few things I learned quite early on by traveling around a lot is that in our part of the world we tend to keep people children for as long as we can. To drag childhood out. We're very reluctant to relinquish parenthood or responsibility, or give rights to the child. It used to be twenty-one. Goddamnit—you do twenty-one again, you're forty-two already. Especially when you go to different parts of the world and see kids six, seven, absolutely capable of taking over their dad's business. 'OK, mind the store.' And you find that the old man is easier to bargain with than the kid. Just by traveling around you get very hip to the fact that kids are capable of growing up. Then you can say, 'Well, is it good for them to grow up too soon?' Whatever someone's capable of, I would imagine would be good for them. Not 'You can't do this, you're not old enough.' In that respect, I've brought my kids up with the view, 'You're old enough to walk, then you can walk to the fucking john to take a crap. I'm not gonna wipe your ass.' I've given them a lot of independence that way."

20

Beast of Burden
1977–1978

I wanted to come back and prove that what I had gone through had made a difference, to justify this kind of suffering.

KEITH RICHARDS, *from an interview with Vic Garbarini, 1983*

That summer Keith, who claimed he depended on domestic life but never spent much time enjoying it, was desperate for something to do. Keith was not allowed to travel more than thirty miles from the clinic, so in order to mix the El Mocambo tapes for the *Love You Live* album, Mick had to meet him in Philadelphia that summer. In the studio Mick lectured Keith about how much they had to do and begged him not to pass out. Several hours later, after drinking a fifth of tequila, Jagger had to be carried out of the studio on a couch. While Keith remained in the studio working industriously through the night, Mick was delivered back to Richards's house, where Anita taunted him.

Richards's cleanup did not, however, last long. After working with Jagger he moved to a house, Frog Hollow, in South Salem, New York, and commuted to New York City to work on a solo album by John Phillips, formerly of the Mamas and the Papas. Phillips's drug habit quickly rubbed off on Richards, who was soon, according to their shocked producer, scaring the secretaries with his derelict appearance as they arrived at 9:00 A.M. while he was leaving the studio. Keith Harwood, the engineer who had mixed *It's Only Rock 'n Roll, Black and Blue*, and *Love You Live*, died in a car crash on his way home from the studio during the disastrous Phillips-Richards sessions, which never saw the light of day. Elvis also died while Keith was working with John.

On September 13, the Rolling Stones celebrated the release of *Love You Live* at the Marquee in London. They dedicated the double album to Keith Harwood, who had done his best work for them on it, with the strange inscription "Those whom the Gods love grow young." Richards did not attend the release party. "The most fascinating thing about *Love You Live* is that it is so much against the grain of the general atmosphere of the last few Stones albums," wrote Billy Altman in *Creem*. "Maybe it's because this band that has meant so much to rock 'n' roll isn't worrying about anything, but is just doing it by instinct. And maybe their contention that they really do care more about playing live than they do about making studio albums is a bit more valid than previously thought. I don't know how long it will last but it's great to feel close to the Stones once more, if only for these few fleeting moments."

Despite the success of the live album, which went to number five in the States, the reviews sounded like an epitaph. The Stones were under a great deal of pressure to produce a strong studio disc after the sloppy erraticism of their last three. They decided to return to recording as a five-man band, and for the first time on record Ron Wood joined them as a full-time member. The heat was on Keith in particular to prove that he was no longer incapacitated by addiction. His love of playing with the Rolling Stones was his motivation for staying off heroin. The recording of *Some Girls* marked the true beginning of the end of his life as a junkie, if not as a drug user. "The Rolling Stones always work best under intense pressure," he said. "Most people do, and that's very true of the Stones. We were feeling a little under pressure to come out with something different . . ."

On September 30, Keith and Ronnie took the newly inaugurated Air France Concorde from New York to Paris to commence recording *Some Girls*. It was not just because he was no longer seeing Uschi that he moved the band from Munich to Paris for the next five albums. Keith was so sensitive to the acoustics of studios that he could judge them by the echo from snapping his fingers. At Pathé-Marconi in Paris he discovered a small room off the main studio that was just the right size and had the required sound. When he discovered that the studio also had a big collection of 1950s Lantern microphones, the deal was clinched. Pathé-Marconi would become as significant in the band's history as Olympic Studios in London, Chess in Chicago, or RCA in Hollywood.

Paris, where Keith had had a flat in the Faubourg-Saint-Honoré since 1968, would become his third home. Keith was well connected in Paris. A cameraman, Freddie Hauser, had shot a terrific film of the Stones' 1976 concerts at Les Abattoirs. He became Keith's confidant and majordomo in France. Most of the time he was there Richards was working, but if Keith wanted to go out the Palace was one of his haunts. There he ran into Brion Gysin, who became another regular in his Paris entourage. "Brion saw Keith a lot in Paris," recalled the poet John Giorno. "Brion was a great star there but Keith was a megastar. Any night that Keith was there sitting at a particular round table, Brion would automatically sit next to him. He was totally empowered by being with Keith and he would be treated like a king. Even toward the end when Brion was sick, he could always benefit from Keith's largesse." While the French police did not appreciate the Stones, in the fashion-film-art-lit scene they were considered *très chic*, Richards being seen as a rock and roll Belmondo with his dangling cigarette and his elegant fuck-you cool. For Richards, the only drawback to the City of Lights was the fact that it was filled with Parisians.

RICHARDS: "I love Paris, hate the people. That's a bit of a rough thing to say, but the Parisians must have a huge inferiority complex. They're terrible to tourists but they're even worse to French people who aren't Parisians. They consider them to be peasants. You know that whenever you're going to get up and leave your joint you can almost take bets on how many minutes it's gonna be before you're insulted or some local pisses you off. Paris would be lovely without the Parisians."

For a month the Stones just rehearsed, and in November they began to record. "When we were doing the mix-downs for *Love You Live*, we'd tell the engineers to get on with the mix while Keith and I and whoever was around just started playing the new material," said Mick. Picking up on the work they had embarked on in Philadelphia the previous April, Jagger and Richards hammered out some forty songs or scraps of songs in a creative explosion.

Richards thought the real difference between *Some Girls* and the previous three albums was that they had gotten rid of all the studio musicians, the "clever bastards" such as Billy Preston and Nicky

Hopkins who were superior to the Stones technically and had often led them away from their basic sound. At last, on the "no more fast numbers" sessions, as they had come to be known, with his Brian Jones-like guitar partner, Ronnie Wood, Richards would have a chance to get back to the raw Stones sound characterized by two synchronized guitars.

In the late seventies, the music world was being rocked by two strong trends diametrically opposed to each other—a slick, techno-wonder dancing music called disco on the one side, and raw, antiestablishment punk music on the other. Keith dug in his heels, refusing to be swayed by either trend. He insisted on sticking to his roots—Berry, Diddley, Waters. Mick, though, had kept up with the trends and was leaning toward a punk- and disco-influenced sound. A collision was inevitable, and when it hit this time, Richards was in a stronger position to fight.

Just as he had wanted to make a psychedelic album that outdid the Beatles in 1967, in 1977 Jagger wanted to make a punk record that outpunked the punks. Keith thought that would have been fatal. As far as he was concerned, Led Zeppelin and the Sex Pistols were just passing fads. The point was to stay on course, to keep connected to their roots. Ian Stewart agreed. "When are you going to start playing something decent?" he would ask them in the studio. "Not another piece of tripe like that, I can't stand it." After running through several punk-oriented tunes, he stopped playing piano on the sessions, moaning, "They sound like bloody Status Quo."

Ron Wood's presence acted as a salve for injured egos, and he often intervened in the fights between Jagger and Richards.

RON WOOD: "Perhaps if time doesn't make it possible for Jagger and Richards to communicate man to man, I can convey to either what the other is thinking without putting in a negative slant. And help. That's all it is, really. I might be with Mick and he'll say, 'I can't take this any further because I don't know how Keith feels about it.' Maybe he's somewhere in the world where Mick can't get through to him. I can say, 'I know for a fact that he likes this but won't go for that.' It gives him a guide. I mean, they don't take my word as gospel. I'm just—not a middleman, but *diplomatic liaison officer*. It's entirely necessary at times for Jagger and Richards to have someone to explain them to each other."

Apart from developing the two-guitars-as-one sound Keith was so keen on, Wood also encouraged Jagger to play the guitar and patiently taught him a few songs. Jagger filled in for Stu's missing piano with the third guitar and in doing so found another channel on which to communicate with Keith. The man Jagger brought in to coproduce, Chris Kimsey, thought Jagger's guitar playing became very much a part of Keith.

Although two of the final tracks, "Beast of Burden" and "Before They Make Me Run," are pure Richards, *Some Girls* was very much Jagger's album (with strong support from Wood), and is arguably the pinnacle of his musical career.

NICK KENT: "With *Some Girls* there was a new Stones style with the Mick Jagger guitar and all the songs in F. If it's a Jagger song it's in F. Some of them are good, like "Shattered," Mick Jagger's rhythm. But you have to understand also that Keith works within a limitation. With *Some Girls* to an extent he's home, but a lot of it is Ron Wood and Mick Jagger pretending to be home. Keith comes in with the best song, "Beast of Burden," but on *Some Girls* Keith wasn't around a lot of the time."

The success of *Some Girls* underlined how much Jagger and Richards relied on the spark of conflict to ignite their best work. Earlier, with Keith too weak to function as a goad and sounding board, Jagger had produced three weak albums in a row; now that Keith's heroin use was on hold, the collaboration (and the struggle for dominance that went with it) was back in action.

Chris Kimsey quickly realized that he was just another piece of meat in the human sandwich, but like so many prime cuts before him, he welcomed the friction. Keith, he figured, often argued with Mick because it created a better product. Richards, though, believed that Jagger was the one who argued for the sake of argument. The majority of onlookers sided with Richards. Keith, they felt, had the more balanced and accurate feel for the group's sound.

Whatever the case, they worked fast and well in Paris. By the time they broke off in December so that Richards could return to

Canada to make a court appearance and spend Christmas with his family, they had recorded all but one of the songs on the album.

On December 2, Richards was in Toronto; a trial date was set for February 6. Inside the courtroom one hysterical fan threw an ashtray and screamed, "Free Keith!"

At Christmas Keith attempted to have a family holiday with Anita and Marlon in New York. Unfortunately, by then, according to John Phillips, Keith was strung out on heroin again and barely capable of lugging a Christmas tree up to the apartment, and once there he was too fatigued to decorate it properly.

Anita's recovery was not going any more smoothly than Keith's. Instead of doing hard drugs, she had taken to drinking heavily.

ANITA PALLENBERG: Keith would still come and see me, but not often, so I just dived into another huge binge of alcohol and drugs. But I remember on Christmas and birthdays he was always there—that's how hard it got. If we wanted to be together, the lawyer couldn't have stopped us, but then there were also Keith's friends. There was Freddie Sessler, and he was a very close friend to Keith and he used to always supply him with women out of his own kind of ambitions. And then Keith had some girlfriends as well, and I was basically in the country by myself. One night I found his phone book and I'm going through the whole of his phone book to try and find him, like in a complete state. I didn't really accept the fact that it was over, but the lawyers had started to say you have to have a separation for a while. They thought I was like a hot potato, I was the weak link in the chain. They thought if he stuck with me he would end up God knows where. And I felt all that stuff very strongly. The way I dealt with it was drinking and drugging. That was the only way I knew.

"Jack Daniel's and ginger ale. That was my favorite. Vodka . . . wine . . . tequila . . . anything. Basically I felt everything had been taken from me. My freedom. We hadn't actually been living together, ever, basically. You know—as I say, Keith was never there and I was here and he was doing a record and then I had Marlon. Marlon was like nine years, ten years old and he hadn't gone to school. So we had to find a way of like inserting ourselves into society. I didn't want to have this regular life, with Marlon going to school, but I had to. There was no other way. So I drank myself into oblivion."

Keith continued to make Marlon a top priority. He loved to transform himself into any number of characters, from Captain Hook to Captain Blood, and chase Marlon around the house as Marlon screamed with laughter. He made a point of spending playtime with Marlon every day and seemed to have abundant energy to do so.

Even a short visit with his son seemed to breathe new life and greater resolve into Keith. Donning a Father Christmas suit over his scrawny frame and pasting a long white beard onto his gaunt skull, he ho-ho-hoed his way through the celebrations and felt pleased to believe his son, aged eight, still believed in Santa Claus.

In January of '78, he and the Stones wrote and spent three days recording the last track for the album. It was an eloquent statement on his embattled relationship with drugs and the law: Declaring his resolve to kick, he vowed that he was going to walk before they made him run. Well, eventually, anyway. In "(I'm Gonna Walk) Before They Make Me Run," his words belie his happy-go-lucky demeanor: He was going to ascend to heaven, he wrote, because he had already been in hell, adding that although he might not have looked particularly healthy, he was feeling terrific.

At the beginning of March 1978, the Stones completed recording *Girls*. Richards and Jagger flew to New York to mix the album and plan a summer tour of the United States. By then, however, Keith had been back on heroin for several months.

In May, under a heavy veil of secrecy, the Stones organized rehearsals for the tour at Todd Rundgren's Bearsville compound in Woodstock, New York. The first step was to resurrect Keith. Tom Edmonds, a tall, skinny, twenty-three-year-old Bearsville recording engineer with blond hair falling below his shoulders, was assigned to see that Richards, the first to arrive, was taken care of. For Edmonds, this was an exciting gig; the Rolling Stones had been his favorite band since the 1967 U.S. release of *Flowers*. Keith was his guitar hero. When Richards's beige Jaguar pulled up outside the studio with Keith, Anita, and Jane Rose inside, he discovered that his first duty was to carry his semiconscious hero upstairs to the apartment above the studio where Jagger and Richards would be staying. In fact, Keith was in such bad shape Tommy was afraid he was going to die before he was laid out upon the bed.

Jagger had asked John Phillips, who had spent that spring in his New York apartment on Seventy-second Street hanging out, playing guitar, and taking drugs with Keith, Mick, and Bobby Kennedy, Jr., to help get Keith four hundred methadonelike Dolophine tablets to see him through the tour. Keith, however, opted for a self-administered black box cure at Bearsville. The difference was, in Richards's version of the Paterson cure he was allowed to smoke pot, snort coke, and drink booze while the receptors went about their pulsing business.

Having separated from Bianca in 1977, Jagger had acquired a new girlfriend, the tall, leggy model Jerry Hall. Keith loathed her on sight. According to one witness, talking to her was like talking to a window. Though partial to models himself, Keith was quick to condemn Mick for what he saw as the superficiality of his tastes. The only girlfriend of Jagger's Richards ever liked was Marianne Faithfull. It was no coincidence that Richards and Jagger did their best work when Mick was with her.

According to Jerry Hall's book, *Tall Tales*, Mick had sworn off drugs but was so concerned about his best pal Keith that he and she devoted themselves to taking care of him for the better part of a month in Woodstock.

JERRY HALL: "Millions of dollars depended on it. And the whole thing was going to fall through if Keith didn't get off heroin. Mick loves Keith, you know. They're like a married couple and they're dearest friends. And it gave Mick a very good feeling to be able to help Keith. He did it staying with us in Woodstock. He got off heroin right on our couch. I don't know if Keith even remembers this, but for a few weeks he was just lying there. Mick and I would feed him. And every time the clips fell off we'd hook them back on. And we'd cover him with a blanket at night. It must have been so painful. He just slept and slept all the time. And he lost a lot of weight and when he got up he'd be so weak. And then he started getting better. You know the feeling you have when you have a child and you watch him grow? We were like 'Look, he's having a bath!' and 'Oh, did you see what he was doing today? He's really much better.'

"Then when he started getting more together you could see him getting more macho. His ego thing was coming back and he'd start going out and throwing knives at trees. He started getting his temper back and we didn't mind that because it was a good sign. And he started suntanning and started exercising and Mick talked to him a lot and it was so sweet to see. For Mick, seeing his friend get himself together is what made him really never want to take strong drugs again."

According to the Bearsville staff, Keith stayed with Mick and Jerry for a total of three days. As soon as Ron Wood arrived, Keith had Tom Edmonds move him and all his stuff to the house where Woody was staying, and throughout the cure Keith was looked after primarily by Edmonds and other staff members. Far from forming one big happy family with his bandmates and their companions, Keith continued to distance himself from Jerry Hall, and when Mick arrived, Anita left. Tommy, who drove her back to Frog Hollow, received a lecture on what hanging around the Stones could do to a once-beautiful young woman, and she gave him warnings about the potential consequences of his accepting a gig as Keith's guitar roadie.

Meanwhile, back at Bearsville, as Edmonds recalled, "The rehearsals were different from any rehearsals I'd ever done ... Mick would say, 'Well, we're going to start at nine o'clock.' So Mick would be there at nine playing the piano and singing. So I called Bill Wyman up and said, 'Bill! Want me to come and get you? Rehearsal's at nine!' Bill said, 'Don't call me or come get me until Keith's there.' The whole thing seemed to center around Keith. If there was no Keith, there was no Stones." Tommy observed that the scale of power balanced Mick and Jerry on one side and Keith and Woody on the other.

As soon as Keith concluded his self-administered black box cure in Woodstock, Ronnie Wood's girlfriend Jo Carslake brought a Swedish model named Lilly Wenglass Green, who had spent so much time in London she spoke with a raucous cockney accent, up to meet Keith. Keith and Lil immediately hit it off and he commenced a hot affair with her reminiscent of his experience with Uschi, to whom she bore a marked resemblance. According to one friend, Lil was "a great character, a real strong personality, and a beautiful girl. She was also a very sexual person, and there was a lot of sex with Lil. A lot! She didn't really do drugs at the beginning of their scene. In fact, she helped Keith a lot when he was trying to get off hard drugs in Paris by keeping people away. She gained a lot of enemies by keeping people away."

Lil, who would be Keith's girlfriend through 1980, liked to think that Keith was inspired a little bit by her, and it makes sense that he was, because her most outstanding feature apart from her smoldering good looks was her laugh—Lil couldn't get through a sentence without cracking up.

As the tide began to turn in his favor in the struggle to pull himself together, Keith went to great lengths to help other artists in a similar predicament. When constructing the 1978 tour, for example, he insisted that the great R&B artist Etta James, who had been struggling with drugs and alcohol for twenty years, be given the chance to open some shows.

According to Penny Stallings in her book *Rock 'n' Roll Confidential*, "Etta James couldn't tell the difference between him and what she calls 'those other skinny little British fags' when he first got in touch with her. As she recalls it now, 'I didn't know nothin about nothin. Most of the time people had to lead me up on stage to perform. But when the Stones were getting their 1975 tour together, I was in the hospital trying to detox, and I got a nice letter from Keith Richards saying he knew I was having trouble and asking me if I would open their show for them. He said that they always felt like the best way to get your head together and deal with your troubles was to go out and tour. I wrote back and told him I was too sick just then and he wrote me and said he understood and that they wouldn't forget me. They didn't either.'" Three years later Etta James was hired to open for the Stones' 1978 summer tour of the U.S.

They also signed Peter Tosh to Rolling Stones Records and selected him as another opener for the tour. Tosh was present during rehearsals in Woodstock. Keith recorded an unreleased album with Tosh and his band.

MICK JAGGER: "He got us involved rather than vice versa. Basically, the Tosh band are rhythm guitar players and use the synthesizer lines to play lead and harmonies. So there we all were up in Woodstock, Tosh didn't have a lead guitarist, Keith and Woody were available, and so Tosh suggested that why don't they play on a couple of things? Keith and Woody are very familiar with the whole reggae thing so it turned out to be really good."

RICHARDS: "I'm drawn to reggae because there's nothing happening in black American music. They're going through the disco phase. It's very popular and no wonder people are drawn to it. The temptation to make those records is strong. Reggae took off because there are more Jamaicans in Britain and America than there are in Jamaica! Bob Marley has created an international status for reggae and now Africa will be a big market for the music too. Trouble is, I don't know if roots reggae is what people want to hear from me. When I've got an album's worth of material in front of me, then I'll think about releasing it. I've got Robbie Shakespeare on bass, Sly Dunbar on drums, and Robert Lyn on piano.

"As far as I'm concerned, I'm not white and they're not black. It's just something you don't think about. They make me feel very comfortable when I'm working with them. I've been going to Jamaica for over ten years."

Despite Richards's long flirtation with reggae and Wood's habit of calling him Jah Keith, things never seemed to click between Richards and Tosh. They spent little time hanging out together on tour. In fact, in the summer of 1981 Tosh's friendship with Keith ended dramatically. Disgruntled with his limited commercial impact beyond Jamaica, Tosh had begun to blame the Stones, attacking them in the press (as had Bob Marley) for allegedly thwarting his career. Richards allowed Tosh to use his Jamaican home for an extended period, but then lost his temper when, after landing on the island for a vacation, he discovered that Tosh had ignored all prior notification of his arrival and refused to leave Keith's hillside villa in Ocho Rios, claiming it had become his property.

Reaching Tosh by phone, Richards engaged him in a brief swap of Kingston bark and coarse London bite: Keith: "I'm coming down to the house. I need it for myself." Peter: "If yuh come anywhere near here, I'll shoot yuh." Keith: "You better make sure you know how to use that gun, and make sure you got the magazine in the right way round, 'cause I'm gonna be there in half an hour!" Tosh left the premises, which he had virtually destroyed, and found himself no longer welcome at Rolling Stones Records.

Richards didn't have much luck in his personal relations with reggae musicians. In the summer of 1981, Max Romeo, who would sing backup vocals on the Stones' "Dance," released an LP entitled *Holdin' Out My Love to You*, which featured Keith. Shanachie Records, which released the LP, used a poster of Keith, a photo of Keith on the back cover of the LP, and a sticker with Keith's name on the front cover to promote it. Another friendship was ended when Keith sued the label and the endorsements were discontinued.

On June 9, 1978, after the U.S. summer tour plans had been completed, *Some Girls*, with its Warholian montage cover of the Stones in drag yet again set against photos of numerous female stars, was released to great acclaim. It yielded two top-ten singles, "Miss You" and "Beast of Burden," with "Shattered" also in the top forty. Keith later told an interviewer that the album was called *Some Girls* because "there were so many I couldn't remember all their fucking names." It even sparked two controversies when Lauren Bacall, Raquel Welch, and other celebrities objected to their photos appearing on the cover alongside the Stones in transvestite poses, and then Jesse Jackson objected to the lyrics "Black girls just want to get fucked all night." "OK, so over the last fifteen years we've happened to meet some extra-horny black chicks—well, I'm sorry, but I don't think that I'm wrong and neither does Mick. I'm quite sure of that," retorted Richards. "If you can't take a joke, have a good laugh, then you shouldn't be here in the first place. We write our songs from personal experiences." The album went to number one in the U.S. and number two in the U.K., and it sold eight million copies worldwide to become their best-selling album so far.

RICHARDS: "We enjoyed making *Some Girls*. It was the most immediate album we'd done in ages, and you can't argue with seven million sales [*sic*], as far as the acceptance goes. I don't think there's that much between it and *Black and Blue* or *Goats Head Soup*. It's just that suddenly the timing clicks. That's the thing in this lark, it's the timing. It could just as easily have bombed. 'Miss You' wasn't specifically recorded as a disco single, it was just another track for *Some Girls*. 'Hot Stuff' [from *Black and Blue*] was discoish too, and so were some of the others, if you want to dig down. All that really matters is that it took off, at the right period in the band's evolution."

Interviewed by Geraldo Rivera on television in the United States just prior to the summer tour, Richards stated that he was "thirty-bloody-four" and "fantastic" physically. Asked why the Stones were still in the vanguard after fifteen years, he replied. " 'Cause we've changed, too, I mean, we're not in 1962, we're in 1978 same as everyone else. That's the reason. The other reason is that we're a band and we all still really want to do it. That's my answer and I'm sticking to it." Asked how he had changed since 1962, he answered, "I haven't changed much. That's my version." He also claimed that his relationship with Jagger was basically the same. "We both still play the same roles to each other." The question "Can you define that?" received a defiant "No! It's something that's been going on so long I'm not gonna attempt it. You can try and get me out of him, but you won't get him out of me. Somebody else might have plans for us to stop," he concluded, "but as long as Charlie Watts can hold up, we haven't."

After a warm-up date in the three-thousand-seat Capitol Theater in Passaic, New Jersey, the Rolling Stones began the six-week U.S. tour. It officially opened in Florida on June 10. No sooner had the band arrived backstage than the police busted the man who was carrying their drugs. Edmonds, who stumbled in on the arrest, hurried to relieve Keith of his personal stash and the .357 Magnum Colt he was carrying for protection. Luckily, it turned out that the police were willing to accept cash payment, literally selling back to the dealer the stuff they had confiscated. The gig went off without a hitch.

TERRY SOUTHERN: "Keith Richards reminded me of Charlie Parker because of the combination of humility and arrogance—Keith had humility and at the same time the kind of arrogance that comes with some inherent awareness of the mastery of your craft—

and because of the impression I've gotten over the years of his gigantic, gargantuan tastes. An example was when we stopped by his apartment in New York after the 1978 concert. I was on the tour writing about it. Gael [Southern's longtime companion] mistook Lilly from behind for Anita. Which is indicative of something. He's always been attracted to the same sort of woman. We're sitting in this alcove which is like the breakfast nook. The great thing was that he was already so whacked out and I had brought him some 'ludes as a kind of present. I got them out with the notion he would take them at his leisure, you see. So we're drinking Jack Daniel's and I said, 'Look, I got these for you, you know, be cool.' I didn't want people to see this as a dope deal. I handed them to him thinking he's going to stash them, but he just went *bop*!, taking six 'ludes, see, meanwhile drinking out of the bottle of Jack Daniel's. It was like something out of a movie. We're talking another ninety seconds and he gradually falls over right there but meanwhile we're still having a relationship, a conversation, even though he's out of it. I mean he was out. So when it came time for us to leave I was reluctant. I said, 'I can't leave him right away because I may have to walk him around if he starts turning blue.'"

Keith laid off the heroin initially during the '78 tour. "Suddenly I was willing to resume my responsibilities," he recalled. "I showed up saying, 'OK, I'm here to take some of the weight off your shoulders.' I thought I was doing Mick a favor, but he saw it as a power grab. In his mind I'd given him up, and why should I think I could just waltz back in there where I'd left off? He resented it. He'd gotten used to wielding the scepter. And when I returned, I don't think either one of us understood the ramifications of it."

Richards would be brought up short on the tour when it became apparent to him that Jagger was generally perceived to be the Stones by the mass public. In Tempe, Arizona, Jane Rose recalls pointing out a marquee to Richards that read, "Mick Jagger and the Rolling Stones."

JANE ROSE: "All those years with the Stones Keith was pushed into the background. That marquee hit Keith very hard. It dawned on him right there that the Stones had become Mick's band, and over a period of time it became apparent that Mick didn't want to change that. Mick was the one person who never stopped believing in Keith. He visited regularly and went out of his way to make sure Keith got everything he needed to get well. Only I don't think Mick intended for him to get this well."

Critical opinion of the first dates of the '78 tour was low. The split between Richards and Jagger was evident a mile away. Tommy complained to Keith that Jagger ignored him and Keith advised him that Jagger was a fucking cunt and to ignore him right back. So Tommy tried it. Later, he recalled, "No more than an hour or two went by. Jagger showed up in Keith's room and I really totally ignored him. I acted like he was invisible just like he said. And sure enough, Jagger came up and sat down next to me on the couch and put his hand on my leg and said, 'You're doing a really good job. By the way, are you gay?' So I thought about it for a minute. You know, this is Mick Jagger. And I said, 'No, man, I'm not gay.' And he got pissed off and stood up and said, 'Well, I'm not either!' Jagger sort of hung out on his own. He would cruise in and out every now and then. Basically, the band and Jagger didn't seem like they were traveling together." This story seems out of character, since although Jagger appeared to attract men he always rejected their advances.

But from Edmonds's viewpoint behind Richards's amplifier, "Keith was always ready to rock. He was always pumped and happy to be there rocking. It was just a crazy time, one big fucking endless party . . . Traveling with the Stones was like living inside a bubble. Inside that bubble, I felt like I was totally shielded, I could do anything I wanted, drugs, drink, I could hit somebody with a pool cue and get away with it . . . Keith was having a great time and the fucking people were going crazy at gigs—he was *there* in 1978 . . . He was bummed about Toronto. I think it was really tough on him financially, and it was an unhappy period, but I think the tour might have pulled him through." Keith himself observed, "I've started to notice the difference more and more since I quit using junk . . . No hassles, because I've managed to keep myself together. I've done what they wanted and done what I wanted both at the same time. And I've only fallen over twice in fifteen gigs, but still kept playing. That could be some kind of record."

The new, improved Keith was mending fences. He made some attempt to befriend Wyman. "Woody brought Keith and me together in 1978 in a hotel room on the U.S. tour," Bill remembered. "Keith insisted that I had never liked him, and it was like two kids making up after a fight. 'I never disliked you, Keith,' I answered. 'Remember when you went to live in Switzerland [for a drug cure]—I sent you letters, and you sent me a lovely letter back with pressed flowers in it? It was you who never made any attempt to keep the relationship going . . .' 'Oh, well, let's be mates now, then,' he said. And we were."

Keith was pleased to find that he wasn't the only one to blunder during performances. When Bill Wyman fell off the stage in the middle of the tour and, badly hurt, continued to play against doctor's orders with his two fingers taped together, Richards nominated him for a Purple Heart.

Tommy's job was to watch Keith throughout the show, making sure he had the right guitar for each song, replenishing his glass of Jack Daniel's when it got low, lighting his cigarettes, and sticking a straw in the right pile of drugs on top of the amp as Keith indicated what he wanted. After the show, he and Keith would return to the hotel and party through the night, listening to ska, Warren Zevon, and reggae, while Keith proclaimed, "Oh, man, that's fucking cool."

The tour ground profitably on, causing Prince Rupert Loewenstein, the Stones' financial adviser, to beam, "The Rolling Stones' ship of state is on a very even keel. Tip-top. Yes indeed, on to 1987 and 1991 and on and on." Chet Flippo, who covered the tour for *Rolling Stone* until he was thrown off because the magazine published unfavorable reviews, wrote that at this level "the truth is that, on any rock tour, the public does not really exist for the performers. The audience is an abstract, picked up and packed into the tractor-trailer trucks along with the lights and amps and backstage ferns, and unpacked in the next hall. There is always another audience. The audience exists only as box-office receipts, only as dollars passing through the gates."

As the tour neared its final dates, Keith reflected on the new Richards.

RICHARDS: "Even people I know extremely well don't come to my hotel room door without first passing through our own security. But truthfully, going on stage each night straight doesn't feel that different to me because I always know what I have to do and what is expected of me. For instance, part of *Some Girls* was made in a totally different condition to what I'm right now. I play my guitar a lot more than I did! With any tour you invariably reach a point where you become almost automatic, even though there are nights which really turn you on and nights that don't.

"Usually, you hit this middle level that you sort of expect and live up to and if it reaches that level then it's OK. You can go home satisfied. But on this tour, every show is different, every show is alive, each one has been a turn-on. And as far as I'm concerned, the timing just happened to be right. The fact is that before Toronto it was extremely difficult for me to get into the States, but after taking the cure, it has proved to be much more easy. Furthermore, it has been good for me."

Keith's dread of coming off the tour and having nothing to do was compounded by the Stones' arrival in Hollywood, where he succumbed to the end-of-the-tour blues and the ever-present lure of heroin. "Hollywood is the end of the line for so many people," he said. "It's a killer, and if you're weak you can be sure it'll get you."

L.A. almost did get Keith that August while he was resting up at a friend's house in Laurel canyon.

RICHARDS: "There was a big party one night and somebody had turned the gas fire off—but not all the way. So the gas was still going and there was some incense burning and then there was a spark . . . Boom! I'm in the bedroom with the flavor of the month, my girlfriend of the hour. I wake up and the room's full of smoke and she's crashed out and I sniff. I open the door to the bedroom and I'm looking at a fireball rushing down the corridor towards the oxygen . . . and me!

"There's the two of us, stark naked. Half the house is already destroyed, the roof is falling in on us, but we've managed to get through—with a few burns here and there—to the swimming pool, and there's all the neighbors. And they don't give a shit about us, they're worried about their houses. Stark fucking bollock naked with this blond, bless 'er heart, good girl, solid gold, saying to me, 'Do something.' And I said, 'What d'you want me to do, piss on it?'

"Suddenly this car stops and it's Anita's cousin! And I never knew how she recognized me, because she could only see my cock! I'm standing in the driveway with this blond chick, saying, 'Shall we just run for it and see what happens?' when she pulls up and goes, 'Get in!' And she just scooped us up and whisked me off so nobody could find me for a couple of days.

"The other weird thing is this house burned down totally, except for one wooden stump of a pillar, and in the bedroom this little portion of a chest of drawers which had like my passport, all my favorite tapes, jewellery, a shooter with five hundred rounds of ammunition. All untouched. And a friend of mine went back the next day when everything else was still too hot to touch, smouldering, and came back with all my stuff.

"I'd say my life-style is one of semifreedom. It's freedom in one way, but looking at it in another way, what other people have that I don't is anonymity. There are times when I could cry out for that kind of everyday freedom. I can never remain anonymous—that's the reason I've been picked up by police so many times. If you worry about it, you're finished. That's what happened to Brian."

On Sunday, October 22, Keith and Lilly flew into Toronto on a Lear Jet and checked into the Four Seasons Hotel. His timing was uncanny. The Sex Pistols had toured the U.S. in September and disintegrated. Their bassist, Sid Vicious, had moved into the Chelsea Hotel with his girlfriend, Nancy Spungen, and had allegedly stabbed her to death. As Keith was awaiting trial in Toronto on drug charges, Vicious was on trial for murder in New York. They shared headlines. Keith thought it ironic that if convicted, Vicious could receive a lighter sentence for murder than he faced on drug charges. Johnny Thunders thought it was ironic that Vicious "beat out Keith Richards for the story of the year."

Since Richards had last been in a Toronto court, ten months earlier in December 1977, a good deal had transpired in his case. Keith had missed court dates in February and March. In most cases such disobedience would have resulted in revocation of bail and jailing of the suspect, but not in Richards's case. Then on February 15 the arresting officer, William Seward, was killed in an automobile crash. Considering who some of Richards's allies were, that might have given some judicial authorities pause for thought, but rather than bearing down on him, they released their grip. As the October trial date approached, the Royal Canadian Mounted Police found themselves barred from making use of Richards's previous arrest record and the crown prosecutor was informed that Richards would face a charge of only heroin possession, not trafficking, and that the cocaine charge would be overlooked. It was obvious to reporters who covered the trial that the prosecuting attorney had been muzzled by the Department of Justice. It looked as if the Canadians simply wanted to get rid of this hot potato.

Richards's trial took place on October 23 and 24. On the first day a doctor testified that Keith and Anita were in a "desperate condition from opium abuse." An affidavit signed by Prince Rupert Loewenstein stated Keith's casual spending had totaled $175,000 in 1975, $300,000 in 1976, and $350,000 in 1977. Keith's lawyer, Austin Cooper, read lengthy testimonials from the Turning Point Clinic, which had sponsored his black box treatment, describing how well he was doing. Witness after witness testified under oath that Keith had kicked drugs. At one point, when Canadian composer Jack Betten stated that most of the Stones' music came from Richards's head, the audience applauded as Keith smiled and tapped his head.

Cooper pleaded for probation, describing Richards's nine-year battle with addiction: "In 1969 he started with heroin and got to the state where he was taking such quantities of the drug and getting no euphoria from it. He was taking such powerful amounts—as much as two and a half grams a day—just to feel normal." He listed numerous unsuccessful attempts to cure the addiction but insisted the current one was working. "He should not be dealt with as a special person, but I ask Your Honor to understand him as a tortured creative person—as a major contributor to an art form. He turned to heroin to prop up a sagging existence. I ask you to understand the whole man." According to Chet Flippo, who covered the trial for *Rolling Stone*, Cooper said that Keith was a very creative person racked with emotional pain, that his everyday life could be hell, and that art was often created from pieces of the shattered self. To support this thesis he cited the shattered selves of Sylvia Plath, Vincent van Gogh, Aldous Huxley, Judy Garland, and F. Scott Fitzgerald. He asked the court to assess Keith "not only for his weakness, but for the tortured creative spirit within him. He has fought a tremendous personal battle to rid himself of this terrible problem." Richards also promised to donate one million dollars to a rehabilitation clinic.

Judge Graburn said that he would give his judgment at ten the next morning. "This is a matter of great importance to Keith Richards and Canada," he intoned. Keith Richards took his shattered self back to the hotel, where all the pieces went to sleep.

On the second day of the trial, after calling for order in the gallery, Judge Graburn announced that "the Crown seeks a jail term" noting that Keith had been arrested with an extremely large quantity of heroin. "But I will not incarcerate him for addiction and wealth," he continued. Citing an artistic sensitivity which compelled Keith toward drugs and alcohol, and a successful drug cure, the judge ordered that Keith should remain free to create his music and finish his treatment.

The verdict was: one year's probation, no fine, no jail; to be on good behavior; to report to his probation officer within twenty-four hours, and on various subsequent dates; to continue treatment at the Turning Point Clinic; and to give a benefit performance for the Canadian Institute for the Blind within six months, either by himself or with the group of his choice.

As soon as the judge made his decision legal, Richards slowly raised a clenched fist above his head, the courtroom erupted in spontaneous cheers, and he left the court with the fist raised in triumphal salute.

He flew back to New York the same day and watched himself on TV. "I feel good about the sentence," he said. "It's very strange . . ." Later he theorized that the judge had made his decision because of "the Blind Angel": "This little chick from Toronto was totally blind, but there was nothing that would stop this girl from turning up at gigs. So I'd fix her up, 'give the girl a ride,' 'cause I just had visions of her being run over. God knows what could happen to a blind chick on the road. This chick went to the judge's house in Toronto, personally, and she told him this simple story. And from there he figured out the way to get Canada and himself and myself out of the whole mess."

That night, Richards went to see Dave Edmunds and Nick Lowe's band Rockpile at a small club, the Bottom Line. He was cheered by the audience and given complimentary champagne and a bodyguard. He jammed on "Let It Rock" and "Down Down Down," and the audience screamed for "Happy." As he left the club, a number of cops shook his hand and congratulated him.

21

All About You
1979

Keith has the constitution of concrete. He's like a cliff. The sea comes and washes up against it and it stands. But so many people who were around him would just collapse. Keith is the sort of person who can stay awake for three days without substances and all of a sudden fall asleep in midsentence sitting up and not moving for a few hours. He would just be up and up and up and up and up and all of a sudden it would be like a light switch, *bing!* But in certain strange positions. Then you would walk around him.

RICHARD LLOYD, *from an interview with Victor Bockris*, 1992

In December 1978, Keith, Anita, and Marlon flew the Concorde to London to spend Christmas and the New Year there as well as to see Keith's mother and daughter. Anita's appearance would have shocked anyone who had not seen her in a year. Bloated, with hairy legs, blotched green-hued skin, missing or rotting teeth, and unkempt hair, she drifted through time making half-hearted efforts to fulfill such motherly functions as pulling a meal together. When Marlon asked for dinner, he was often presented a plate of ice cream. But Keith still spoke reverentially about her. "She's everything, man," he told an acquaintance. "It all comes from her, the Rolling Stones." In truth, though, instead of being the great Rolling Stones catalyst she once was, she now had an effect on Keith that was altogether negative.

Keith's focus during the holidays was on collecting tunes for the next album. The London music scene was very hot. Punk was self-destructing in a blaze of publicity over the breakup of the Sex Pistols and Sid Vicious's alleged drugcrazed murder of his girlfriend, but there was still a lot of energy pumping up from the underground. Groups such as Siouxsie and the Banshees, the Buzzcocks, and the

Clash were hotter than ever. On top of that, there was a virtual heroin epidemic sweeping the scene, as cheap Iranian heroin poured into town. When the seventies reached their apotheosis around the world, revelers found themselves in the forefront. Instead of picking up on the action, Keith holed up in an opulent suite at the Ritz Hotel in Piccadilly, overlooking Green Park. There, he and Anita kicked back behind a wall of cocaine, marijuana, booze, and the music that still played continuously on tapes and in his mind. He was immersing himself in what would become *Emotional Rescue*.

Keith had discovered how to use the press as a line of communication to the rest of the band in a 1971 interview in *Rolling Stone*, and he now took the opportunity to mend some bridges and let everybody in England know he was alive and well. He opened a new campaign to keep the Stones together by summoning to his suite the rock critic Chris Welch, who had written extensively about the Stones for *Melody Maker* in the sixties, for a major interview. "Keith, who now kept life at bay with hearty draughts of vodka, was an extraordinarily charming man, possessing infinite patience," wrote Welch. "While his speech and thoughts were sometimes held in check by the flow of soporifics and stimulants holding their own press conference inside his head, his acerbic wit and hard-bitten worldly wisdom remained intact." While talking about the flourishing London music scene, Keith fended off the standing criticism that he dismissed punk, new wave, and other rock trends.

RICHARDS: "I think punk rock was great theater, and it wasn't all crap. The music was all incidental, like background music. You just had to see it. It's a little too image-conscious from my point. It's like in the 1960s, 'We'll put this band in these clothes, we'll dye his hair.' As long as the band's good, I don't care what color they dye their hair. But anything other than California rock, anything but complacency, yeah, sure.

"I'm probably a little out of touch with the music scene here, but most of the stuff that's happened has lost touch with itself anyway. It's back to fads. One minute it's the Bay City Rollers, then it's punk rock, then it's power pop or new wave, then it's finished. People are back to sticking labels on things. Elvis Costello. I've 'eard his stuff. I'd sooner see him live, that's all I care about. I don't care about album production. I like Ian Dury, he's down to the bone. As long as there's something happening here, that's all that really matters. Where they went wrong with the punk thing was they were trying to make four-track records on thirty-two-track. We were trying to do the same thing in a way. We tried to make 1964 sound like 1956, which wasn't possible either. But we did end up with something that was our own."

Throughout the interview Anita chided him with sarcastic remarks and called him a baam claat man (a baam claat was a cloth used in Jamaica to mop up the blood of whipped slaves). Just as Linda Keith had ended up deploring Richards's musical direction, Anita attacked his refusal to develop a solo career. To the interviewer she insisted that he had future plans to get out a solo album. Keith demurred, saying he didn't give a shit.

RICHARDS: "I don't have time to think about doing stuff on my own. I'd just be cutting myself off from the Stones in one way, and that's not going to help anybody. I'm not interested. The basic thing about the Stones is that there is an understanding that there are five guys in the band, and there might be a few others involved in the making of a record, but what comes out of the speakers is basically one sound. It's like a watch—there might be fifteen little jewels in there, and all kinds of things ticking around, but if it don't make the hands go round it's no bloody good." In fact, he had released a poorly received single ("Run Rudolph Run"/"The Harder They Come") in the States in December '78, and there were persistent rumors in the press throughout 1979 that Rolling Stones Records was going to put out a Keith Richards solo album based on the Toronto tapes called Bad Luck. The question was whether Keith would work without the Stones. He would duck the issue for the next eight years.

"For what I do and what the rest of the band does, I don't think I could do it any better elsewhere, in a different setup," he told Welch. "Sometimes I might do the odd song alone, and that's the way we've always worked. Mick might say, 'Your rough tape has got the best feel, why don't you do that one?' But we still work closely on songs."

In 1979 Keith's songwriting output was prodigious. Apart from the songs that later appeared on *Emotional Rescue*, particularly the outstanding "All About You," on which he sang the lead vocal, and "Little T & A," on which he also sang lead and which would wind up on *Tattoo You*, he wrote a number of exceptional unreleased songs that year, such as "Let's Go Steady" and "We Had It All."

Richards's biggest headache in these choirboy days was the possibility of a reopening of the Toronto case. In November 1978 his worst fears had surfaced. The crown prosecutor had won an extension to appeal his sentence, and now Keith was back to attributing the whole brouhaha to political squabbles.

RICHARDS: "It's Canada vs. the Rolling Stones. I mean, I didn't screw Margaret Trudeau. Ah ha! But in that case—who did? Who ripped the flimsy bathrobe aside? I end up feeling like I have to pay for the rape of Canada. But I didn't have nothin' to do with it."

Keith was still reveling in the international success of *Some Girls* when he flew into Nassau in the Bahamas on January 20, 1979, to begin work on the sessions for the album *Emotional Rescue*. His head was full of ideas and his pockets jammed with cassettes of outtakes and rehearsals he had collected in England. But Keith's ideas met with opposition from the band.

RICHARDS: "You write a song, you have a certain feel, it's supposed to go this way, or you feel it's supposed to be very minimal lyrics, just sort of a chant, and here Jagger comes zoomin' in to the studio with a goddamn opera! You can't always click exactly right. Those things happen all the time. You say, 'I just can't see it any other way. I'm sorry.' And you go through all of that. When you're writing songs twenty years with a guy, you go through loads of these sorts of things. It's part of the process."

Richards was so determined to get the recordings just right that he would eventually delay the release of the album until he could be sure that the track "All About You" hadn't been subconsciously taken from another artist. And yet he was critical of Jagger's similar hands-on approach. Keith thought Mick was too involved with the businesspeople.

RICHARDS: "One of my points was that he had his hands on everything. Mick, nobody can do everything. And you're also wasting the big gun. I remember with Allen Klein renegotiating our record contract, we sat there in front of this board of directors and did not say a word. That's one of the greatest weapons the Stones have, the fear we inspire. If you're dealing with these people all the time, they get to know you too well. One of the Stones' greatest strengths in doing business was that we never said a word."

MICK JAGGER: "I read these things always: 'Mick's the calculating one; Keith's passionate.' But, I mean, I'm really passionate about getting things right. And if I'm not passionate about the details, some slovenly person that's employed in this organization will just let everything go."

"There was this awful inability to lead a separate existence," observed the British rock critic Michael Watts. "They were tied to each other creatively. They may have liked each other, but they really didn't want to be married and I don't think they ever really talked about the horror of it. One can imagine what a horror it must have been. It wasn't even like being brothers—they depended on each other for their livelihood. This operated far more in their case than it did with Lennon and McCartney, who were separate individuals. They had to work out some kind of *rapprochement* together. As they went into the 1980s I think that was the perception that a lot of people picked up." *Punch* magazine humorously likened the pair to other iconic, homoerotic duos, placing them in league with Gilbert and George, and Laurel and Hardy.

"It's a true friendship when you can bash somebody over the head and not be told, 'You're not my friend anymore,'" said Keith. "You put up with each other's bitching . . . He's my wife. And he'll say the same thing about me."

"Mick and Keith are going to have to face each other eventually," said Anita. "They should get married. The mayor of New York should marry them." Earl McGrath, who had replaced Marshall Chess as president of Rolling Stones Records, was of the opinion that "Keith didn't care about *anything* except Mick Jagger."

Keith particularly resented Jagger's refusal to tour in 1979 not least because it left him not knowing what to do. He also continued to resent Jerry Hall, knowing she would keep dragging Mick into the celebrity-studded disco world of Studio 54, which Keith saw as "a room full of faggots in boxing shorts waving champagne bottles in your face." The conflict that had made for creative tension had become a power struggle that would undermine their work throughout the eighties.

Keith had found a new drug partner in the comedian John Belushi, and as soon as he hit New York from Nassau in late February, he was spending nights staying up with John. Keith was a student of comedy, John was a champion of blues, and both were dedicated users. Keith sensed the same "I won't make it to thirty" quality in John he had in Brian Jones. Others saw Belushi as another victim of the Keith Richards lifestyle. When James Brown played Studio 54, Keith showed up in his dressing room with John, who had featured Brown in his film *The Blues Brothers*. They "sat around talking to me," Brown recalled, "but John was well out of it that night, and I remember thinking I wish I could be with him more and talk to him and help him straighten out."

Rolling Stones Records announced plans to release a Keith Richards solo single, "Bad Luck," in April, followed by an album of the same title but the disc was never released. In March Jonathan Cott saw Keith at Peter Tosh's show at the Bottom Line. "He looked as if he had just been taken down from the cross," Cott wrote. "He was incapable of getting around the room by himself and had to be virtually carried out of the club." Richards's survival instinct told him to get busy or die.

Richards did the previously unthinkable when he decided to tour in 1979 without the Rolling Stones. Ron Wood, who had less invested in his identity as a Stone, was putting together a band, the New Barbarians, with Ziggy Modeliste of the Meters on drums, the seminal jazz musician Stanley Clarke on bass, Ian McLagan of the Faces on keyboards, and Keith's old buddy Bobby Keys on sax, to do a brief spring tour in support of Wood's latest solo album, *Gimme Some Neck*.

RON WOOD: "It was easy to get Keith to back me up because he wasn't doing anything else. 'Hey, Keith.' I rang him up. 'You gonna sit on your ass for another few months or what?' Keith just said, 'If you're touring, I'm in on it.'"

Keith had been in a dilemma about going into Canada to play the

April 1979 concerts for the blind since the Canadian authorities could serve him with a subpoena on the appeal of his sentence and confiscate his passport. However, while he was rehearsing with the New Barbarians, his lawyer worked out an arrangement so that he could go into Canada and play the concerts, if he agreed to appear in court the following day to acknowledge the appeal.

On April 22, backed up by the New Barbarians and, in a surprise appearance, the Rolling Stones, Richards played two shows for the blind at the five-thousand-seat Oshawa Hall outside Toronto. Backstage before the first show Keith was bubbling with excitement. "It'll be a good show!" he promised Chet Flippo. "We'll just do 'Some Girls' and see how it works."

They were introduced by an ebullient John Belushi, who screamed, "I'm a sleazy actor on a late-night TV show, but I'm going to present some real musicians!" The high point of the show came when Keith and Mick sang "Prodigal Son" together on stools in front of microphones with an acoustic guitar, just as they had done when they started out together in a pub in Devon in 1961. The show raised fifty thousand dollars for the Canadian Institute for the Blind. Though still prodigal, the sinner had received full public absolution.

From April 26 through May 21 Richards went on the New Barbarians' tour of the States, playing from Washington and New York to L.A. As they traveled across the country, Blondie's "Heart of Glass" was topping the American charts, Bob Marley had picked up his biggest listening audience ever, and Elvis Costello was taking America's forward-looking youth by storm. Ron Wood's all-star band didn't measure up to the standards set by these innovative artists. "We hit about fifteen U.S. cities in a month," said Wood. "Unfortunately, there were all these fans yelling, 'Mick! Rod!' That was a bit of a blow to the ego. In fact, when we did Milwaukee, the kids literally tore up the place when no surprise guests came on. And we got slapped with a lawsuit." But the critics, ranging from the acerbic Lester Bangs to *The New York Times*'s Robert Palmer and *New Musical Express*'s Charles Shaar Murray, were impressed with Richards's stage presence, newfound energy, and apparent good health. There was, noticed one witness, "a new willful, jaunty bounce to his gait and an ease to his manner in general." By some miracle, it was noted, his teeth had grown back!

For Keith it was a double pleasure all down the line. The Toronto problem was off his back for now. Instead of being in jail, he was off in his favorite place—on the road with a bunch of, in his opinion, "great musicians." Despite drinking two fifths of vodka a night on stage, he had no trouble coming up after playing at his characteristic ankle level.

His visibility as an artist, not a junkie, had never been higher. His image was rehabilitated to the point where it was acceptable but still rough enough to be impressive. Keithmania prevailed. Bill German, editor of the Rolling Stones newsletter, *Beggars Banquet*, described the show at Madison Square Garden: "The handful of songs in which Keith had lead vocals had the crowd on their feet. Getting 'a little variety,' Woody played sax as Keith sang the old Sam Cooke song 'Let's Go Steady.' Keith took up the piano for 'Apartment No. 9,' a sweet ballad taken from his upcoming LP. Keith also sang 'Worried Life Blues,' a song the Stones did at the El Mocambo. Keith of course did 'Sure the One You Need,' in which he had to quickly ad-lib for forgotten lyrics in the third verse. If you wanted to see 20,000 people go bananas all at once you should have been there as Keith sang 'our rendition' of 'Before They Make Me Run.'"

"Behind Wood, nearly at the epicenter of the stage, the renewed man who has always played with the Rolling Stones is writhing in the music, backwards, forwards, almost falling to his knees as if it were his blood and not paint spilled on the stage, striking at his guitar in small, startled circular gestures as if it were too dangerous to really touch and, at the same time, as if it were irresistible— sweet pain—and showing (and showing off) that, the Rolling Stones aside, he'll take his rock and roll where he gets it," wrote Robert Duncan in *Hit Parader*. "Woody skitters back to the mike stand, which holds two mikes, and Keith writhes up next to him, directly on cue, as Zig Modeliste jams the band into overdrive and Ron and Keith and, off to the other side of the stage, Ian McLagan repeat chorus, repeat chorus, repeat chorus. Crash: 'Sweet little rock 'n' roller/Sweet little rock 'n' roller.'"

Charles Shaar Murray saw the Dallas show and wrote: "Richards was goofing off more than any other big-time guitar player. Even when they laid down a 'Jumpin' Jack Flash' encore sharp enough to perform open-heart surgery with, he still slid up to a climactic chord and missed it by a good three frets. He did everything but drop his pick, and stared down the audience as if daring someone to make something of it."

The tour gave Keith his first taste of working outside the Stones. "The thing about being in the Stones—and baby, when you're in the Stones, you're in the Stones—you don't get that much chance to go out on the road and play with other people, as a part of another band, just to keep your hand in," he told Lisa Robinson. "It was a delicate situation, not to come on too strong. I was there to back Woody up and that's what I tried to do. If you come on upstaging everybody, then there's no bloody point in being there, because you might as well go out on the road on your own."

Behind the scenes, however, the band had problems. In an unrealistic attempt to keep up his image as a Rolling Stone, Wood and his manager set up a tour that couldn't make any money. Despite selling out their sixteen concerts (largely, some griped, on the strength of the hinted-at appearances of Jagger and Bob Dylan), the luxurious private jet, the fleet of limousines, and first-class hotels ate up the profits. Furthermore, although Wood's album came out during the tour, it did not sell particularly well, and Keith's much-heralded solo album, *Bad Luck*, was canceled. Consequently, imagined profits turned into a mirage, which particularly annoyed Richards, who was in need of money due to his enormous legal bills for Toronto. Lil, who accompanied Keith throughout the tour, said that it was different from a Rolling Stones tour in every conceivable way. "Of course he enjoyed it," she said. "But there was also a lot of bullshit going on."

Offstage, in the luxurious cocoon of limousines and first-class hotels, Richards showed signs of being lost. Witness after witness reported scenes of Keith, bottle in hand, spliff in the other, his puffy, lined face and graying hair showing age far beyond his years, staggering from hotel room to hotel room, barefoot and bare-chested, while a tape of the night's performance roared out of his cassette player. "Do anything you want to do," Keith told one visitor in his Dallas hotel room after a show, "just don't touch me." According to another witness, "He looked around as if he'd only just realized where he was and passed out, schlumpfed in a corner, cheeks drawn, mouth open, eyes shut, while a bunch of people he hardly knew rang room service on his tab, smoked his dope, and made free with his room." His relationship with Woody, whom he now referred to as Squirt, was strained, as Keith's buddy and biggest fan edged closer to becoming a casualty of the drug lifestyle.

On May 21 the New Barbarians finished the month-long tour at the L.A. Forum. For a treat, in the town that seemed to be his nemesis, Keith bought some Persian Brown heroin from Cathy Smith, who would later be involved in John Belushi's death. "I was reliving a second rock and roll childhood," he said. "I could have gone back. Easy. It could have gone either way for me, life or death."

"I have grimly determined to change my life and abstain from any drug use" was the opening line of a statement by Richards that was read by his lawyer in front of a panel of judges in a Toronto court on June 27. "I can truthfully say that the prospect of ever using drugs again in the future is totally alien to my thinking. My experience has also had an important effect not only on my happiness, but on the happiness at home in which my young son is brought up."

On the basis of this statement and a positive report from the Turning Point program, the panel drew the conclusion that Richards had overcome his heroin addiction once and for all. In October it handed down a decision refusing to reopen the case. For the first time in nine years, Richards was totally free from the threat of incarceration. His ability to live beyond the law enhanced his legend and kept him in the world of make-believe. The same year Chuck Berry was sentenced to four months in prison for a minor case of tax evasion. He was one of many black R&B stars to suffer jail terms. Keith's mojo was still working.

The extent to which Richards was protected was emphasized by two things that happened while the court was considering the appeal. Tony Sanchez published *Up and Down with the Rolling Stones*, a lurid account of his career as Keith's drug procurer, which was serialized in the *New York Post* and syndicated across America. Sanchez portrayed Keith as a callous drug abuser, verging on evil, and Anita as a drug-crazed beauty turned hag. "She had been prey to the gross enlargement of conventional insecurities," wrote one reviewer. Sanchez's book was a grueling testament to the ten years of heroin addiction that had led to these tragic images.

RICHARDS: "I couldn't plow through it all because my eyes were watering from laughter. But the basic laying out of the story—'He did this, he did that'—is true. Tony didn't really write it. He had some hack from Fleet Street write it; obviously, Tony can hardly write his own name. He was a great guy. I always considered him a friend of mine. I mean, not anymore. But I understand his position: He got into dope, his girlfriend OD'd, he went on the skids and . . . it's all this shit. As far as that book's concerned, as far as, like, a particular episode, just the bare facts—yeah, they all happened."

It was, wrote one critic, "the most nightmarish book on rock yet written. Mr. 'Elegantly Wasted' emerges as a self-centered skinflint, paranoid, the sort of man who toys with the idea of using his child as a smack courier. This desperate kiss and tell is a portrait of malevolence and imbecility."

On July 20, just as the Sanchez book hit the newspapers, a seventeen-year-old boy named Scott Cantrell blew the back of his head off in Richards's house, Frog Hollow, in South Salem, New York.

According to shocking press reports, Cantrell had killed himself in Keith and Anita's bed with one of Keith's stolen guns. The fact that Richards was living in his Paris flat with Lilly making *Emotional Rescue* notwithstanding, the negative publicity seared him like a lineup spotlight, bringing with it all the old charges about the Rolling Stones' relationship with Satan, drugs, and death. Anita, who appeared in photographs and nightclubs around New York looking bloated and deranged, did little to quell rumors that she was involved with dispensing drugs to teenage boys and sex orgies, although she denies having sex with Cantrell. According to Anita,

Keith called from Paris and was upset about the incident, but not because of the death. "He didn't say anything about the guy, he just got annoyed with my negligence, being so sloppy and flopped out. He just said, 'Oh, you managed to lose a piece, didn't you?' I thought that was very hard, because it was not a life, just the gun that had gone with the police he was concerned about." Anita knew that this was the last straw, and that their common-law marriage, if not their fifteen-year relationship, was over. "That boy of seventeen who shot himself in my house really ended it for us," she said. "And although we occasionally saw each other for the sake of the children, it was the end of our personal relationship."

In and out of the court and the glare of the public eye for the rest of the year, Anita was finally cleared of any involvement in Cantrell's death, pleaded guilty to possession of a stolen gun, was fined one thousand dollars, and was given a conditional discharge.

ANITA PALLENBERG: "For a while it was a nightmare. The lawyers told us we were no good for each other because of the drugs. They said we were a bad influence on each other. I always had my boyfriends on the side. It was loneliness. I didn't think anything bad. I used to introduce them to him. He met them all. But I think the relationship was good. It wasn't like Bianca and Mick or Angie and David [Bowie]. It was nothing like that with Keith. He's a very understanding, a very human person and he appreciates home and he's a really rewarding person."

Anita was more dangerous than ever—fat, strung out, and horrified by what her life had become. She lived in hotels, apartments, and houses in New York or Long Island paid for by Keith, watched over day and night by surly "friends of Keith's," large, silent English bodyguards and roadies whose conversations were at times so psychotic she was thankful for their silence. She cried to friends that she really wanted just to get back together with Keith and have a family, but when they recommended that she lose weight, see a hairdresser, and go to the gym, she scoffed that she had already *been* a top model. To his entourage she seemed a pathetic wreck, but Anita knew Keith was still frightened of her and attracted to her. Some time after Cantrell's suicide they met in a New York hotel room. "I was really overweight," Anita remembered, "and I really didn't think he liked me, but I guess he loved me because he still wanted to make love to me. But I didn't feel worth it," she recalled, "for him. I said, 'You bring out the worst in me.'" For Keith, Anita still had the lure of the divine mother. She inspired one of the best songs on which he sang the lead vocal, the elegiacal "All About You," which would come out on *Emotional Rescue* and feature the telling line "I'm so sick and tired hanging around with dogs like you." It would mark a turning point in his songwriting career, prefiguring the more emotionally expressive style of his solo album. Keith was still as vulnerable to Anita as he was to junk. Everybody else Keith hung out with was in the drug world. He was surrounded by creeps and dealers who spent the majority of their time trying to hustle him.

Before continuing to record *Emotional Rescue* in Paris, Keith took a vacation in Florida with Lil, Freddie Sessler, and Sessler's new girlfriend, Terry Hood. Having lost the anchor of his family, Richards stumbled through the second half of 1979.

TERRY HOOD: "Keith is a very sensitive person and can be very emotional. He is a very interesting character, a bunch of complexities but really a very old-fashioned person. He has a lot of very interesting perceptions and sees life from different angles from being at the same time old-fashioned and sensitive. A lot of his sensitivity used to come out when he was stoned. Sometimes he would talk about the death of Tara in a roundabout way and he would get very emotional. He was very romantic, very big on flower petals on the floor in the bedroom. One night, I remember, we got flowers for the room for him and Lil. They were like confetti on the floor and he came out and went to the refrigerator and took out a carton of chocolate milk. He had had a bath and he had a box of Oreos under his arm and he was heading out the front door. I said, 'Where are you going?,' because if he went outside the building there was a security lock and he wouldn't be able to get back in. I said, 'You don't want to go out there, you don't have a key.' And he lay down on the floor and said, 'You know, these are my stage pants.' He'd been up for a few days. I said, 'Don't you want to get in bed or let me put a pillow under your head? You look like a gypsy down there.' And he said, 'It's a privilege to be a gypsy and be comfortable and to lay your head wherever you are.' He's one of those great storybook characters."

On October 26 Richards and Jagger flew to New York to mix *Emotional Rescue*. They continued arguing over the selection of tracks and mixes. Keith wanted to stay raw and take chances. Mick wanted to play it safe, go for mainstream pop success, and make as much money as possible. In November, in between periods of working with Jagger, Richards let out frustration by playing on albums by Steve Cropper, Screamin' Jay Hawkins, and Ian McLagan.

Keith was like a man on the run trapped in a maze of trick mirrors. Everywhere he turned he saw people he loved disintegrating or disappearing, and he couldn't do anything to help them. Since the New Barbarians tour he had stopped spending so much time with Wood. Ronnie was freebasing cocaine and losing his grip on reality. All Keith could do was turn away from the problem. Jagger had become embroiled with Bianca in a publicized divorce and had disappeared deeper into the jet set. The Glimmer Twins rarely saw each other or talked when they weren't working. "Keith thinks the same as when he started, but I don't," Jagger noted. Keith's lifestyle had taken its toll on Lilly. They continued to have a great sexual relationship, but she could no longer offer him a haven. There was no home he could go to and feel grounded except Freddie Sessler's apartment in Florida. He visited Freddie frequently during this period, but for someone struggling with drug addiction, Freddie's world was not a particularly healthy one. Freddie Sessler was undoubtedly a father figure to Keith, but as Keith tried to straighten out he would often become annoyed by Sessler's behavior.

Keith had always made a point of celebrating his birthday to the hilt. His thirty-sixth birthday, in 1979—despite the unsettled nature of his life at this point—would be no exception. One friend who shared Keith's birthday commented, "Being a Sagittarius is not an easy sign. He's got an angel on one shoulder and a devil on the other. It's given him beautiful women and riches, but it's also given him a lot of pain. His personality was split. Half of him wanted to take the dark path, half the light."

A number of friends gathered in New York for the occasion. Bobby Keys was there. John Dunbar flew in from London. Keith was again on the trot for three days at a time. With a bottle of Rebel Yell in his hand and half an ounce of cocaine in his pocket he would crash out wherever he fell, then wake up several hours later and just party straight on with whoever could keep up.

David Courts, Keith's jeweler, arrived from London with a special gift he had made: a beautiful, thick, funky silver ring in the shape of a skull. Keith became enamored of the ring and wore it from then on because, he told a friend, it reminded him of his own mortality and of the fact that we are all the same beneath the skin. He was wearing the skull ring that week when he met the one person who could fill the void left by Anita and Mick.

Patti Hansen, born on St. Patrick's Day, March 17th, was a feisty model with apple-pie looks. Trying to get Keith to move on with his life, several friends had urged him to call up Patti, who they thought could be the right woman and soul mate he desperately needed. They shared a forthrightness, a sense of humor, and working-class roots. "For a year before I met Patti," Keith recounted, "every other night someone would say, 'Oh, you should meet this Patti Hansen.' I kept asking. 'Why should I meet this Patti Hansen?' I found out." Jerry Hall invited Patti to meet Keith at his birthday party, which took place at the Roxy roller rink in New York, but Anita, who was hoping to get Keith back if he broke up with Lil, was there too. Further complicating the setup was the arrival of one of Keith's presents, a renowned call girl who arrived naked in a limo with a big ribbon tied around her. The poet Jim Carroll, who had recently embarked on a rock and roll career and become friends with Keith, remembered the comedy: "When Anita arrived she immediately started screaming, 'I want to see Keith now! Where the hell is he? It's his party! I have his son here, for God's sake! He wants to go roller-skating with his dad!' She wasn't looking as good as she used to, but she still had this incredible Teutonic presence and I think Keith still had the fear of God in him about Anita's jealousies. When he finally came out of a back room where he had apparently been with his 'present,' Keith had to do a little shuffle himself. It was a funny night."

But it was Hansen who won out. When Keith called in the middle of the night and asked her to meet him at a club, they finally got together. For the next five days they ran around New York in a limousine accompanied by an entourage, playing loud reggae music and stopping at clubs, record shops, restaurants, and other people's apartments along the way. On the fifth day without sleep they wound up at a party at Mick and Jerry's, but Patti felt like a zombie and decided to leave. Keith turned to Mick and said, "I'm outta here too, I'm going with this lady."

A limousine driver named Bernie Cohen who occasionally ferried the Stones around New York remembered one journey in which Keith was sandwiched between two people who spent the whole time trying to persuade him to buy drugs. Keith had fended them off but sounded more and more uncomfortable. Three days later Cohen found himself driving Keith around with Patti Hansen. He noticed that with her Keith seemed to be a whole new person, balanced and calm.

PATTI HANSEN: "When I first met Keith all I could think was: 'This is a guy who really needs a friend.' I gave him the keys to my apartment after only knowing him two weeks. There was no sexual thing going on. I knew he just needed a secret place where he could get far away from the madding crowd. It wasn't love at first sight, though it feels like that now. It just sort of mutually grew. But he is the most romantic man. So romantic. I remember New Year's Eve '79 going into '80. I came back from Staten Island in my brother's Oldsmobile because I knew somehow I was going to see him. I just knew it. When I got to my apartment, there he was sitting on my stairs, waiting for me. Keith and I have never been apart on a New Year's Eve since."

22

Wanna Hold You
1980

Patti Hansen—like Keith—is totally free of artifice. She is a relaxing and stabilizing influence on Keith.

FRAN LEBOWITZ, *from an interview with Kevin Sessums, 1989*

The Hansens lived on Staten Island, where Patti had grown up as the youngest of six children in a working-class family. Her father was a bus driver. The close-knit family was devoutly Lutheran. One brother was a minister. Patti was a bold, confident, no-bullshit person and she shared with Keith a raw, earthy humor. "She's from great stock," said her friend and hairdresser, "and has been unconditionally loved all her life." Patti's modeling career began when she was spotted, at age fifteen, by a talent scout at a Rolling Stones concert on the 1975 tour. By the time Keith met her, she was a top model who had been featured on the cover of *Vogue*, and was starting a movie career. She had built a reputation in both fields for being reliable, hardworking, enthusiastic, and loyal. As one friend said, "Patti Hansen is Marilyn Monroe without the neuroses."

To Steve Rubell, one of the owners of Studio 54, Patti was like one of the Gabor sisters, a "real pro" who "knew how to look after her man." She had a golden glow about her, somewhat like Anita's when she had been twenty-three, but without the dark side. Patti had a great sense of humor that matched Keith's—they laughed a lot. She loved reggae. She was smart, levelheaded, someone he could talk to. As he put it in "Little T&A," "the little bitch got soul." Not since Anita had he found this combination. Patti was everything Keith desired in a woman. But she was letting herself in for a hard time—fending off the allure of drugs with one hand and grabbing Keith's attention with the other. The question was, could she maintain the pace and stand the pressure that had burned out so many women before her?

Patti had several advantages. A star herself, she didn't take Jagger's bullshit, and, as one friend pointed out with relief, he wouldn't be able to fuck her. She was the top model of the year when Keith met her, and was about to start work on a film with the eminent Peter Bogdanovich, with whom she had previously been involved. She was also very protective of Keith. Whereas Lilly had valiantly tried to keep the drug people away but ultimately failed, Patti put her foot down and kept it there. For a while people such as Freddie Sessler would find themselves less needed than they had been.

The worst thing about being supposedly straight, Keith told David Courts, was that he often had to go down to the Lower East Side by himself, carrying a gun, to make the connection.

RICHARDS: "I mean, my view of the world is totally distorted. Maybe the whole dope thing was a way of negating that superstar stratosphere—'cause that put me down in the gutter. One minute I'm operating as a superstar and the next I'm shooting up with some guys on the Lower East Side. There was a time the dope scene was pretty rugged. And when scoring I packed a piece to shoot the lights out and go. They'd wait downstairs to rob you of your stuff. They had a two-way street going—you'd go up and buy it and they'd take it back. I've done chandeliers, just to get out. Just go down blazing. Suddenly I realized—what the hell am I doing? I'd be taking apart a cheap hotel room to hide this shit."

On a number of occasions, muggers who were about to rip him off flashed on who he was and smiled apologetically. Patti inspired Keith to make a last-ditch effort to completely stop taking heroin, which he was still dabbling dangerously in when they met. "Patricia is a remarkable girl," he said. "I could have just drifted at that point when I met her. I could have relived my forgotten youth or I could have gotten it together. Patricia turned me around just when I needed turning."

"Keith met her at the perfect time," said one friend. "She had everything Anita and Lil had but she also had the other side, and she offered Keith the opportunity to see his positive side. She is as spirited and emotional as he is, like a wild horse—they were so alike—but above all, Patti had balance."

One of Keith's pleasures was seeing the looks on the dealers' faces when he turned down a free taste. "After ten years of trying to kill myself," he said, "I decided I'd better get on with my life." However, as soon as Richards stopped being a junkie, he became an alcoholic. Keith's rationale for being addicted in the past had always been that he could never get enough time off to clean up. Clearly this was not the case in 1979 and 1980, when he had virtually two years off except for a few scattered months of recording. He certainly knew alcohol had more deleterious effects than heroin, which by itself harmed neither body nor brain.

RICHARDS: "I consider booze to be far more harmful than any other available drug, far more damaging to the body, to the mind, to the person's attitude. The way some people change on it is amazing, and then, goddamn it, every morning when you wake up you've got a cold turkey whether you like it or not. You know, just because it's called the 'hangover.' It seems to me the most uneconomical and inconvenient high you could possibly have, 'cause every morning you've got to pay for it. I mean, even a junkie doesn't have to do that unless he decides to stop or runs out of stuff, but even if you've got bottles of booze in the morning you've still got a hangover. And it just seems so vague putting yourself through those constant incredible changes. That's what I think really does you with booze."

The continued dependence had deeper roots: Keith needed alcohol or drugs to maintain a state of mind conductive to total devotion to his music. Under the influence, he could remain, indefinitely, in his private world. As Dr. Joseph Gross explained the syndrome: "Some alcoholics get to a state of mind which is like an acid trip. They enter into another kind of reality and enjoy the agonies and ecstasies of their trip. They couldn't care less about anything else that's happening, and in fact when they're in that state they can actually do all kinds of wonderful, crazy, impossible, and real things. Particularly for introverted and expressively inhibited people, alcohol initially projects them into a whole spectrum of reality from which they're otherwise cut off."

Keith clearly enjoyed his debauched image. In a 1980 *Hit Parader* interview with Lisa Robinson he boasted, "I've been drunk for twenty-seven years!" From 1980 on he was constantly photographed on and off stage waving a bottle of Jack Daniel's or Rebel Yell around. He told one friend that he had gotten over the hurdle of missing heroin all the time and thought he really didn't have to worry about it anymore. To this self-deception his interlocutor replied, "It isn't too hard not to worry about it when you're drinking a couple of quarts of Rebel Yell a day, Keith!"

His habits died hard, and he continued to party and stay up for days, occasionally with unfortunate consequences.

RICHARDS: "I'd been up for nine days. I was working on something in the studio and I put a tape in the machine to hear the latest blast I'd gotten. I turned around and fell asleep for a milli-second and I collapsed into the corner of a JBL speaker. You know what noses are like. Great nap, waking to this red shower. I think I gave it a slight curve to the left. It was just that life was so interesting for nine days that I couldn't give it up. Not even for a minute."

Richards was excited about making 1980 a Rolling Stones year. After one and a half years off the road, and with *Emotional Rescue* due for release that summer, he was sure they would tour. It was always one of the ironies of the Rolling Stones that as soon as one of the band rose to the top, full of fresh energy, another simultan-eously sunk to the bottom. In February 1980 Ron and his girlfriend, Josephine Carslake, were arrested on the island of Saint Martin with two hundred grams of cocaine.

Jagger was set on making the eighties their greatest financial decade and the last thing he wanted was legal screwups with visas. The Stones' drug convictions had already cost them millions of dollars in unearned revenues from markets such as Japan that barred them from playing. Despite the agility with which the Rolling Stones' legal machine sprang Wood and Carslake from five terrifying days in a Saint Martin jail and flew them out on a private jet, the image of the Stones as drug outlaws was once again in the headlines, although this time without the rebellious context of the sixties or punk glimmer of the seventies—the busted Wood just looked foolish. At a dinner in New York a week later, Mick Jagger told Andy Warhol and William Burroughs that there might not be a Rolling Stones in 1982 (their twentieth anniversary). He was clearly asking himself how much longer he could afford to be associated with this sort of juvenile scene.

However much Wood protested that he had been set up, he now became, in the eyes of the public and opinion of the band, the group's troublemaker, moving ominously into the fall-guy position Brian Jones had occupied. Ron Wood was as addicted to the Stones as he was to drugs and he couldn't afford to lose them. It became apparent that he had made a mistake in taking the advance rather than the salary when he officially joined the band in 1975. He was getting paid half of what the others received per year, and as he was receiving no songwriting royalties from the Rolling Stones (he did get some royalties on his solo album) he was in a different financial bracket from Mick and Keith altogether. In the last five years he had gone broke trying to keep up a style of living that was suitably lavish for a Rolling Stone. Psychologically, Ronnie was hanging onto his position in the Stones by his fingernails. For the next three years he would remain on the verge of being expelled from the band.

By the time the Stones met in New York in April to shoot promotional films and put finishing touches to the album, there was little feeling of unity among them. Wyman had been quoted in a British tabloid as saying he intended to quit in 1982. Even the stolid Charlie Watts was growing weary. "I can't keep up being a Rolling Stone all the time," he told a reporter. "Plus the fact that I hate rock and roll. Rock and roll is a load of old rubbish, isn't it?" In a later retraction, he told another reporter, "I didn't say I hated rock and roll. That's why I never give interviews." Richards, the perennial enthusiast, was the only one raring to go. "I still find that we—as a band—are doing things that are improving, amongst ourselves, and everyone in the band is still interested," he said. "It's collective interest that keeps it going." Richards now really stepped out of his ten-year fog to wrest his share of control of the band away from Jagger, who was in charge of when, where, and how to tour. As for the other band members, skeptical as they may have been about the future of the band, they were all keen to tour because they needed the money. Jagger dangled the possibility before them, implying in interviews at one point that the band would tour in 1980. Discussions were under way for a U.S. tour in June or July. Later it was rumored they would play one New York date to promote the album. There was even talk of touring China. When Keith became more aggressive on what he considered his turf—the recording studio—Jagger tried to block him, and the fights turned nasty.

All this on-again, off-again uncertainty put a strain on Richards.

RICHARDS: "When I did clean up my act—'OK, now I'm ready to shoulder some of the burden again. God bless you for taking it all on your shoulders when I was out there playing the freaked-out artist and getting busted'—he [Mick] supported me every fucking bit of the way. I ain't knocking the cat at all. But when I came back, I didn't want to believe that Mick was enjoying the burden. He could now control the whole thing; it became a power trip. I heard that shit from the john like 'I wish he was a junkie again.'"

In June 1980 *Emotional Rescue* was released, and the band members presented a united front to the press. The boys-together theme was still the magnet for their predominantly male audience. To one New York reporter Richards revealed, "We did about forty songs for this album. Then Mick goes back and listens to them, trying to pare it down to the ones which seem to fit together as one album. Then I'll listen to his choices; then we'll listen together. Usually, though, he knows what will make the best Stones album."

Perhaps Keith said this because he figured that he and Jagger had reached a truce after the release of the album, and that Mick was about to give in on the tour issue. People who witnessed his behavior that June saw a man leading a carefree—if not careless—existence.

But the split was quite obvious to outside observers. On June 23, while the band hosted a release party in London, Keith was on his way to an appointment with *Rolling Stone*'s top Stones reporter, Chet Flippo, in New York.

CHET FLIPPO: "Keith marched into the Rockefeller Center offices of Rolling Stones Records at 6 P.M., loudly announcing, 'I'm ready for my bacon and eggs.' He was waving a fifth of Jack Daniel's. He had just awoken and wanted breakfast—the sourmash bourbon kind. He seated himself with a flourish at Earl McGrath's desk and tried to crack the seal on the Black Jack bottle, without success. 'I've got a key we could try,' I ventured, but Keith cut me off by whipping out this enormous gravity knife and—kachunk!—snapping it open. He winked at me and held up the knife: 'This is the key to the highway!' He poured us both hefty tumblers of Jack and toasted me . . ."

"My idea is to get out another album this year and then we can get those motherfuckers out on the road! Instead of the same old treadmill of the road, studio, road, studio, we can take extended road trips or do anything we want to do; be movie stars or make solo albums," he told Flippo.

Three days later, June 26, the Rolling Stones (*sans* Charlie, who missed his plane) gave an afternoon party for the album's release in a New York new-wave club, Danceteria. The atmosphere was far from relaxed. Each band member was given a bodyguard; Jagger took his into the toilet and proceeded to snort half a gram of coke, smoke a big joint, and bolt half a bottle of whiskey in order to become "Mick Jagger" for forty-five minutes. For Richards, the party was just another pit stop on his long day's journey into night. The poet-singer Jim Carroll, whose first album, *Catholic Boy*, had recently been signed to Rolling Stones Records, was performing that night at another club, Trax, where Richards was to guest on the song that was the album's single, "People Who Died." Jim spent the majority of the day with Keith.

JIM CARROLL: "We met up at Rolling Stones Records' office that morning, Keith had been up all night with Patti Hansen, who was on the couch, totally zonked out, and we just cleaned up the desk and did one of those big mandala jobs of coke. Keith had the best-looking coke I've ever seen, that's for sure, pure-crystalline-new-age-quartz-crystal coke! It was very good, too, and so we were all getting wiped out, or wiped up, and I'm thinking maybe I shouldn't be doing this before my show, but when I expressed this concern Keith gave me a little two-gram bottle and said, 'Save this for the show tonight.'

"I had a bottle of methadone. I signaled to Keith to go into the other room, Jane Rose's office. She worked for the Stones but she mainly was a flack for Keith, and we locked the door behind us 'cause this was something I did not want Earl to see, and I said to Keith, 'I've got some methadone, do you want some?' He said. 'Oh, man, God—this is like a blessing from God, Jim.' He says, 'I've been up all night, I got drunk, I'm wired from this coke,' he says, 'and since I'm clean I can really feel this stuff now!' So he said, 'How much do you think I should take? You know, what's the dosage here?' And I said, 'It's a hundred milligram bottle,' which is like the strongest you could get, and so he said, 'Oh just give me two capfuls.' I marked some and poured it out and so Keith said, 'Oh, this is just great, and I can really feel this stuff now, you know.' When you're wired from coke it's perfect, because if it's good coke the methadone just sets it up and it feels like heroin. So at any rate, it gave Keith his second wind and everything was hunky-dory.

"Then at the *Emotional Rescue* party around four that afternoon he said, 'Do you have any more? It really kicked in nice.' He said, 'I think there's no sense in being too cautious about this.' So at the party I gave him a little more."

It was one of those days, and they were increasingly frequent, when Keith and Mick had nothing to say to each other even when they were pressing up against each other in the media crush. Jagger was seen leaving the party hastily after a brief altercation.

JIM CARROLL: "We were going right to the sound check at Trax from there. Keith didn't go. Mick came. He was particularly helpful and enthusiastic about the show, checking out the sound, giving me little pieces of advice.

"We planned that Keith was going to come up and play these very Chuck Berryish solos on 'People Who Died.' First of all, we were trying to get down the chords with him beforehand. It was a pretty basic song and he got it, but I think he forgot it by the time ... at any rate, Keith came out and was so completely drunk and wiped out by then it just sounded terrible. So we started out and there were these brilliant notes coming out, you know, and he was playing chord-lead-notes type of Keith riffs, it did sound like archetypal Keith Richards solos, but it was off to the point where I think he might have been playing in a different key. I only listened to it like once and that was it for me, but it didn't matter, I mean it was great, like Keith Richards was up there making these great moves."

From the audience, the photographer Bob Gruen noticed that "seeing Keith play without the other Stones made me realize that *he* is the reason the Stones' sound is so unique. I mean, the minute he started playing with the Jim Carroll Band, the music took on an enormous heaviness, like an elephant running. The Stones always sound like that, but you don't realize that Keith is the reason, because he's up there with them for the whole show. If the Stones played even one song without him, you wouldn't recognize their sound."

Jim Carroll found out that Keith also recognized his own impact when Richards read an interview with Carroll in which he said Lou Reed told him that working with the Stones was the kiss of death. "Keith got very angry," Carroll recalled. "He left a note with the article pinned up on the wall and he told Earl not to take it down and he wrote on the bottom of it, 'Dear Jim, lucky thing you put this on Lou, piss de breath kiss of death.'"

When Keith played at Trax, it was clear how eager he was to play, but it was also apparent just how frustrating it must have been for Jagger to have put up with this guy who was very drunk almost all the time and was never somebody who could be reasoned with. A week later, Keith's hope for a Stones year replete with tours and celebrations came crashing down. As *Emotional Rescue* went on the British and American charts, on its way to number one in both markets, Jagger, who was departing on an extended vacation with Jerry in Morocco, sent a telex to the New York office saying he had no intention of going on the road in 1980. Keith was enraged. "Mick waited until he was three thousand miles away and just sent a telex," he fumed. "I mean, he could have told me this, in person, two days earlier, before he flew away! During that period we almost came to blows—or worse."

Their attitudes toward their music were also increasingly disparate. Richards passionately believed in rock music's longevity. As he put it: "Rock and roll is as healthy as ever. We all tend to forget that it's ninety percent crap anyway. But the ten percent is good.

The younger kids have sort of got the right idea on how to play it; they have the right attitude. And that's what rock and roll is, an attitude."

"There is no future in rock and roll," Jagger said. "It's only recycled past."

From a practical point of view, Jagger was in a stronger position than Richards. He had built the business machine that ran the organization. The men in power—Rupert Loewenstein, Earl Mc-Grath, and Alan Dunn, to name but a few of the top people among the Stones' one hundred full-time employees—were his men. Richards had never learned to work with the people who ran much of his life. He had access to them, but was rarely able to keep his appointments with them, sometimes strolling in as much as two weeks late for a meeting and then acting dismayed that nobody else was there. He never made any serious efforts to get involved in the Rolling Stones' business organization. He just constantly tried to make Jagger see things his way. Keith had always understood their need for each other better than Mick and was less willing to risk breaking that tie. Not being a musician, Jagger was not as aware of the dynamics of the music and began to believe (encouraged by as many sycophants as he could accommodate) that he could be just as successful—or more so—without the Rolling Stones. There was so much more money to be made if he worked on his own, the idea gnawed at him.

Meanwhile, *Emotional Rescue* hit top-ten charts worldwide. It reached the number-one spot in Britain and America, and held steady for seven weeks in the U.S. and two in the U.K. The Stones' audience had grown so large that almost anything the group released would reach the top ten. But hard-core fans were not fooled by the album's popularity. The listeners who waited for each new Stones album the way some people wait for instructions from God were disappointed. The Stones, too, were far from satisfied with the album. It was a nagging reminder of their flagging drive and spirit.

In March 1980, Keith moved his clothes and guitars into Patti's Greenwich Village apartment. He even made the gesture of meeting her parents and family. They were worried about Patti's involvement with a man they saw as a decadent, self-destructive rock star. Patti, who was close to her parents, was keen to allay their fears about Keith. Thus it came about that one night the thirty-six-year-old Rolling Stone found himself trembling in his boots as he made his way to Staten Island to meet Mr. and Mrs. Hansen.

RICHARDS: "After all this time, I'd never been through this trip, meeting a girl's parents, so it was important to me. But the first time I went to meet Patti's parents, I was out of it. I tried to be real cool, and I overdid it. I'd been up for days, got drunk, figured I'd keep myself real mellow. Instead, I wound up out of my brain smashing up stuff. But they dug it. I went crazy and it didn't offend them. I could have blown it, you know, 'Never come back here again!' I was my worst. I went totally over the top. But they dug me for it. That was the first indication that if they can take that, 'this family I can do with.'"

"After I met him," said her brother Harry, "I knew she had made the right choice. He's so different from what you expect. I was amazed at what a well-mannered, intelligent, poetic man he is. They are a perfect match—both are blunt, bold, no-bullshit people."

However, Keith was reticent about their relationship. Patti was very young and in many ways resembled the youthful Anita, and Keith was worried about making another commitment of that nature. If the pattern were to repeat itself, Keith wouldn't be able to survive the consequences.

Keith was loath to break up with old girlfriends. He continued to see Lilly and Anita on the side, neither one of whom intended to let him go without putting up a good fight. Shortly before meeting Patti, Keith had told Jane Rose to find a New York town house for him and Lilly, and they had moved in together. Keith continued to visit her there throughout 1980 and into early 1981. In early 1980, on one of the first occasions Keith went out with Patti in public, to the Ritz nightclub in New York, an inebriated Anita came in and saw them sitting at a banquet table in the roped-off celebrity section. Creeping up behind them, she climbed onto the top of the table and, before Keith knew what was happening, wrapped both her legs around his head and squeezed it between her thighs, giving him what one observer described as "a muffie." While Patti, not knowing what to do, looked on horrified, Keith begged Anita like a child to "please, please let me go."

"Keith and I still love and respect each other," Anita told friends. "The trouble was, we couldn't live together. The people who really love Keith are waiting for him to grow out of the kind of life he lives and the creeps he lets surround him. I've always been his greatest fan."

RICHARDS: "I don't consider myself separated from Anita or anything. She's still the mother of my kids. Anita is a great, great woman. She's a fantastic person. I love her. I can't live without her, you know?"

Actually, Anita's relationship with Keith remained quite amicable through this transition. "He doesn't ignore me. He didn't put me through any bullshit like Bianca," said Pallenberg. "We already had so many legal hassles as it was. Who wants to go through any more? Now the problem is Doris is keeping Dandelion in a shell. She seems to be more conscious of who she is, who Keith is. Like, Marlon is Keith's mate, and they've always been mates, but it seems to be more difficult with her. I meet Keith now and talk about it and see what we can do. We're trying to redeem her. He comes and visits and says, 'Hello,' brings goodies for Marlon, brings me tapes to play. He's mellowed out a lot. He's had lots of girlfriends from when we kind of split up, and I met them all. There was no way out of it. And I've been around him so long anyway. But Patti's the only one I think is OK. She takes care of him. I'm really happy, because you do feel you have to look after them."

That August Keith took Patti to Redlands for the first time. Lilly was stashed in a suite in the Savoy where Keith would visit her during trips to London. On one occasion Lilly even went down to Redlands to suss out the situation regarding Patti for herself. According to Terry Hood, Patti behaved very well throughout the entire period, but after one night when Keith went to London and returned the following morning, she told him that she was a star in her own right and did not have time for this jive rock and roll bullshit.

However, despite rumors in New York that they had broken up and the fact that Keith did continue to see Lil, Patti appeared mollified. By the time Richards went to Paris to meet Jagger in October to start work on the next Stones album, *Tattoo You,* everything between them was copacetic.

"Would it be fair to say you're in love?" asked the reporter Kurt Loder.

"Oh, yeah, but I've always been in love," Keith replied.

"It seems like you and Patti, though . . ."

"It's a big one, it's a big one. Yeah. It doesn't matter, I'll tell ya—yeah. I'm in love. Those are the things that, when you're on the other side of the scale, you know and you think, 'Oh, goddamn, you can only be in love when you're eighteen or twenty-three or . . . But when you get older, suddenly—bang! Once again! And you realize that was all a load of crap. All those things that turn you on, you know? Those are the things that make you look forward, keep you going. You say, 'Well, it can happen, keep on going.' I mean, it's the greatest feeling in the world, right?"

"Love is good!"

"Love wears a white Stetson."

Meanwhile, as Patti became more interested in acting than modeling, Keith got interested in working with her on a movie, for which he would write the score and in which he would play a small part.

The good feeling seems to have spread to Jagger also, because two of the four songs they recorded in the October–November sessions at Pathé-Marconi in Paris were celebrations of their friendship, the loving "Waiting on a Friend" and "Neighbors," Jagger's affectionate description of the problems Keith encountered trying to find a place to live where the neighbors could put up with his twenty-four-hours-a-day-at-top-volume rock and roll life. By the time Richards joined with the other band members in the fall of 1980 to hammer out songs for a new album, everyone noticed the change in him. "There was a big difference in Keith's personality," said the associate producer of *Tattoo You,* Chris Kimsey. "His attitude toward the band is much more relaxed. He's more secure. And, of course, he's in love." However, what started out as a challenging and fun playtime for Keith turned into a disappointing barrage of conflicts with Jagger. Instead of coming up with a new album that would stake their claim on the rock and roll turf of the 1980s, the group managed to record only three new songs.

Though the creative spark may have been missing between the two leaders, the Stones turned to their rich inventory of material and, relying on tracks recorded between 1975 and 1979, put together an album that would be their most successful of the decade. *Tattoo You* marked a departure not only because it was their only new studio album cobbled together from outtakes but because it was largely crafted and produced by Jagger. It was Jagger, for example, who dusted off a 1979 Richards tune called "Start Me Up" and, by turning it from a reggae song into a rock track and speeding it up, made it into one of the most successful singles of their career. "I found it," Mick remembered, "put it together, wrote the lyrics, put it on, and Keith said, 'I can't believe it, it's just wild.'" And it was Jagger who made the bold move of calling in an independent producer, Bob Clearmountain (who had worked successfully with the Psychedelic Furs) and had him reedit the final mix without Richards's input.

Clearmountain made two crucial decisions: He mixed Charlie's drums way up front and also brought the dual guitars to the fore more than they had been since Richards and Jones fueled the first albums.

RICHARDS: "Mick is a great friend of mine, and our battles aren't exactly as perceived in the press, but I'd say from '80 to '85, people who worked with us for years and years were forced to choose which side to be on. I hated it. In the twenty years of workin' with these guys, we prided ourselves that we didn't have those problems. It got to the point where other cats in the band would come up to me and go, 'So what's he doin' here? We're not too happy about this here.' And I'd be the one to have to go off. It didn't necessarily bother me, but it bothered the boys in the band. My attitude was, 'Let's work together.'"

Even as *Tattoo You* was taking shape, however, Jagger announced that he was once again pursuing his movie career.

This time he chose a project even riskier than *Performance* or *Ned Kelly*. He hooked up with the avant-garde German director

Werner Herzog, who was planning a film, *Fitzcarraldo*, about a man who tries to drag a large ship over a mountain in the jungles of Peru. The film was to star Jason Robards. As a costar, Jagger would be required on the set for six weeks. Conditions were supposed to be hazardous and communications with the outside world virtually non-existent.

Naturally, Keith was not happy. It had been three years since the Stones had hit the road. Jagger's going to Peru would cut their rehearsal schedule and disrupt plans to catch the summer audiences in outdoor stadiums. Jagger was torn between his age-old fear of looking out of it and foolish on stage and choosing another lemon of a movie. Back in September 1980, he had been stung by John Lennon's comments on the Stones' longevity in a *Playboy* interview. Lennon, who had always been pissed off that the Stones had been able to stay raunchy and more blues-oriented than the Beatles, noted acerbically: "You know, they're congratulating the Stones on being together a hundred twelve years. Whoopee! At least Charlie's still got his family. In the eighties they'll be asking: 'Why are these guys still together? Can't they hack it on their own? Why do they have to be surrounded by a gang? Is the little leader afraid someone's going to knife him in the back?' That's gonna be the question. They're going to look at the Beatles and the Stones and all those guys as relics ... They'll be showing pictures of the guy with lipstick wriggling his ass and the four guys with the evil black makeup on their eyes trying to look raunchy. That's gonna be the joke in the future."

Jane Rose told friends that as a rock and roller, in terms of his attitude, way of seeing things, and personality traits, Keith was much like John Lennon. They had, she would say, identical personalities and intelligences. When Lennon was shot to death outside his New York apartment house, the Dakota, on December 8, Jagger, who lived next door at 135 Central Park West, made no official comment. Richards was saddened. "If there was one guy that shouldn't have gone like that it was Lennon," he said on NBC's Friday Night Videos. "Look what that guy gave and what he got in return."

In the winter of 1980–1981 Keith would find himself with a lot of time on his hands. Considering his habit of playing rock and roll music at earsplitting volume day and night, often for up to 120 hours nonstop, it is hard to imagine how Keith found anywhere to live. He managed to stay at Patti's apartment on and off for nine months before the neighbors (one of whom was particularly annoyed by his repeated broadcasts of "It Had to Be You" at 4:00 A.M.) succeeded in getting Hansen evicted. They moved into a hotel, and Jagger's song "Neighbors" was made prophetic. Regardless of Patti's reaction to losing her home, Keith, who was so used to living in a hotel that he hardly ever knew where he was when he woke up, did not let a trifle like getting evicted cut into his winter program. At the end of January 1981 he saw Jerry Lee Lewis at the Ritz. In early February he jammed with Etta James at the Lone Star Café.

RICHARDS: "To get the most out of New York is not to get stuck in one thing. I've been traveling back and forth to New York for years, but it's not the same as living here. Then you really get a feeling for what it's like to walk out on the streets each day. I have a staggering number of things I could get into. One night it's good blues or reggae, another it's rock and roll. If I wanna go out, it's usually to see someone play. If I know the place they're playing, I'll get someone to call them up and see if I can get in the back door. I don't want to queue up. That's about the only concession I make to all that stardom because I hate pulling rank and all that crap.

"You can't afford to be paranoid anywhere. Being run by fear is the worst thing anyone can do to themselves. If you're afraid to come out of your house because you're afraid of walking the streets, you're assigning yourself to some kind of purgatory. It's not quite hell, but it might as well be."

23
Start Me Up
1981–1982

Sometimes Ronnie and I are together for five or six days on the trot. Other people have been to sleep six times and we've seen six dawns. You can't even remember the last time you slept because you've got this memory. After about two and a half or three days, it doesn't matter any more. You're not tired—you're not even really on the same planet. It's funny, when you sleep everything is so neatly put into compartments of that day and that day, and I did that on that day, but if you stay up for five or six days, the memory goes back into one long period with no breaks at all and the days don't mean anything anymore. You just remember either people or specific events. That's how you time it, it's no longer Thursday. You know, "Do you remember last Wednesday we did that?" "Oh . . . that was, um . . . that was Cathy's time . . ."

KEITH RICHARDS, *from an interview with Victor Bockris, 1977*

"'We are going on tour this year,' Mr. Richards insisted. 'And I hope we'll be able to warm up in Europe and hit America when we're really hot.' Beyond the tour," wrote *New York Times* music critic Robert Palmer in April 1981, "Keith was projecting his optimism into the future: 'I've been to hear Jerry Lee Lewis and Fats Domino recently,' he said, 'and they're playing as great as ever.' Mr. Lewis and Mr. Domino are more than ten years older than Mr. Richards. 'I intend to be like them. I'll be out there playing if they have to wheel me out in a wheelchair.'"

Due to illness and hostile Indians, Herzog was forced to close down the *Fitzcarraldo* set, and Jagger quit the project. In early March, Keith and Patti joined Mick and Jerry for a vacation in Barbados. There, Mick told Keith that he was ready to consider touring. They returned to New York to oversee the release of a greatest-hits album, *Sucking in the Seventies*, and put some finishing touches on *Tattoo You*.

While waiting for the final word on the tour, Richards got feedback on *Sucking in the Seventies*. "I knew [*Sucking in the Seventies*] was a piece of shit the first second I saw it," said Lester Bangs. "So do the Stones, of course, why else'd they call it that, though I don't imagine they expected to lose the sales. But they really rubbed our noses in it this time . . ."

"The Rolling Stones' *Sucking in the Seventies* is a substandard compilation from a decade in which the band made its worst records, as the album's self-deprecating title cheerfully admits," wrote Robert Palmer in *The New York Times*. "But the Stones' Mick Jagger and Keith Richards are the group's producers, and even when the songs or performances are below par, the music has a raw, intentionally ragged sound that's instantly appealing.

"If *Sucking in the Seventies* is a holding action, at least it's honest about its intentions. It begins with the admission that 'I'm in tatters . . . shattered,' and includes the ballad 'Time Waits for No One,' which adds, 'and it won't wait for me.'"

Finally it was officially announced that they would tour the U.S. in the fall of 1981 and Europe in the summer of 1982. But there were still many obstacles to overcome. While Richards favored playing smaller halls and connecting with their audience, Jagger as usual was more interested in making a big splash. He wanted to create spectacle, outdoing all of the spectacular acts of the day, from Prince to Duran Duran. To this end he ordered up a tour of the biggest stadiums in the country on a specially designed stage that would allow him to put on a grandiose performance. Among other devices, he planned to have a cherry picker ferry him above the heads of the audience, like some electronic bird, so that he could sing down to them. Next, Mick ordered a variety of costumes for endless changes on stage. Keith, who saw shades of the circuslike 1975 tour in all this, fought tooth and nail to stick to their roots and just play without adornment. Jagger, backed by dollar-happy managers who were more interested in the cash receipts than customer satisfaction, got his way. In fact, Mick made most of the arrangements without Keith's knowledge.

Jagger had sat down with his team the year before and laid out the plan, getting Charlie Watts to design the stage, then called the band together and presented it as a *fait accompli*. Meetings had been arranged for Richards to be informed of what was going on, but he never showed up to any of them. When he discovered Jagger's plans to make a spectacle out of himself in a pair of yellow tights on top of a cherry picker, he flipped out, screaming, "We're a rock and roll band, not a sideshow! What do you need this for?" Jagger immediately got his back up against the wall. As far as he was concerned, he had done them a favor not only by agreeing to tour but by making all the arrangements, and a lot of money, for them. Allegedly, he offered to cancel the cherry picker in exchange for Richards's promise that there would be no drugs on the tour. That was the end of that conversation.

When asked how he felt about the perfume company, Jovan, sponsoring the tour, Richards replied, "We don't usually do this kind of crap, but in this case it will enable us to cover our costs so that we can play in smaller places." (In fact, the Stones played only one small date during the tour.) While Richards was not touring just for the money, somebody who has remained among the highest-paid members of his profession for thirty years cannot be believed when he claims to be completely unconcerned with it. Richards certainly needed more cash. Going to court in the 1970s had been an extremely expensive habit. He was only too aware of how much more money Jagger had than he did because Mick had not squandered a fortune on drugs and the law. Richards was known to be a generous host, but he didn't waste money on anybody. And when he lent people money, he expected to be paid back, more on principle than necessity. Keith did want to make money in 1981.

"Selling out" was another sensitive point between Richards and Jagger. But without Jagger's business acumen, the Stones would never have made the money that they did. The several fortunes Richards earned and squandered had come to him as much because of Jagger's business dealings as because of the songs Richards wrote. And yet he was never grateful to Jagger on that score, and never tired of pointing out that if Jagger was such a great business-man, why had they lost fifteen million dollars in the 1960s?

"I don't think Keith's interested in much else besides music,"

Jagger said, "but he realizes that there are things to be taken care of, decisions to be made that involve a whole lot of money. The Rolling Stones is a huge business machine that has to be kept track of. I really don't mind doing it."

"Mick needs to do that," Richards said. "He's a workaholic. Me, I like to know what's going on. I don't have that thing that makes me wake up in the morning and can't wait to make a phone call and say, 'Hey, what's been happening since last night?'"

As soon as he was unleashed to do his share of the work rehearsing the band, Rip Van Richards sprang into action with all the pent-up energy of a man who had awakened from a ten-year nap. He wanted to whip the Stones into the kind of shape that would enable them to produce the crisp, hard sound they had achieved on *Tattoo You*—a tall order in open-air stadiums in front of eighty thousand people. Richards believed that in order to weld themselves into a tight unit, it was essential for the band to live together before going on the road. It had been three years since the wrinkled warriors had toured, and Ronnie was still teetering on the edge of self-destruction. They were seriously considering replacing him with the young American R&B virtuoso George Thorogood, who would open most of the shows for them.

After considering various prospects, Richards decided to inspect a recording and rehearsal compound in Brookfield, Massachusetts, Longview Farm. Run by an imaginative and gracious entrepreneur named Gil Markle, it was close enough to New York for them to oversee tour preparations and the release of the record, but secluded enough for them to avoid fanmania. Markle, who had hosted the J. Geils Band and was keenly aware of how prestigious it would be to have the Stones rent his place, sent a private plane to fly Keith, Patti, Jane Rose, and longtime Stones aide Alan Dunn up to Longview. As soon as they arrived he handed Keith a Stoli and orange juice and took him on a tour. When they ended up in the recording studio, Richards started blasting some tapes at full volume. According to Markle, he and Keith were getting along famously when Jane Rose burst in the room. In his entertaining unpublished journal of the Stones' stay, Markle described the scene this way:

"'Oh, Keith! Keith!' Jane Rose tends to shriek a bit when she talks. Her job is to take care of Mick Jagger and Keith Richards, and she is very protective of them.

"'Oh, I knew I'd find you in here, in this ice-cold control room, talking to Greg and listening to records.'

"Keith hit the 'mute' button on the console, lowering the volume level in the room.

"'Gil's his name,' he said.

"'Gil, then. Listen, Keith-eee, we simply must begin to think of getting on our way. Greg, here—Gil, I mean—has those two pilots waiting inside that gorgeous airplane, and we simply can't keep them waiting, can we? You know what you have to do for tomorrow. There's the dentist again, and there's the consulate, and there's Renaldo, in Rome, and we're way up here in God-knows-where. And I know Patti must get back to the city too, mustn't you, dear, and I know . . .'

"'We're not going anywhere,' Keith said, returning the studio monitors to full, undistorted blast.

"I smiled, having only moments before taken Keith behind the moose head in the library, with our two full glasses of Stoli and orange juice. 'You don't have to go anywhere tonight, Keith,' I had said. 'It just starts to get fun around here after supper. You can hang out, listen to some records, fool around, anything you want. The place is yours.'

"'Yeah,' he muttered through a smile, 'I don't have to go anywhere, do I?'"

Having been offered uninterrupted time and every instrument and recording device he could hope for, Keith was happily playing in his favorite place.

After Jane Rose left, he sat down at the piano and started to play a sentimental Hoagy Carmichael ballad called "The Nearness of You." Excited to hear Richards live and eager to illustrate how state-of-the-art his equipment was, Markle set the recording tape rolling. After recording several of his favorite country and western ballads, Richards turned to Markle and delivered himself of the following revealing statement: "I suppose you think it's all fun being me. Listen, I never get a chance to sing by myself like this, play the piano, without some bastard weirding out and asking me why I wasn't playing the guitar and looking mean. People have their ideas about me. I bet you didn't think I could play the piano, did you? Or sing classics from the thirties? Well, I can. People think I get my way a lot more than I do. You don't know what it's like dealing with the people I've got to deal with. If it wasn't for the music, I wouldn't be doing it."

Three days later, after recording numerous versions of his favorite country and western songs for seventy-two hours, Keith emerged from the studio to inform Alan Dunn that they would take the place for five weeks in August and September. He loved everything about it. Joining Jagger back in New York on June 1, Richards sent telegrams to Wyman, Wood, and Watts announcing that if they were not in New York within twenty-four hours they wouldn't be on the album cover, and if they weren't there within forty-eight hours they wouldn't be on the tour." The three immediately flew to New York. Having ascertained that they were all in place waiting for him, Keith took Patti down to Florida to spend a week with Freddie Sessler.

Despite the fact that Keith's dramatic truancy delayed the beginning of rehearsals, disrupted the tour plans, and forced a lot of Jagger's people to frantically rearrange things, when Keith returned to New York ready to set up shop at Longview Farm he was well rested, well pleased with himself, and ready to embark on the greatest test the band had ever endured. The 1981 tour of America from September 25 to December 18 was to amount to fifty concerts in front of three million people and gross $50 million. In comparison, their most successful tour of the 1960s grossed $1.5 million.

On August 14 the band and its entourage of families, technicians, tour managers, and accountants arrived at Longview Farm for five weeks of rehearsals. The fragmentation of the band was blatantly clear to the staff of Longview Farm. While Richards and Wood played loud rock music all day and night for as long as they could stay up, and crashed wherever they happened to fall out, Jagger was never without a calculator, a notebook, and a list of appointments, and he kept regular hours, exercising, rehearsing, and organizing the tour. Mick and Keith rarely spoke outside of rehearsals, which took place when Keith called them. Bill and his girlfriend Astrid Lundström kept to themselves. When he wasn't working with Jagger on the design of the stage or laying down his inimitable beat during rehearsals, Charlie drank. But when they got together on the hundred-foot-long stage Markle had installed at Richards's request and went through their set, working themselves back to performance peak, the staff and entourage were amazed by the power of their sound.

At Longview Farm Keith lived out his every fantasy just as he had done at Nellcôte. He had his drugs flown in on a private plane once a week. Patti was with him. He had Jagger pretty much where he wanted him. Whenever he felt like it he could play with parts of and sometimes all of his band. Keith and Woody commandeered the basement rec room and made it their Boy Scout den. There they would spend days drinking, rapping, listening to records, and playing together. One day, when they barged into the room and came upon a meeting of elegantly dressed gay fashion designers going over Mick's costumes, Keith told Markle that if he ever came across anything like that again in *his* rec room, he would beat him up. Looking up from the pool table where he had just sunk three balls with one shot, Ronnie drawled, "Ah, don't listen to him, Gil, he doesn't mean it."

One of the many issues Jagger and Richards fought over before the 1981 tour was whether Ron Wood and Bobby Keys, who were both getting really fucked up on drugs, should be allowed to accompany them. Jagger in particular didn't want Bobby Keys on the tour, but Richards, whose undying lifelong loyalty to his friends is among his more admirable traits, was adamant about taking both of them along. At the same time, though, he could be very tough on the people he loved. When Woody's wife, Jo, would go crying to Keith, he'd get right on Ronnie's case. This made 1981 a pretty bad time to be Ron Wood.

"'Woody,' as lead guitarist Stone, survives in the niche where Brian Jones and Mick Taylor could not, chiefly through being this ideally complete and recognizable rock star parody," wrote Philip Norman, "a cartoon trailer, as it were, to his friend and confederate, Keith Richards."

Despite the fooling around, all was not fun and games for Ronnie. Visitors were instructed, "Don't give any drugs to Ronnie," and he was reduced to begging old friends to bring him something back the next time they passed through. "During the rehearsals at Longview Farm, several reporters noticed that Richards and Jagger had little to do with Wood," wrote Nick Kent. "During an interview, Richards, disgusted with Wood's behavior, fixed him with a withering glance. 'Just disappear!' he ordered, and Wood promptly obeyed. Turning back to the journalist, Richards remarked caustically: 'That's one boy who hasn't got much longer the way he's going.'"

Keith had no such problems with Charlie. "As soon as Keith walked into the room we'd be twenty years old and have a really funny time," Charlie Watts recalled. "And it never stopped." For Keith, jamming with Charlie was how he found the sound: "I just go in the room, Charlie's usually there, and I'll just start playing. I'll pick up a slight germ, and then I'll infect everybody else. I'm like a housefly!"

While Richards was concentrating on the music, Jagger and his advisers, Loewenstein, Dunn, and Bill Graham, who had replaced Peter Rudge as tour manager, were putting together the tour package. "In 1981 everybody in the Rolling Stones felt good, and we all decided to kick some ass," said Bill Graham. "These guys rehearsed strong. We started in Philadelphia with outdoor shows, and my goal was to build a great stage and make it a great event. They are an awesome rock and roll band. There are a lot of flaws, but those guys are a great mix. They also had a physical attitude—a jungle-cat attitude—that prevailed." Jagger became extremely nervous about getting ill, losing his voice, or screwing up in some other more self-inflicted fashion. Richards acted as if he couldn't have cared less. One morning at Longview he careened off a porch. After he fell he felt a sharp pain in his ankle. At first it was thought that he had broken it, a possibility that would have scotched the tour and cost them all that money. Fortunately it turned out to be only a sprain.

Brought up by a physical training instructor, Jagger had been used to working out since he was a child. Employing a series of instructors, he went through hours of exercise each day. Keith appeared to do nothing except a little horseback riding and an occasional run. He saved his energy for chain-smoking and drinking at least a quart of alcohol a day. The only sign of his indulgences appeared on his face. But this too became his asset. Hailed as "the face of rock and roll," it appeared to map years of hard experience in its marks and creases.

ALBERT GOLDMAN: "Look at his face! Keith has one of those great I've-done-it-all mugs you see in French movies of the thirties. Almost from an ethical standpoint I could say authenticity is there in his face, in his style; also a certain grace. He does have soul, he does look like what he is, and there's a very beautiful, delicate, tender, and lyrical style that he has. There's a lining of a different sort inside of Keith. It's a matter of being all of a piece.

"Richards struck me as being, in some weird, almost mystical way—and you find these people in jazz, too—someone who gave himself up so completely to the rock life, who is identified with it so completely, who did so little to protect himself from its dangers and its traps, that he eventually developed a strange purity amidst filth. He obtained a kind of blessedness in the gutter."

Despite a painful shoulder problem during rehearsals, and the diagnosis of a local chiropractor, Billy Mykel, that he was in unequivocally terrible shape, Richards passed all the medical tests required before the tour. Still, Patti, who stayed with Keith throughout the rehearsals, worried about him. She couldn't believe how much he drank, snorted, and smoked. Patti, Keith has said, "is always asking me: 'Why are you lighting up another cigarette?' I tell her it's because the last one wasn't long enough. I've taken worse things than cigarettes and whiskey." Patti also had to look out for herself in trying to keep up with him. On the days that Richards slept, the Longview staff noticed, a pale and wan Hansen would emerge from their room around 10:00 P.M., give the high sign for Keith's simple breakfast of hamburgers and home fries with HP sauce, then bus it back herself. Half an hour later, pumped up by the red meat chased by a belt of bourbon or vodka and some lines of that super pharmaceutical C, Keith was bouncing off the walls before he hit the rehearsal stage. However, looking into his unpinned eyeballs, you could see that the Keith Richards who made Longview Farm his playpen that summer was very much at home.

When Kurt Loder made it up to Longview during the last week of rehearsals to interview Richards for a cover story in *Rolling Stone* (almost exactly ten years after the memorable Robert Greenfield rap of 1971), he found a man "looking very teenage-wasteland in a black bomber jacket, black T-shirt and black jeans, with blue suede boots scrunched down around his ankles and a dark green scarf knotted at his waist, who appeared healthy and in high spirits.

"After wrapping up the interview, he wandered off to an upright piano and began noodling around in the rolling, bluesy mode that seemed to fall somewhere between the style of Memphis Slim and Keith's own favorite, Johnnie Johnson. Richards' playing had a buoyant stride to it, transparently subtle—the music of a man tapped into the source."

On August 31, at the end of the first month of rehearsals at Longview, *Tattoo You* was released. That Keith was still weakened by his drug use in the early eighties was made abundantly clear by the release of the album. It was originally titled *Tattoo*, and when it came out Keith was brought up short by the change, exclaiming, "What's this *Tattoo You*?" Many decisions were still being made around him and for him. However, the results were unmistakable. The record sold one million copies during its first week in release in the U.S. alone. It would be one of the best-selling albums in the Stones' catalog, going to number one in the U.S. and number two in the U.K., and "Start Me Up" would become the song of the fall of 1981 in America.

ROBERT PALMER: "The Rolling Stones sound like a great rock and roll band again, but they aren't the old Stones magically revitalized, they're something new. If much of their seventies work seems futile or depressing in retrospect, the futility and depression were inevitable. The Stones were growing older and learning to cope with it, as were their fans. If they were no longer snotty young outsiders looking to get inside and intending to trash the premises upon admittance, who were they exactly? It has taken them much of the past decade to find out, but the Stones of the eighties seem to have a handle on who they are, and a clear understanding of who they aren't. They aren't kids or rebel anarchists or demons anymore. But they're still supremely self-confident, even a little arrogant; they're still a rock and roll band.

"Only they're a grown-up rock and roll band, with fans ranging in age from under ten to sixty or more, and with a history as rich and various as the histories of the early bluesmen and first-generation rockers they've always admired. They have something else in common with those blues singers and early rockers, too: they have their dignity."

On September 25, the Stones' three-month tour began in Philadelphia.

JERRY HALL: "To look out into that crowd is just mind-boggling. The energy that shoots back at you nearly knocks you over. It just goes right through you like a bolt of lightning. It must take incredible courage to go out there."

Preparing for each show was an elaborate psychological process as important to Keith as tuning his guitar. Richards had always joked about how much attention Brian used to pay to his hair and how much time Mick spent putting on makeup. Jagger spent a good forty-five minutes in front of his mirror before leaving his dressing room. Richards put the bits and pieces of his costume together more casually, as if he were going to a friend's party. His 1981 look consisted of his jeans or black leather pants tucked into scrunched-down suede boots, a T-shirt, the skull ring, a bracelet of handcuffs, a bandanna around his unruly salt-and-pepper hair, a cigarette clamped between his grinning teeth, and a two-day growth. While it was true that he was more naturally himself in performance than Jagger, who basically had to create himself for an audience, Richards was not unaware of developing his own image and strengthening it. He always checked himself out in a full-length mirror before going out onto what he called the killing floor. "Every time you walk out, the pressure's the same," Keith said. "It doesn't matter whether you're the front man or the guitar player. It's 'Get the fuck out there, you goddamn cretin, get your frock on and go!'"

As had become traditional for them, despite the fact that they were playing in front of one hundred thousand people, they treated the opening show as a rough-cut dress rehearsal to be polished later.

PATTI HANSEN: "I started crying. People were looking at me wondering, 'Boy, she must really be exhausted.' I was so emotional . . . I was so proud of Keith. He'd been doing this for twenty years and all of a sudden there's this kid proud of him. Before, I just saw Keith as some ordinary guy. But the more I watch him, the more I respect his craft. He really is the best at what he does."

When Keith went back on the road in 1981, his reputation and following had visibly grown.

CHARLES SHAAR MURRAY (New Musical Express critic): "You know the riffs: There's the one that goes, 'When Keith Richards comes into a room, rock and roll walks in the door,' and 'Keith Richards, the world's most elegantly wasted human being,' which comes equipped with hyperbolic virtuoso prose which attempts to outdo the last writer's description of how utterly, utterly out of it and cadaverous Mr. Richards looked at the time. Then there's the scholarly bit about Keith's pitiless open-tuned riffing and [Ted] Newman Jones III [Keith's guitar roadie] and the four hundred and ninety-seven guitars. All of it boiled down to a single one-liner terse enough to stick on a telegram. That one went, 'Keith Richards is Rock and Roll.'"

RICHARDS: "There is an image projected that people come for and take away with them and give to their readers if they're journalists, and obviously there's a lot to me in that image. I've never tried consciously to project it, but there's not really much you can do about it. It's like a little shadow that you live with."

By the next performance in Buffalo, the band's playing was inspired, largely due to Keith, according to several witnesses.

PHILIP NORMAN: "They are playing with the percussion of inspired lawlessness, smashing the high-hats like policemen's helmets; a bass line below it, groping up the little girls' skirts. They are playing with one heartless heart, one vicious voice, one thin, bare arm pumping a guitar with renewing force as light streams into the vampire's red-rimmed eyes. The Human Riff is awake at last. The World's Greatest Rock 'n' Roll Band is in business again. The Rolling Stones are back in the bloodstream."

JERRY HALL: "The tension around the Stones on that tour was incredible. People went crazy around them, but among the members of the band it was professional and businesslike. It was very smooth and everything was done by the minute."

Jagger's voice had also improved immeasurably, drawing compliments from even Keith Richards. "He used to come out leaping about and after twenty minutes he'd be too winded to really sing," Keith said.

"Now he's learnt not only how to pace himself, but his voice is so much stronger. The fucker's actually singing, man! I can't believe it, but there it is . . ."

"Every city they went into became the rock and roll capital of the United States for that one day," said Bill Graham. "When the Stones performed, every man felt like a man and every woman felt like a woman. And they all wanted to take the Stones home."

By the time they played the Fox Theater in Atlanta on October 26, according to Robert Palmer, Keith was making perhaps the most riveting music of his career: "When the Stones were good and ready, the Stones hit the stage. The sound was clear, and so beautifully balanced that even the casual listener could distinguish Keith's guitar from Ronnie's, and Ian Stewart's hammered boogie-woogie from Ian McLagan's Jerry Lee Lewis rock and roll. Mick was singing hard and true, but it was Keith who pushed the band into playing its best and then playing better. Nobody was sitting down, and the momentum kept building, song after song, until the Stones were rocking harder than Little Richard or Chuck Berry, as hard as anyone ever rocked.

"Charlie, not used to playing so aggressively, kept trying to bring the ferocious energy level down a hair, but Keith would turn on him, jump onto the drum riser and pump his guitar wildly up and down until Charlie broke into one of his megawatt grins and gave in. Wyman was reeling off brawny lines that heaved at the rhythm from underneath, and he flashed Keith one of his rare smiles. When the curtain went down, it was Keith who accepted the bouquet of roses, who took the final bow. He'd been the spark plug of the tour's hottest show—and the Stones had rocked and rolled and raged like a hurricane."

Despite playing well with Ronnie, Keith refused to abide his drug habit, denying him the indulgence he himself had received for most of his drug-drenched years. "There was one tour where the powers that be in the Stones were worried about Ron's habits at the time," Keith recalled. "And I personally guaranteed that I would take care of him. But he let me down once on the road. I went berserk. I punched him in the hotel on that tour. I'd guaranteed that he wouldn't do this shit and then I found out he was up there doing it. So I said, 'Right, I'll go get my pound of flesh now.' My old lady was going, 'Keith, don't make a scene,' shouting, 'He's going to kill him, he's going to kill him.' And by the time I'd gotten across there, she'd ripped the back of my shirt off. So I arrived in Ronnie's room with these few shreds of shirt hanging off me, grabbed hold of him—'You fucker!' Smack! . . .

"I just had to, because I knew that I had guaranteed him. I know Ronnie Wood real well, but this was the one time he'd let me down personally. Freebasing coke, people do crazy things, things don't click. Still, as I'm turning round to go back, Big Joe Seabrook, who's my man on the road—great character, hard as nails—says, 'I didn't know you were a southpaw, Keith.' Running a band is a funny business."

As Wood remembered it, "He'd been up for days and he thought that I'd been cheating on my wife and doing dope and suddenly there was this madman leading a posse of my wife, his wife, a huge string of people. God, when we collided! Boom! He got the first one in—hit me in the nose—and I got up and smacked him. It was all over in ten minutes and it actually cleared the air. We got very close after that. I was covered with blood and walked into the next room, where Mick and Charlie were working on a set list, and I said, 'What do you think of this?' And Mick said, 'How does the middle eight of "Summer Romance" go?'"

TERRY HOOD: "Keith put himself in the role of caretaker of Ronnie. He has a very paternal sense about everyone and he's very bossy but very insecure and very emotional. They were all very pissed off with Ronnie and Bobby Keys for getting fucked up, but Keith had a great love for Woody and just out of loyalty stayed at his house in L.A. on the tour. Keith stood by his friends and tried to play the policeman and straighten them out whatever the cost. It was a pretty hard time for Woody."

Even without heroin, Keith had his quirks, most of them having to do with habits that gave him a sense of security and a link to the past. Keith's diet consisted of eggs and bacon with HP sauce, hamburgers and french fries with HP sauce, fish and chips with HP sauce. He bought the sauce by the crate. Then there was the matter of a pair of boots he grew so attached to he wouldn't step on stage without them.

BILL GRAHAM: "Every time I saw Keith walk on stage during the Stones' 1981 tour, he wore a different outfit, but he always wanted to wear the same handmade Spanish boots. After a while, after playing many cities, a little piece of suede came loose, and they had to glue it down. In another city the stitching or the sole might come loose, and they'd put some tape on it or nail it together. There was tape here, gauze there, glue there, nails . . . But it got to the point where the boots were a major concern of mine, because he loved them and wanted to wear them all the time. Finally, at Candlestick Park [in San Francisco], the Stones were about to go on and a heel snapped off and broke.

"I said, 'Aw, jeeze, do you really want to wear those? Do you have something else?' He said, 'Yeah, but I just feel like . . .' He didn't go crazy. And I said, 'Well, I'll try.' So I left the trailer and I asked everyone who works for me, 'What are you wearing? Let me see your heel.' 'What do you want?' 'Let me see your heel!' I couldn't find anything.

"But there was a guy at a table in the other backstage area who had a pair of boots on, and the heel was just about the same size—a little higher, but the same shape. And I said to him, 'Do me a favour, I can't explain it to you now. Let me have your shoes for fifty bucks.' He didn't know what I was doing. I got them and took them back to the tech area. Two of the guys got a nail and a hammer, shaped the heel down a little, and put it on Keith's boot. Up and away it went. He used it. After that date there was more paper, more glue, more spit, more rubber bands. He always wanted to wear those boots."

By this time the Stones on the road could get away with a lot; all they really had to do was show up and evoke some memories without making any egregious errors. But by the time they rolled to a halt, Keith was still nervous about the HBO taping of the tour's last show at Hampton Roads, Virginia, to be played on his thirty-eighth birthday. Keith argued that it would be impossible to play to the audience and cameras at the same time. Pacing around backstage that night, he wondered what they had got themselves into. Everybody started blaming everybody else. However, according to Bill German, the show was virtually the best of the tour, and it also contained its most memorable image. During the encore of "Satisfaction," as hundreds of huge balloons and tons of confetti rained down on the band, a fan jumped onto the stage and, eluding security, made straight for Jagger. Standing next to Mick, Keith spotted the fan, unstrapped his guitar, clubbed him across the head, and continued playing without missing a beat.

RON WOOD: "I said, 'Hey, Keith, he's only a fan. No reason to fuckin' hit him.' And Keith went, 'Oh, yeah? What if he had a fuckin' gun in his hand or a knife? I mean, he might be a fan, he might be a nutter, and he's on my turf. I'm gonna chop the mother down!'"

BILL GRAHAM: "On the plane back to New York after the last date, Keith said, 'Hey, Bill, I want to see you for a minute.' And we stepped into the toilet area. 'Man, I just want to tell you, I really drove you up the wall. Sometimes it was insane. But . . .' And he had this package wrapped in newspaper with a rubber band around it and a rose attached, and he just said, 'Thank you.' And I knew what it was. It was the boots."

Richards took a break at Christmas, spending the holiday with his daughter, Dandelion. He didn't rest for long. In January he produced some tracks for the newly reformed Mamas and the Papas. In February he flew to L.A. to work on a film of the concert tour with Jagger and its director, Hal Ashby. In March he was in New York editing the sound track of the live shows. One year before their twentieth anniversary the Rolling Stones made a clean sweep of *Rolling Stone* magazine's reader survey: The Rolling Stones were the best band, Jagger was best vocalist, Richards was best instrumentalist, *Tattoo You* was best album, "Start Me Up" was best single, Jagger and Richards were best songwriters. They were also at the top of the critics' awards: The Stones were artists of the year, *Tattoo You* was best album, "Start Me Up" best single.

*

On April 28, 1982, the Stones held a press conference to announce the European tour. "I need this to keep me young," said Richards. "When we started this band we thought we had about two or three years. Now it's habit and it's absolutely vital that it works on the road. We need constant contact with a living audience. We're so excited about the prospect of doing Britain again after so long. Wherever we might make our home now, Britain is where our roots are."

From May 26 through July 25, 1982, the Rolling Stones toured Europe. "During the tour's London stopover, while Jagger, Richards, Watts and Wyman—not to mention the other band members—were sequestered in a hotel in London's Knightsbridge district, Wood was 'elsewhere'—holed up in an apartment," wrote Nick Kent. "Several excuses were proffered, but the main reason was a clause that Jagger had placed very high up in the Stones' official contract that read, 'If anyone is found in possession of drugs in any part of the backstage area, that person will immediately be banished from the vicinity, whatever their capacity.'

"Vexed at Wood's inability to control his problems, the Stones put him on an allowance during the tour in order to prevent him from buying drugs. But Jagger wanted him out of the band altogether and, whenever possible, forced him to stay in different quarters than the rest of the group—even the roadies. According to insiders, George Thorogood, a supporting act on many European dates, was secretly rehearsing to take Woody's place."

At the end of May, Richards, mindful of the time when the Stones would stop working, turned his attention toward assembling a new family-*cum*-entourage. "This is a very rootless life," he said. "The only thing you got to hang on to is family." The surprise family member on Keith's new team was his father, whom he had not seen since the day he had slammed out of his Dartford house in 1962 screaming, "I gotta go!" Patti, who had a strong relationship with her ailing father, urged Keith to at least try to make a connection with Bert, who was now in his seventies.

RICHARDS: "This was the father I'd left because we couldn't stay in the same house together anymore. After my parents divorced I was closer to my mother. I hadn't seen my father since 1963 [*sic*]. I wasn't anywhere capable or geographically near enough to deal with it, so I got very used to it. 'Oh, I haven't seen my dad in two years. I haven't seen my dad in five years. I haven't seen him in ten years. Fifteen years.' It could have gone on forever."

As he waited for his father to show up, Keith was full of mixed emotions. In fact, he was so nervous that he had Ronnie accompany him for emotional support. When the car pulled up he thought the old geezer was going to leap out and whack him over the head. But as Bert emerged and said, "'Allo, son, 'ow ya doin'?," Keith was, in his words, "breaking up already. That's when I knew it'd be all right."

NICK KENT: "Keith said to me, 'It's great. I phoned him up and he said, "Well, son, meet me in this pub, right?" And all I could say to him was, "Public bar or . . .'" That was the first thing he had said to his dad after twenty years. Three days later I visited Keith in his hotel room in London, full of people, and his dad came into the room. It was very weird because they didn't talk. His dad was on the tour so it was 'Dad's coming.' Dad had been to the pub with some of his bodyguards. 'Get Dad.' Dad's really drunk and everyone's going up to Dad. 'Mr. Richards, you've got a great son.' And the guy was so pissed. He was probably thinking, 'Well, I fucking made it. I used to be down the pub with all the old age pensioners and now these guys are taking me for free drinks!' I mean, it was just like no one at home. You could go over and say, 'Mr. Richards, how does it feel?' but there was no communication. His dad was drinking more than Keith.

"Funny thing was, all these guys like Peter Wolf and the J. Geils Band came in because they wanted to play with Keith, but there was Bert. Keith had been shoving drugs around, but suddenly it was 'No, me dad's here.' There was a guy employed to roll joints and he'd stopped. It was like 'My dad's here, so what are we gonna do? Well, I know what I'm gonna do.' Keith suddenly got the guitar and he was like 'OK, we're gonna have a musical session. I've gone and taken my cocaine in the bathroom, I'm ready. You guys, you're on your own. I've got this guitar and I'm gonna sing this song and what I'm gonna sing is for my old dad, "Danny Boy".' It was so funny. These guys were like 'Where's the fucking drugs? Oh, man, now we're gonna have to sing "Danny Boy". This bastard! This fucking idiot!' And Keith's going, 'Oh, Danny Boy . . .' and eventually they led Bert off."

FREDDIE SESSLER: "Patti arranged for Keith and his father to get back together. It took a while for the relationship to develop. Now they have a fabulous relationship—he wouldn't go anywhere without his father—although he suffered because his mother is very jealous of her husband. She doesn't want him to have anything to do with him. She resents him being around Keith."

In 1983 Keith moved Bert to the house on Long Island where Anita and Marlon lived under the protection of some English bodyguard friends, which was fast becoming the home of secondary family members. Marlon and Bert took to each other like long-lost friends. His grandfather's presence undoubtedly benefited the young teenager. Keith and Bert soon established a relationship based on drinking. On Friday nights when Keith was in New York he would sometimes drive out there and spend the evening playing dominoes with Bert over bangers and mash and a bottle of rum, and they matched each other drink for drink. "All the things we couldn't stand about each other twenty years ago are all water under the bridge," Keith said. "In a way he's given me a lot of insight into why I'm like I am. Now we really appreciate each other."

Anita noticed that Keith was like Bert in many ways: "To a certain extent Keith had gotten very much like his father. He's very narrow-minded, very sheltered and shuttered, and that helps to keep him going. He doesn't want anything from the outside. Everybody knows what he wants and what he likes and what he needs. Whether he's in Berlin or Tokyo, if you look in the fridge there is always a shepherd's pie. His father also only eats that kind of food and won't do anything he doesn't want to do. I can see the resemblance, this kind of unmovable, unchangeable figure everybody flitters and moves around. And Keith flies off on tantrums and gets very threatening. I've seen Keith pointing guns at people, which is very scary stuff, especially if they're loaded. Once a member of the crew ate his shepherd's pie and Keith threatened to cut him up and put his legs in a shepherd's pie. So he gets his shepherd's pie, miles of shepherd's pie everywhere. He's always got shepherd's pie, and he doesn't have to worry about it."

On June 1, 1982, the Stones released the single "Going to a Go-Go," which had been recorded at the Capital Center in Landover, Maryland, the previous December, along with the album *Still Life*, which featured ten cuts recorded throughout the tour. The single went to number twenty-five in the U.S., while the album reached number five and went gold. Album sales were reflected in the audience's response to the Stones tour as it made its way across Europe. The German Stones expert Dieter Hoffman noted the growing reaction to Keith.

DIETER HOFFMAN: "After the '76 tour, that was the big break in his reputation in Germany. On the '82 tour Keith was the most popular. For me personally, I love Keith and his work because it's not a lie, and he plays rock and roll. If Keith makes a mistake, it's authentic. He stands for rock and roll. His face is the image of rock and roll in Germany for sure."

On June 26, at the second of two victorious homecoming extravaganzas performed before more than seventy thousand fans in London's Wembley Arena, Richards forgot the main riff at the beginning of "She's So Cold." He immediately tossed his guitar aside and leaped on Watts's drum riser, his whole body conducting the rhythm. Charlie was there like a shot, as was Wyman, right on cue with the song's brawny bass line. Richards then spun around expecting to hear Wood covering him, but Wood wasn't there—he seemed momentarily oblivious, a cigarette in his mouth and his eyes closed. Richards leaped off the platform and drove his fist into Woody's face—so hard that Wood almost tumbled off stage.

Though the Stones were carrying on business as usual, differences between Jagger and Richards deepened on the European tour. "On stage, Jagger would try to unnerve Richards, whose rhythm guitar set the pace for the twenty-six-song set, by hurrying things along," wrote Nick Kent. "Keith would glare back, methodically changing his guitar until he was ready to begin. During Richards' solo vocal number, 'Little T & A,' Jagger was forced to vacate the stage; it was written into the contract. The rift began to show up on stage in one show during a version of 'Time Is on My Side'—originally recorded in 1964. Evidently bored and ill at ease with his bygone era, Jagger donned an absurd outfit and minced around the stage, a purse hanging from an exaggeratedly limp wrist. Richards fixed him with a withering glare that he made no attempt to conceal before striding to the mike stand for the vocal duet. At another show, in Scandinavia, Richards deliberately hijacked the cherry-picker platform used to lift Jagger over the crowd during 'You Can't Always Get What You Want' and performed a twenty-minute guitar solo. Furious, Jagger dispatched Wood to try and coax Richards down, but Richards refused and, according to the tour photographer, 'Woody nearly ended up getting booted for his role as go-between.'" In Göteborg, Sweden, fifty-four thousand fans saw Keith play the solo of "Beast of Burden" lying on his back drunk after having fallen over.

Kent saw most of the English shows and spent some time with Keith in London. "Wolf and these other guys from the J. Geils Band wanted to play with Keith, and Peter Wolf had actually brought his Hank Williams songbook with him. He told Keith he had just seen Jagger outside the door, and when Jagger saw that he was going to Keith's room Wolf said, 'Mick came up to me and said, "Hey, Peter, man, professionals don't use those books."' This was Jagger as Nijinsky, turning on his heel and disappearing into the lift with the attitude, 'You want to go with Keith, all right, I've fucked with you.' Wolf was really shaken by it. And in front of a room full of journalists Keith said loudly, 'Yeah, that's a fair example of the kind of cunt I've had to deal with for the last twenty-five years.'"

24
Sleep Tonight
1982–1986

It's no fun being at loggerheads with me. I can drain the energy out of anyone if you're gonna fight with me. I don't enjoy it, but I can be a hard fucker.

KEITH RICHARDS, *from an interview with Adrian Deevoy, 1989*

At the end of the 1982 tour, Keith and Patti flew to Cabo San Lucas and took up residence at the very tip of the longest peninsula in the world, Baja California, Mexico. Over the next year and a half Richards would make Cabo, once the exclusive playground of Hollywood stars John Wayne, Frank Sinatra, and Bing Crosby, his resting place. Renting a beautiful house on the main drive in Cabo Bello, he soon made contact with a local American couple who, like the Sursocks in Switzerland, became his conduit to the scene and provided him with a haven when he wanted to get away from it. And as he had done in Switzerland, Keith imported his family, entourage, and drugs.

While in Cabo, Keith was reunited with Uschi Obermeier, whom he had last seen in a Chicago hotel room in 1975. "I heard he was in town," she recalled, "so I went by the hotel and left a message. The next day my boyfriend Dieter and I were leaving for the mainland so we had a big party on the beach for our friends. Keith came and we had a long talk. He asked me why I had left him and I told him how I had feared becoming a victim of the road."

Reinvigorated by the momentum of the hugely successful '81–'82 world tour and his Mexican sojourn, and anxious to continue playing with the Stones, Keith next turned his attention to the new album, *Undercover*, while Mick went off to negotiate a new distribution contract for Rolling Stones Records. In the wake of the record-breaking U.S. tour, Jagger was hailed in the American press as "the greatest businessman in rock and roll history," an apt accolade for the money-hungry 1980s. Charged up by this good publicity, and determined to take full advantage of his position of strength, Jagger looked forward to negotiating the new contract. He began preparations in the fall of 1982, when even a bad businessman would have been in a good position to deal for the band. Their last three albums had been worldwide hits. They had just completed the top-grossing tour in rock history. Their entire back catalog was selling internationally. And Jagger's reputation was at its height; he was more famous than ever, still able to arouse fear, outrage, adoration, excitement, sex, and chaos. On top of that, businesspeople saw him as a responsible adult. While researching the new contract, Jagger had other thoughts in mind. Given all his hard-earned prestige, why should he throw his fate in with the band's? What better time to jump into a solo career, as Michael Jackson had recently done so successfully? After making exploratory probes, Jagger zeroed in on the president of Columbia Records, Walter Yetnikoff. He and Yetnikoff seemed well matched. Like Jagger, Yetnikoff was at the height of his career. He had won fame pushing the careers of Michael Jackson and Bruce Springsteen, the two biggest solo stars of the era. An obese, brawny, uncouth man, Yetnikoff exuded the aura of a sleazy record executive you might expect to find in a Terry Southern novel.

Richards was eager to sign the Stones' next contract, sure that it would open the door to another tour. Only later did he realize that Yetnikoff wanted a solo Jagger, not the Stones, as his next superstar "product."

Not yet aware of the extent of Mick's plans for a solo career, Keith set up recording sessions for the Stones' last studio album to be distributed by Atlantic Records, *Undercover*. He even got in a few good weeks of rehearsal with Jagger alone. They met in Paris, rented a basement studio from a friend, and bashed out "Wanna Hold You" with Mick on drums and Keith screaming into the microphone and playing guitar. The song, Keith said, "has a very universal desire, especially when you're very frightened, or lonely, or cold."

"Wanna Hold You" ended up being the softest number on an

album characterized by violent themes and lyrics. It also represented the last time for a long while that Keith and Mick collaborated in an intimate and informal way. Within a few months Mick's inflated ego would place him on bad terms with all the Stones. During November, while Jagger was laying the groundwork for going solo, the band met in Paris to record *Undercover*. Keith believed that making the record after two consecutive years on the road had a lot to do with its sound.

They finished the first *Undercover* sessions in December. On the eighteenth, his thirty-ninth birthday, Keith flew from Paris to London, where he spent a few days before flying on to New York to be with Patti. Rumors abounded in the press that he was going to marry her in January. Richards's spokesman admitted the gossip was true, and a wedding date was set.

ROBERT PALMER: "Keith had some rooms at the Plaza Hotel. I called to see him and Ronnie was there jamming. I thought, 'Shit, I wish I had my horn.' Just at that moment Keith and Ronnie said, 'Hey, can you get your horn?' So I called up my girlfriend and asked her if she could come over with the horn. While she was on her way, Patti came in extremely distraught. She had just gotten a call that her father had died. Keith went into another room to be with her and we all sat there feeling like deflated balloons." When Patti's father died the second week of January, the wedding plans were indefinitely postponed. Patti had been very close to Alfred Hansen, and although he had been ill for some time, his death was a heavy blow.

Despite some misunderstandings with the Hansens, who had given interviews announcing that Keith was "an enthusiastic disciple of Christ" and that he "embraced Christ as a way of life," Richards proved to be a pillar of strength throughout the ordeal. He attended Hansen's wake on the eighteenth (that night the 1981–1982 concert movie, *Let's Spend the Night Together*, premiered in New York) and served as a pallbearer at his funeral the following morning. Wedding or no, Keith was clearly considered part of the Hansen family. By the end of the month, Keith and Patti were out and about again. On the twenty-seventh they attended a Tina Turner concert at the Ritz in New York. Afterward, Turner and David Bowie accompanied them to Richards's suite at the Plaza Hotel.

TINA TURNER: "He had this great big tape machine set up there, and you could see that he used it constantly. We had some champagne, and Keith cranked up his machine and started playing all this old music, and it suddenly dawned on me: This is what these guys did. They would go back to this old music that they loved—blues and R&B—and they would change it around and make something of their own out of it. Because the feeling that was in that old music was something they felt, too. But they made it new again, and that was what had always attracted me to the Rolling Stones' songs. I had never actually realized it before. That was a magical evening."

On January 30, Keith left for Paris with Ronnie and Jo to resume work on *Undercover*. Meanwhile, relations between Richards and Jagger had deteriorated.

RICHARDS: "When it comes down to what you're going to put out, he goes for the safe mix. I'm less inclined to go for the verse-chorus-verse-chorus approach. I don't mind a five-minute intro or knocking out a verse or some vocals. I go more for the aural excitement. I mean, we're the ones who brought out our first album without a title, with an instrumental, put out 'Little Red Rooster,' a real barnyard blues, when everybody thought it was time to bring out a smash hit. 'Why be conservative now?' I said it to him, and he damn well knows it. And Mick, bless his heart, even agrees with me. He knows he has a problem from that point of view, and he's working on it."

A good measure of how profound the conflict really was was the fact that Keith suddenly showed less interest in working with Mick than in being with Patti. In May, while Jagger and Wood mixed the album in New York, Richards went to San Francisco, where Patti was filming *Hard to Hold* opposite Rick Springfield. After returning to New York briefly, he flew down to Jamaica in June, leaving Jagger to continue alone. Speculation that Richards was becoming disillusioned with Jagger was now rife on both sides of the Atlantic.

Back in New York at the end of June, Richards paid $750,000 to buy a home for himself and Patti—four floors of an apartment building on East Fourth Street in downtown Manhattan. They planned to take a year to renovate it before moving in. In July he flew to L.A. with Patti to appear with Little Richard, Mick Fleetwood, and Gary Busey on a TV special saluting Jerry Lee Lewis. Richards had been a Lewis fan for some time, but this was the first opportunity they had to perform together. When Keith showed up for the rehearsal, he was astonished to discover that he had donned the identical outfit—turquoise T-shirt, shades, black jeans, and white shoes—Jerry Lee was togged out in.

In August, when the Stones signed a record deal with Columbia, Keith realized that Yetnikoff saw Jagger, not the Stones, as the hot property. It turned out not only that Jagger had agreed to make two solo albums, but that Yetnikoff, who clearly did not understand the dynamics of the band, was encouraging him to make one of the solo albums first, before the next Stones' album. Yetnikoff's attempt to turn Jagger into a solo star effectively crippled the Stones creatively for the next five years, while Columbia paid them only their approximate market value. Still, the money involved was staggering. "Walter must have been feeling his oats when he bid for the Stones," wrote Fredric Dannen in *Hit Men*. "His offer, which included some of the Stones' catalog and the right to Mick Jagger's solo career, came to $28 million. Atlantic's Ahmet Ertegun, who had outbid Clive [Davis] for the group a decade earlier [when Davis was president of Columbia Records], was stunned by Walter's bid, which was twice his own." According to Marc Eliot in *Rockonomics*, Columbia actually got the better of the agreement, recouping its initial investment in one year by releasing the Stones' backlist on compact disc.

In October Keith was in Paris to shoot a promotional video for the Stones' upcoming single, "Undercover of the Night." According to the video's director, Julien Temple, Keith liked to test the nerve of the people he was going to work with. In their first meeting he held a sword stick to Temple's throat. Later he took him for a drive through the streets of Paris at more than 100 mph. Temple obviously passed the tests because not only did he continue to work with Keith, but they became good friends. From Paris, Keith flew with Patti, Mick, Jerry, and Julien Temple to Mexico City to shoot more videos.

On November 7, *Undercover* was released in the U.S. and the

U.K. The album turned out to be one of their most controversial and least successful. Many of the songs—"Too Much Blood," "Pretty Beat Up," "Tie Me Up," "It Must Be Hell"—had violent themes and lyrics. Several, considered to be misogynist, provoked the wrath of women's groups once again. The BBC banned the promotional video for the single "Undercover of the Night" for being "exceedingly violent."

In an interview with Bill German, Keith admitted that it was a gory album, but pointed out that it also had the kind of classic, archetypal Stones imagery that mirrored society. "If there's too much blood, there's too much blood," Keith said. "And it'll come out. I thought Mick has done an incredible job. I think he's taken quite a leap forward, lyricwise, on this album. You can put out 'Tie Me Up,' which is kind of funny because of all that shit that went down—some mouthy feminists. It's just a point of view. They take it on the literal level. 'Oh, "Tie Me Up," the Stones just want to enslave you.' Most of those chicks probably never had it anyway. But they scream their mouths off even if they don't know what it's like."

The violent lyrics in the album probably had less to do with reflecting the world at large than the hostility in their recording studio. However, this time the competition among group members did not produce a great album. In the U.K. the single "Undercover of the Night" only reached number three, the album going to number eleven. On the U.S. charts the single only reached number nine while the album stalled at number four. It was the first time since 1969 that a new Stones studio album failed to reach the number-one spot in their largest market.

After shooting the videos in Mexico City, Keith and Patti returned to Cabo San Lucas for a long stay. Once again Keith took up with his local friends, putting the color that the difficult birth of *Undercover* had drained back in his cheeks. People noticed that Patti seemed somewhat distant and less friendly than Keith. She had found it hard to keep Keith off junk, stay straight herself, and put up with his womanizing. Early in their relationship Patti had been determined to maintain her own career as a model and actress, but just as Anita had found it an impossible task in 1967, Patti was pulled into the vortex of Keith's lifestyle. Although some held that "she would do anything for Keith," there were dissenting opinions. "The bitch needs help," commented one observer who witnessed the decline of her career. Patti had given herself completely to Keith, and her sacrifice turned him around in some vital ways. He had come to trust her and see that he could have a second chance at having a family, that she wasn't going to turn into Anita. While they were in Cabo San Lucas, Keith and Patti secretly told friends and family that they were getting married. The wedding was scheduled to take place in Cabo on Keith's fortieth birthday, December 18, 1983, thus ensuring that he would not forget their anniversaries. Arrangements were made in a frantic rush. Patti returned to New York briefly to fulfill a modeling assignment and to pick her gown. Doris Richards scrambled to find Keith's birth certificate. By the seventeenth, Doris, Bert, and Keith's kids, Marlon and Dandelion (who had recently changed her name to Angela) were all in Cabo San Lucas. The event brought Keith's parents together for the first time in twenty years. The Hansen family was represented by Patti's mother and her brother Alfred. Mick, *sans* Jerry, showed up as Keith's best man. Anita, who was in terrible shape in London after breaking her leg and being busted once again, didn't attend; but later she graciously acknowledged the end of her "marriage" to Keith by presenting him with a beautiful 1934 Gibson guitar. By this time, she not only approved of Patti but had come to genuinely like her.

Uschi and Dieter were also once again in Cabo. "Keith was really one of the most important men in my life," she said, "and of all places in the world there he is getting married right under my nose."

At the bachelor party the night before the wedding, the Glimmer Twins played and sang their old favorites: "Great Balls of Fire," "Whole Lot of Shakin' Goin' On," "Blue Suede Shoes." Keith, close to his roots as ever, was wildly happy. "Nothing like a good woman!" he crowed, adding, "I know I couldn't have beaten heroin without Patti. She's been of inestimable value. I ain't letting that bitch go! And besides, shit, I'm gonna try anything. And if I'm gonna try anything like marriage, I'm only gonna try it once. 'Cause

I'm not about to try it twice. And if I try it once, it's gonna be with this chick. Patricia's a wonderful girl." The woman who was about to become Mrs. Richards had been nine when "Satisfaction" was number one.

In full evening dress and blue suede shoes, holding his head high, Keith had never looked prouder or better than he did on his wedding day. The Lutheran ceremony was conducted in Spanish and held outside at the Finisterra Hotel, in balmy breezes under sparkling ocean skies. Keith shunned all organized religion, particularly Christianity, whose "logo of a guy nailed to a piece of wood" he thought particularly odd, but in order to spark things up a bit he performed the Jewish wedding custom of stamping on a wine glass wrapped in cloth. At the reception afterward in a bamboo hut at the Viejo Trailer Camp, observers watched as Keith flung himself down at Patti's feet and serenaded her with Hoagy Carmichael's "The Nearness of You," his voice cracking with emotion.

In January 1984, one week later, Uschi's boyfriend Dieter was killed in a motorcycle accident. Keith was there like a shot, asking if there was anything he could do, but because he was committed to Patti he was careful not to get too involved. Uschi never saw him again. Nor did anyone else in Cabo San Lucas. By the end of the year, Keith's wild ways had caught up with him: According to one witness who was a close friend of Richards's main contact, Mexican authorities quietly advised him that it would be to his advantage to leave Cabo San Lucas.

Keith went to Mexico City to work on more videos with Temple and the Stones, and then returned with Mick and Patti to New York, where he remained for a month. On February 25 he took the Concorde to Paris to inspect a new studio for the Stones to work in, since Pathé-Marconi had demolished his favorite room there. Keith was working on holding the band together; Mick had begun to work on his solo album. When Jagger informed Richards that he intended to take solo credit for the songs he was planning to record on his first album, thus breaking the tradition of using the Jagger-Richards byline, Keith was angry: "My attitude when he said he was going to do that was 'Fine! Since I'm not going to have anything to do with it, I don't really want my name coming into it anyway! Since I'm not going to be involved, maybe I won't like it. I don't want my name to touch those songs! If this is your album, you stick your name on 'em.'"

Keith and Patti returned to New York in March and joined her family to celebrate Patti's birthday on March 17. On March 28 they saw a screening of *Hard to Hold*, which was a flop. Although this was primarily the fault of the director, Patti's hairdresser's comparison of her to Marilyn Monroe was not borne out on the screen.

On April 10 the couple flew down to Jamaica for a two-and-a-half-month holiday at Point of View. Julien Temple, who visited Richards in Jamaica, noted that getting married didn't slow Keith down at all. According to Nick Kent, when Temple arrived at Montego Bay "he was picked up at the airport by these three mates of Keith's. They drove to Keith's place smoking joints. First thing they do is run over a goat in the road. People are shooting guns at them. Finally they arrive on this back road at this mansion where Richards lives and the first thing Temple hears is somebody screaming. Freddie Sessler is fucking drowning in the fucking swimming pool and like Keith comes out of a balcony window, this Errol Flynn-like appearance—'Mr. Danger, here I come to save Sessler. Here I am still living that dangerous, cutthroat life.' But the guys that surrounded him were real roughneck, unpleasant dope people."

Jagger spent the first months of 1984 working on his album. As if scared by the prospect of solo flight, he cut a single, "State of Shock," in collaboration with Michael Jackson. The two singers recorded the single in May, backed up by the Jackson family. Jagger is said to have shocked Jackson by singing flat. "How did *he* ever get to be a star?" Jackson supposedly asked. On June 30, a day after another Stones greatest-hits album, *Rewind*, was released, "State of Shock" started to climb the U.S. charts, where it would peak at number three. It was not a bad start for a solo career, except that it wasn't solo. Meanwhile, both Mick and Keith were keeping an eye on the Olympic Games in Los Angeles because they had donated money to the British gymnastic and decathlon teams. Keith was a big fan of the British track star Daley Thompson, who won a gold medal in the decathlon. Richards sent him a telegram stating, "You've made us Brits exuberant."

In July, Patti became pregnant. "When Patti and I got married she said she couldn't have babies," Richards recalled. "I said, Fine, I'll marry you. Within six months: 'Guess what, I'm pregnant!'" Having children had always seemed to make Keith extraordinarily happy, and now it increased his new-found devotion to his home life. He went home to New York to spend August with Patti and Marlon. But there were strings attached. Having a baby was about to bring new responsibility. It soon became apparent that Patti was less keen than before on having Keith drink and stay up all night. She became increasingly impatient with his wild, drug-happy buddies. Ron Wood, who had just emerged from a detox clinic, recalled that when Keith stayed out late he got scolded: "Patti never hassled me, she just yelled at Keith."

With a gap left by Jagger, Ronnie became a mainstay of Keith's life in the mideighties just as he had in the midseventies. Ronnie installed a private recording studio in his basement, and Keith spent many hours there playing with Ronnie and numerous friends. Keith took to dubbing his mate "the holy host."

Richards spent the fall of 1984 bouncing from one home to another. In the first half of September he was in Jamaica with his father, who had been staying at Point of View since June. Keith did have many things in common with Bert apart from being stubborn, drinking, and liking the same food. Both men had a strong sense of humor and loved playing games. They played a lot of checkers together. Keith would sometimes play Yahtzee with his children for hours at a time. Marlon also benefited greatly from Bert's presence. Keith, who often gave people pet names, referred to them as Batman and Robin. At other times he would introduce his father as Popeye.

In late 1978 a New York high school kid named Bill German had started publishing a Rolling Stones fanzine called *Beggars Banquet*. In 1984 the Stones adopted it as their official fan magazine. Over the years Keith was the one who supported it most and was most willing to keep in touch with the wide spectrum of subscribers, ranging from twelve to sixty-year-olds. "Keith has stepped out a lot in the eighties," German said. "He likes being interviewed now and without a doubt he's the best interview in the band, probably in all of rock and roll. He has consistently supported my efforts through-out the years. For the things he's done for me personally I could never thank him enough. Marriage has mellowed him out in a good way. There's a side to him that a lot of people just aren't aware of."

At the end of October 1984, Keith, Mick, Bill, and Charlie had met in Amsterdam to discuss once again the future of the band. By then the others were at the end of their tether with Jagger, who was lording it over them from his exalted position as Walter Yetnikoff's golden boy and, as he saw it, "the undisputed leader" of the Rolling Stones. Even the gentle drummer lost his cool. As Keith described it, Charlie "dished Mick out a great fucking left hook, and that was Charlie's way of saying, 'You and I have had it.' I had taken Mick out for a drink, so at five in the morning he came back to my room. He's drunk by now. Mick drunk is a sight to behold. Charlie was fast asleep. 'Is that my drummer? Why don't you get your arse down here?' Charlie got dressed—in a Savile Row suit, tie, shoes, shaved—came down, grabbed him, and went boom! Charlie punched him into a plateful of smoked salmon and he almost floated out the window into a canal in Amsterdam. I just grabbed his leg and saved him from going out. Mick was wearing my jacket at the time. It really pissed me off. Meanwhile, my jacket, my favorite jacket, got ruined. Why did I lend him that jacket? 'Don't ever call me "your drummer" again. You're my fucking singer.' That was Charlie's way of saying, 'It's over, man.' If there was one other friend Mick had, it was Charlie. On top of that, Mick was very stupid. He forgave Charlie. There was nothing to forgive. Nothing left to forgive."

In January 1985, recording for the new album, *Dirty Work*, began in Paris. They all knew this recording period would not be easy. Richards was enraged when Jagger showed up with hardly any original material to contribute. He was completely absorbed by the March release of his album, *She's the Boss*. "I thought the timing was very strange, bringing out something like that, an obviously commercial album, just before we were starting to work on the new Stones album," Keith said. "I mean, if he had done his favorite Irish folk songs with a lady harpist . . . or had Liberace accompany him on Frank Sinatra songs, whatever, something you couldn't possibly have done with the Stones, that would have been fine. To my mind, a Mick Jagger album should have been a ginormous event, not just another record. I told him it was dumb timing and not an inspired piece of work." Keith began referring to Jagger less than affectionately as "Brenda." As he explained the name, "'Brenda' was a momentary thing. In Paris, I lived around the corner from the English bookshop and there was this book in there and in great gold letters it said 'Brenda Jagger.' So he became Brenda for a bit."

Suddenly, just as Jagger had once had to coax Richards into songwriting, Richards found himself trying to pull at least some kind of collaborative response out of Jagger. Thinking that Mick would be a natural for a track that had been a top ten U.K. hit in 1969 for Bob & Earl called "Harlem Shuffle," Keith copied versions of the song onto every tape he gave to Jagger. Eventually, as the band played the track over and over during a night of rehearsals, Mick took the bait and put down the vocal track.

RICHARDS: "He was spending more time doing his solo stuff instead of doing *Dirty Work*, which really pissed me off. He shouldn't have been making the album if he wasn't into it. I very nearly stiffed him at the time. But there's no joy in punching a wimp. I like him, and I say these things, and they come out and they sound kind of cruel, but I've known Mick since I was four years old, and despite myself I do love the guy. Mick and I have always prided ourselves on recognizing the point when you thought you had become bigger than the Rolling Stones. We fell out during the making of the record when he was around. We hardly got the chance to fucking fall out, he was there so infrequently! It was just Charlie, Ronnie, and me trying to make a Stones record. It was very unprofessional of Mick, very stupid."

Keith and Charlie were not the only ones fed up with Mick. Bill Wyman complained, "I've lost touch with whoever Mick is now. I'm sure he has as well. Seven or eight years ago I could talk to Mick about books, films, and intelligent things, but now I just talk to him in asides. Mick is a very difficult person to know now. I'm not worried saying what I think about Mick. He's not my boss. We are a band, and Keith Richards runs the Rolling Stones, really. Mick is a brilliant man, but in the final count he just has his share of five votes, no more."

Only Jagger, who was far too PR-conscious to take any other tack, maintained that nothing had changed. "The other Stones might think it's possible that if the album did really well it might be the end of the Stones," he said. "But I know it won't be. But it was still strange working without the others. It's rather like having a wife and a mistress. The Stones thing is a long marriage. I know them very well. I know their strengths and their weaknesses. I almost have telepathy with them after all these years."

On March 1 Keith flew from Paris to New York to await the arrival of his first baby with Patti. He soon got word of two births: On March 4, Jagger's solo album, *She's the Boss*, was released. On March 18, while Mick's album was climbing rapidly up the U.K. charts, Patti gave birth to their daughter, Theodora Dupree (in honor of Gus) Richards.

RICHARDS: "Just after Theodora was born I was walking from the New York Hospital and decided to stroll home, because I felt like it. It was night and there was a railway arch and I see these two guys cross over and start walking towards me. I thought, Ah, here we go, let's see the size of them first. They pull a knife out and they walk under the light and they say, 'Oh, sorry, Keith, didn't know it was you. On your way, son.'"

Keith was now older and more reflective, and his fourth experience with fatherhood gave him a new perspective. "What children do is grow you up, make you think," Keith said. "What the hell am I going to leave behind when I'm gone? It's throwing them into a fucking caldron of pollution and fear. But a lot of people don't take any notice of their kids, they just think of them as possessions, or something like 'I fucked up that night; I forgot to pull out,' and 'OK, we can do plenty more; if that fucks up we can have another one.' We can be incredibly callous about ourselves. There are so many of us, and the forces of nature are relentless."

On April 11, the Stones resumed work on the album, whose release date had been pushed back from June to September because of Columbia's concentration on Jagger's album. Richards countered

Jagger's decision to take sole credit for the songs on his solo album by involving Ronnie heavily in the work on the Stones' album, and he was determined to make sure that Wood got credit for at least half the songs. For Keith, the only good thing about making the album was his collaboration with Ronnie, who also benefited from working with Keith. "While we were doing *Dirty Work* I said, 'Do you realize, Ronnie, that you've been in the band longer than Brian was? Longer than Mick Taylor? And you're still the new boy!' He's got a very superficially flippant character, but he's got a lot more depth to him than people think. And I've always enjoyed working with him very much. I love his enthusiasm."

"A few times Keith and I felt like killing people, but we picked up our guitars and wrote songs instead," recalled Wood. "That's how we came up with 'Fight,' 'I've Had It with You,' and 'One Hit (to the Body).' We've all been spared long jail sentences by being able to play our music."

Despite the enormous amounts of publicity it received, Jagger's first solo album was a critical and commercial disappointment, although not a disaster. The single "Just Another Night" reached number twelve in the U.S.; the album reached number thirteen and went platinum. Its relative failure was mitigated by Jagger's spectacular success at the Live Aid benefit in July 1985. The Stones had, of course, been asked to perform, but had not even replied to the invitation. According to Richards, this was because they were deeply involved in making an album. According to Wyman, it was "because Keith didn't give a fuck."

"I had no intentions of going near Live Aid," Richards explained. "I don't trust big charity events. The minute rock and roll reaches the head, forget it. Rock and roll starts from the neck down. Once rock and roll gets mixed up in No Nukes and Rock Against Racism, admirable causes though they are—it's not for rock and roll to take these things up as a full-time obsession. Because nukes may obsess your brain, but they don't obsess your crotch. Rock and roll, it's a few moments when you can forget about nukes and racism and all the other evils God's kindly thrown upon us. The Stones were asked to play as a band but they were not a band anymore. They'd already broken up."

In May, Jagger announced that he would perform solo. Bob Geldof guaranteed him a twenty-five-minute spot at the prime time to watch the show, at least on the East Coast of the U.S., of 9.00 P.M., just before the final act, America's poet laureate and the spiritual captain of his generation, Bob Dylan. Jagger booked Hall and Oates's band to back him up, he threw himself into rehearsing, and he looked about for something that would put his performance over the top. He invited Tina Turner to do two songs with him, and arranged to make a video with David Bowie of "Dancing in the Street," which would premiere at the end of his set with Turner. Jagger put on a dazzling show, full of well-staged charm and glamour, but the most notable points of his coup—a raunchy "Honky Tonk Women" with Turner and a suggestive, playful "Dancing in the Streets" with Bowie—were, like his duet with Michael Jackson, collaborations. Part of their appeal was the novelty of two superstars appearing together.

Richards decided to go to Live Aid after all when the idea of Keith and Ronnie playing with Dylan at Live Aid arose, according to Wood, out of a visit by Dylan to Wood's house a couple of days before the event.

RON WOOD: "Bob says, 'I'm playing in Philadelphia the day after tomorrow.' I didn't know about Live Aid. He says, 'It's a big charity thing. Bill Graham's got a band for me and I have to go along with it. Do you think that maybe you and me could play together some time?' I said, 'Sure. Let's do the gig on Saturday. Keith would love to do it too.' So I rang up Keith and I said, 'Get over here because Bob wants us to do Live Aid with him.' Keith knew about it. He said, 'You better not be lying, Woody.'

"Keith comes round to my house, but the first thing Bob says to Keith is, 'Are you going to do Live Aid or are you going to watch it on TV?' and I've already told Keith that we're doing it! And Keith goes, 'You lying bastard!' and starts as if he's going to strangle me. I'm shouting, 'Shut up, man!' and Bob's looking a little confused so he decides to go to the toilet. Keith's shouting, 'You've been telling me all this shit, Woody! Oh, man, you can never do *anything* right.' So I say, 'Look, sit there. Stop fuming.' So then Bob is just coming out of the toilet, so I rush upstairs and say, 'Bob, do you want us to do this gig on Saturday or not?' And he says 'Course I do.' So I turn to Bob and say, 'Well, tell him!' and Bob says, 'Hey, man, will you play this gig with us?' Keith says, 'Course I will.' And we had a great time from there on, rehearsing for a couple of days in my basement, playing through everything in Bob's catalog and everything in the Stones catalog. When we got to the stadium he was saying, 'I wonder what Bill Graham wants me to do.' We were going, 'Do what you want to do, Bob!' Even going up the ramp—we'd decided what songs we were going to play and he turns and says, 'Hey, maybe I should do "All I Really Want to Do."'' We were going, 'Aargh! Oh, my God!'''

Richards and Wood accompanied Dylan in what should have been the high point of the show, but the trio went on stage in a state of confusion. Behind the curtain Ken Kragen and Lionel Richie, two of the organizers of the concert, were arranging a vast chorus of "We Are the World." Dylan, Richards, and Wood started to play acoustic guitars with no monitors as people banged equipment a few feet behind them. Far from eclipsing Jagger's *tour de force*, the set turned into a ramshackle disaster with Richards and Wood playing vague, largely inaudible backup to songs that appeared to have been neither rehearsed nor arranged.

"It soon became clear," wrote Philip Norman, "that Richards and Wood were in a condition which only the most devoted Stones fan of the mid-seventies would have considered appropriate. Unsteady on old-fashioned boot heels, raddled faces confused, skinny forearms clumsily pumping scrub-board guitars, they appeared less like rock immortals than a pair of disreputable charwomen half-heartedly washing some socks.

"The music was abysmal, but still worse the archaic Gauloise and Jack Daniel's reek of the musicians on an afternoon dedicated to altruism and higher thought. To the Live Aid masses, in their conspicuous virtue and wholesome street-cred undress, the whole concept of the Rolling Stones suddenly seemed ludicrous, if not vaguely obscene. The two bespangled old reprobates were all but laughed off the stage."

Nobody but Mick could front the Stones, and every time Keith tried to find a replacement it was a disaster. "I found myself," Keith said, "as they say in the navy, 'on the beach, on half pay.'"

*

In November 1985 Patti got pregnant for a second time. Keith continued to spend days and nights thrashing out songs on the piano and guitar. Bono Vox, the lead singer of U2 visited him in the studio shortly after the Live Aid show and observed: "Keith doesn't talk much. He prefers to play the guitar or piano or sing. That night he beat the ivories with his knuckles and hollered out country and western stuff, old Buddy Holly songs, blues. That's his dialogue; rock and roll music is his language of love. He was talking to me through his songs, then he looked up as if to say, 'Now you sing your songs.' I found Keith to be very much on the main road. He was still in love with the music. You can see that all his infamy and fortune didn't matter much to him. When he put on his guitar, lines disappeared from his face." Meeting Richards inspired Bono to write his first blues, "Silver and Gold," which Keith and Ronnie played on the following day. It was included on *Sun City*, an antiapartheid album by a number of star musicians.

ROBERT PALMER: "About 5.00 A.M. Bono and Miami Steve [Van Zandt] and Arthur Baker showed up. [Van Zandt and Baker were putting together the *Sun City* compilation album.] Bono had just written 'Silver and Gold' and recorded the vocal in his hotel room. At a certain point in a drifting conversation Keith said, 'OK, now let me get this straight: You've got this vocal track here and you've brought it over and you'd like me to do an arrangement to go with it, right?' There was this little pause and Bono said, 'Yeah.' And Keith immediately said, 'OK, Ronnie, why don't you play the acoustic guitar and use your switchblade? I'll play electric guitar, and Palmer, you can play clarinet.' We listened to the vocal a few times and just went out in the studio and did it in two takes. Keith shapes the music without saying anything through a combination of his playing and body language.

"It was particularly interesting because the Stones were spending so much time on *Dirty Work* and he and Mick weren't getting along and it must have seemed like this endless quagmire, so Bono's coming in with the song was a relief for Keith—it was something he could just do. And it was done with a lot of intensity and concentration and real focus. When we were finished everybody said, 'that's great,' and Bono said, 'Yeah, that's happening.' He took the tapes and ran."

As the *Dirty Work* sessions proceeded in New York in the summer of 1985, it became clear that the Rolling Stones were no longer functioning as a band. Bill Wyman played bass on only half the album, while Charlie Watts became so vexed at one point that he walked out and flew back to England. "What we done today?" he complained. "Nothing. It's absurd. In twenty-five years with the Stones I've worked for five years and spent twenty years hanging around. I'd have been dead years ago if I'd thought about it." "Charlie," Keith would later admit, "was going through a weird period, which he does from time to time." Ron Wood stepped in to cover, playing drums where needed and helping Keith find stand-in players. Richards managed to pull together an all-star lineup of special guests for the album—Jamaican singer-songwriter Jimmy Cliff, R&B star Bobby Womack, singers Tom Waits and Kirsty MacColl, guitarist Jimmy Page, plus three musicians he would work with a good deal in the future, Steve Jordan, Ivan Neville, and Charley Drayton. The album's backbone came from the comically named Biff Hitler Trio, an assemblage of roadies and friends whom Richards and Wood enlisted in the absence of regular members.

Playing with so many top stars in the aftermath of Live Aid bolstered Richards's self-confidence. On one occasion during the *Dirty Work* sessions when Jimmy Page came up with a chord progression that was so complex Keith couldn't play it, he went out of the room for five minutes, then returned with the words, "Screw you clever bastards," and played a sequence that stunned everybody with its simplicity and rightness. During the second half of the 1980s, Keith's reputation as a guitar player and songwriter skyrocketed among his peers and also in the rock press. Before the end of the decade he would be voted the most influential guitar player in rock by a jury of his peers in a *New Musical Express* poll. Nils Lofgren puts it this way: "By now I think it's beyond argument that Keith Richards is the greatest rock and roll songwriter."

Jagger did not seem to care about, or, for that matter, feel threatened by, the inclusion on *Dirty Work* of such figures as Womack (which led some wags to set the gossip wheels spinning by wondering out loud if Womack or Jimmy Cliff could do a credible version of "Satisfaction"). "I could never work Mick out," said

Steve Lillywhite, who coproduced *Dirty Work*. "Mick is such a great bunch of blokes. In New York his accent changes; when he's with the lads he's a drunken yobbo. With that talent you would have thought he would have made a great actor, yet Jagger is never quite as cool as he thinks."

On December 12, Ian Stewart, the sixth Stone, who had been suffering from intense respiratory trouble for a few days, went to see a specialist in a West London clinic. During the wait he suffered a massive heart attack and died at age forty-seven. Stu had planned to visit Keith after the appointment to help iron out some of the problems with the album. "He'd encourage me to carry on with *Dirty Work*," said Richards, "to get the record finished. He wasn't too happy with it, either. Making a Stones record had always been a breeze, a laugh. It had never been a hassle. But he was still there every night, never giving up." His passing was, said Richards, who was probably the band member most affected by it, "the final nail in the coffin. We all felt the glue had come undone. Very few people realized how important he was to the Stones. He was the glue that held all the bits together. The combination of that and Mick's defection left me in limbo. Suddenly it was 'What can I do?'"

"We were all at his funeral at Randalls Park Crematorium, Surrey, on 20 December, together with Eric Clapton, Jeff Beck and Glyn Johns," wrote Bill Wyman, "and we knew that Stu's death would leave a huge gap. As Keith said to Woody at the funeral: 'Who's gonna tell us off *now* when we misbehave?' And Keith meant it; we were heavily choked up." Three days after the funeral, Keith and Ronnie Concorded back to New York to spend Christmas with their families.

In New York, *Beggars Banquet* magazine asked Keith for a statement about Stu's death. He came up with the following: "Why'd you have to leave us like that, you sod! At least he went out on an upswing. He was excited about the new album. But I thought he'd be the one holding the shovel, the one to bury all of us. What a hole he's left, such an obvious gap. He would always be there to comment on everything, and sometimes you would think he was crazy. But then you'd go and realize he was right all along. I mean, no one had a bad word to say about him. I'd had other friends pass on, and you go, 'Gee, it's a shame,' but Stu was different. I could think of a hundred other fuckers who should have gone instead of him! He wasn't even on my list!"

On February 23, 1986, Stu's friends gathered at the 100 Club on London's Oxford Street to pay him tribute. For once, re-creating the past, which Keith so enjoyed, was the only appropriate thing, and the Stones took the stage. When pianist Chuck Leavell asked Keith what songs they'd be doing, he replied, "Man, there's no way we can make a set for this. This is for Stu. We can't plan it out." And so the Stones jammed, launching into the sort of R&B covers Ian Stewart loved, the songs that had sparked their careers.

The musician most affected by the Stones' tribute to Stu was Eric Clapton. One of the great guitar players of rock himself, Clapton was floored by Keith's performance that day. No one had dared start the jam until Keith stood up. The power, Clapton said, was devastating. "He's an unbelievable player, one of the best ever."

According to Jeff Baker of the *Daily Star*, "The Stones played with the guts and energy of a teenage band. This was the Stones going back to their roots, playing muddy and dirty, ripping through the old classics." Mick and Keith left the club with their arms around each other.

When, a week later, the Stones were awarded a lifetime achievement Grammy, Clapton presented it in London. The ceremony was broadcast by satellite to the U.S. Jagger, who was annoyed that it took the Grammy judges twenty-five years to figure out the Stones' worth, had considered refusing the award, but Richards insisted they accept to help publicize the new album.

Dirty Work was released on March 24. The album was dedicated to Ian Stewart, who ended it with thirty seconds of the boogie-woogie piano playing that had blown Keith's head off twenty-four years before. Keith sang two lead vocals on the record, the reggae number "Too Rude" (on which he had an assist from Jimmy Cliff) and the quintessential Richards ballad "Sleep Tonight," which garnered the most critical attention. In his comments about the album, Keith tried to downplay the Stones' rift. "Let's put it like this," he stated: "It's a Stones album. If I've had a little more to do with it and a little more control over this one, it's the same to me as the middle seventies when Mick would cover my ass when I was out of it. Because of the timing of Mick's solo album, he wasn't there as much as the rest of us in the beginning when the mood was getting set.

"Even if Mick and I never did another stroke of work together in all our lives, we'd still have to live with each other. Just on a business level we'd still have to face each other, but he doesn't put as much store by friendship and loyalty as I do. Mick happens to be an incredible entertainer. Without Mick, the Stones would never have gone anywhere. I just wish Mick could find a few guys he got along with. A friend, to me, is one of the blessings in life. And I don't agree with that saying, 'You can count your real friends on one hand.' If that's so, then you ain't farming the right acres, because friends are everywhere. My battles with Mick are on many levels. I understand the desperation of somebody like that, the insecurity that says, 'Until I'm sure of myself, I can't let anyone get too close, or I'll get really confused.' To me, one of the best things you can get out of life is to have friends. If you can count more friends than you have fingers, then you're really lucky. Luckily, I can start on my toes. And I don't know if Mick can. I don't know if Mick can fill a hand . . . I feel like I'm his only friend." Despite this avowal of friendship, later in the same interview Richards commented on the oversize egos of Jagger and Bill Wyman, saying the two of them "take it for granted that people love the shit that comes out of their arseholes, quite honestly. And that makes me feel very squeamish. It's horrific to me that I could think that I'm above and beyond anybody else. I'm just a guitar player."

Keith didn't realize it, but his days of being "just a guitar player" were drawing to a close. Difficult as it was to put together, the album served as a bridge to Keith's solo career. As Greg Quill pointed out in his enthusiastic endorsement of *Dirty Work* in an essay on the Rolling Stones' twenty-fifth-anniversary tour, "*Dirty Work*'s greatest achievement was in liberating Richards from his constraining 'number two' position. His contributions here were more honest and heartfelt, more confident than anything he'd done on earlier records. Bitter at times, aggressive and deliberately provocative, particularly in his demands on Jagger, Richards used *Dirty Work* to pave the way for his first solo album."

In January 1986, Keith and Ronnie flew to Fort Lauderdale to talk up *Dirty Work* at a CBS convention. In a spirit of uncharacteristic cooperation with the top brass, they played a tape of some *Dirty Work* cuts and posed for pictures with convention guests. "We've done our *Dirty Work*," Keith told the astonished CBS executives. "Now it's time for you to do yours." Keith's spirits were so high that Jane Rose looked out her hotel window one morning to discover him doing headstands!

Richards was anxious to tour, but once again Jagger threw a wrench into the works. At the end of February Keith was interviewed in New York for a book on songwriters by Bill Flanagan, editor of *Musician* magazine, who had just heard that Mick flatly refused to tour behind *Dirty Work*. Flanagan was so taken by Keith's enthusiasm about the tour that he couldn't bring himself to tell him it wasn't going to happen. "Keith Richards loped into the Rolling Stones' New York office on a snowy evening in February 1986 wearing a wide-brimmed Stetson hat and reaching for a bottle of Jack Daniel's whiskey," Flanagan wrote. "Keith is rock's greatest contradiction, a monument of self-abuse who stays strong and vital year after year; a hard, thick-skinned pirate who behaves like a perfect English gentleman; the guru of hard rock and prototype for the image of the decadent rock star who writes melodic ballads in the tradition of Hoagy Carmichael. And says the measure of a guitarist is how well he handles the acoustic—not the electric— guitar."

Once again Keith was enraged when he got the news. But Keith's disappointment and anger were nothing compared to the way he felt when he heard Mick was considering touring and performing Rolling Stones songs with another band. By now, Keith's comments about Jagger in the press were honest and brutal. "Mick felt he could do better without the Stones, and that to me is like really loopy. Why do that when you've got twenty-five years of integrity and respect behind you? I think the Stones are at a point where they could really grow up gracefully. Be more mature. Make it strong that way. He said, 'I don't need you bunch of old farts. You're just a millstone around my neck. You're too much of a hassle.' There's times I coulda killed him. I mean, it would be one thing to say he don't want to go out on the road . . . but if he were to say he don't want to go out with the Stones and goes out with Schmuck and Ball's band instead, I'LL SLIT HIS FUCKIN' THROAT."

RICHARDS: "Mick and I got a bit frayed in the mid-eighties. A lot of that's a storm in a teacup. But when you're fighting via the press, it's like issuing bulletins at each other. Without the media adding a bit of gasoline to the fire now and then, Mick and I could have probably resolved it a lot quicker and smoother. It's not like having a little row with the ol' lady. Your life is under incredible scrutiny."

It wasn't only Jagger's solo career that deterred him from going on the road. He was tired of the bickering among band members, not to mention their chemical imbalances (even Charlie, it was whispered, had fallen prey to the jazz musicians he was playing with—on one occasion he had shown up at the Oval cricket ground driving a Lamborghini and togged out head to foot in the costume of an RAF officer) and wanted to avoid spending another year of his life with them. Also, since Wyman had released two solo albums, Ronnie had continued to do solo work, and Keith had toured with the New Barbarians and contributed solo songs to Ronnie's albums, Jagger did not think it was fair to bar him from a solo excursion.

MICK JAGGER: "I was completely one-hundred-percent right about not doing that tour. The band was in no condition to tour. It's as simple as that. The album wasn't that good. It was OK. It certainly wasn't a great Stones album. The relationships were terrible. Health was diabolical. I wasn't in particularly good shape. The rest of the band, they couldn't walk across the Champs-Élysées, much less go on the road. So we had this long, bad experience of making that record and the last thing I wanted to do was spend another year with the same people. I just wanted to be out. I mean, we've had a lot of ups and downs in the Rolling Stones and this is one of them. I, for one, hope we regroup. I respect Keith and I feel a lot of affection for him, and I feel protective. He's the kind of person who has a certain kind of vulnerability. He's had a lot of hard times. He's had a lot of good times. We've had a lot of fun and a lot of heartaches together."

Keith's Stones family appeared to be disintegrating before his eyes. Four days after Jagger celebrated his forty-third birthday in London, Ron and Jo Wood left New York to move back to England permanently, ending the era of "the holy host." Adding disappointment to injury, *Dirty Work*'s sales fell below expectations. Despite a promising single, "Harlem Shuffle," and a popular video, the album peaked at number four in the U.S. and number three in the U.K., making it their second consecutive studio album not to reach number one in the U.S.

Fortunately, Keith's real family continued slowly but surely to replace the Stones. On July 28, 1986, Patti gave birth to Alexandra Nicole. As his young daughters grew, the first in the image of a dancer, the second, who took on a remarkable resemblance to Keith, in the image of a boxer, so did his fondness for them.

RICHARDS: "Having babies roaming around your house is one of the most beautiful things in the world. You get a little girl coming up to you and saying, 'Daddy, I love you.' It's 'Ah, break my heart, darling.' They cheer you up like nothing else can. It's always fascinating. They keep reminding you of things you can't remember, those first two or three years. My current family is more stable than the first. Children are like songs to me. You don't bring them up. They kind of show you what they need, and you provide it. Children are far too intractable for you to impose yourself on them. There's no point in having fights, because they beat you every time. Especially girls.

"I mean, sometimes I wake up in the middle of the night and there's both kids in the bed. They've managed to find their way, and we're all in the same bed together. You get more out of it like that, and so do the kids. Family is a special thing. It's almost ... you can't really talk about it, except to say that if you get a chance at it, try it out, because it's one of the most special things that you'll ever get on this earth. It gives you that final missing link of what life's about. While they're looking upon you as the most wonderful person in the world because you're 'Daddy,' they do more for you than you do for them. Your kids give you that bit of love you gave your own parents, the bit of life you don't remember. It's vital knowledge, like a missing piece of a jigsaw puzzle."

Patti grounded Keith, protected him, and was devoted to him. He loved her, loved being with her, showered her with gifts, and maintained their romance. They had moved into a large house in the quiet, wealthy town of Weston, Connecticut, where Keith and family could realize the comforts of domesticity. "Every time I see Keith and Patti," commented the photographer Bob Gruen, "they're laughing about something."

RICHARDS: "This is a very rootless life. The only thing you got to hang on to is family. I can sit at home with the kids and the wife, and to me it's a perfectly rock and roll natural wedding. My wife wakes me up and says good morning to me, even though it might already be evening, then I get down to work. There's no fixed method that I've found to write songs. I usually warm up a little— plenty of times I play the riff from 'Jumpin' Jack Flash.' It's a beautiful riff to play. Or sometimes I sit around with a few friends after a party and just for fun I'll play something on the guitar. Someone will say, 'Oh, do you know that Everly Brothers song?' Then I'll get my guitar out and play it. Then you play some Elvis, Buddy Holly, anything that I can remember. And after that I'll start to branch out and come up with something of my own. But I also like playing when I'm on my own—old things by Otis Redding, for instance. I pretty much do what I want. But I know that for the great majority of people it's far worse than for me. I don't have to go away every day and do something that has nothing to do with rock and roll. My whole life is rock and roll.

"I don't have to get schizoid about what I do and living a family life. We play music, the kids dance around. It's fun for them. And I enjoy, in my way, doing those odd family things, you know, like taking the kids for a walk, going out to play with them. It's fun. Believe it or not, this is the way I always dreamed married life should be. I never have the chance to get bored with it, because I never really get enough of it. I'm away a lot. And, because of that, I never mind coming back to an active nest."

But twenty-five years as the egocentric, macho leader of an all-male gang could not be completely erased. According to one visitor who spent twenty-four hours with Keith and some friends at East Fourth Street, Keith was the indisputable king of his castle. They were sitting in the living room smoking hash, drinking beer, snorting cocaine, and listening to records when "all of a sudden Keith says, 'All the girls out of here!' There was Patti and a few friends of hers and he said, 'All right, all the girls to the basement!' Patti goes, 'Oh, well, OK, we'll go down to the basement!' So they go down to the basement and we hung out for a couple of hours. Then, just as suddenly as Keith dismissed the girls, he goes, 'You guys want some meat? Want some steaks?!' Picked up the phone and said, 'Patti! The guys want some meat! Put on some steaks!' So a few minutes later she comes up, 'OK, I'll put on some steaks!' It's great when you have that much money and success how well your relationship succeeds. It was a total dream-world existence."

In the second half of the eighties, Keith again found himself surrounded by female relatives, just as when he had been raised by his mother and six aunts. "I live in a household of women, which sometimes can drive me totally around the bend, which is why I need to work and get out on the road," he said. "I love them all, but it's weird to be living with a load of chicks—it doesn't matter what age they are. Sometimes you can be overwhelmed by the females. All girls everywhere. For a guy, the only guy in the house, you gotta call up another cat and say, 'Hey, come over,' or 'I'll drop over there!'"

Keith might have remained unreconstructed as far as gender roles were concerned, but he at least maintained a good heart. He did not, like so many men who marry again, ignore his other family: "Anita's doing very well," he told those who asked. "Very well, cleaned up her whole act. Lookin' good. I'm very proud of her. Her and Patti actually talk to each other. I'm either very lucky or I've done something right. There is nothing hidden from anybody. They talk to each other, visit each other. Anita still knits me sweaters."

With his older kids, Keith had Anita to keep the problems away. The breakup of the family was something that Keith did not appear to have a clear perspective on. He was not aware, for example, that Anita really wanted to get back together and just have a family with him and Marlon in 1980. As he passed through his midteens, Marlon had some disciplinary trouble in school, and Keith—the man who just said yes—was reduced to making an appearance before the dreaded headmaster. "I said, 'Marlon, how could you do this to me!'" he recalled. "I hated it." No wonder, for as soon as Keith and Patti got into his office the teacher attacked Keith by exclaiming that it was impossible to discipline the son until somebody disciplined the father. Richards later told friends that he would take care of the problem by going back and buying the school!

Keith's views of his older children's lives were as rosy and unrealistic as his assessment of his addiction had once been. "They've grown up real great," he said. "My kids are the straightest kids in the world. I've got a nineteen-year-old son [Marlon] and he likes a drop of champagne now and again. He was living here for ten years and he just moved back to London last week because he wants to go to art school and the better ones are there. He's looking around, seeing which ones he can get into. He knows what he wants to do. He's a great illustrator. But when he was here we got along fine, we went out for a drink, talked a lot."

According to Nick Kent, "Marlon's a nice kid. He's not a person with a major destiny, but he's come through well. I knew a young kid who was a serious drug user who was a friend of Marlon's and Marlon doesn't go for that shit. He's like into the Eagles and Led Zeppelin, but that's it with him. You gotta understand, with all those Stones kids they're very hip to all that stuff."

Anita saw a more troubled side to Marlon: "I still think he suffers from being Keith's son. I think he's found it very hard. He went through periods when he actually had to buy his friends through selling Keith Richards and giving out records. I saw that, but I just let it be and let him get over it by himself."

Since reuniting with his father, Keith also tried to see a lot more of his first daughter, Angela. His equally rosy opinion of her happiness was also far different from Anita's. Anita complained that Doris was always rude to her when she called to inquire how her child was getting along, and now she saw Angela as having trouble finding herself.

RICHARDS: "My daughter is now 'Angela.' She discarded 'Dandelion.' It's much easier to melt into the crowd with a name like Angela. It's also her name. Give 'em three or four, let 'em choose!

Once she went to school, Dandelion said, 'If you ever call me Dandelion again, Dad, I'll kill you!' She's sixteen, just left school, and lives with my mother in England. She went to an ordinary school and developed a passion for riding. She wanted a pony. Now she's gotten good and she's started to win competitions here and gymkhanas [horse shows] there. My daughter works in a stable and teaches other young kids to ride. She's an equestrian. She's been brought up like I was brought up, so it's a good upbringing. After all, the old lady didn't do too bad with me."

For Patti, having a family around allowed her to cope with Keith's demands and eccentricities. The Stones' women have generally led lives isolated by the nature of their mates' fame and hours. As Bianca Jagger remarked rather bitterly at the time of her divorce from Mick, the Stones themselves are a "secret society." "No marriage is as important to the men, even now, as that mysterious bonding of rock and roll," wrote Kevin Sessums in a profile of the Stones' wives. "The women's best defense is their support system, and each of the enduring Stones women has evolved her own from other female family members. Patti Hansen's mother is her nanny, housekeeper, confessor, and she or another female relative is always there." "Keith likes that kind of tumultuous family atmosphere around him," explained the satiric writer Fran Lebowitz, who had become a regular among Richards's dining partners. (Keith maintained a warm spot for comedians.) "It means he can go off by himself and play his music."

"Keith is actually a quiet person and he doesn't really get up and go out and stay out all night and vanish," attested Pallenberg. "But she's got this huge family that is all around her. She's always got a niece looking after the children, always somebody around. She's never alone."

PATTI HANSEN: "I have no regrets about my life with Keith. He's so good to me. He'd fill my house with servants if I wanted them, but I've got to keep to my roots. I have my mom come in and help with the kids. My niece comes in to help me clean. Got to keep it in the family. Jerry Hall says, 'Why don't you get someone to cook for you? Why don't you get somebody to do your shopping?' But that's not me. I'm happy being a wife and mother. Some of my friends are still after me to go back to work, but I'm totally fulfilled right now. Keith and I are about to build another house out in Connecticut and I want to get busy and have more kids."

As for Keith, he was more open in his acknowledgment of Patti than of any other collaborator down the line. "Thank God Patti came into my life," he told one friend. On another occasion, arriving at a party in his honor, Keith fell to his knees and kissed Patti's toes. "On top of the fact that I love the bitch to death," he said, "she keeps up with me, she keeps me going."

Largely because of his successful relationship with her, Keith regarded himself as a man who understood himself—this despite the fact that Keith had never examined the causes of his addictions, nor had he really given up drugs (he was drinking an enormous amount of bourbon, supplemented with pot smoking and regular cocaine use). And he certainly never discussed his feelings, at least not publicly. "There's always this thing in show business—you have an 'image,' and you play it to the hilt, but you're not really like that 'in private life,' et cetera," Richards explained. "I mean, I'm a family man. I have little two-year-old and three-year-old girls that beat me up. I'm not the guys I see on MTV who obviously think they're me. There are so many people who think that's all there is to it. It's not that easy to be Keith Richards. But it's not so hard, either. The main thing is to know yourself."

25

Make No Mistake
1986–1988

Keith is a guitar player. He's dedicated. He loves what he does and he does it all the time. I've never known anyone who works harder.

STANLEY BOOTH, *from an interview with Dia Stein, 1991*

Keith finally came to understand that his only salvation lay in working all the time. Just having a wife and babies couldn't save him—he had to be active and have structure to his life. If he wasn't working, he was working against himself, and his dark side would take over and lead him down the path to self-destruction. He was always a half step from temptation. "I'm somebody who's always got to have something to do," said Keith, "someone who needs continuity rather than these constantly shifting extremes."

On January 16, 1986, Keith Richards, forty-two, inducted his childhood hero Chuck Berry, fifty-nine, whom he once called "the most charming cunt I've ever met," into a new institution, the Rock and Roll Hall of Fame, in New York. That night Richards acknowledged, "I lifted every lick he ever played." It was an auspicious moment, but did it signal a strong return to Richards's beginnings or the end of the ride? When Keith started playing the guitar in Dartford in 1958, he wanted to be tall, black, arrogant, and elegant, just like Chuck. Now, twenty-eight years later, he saw rock and roll as a life force that tuned us in to realizing that we all live together on one planet. But Jagger, who was being unsuccessfully sued for plagiarism over his single "Just Another Night," skipped the ceremony—he had slipped away to the Caribbean a few days earlier, leaving Richards wondering what he was going to do in the Stones year that stretched before him. They had an album coming out, but it was not known if the band was ever going to record again, let alone tour.

Few people envied the long-suffering Jane Rose her job as Keith's personal manager. She was essentially on call twenty-four hours a day, seven days a week. Being the gatekeeper between Richards and the thousands of people who wanted access to him forced her into becoming Borman to his Hitler. Throughout the eighties she played an increasingly strong role in constructing Richards's career. Many people around him thought she was too protective and complained that she could be incredibly insulting, but they all agreed that she was ferociously loyal to Keith and her heart was in the right place. Now she steered him toward other collaborations with two of his favorite performers, Aretha Franklin and Chuck Berry. Franklin planned to include a cover of "Jumpin' Jack Flash" on her next album and to release it as a single, which would be used as the title song for a film of the same name. She invited Richards and Ronnie Wood to play on the song, produce it, and appear in the accompanying video. Berry was to be the subject of a ninety-minute documentary film (*Hail! Hail! Rock 'n' Roll*) to celebrate his sixtieth birthday, directed by Taylor Hackford, and Richards was asked to be its musical director. Although in numerous interviews Keith repeatedly expressed the desire to grow up with the Rolling Stones, he seemed to be equally interested in going back to ponder his roots. He had been considering a similar film project on Robert Johnson for a couple of years. Just as that collapsed, the Berry proposition fell into his lap. Richards's job was to put together a band to play behind Berry in a concert that would be the centerpiece of the film; the film's sound track would also be released as a record.

On July 7, Keith and Ronnie flew to Franklin's hometown, Detroit, with a young black drummer who had frequently jammed with Keith at Ronnie's house and had also played on *Dirty Work*, Steve Jordan. Keith had despaired of finding another drummer to match his favorite, Charlie Watts, but playing with Jordan on the "Jumpin' Jack Flash" sessions really turned him on. The infectious good time he had is evident in the playful video with Whoopi Goldberg, who starred in the film. The single went to number twenty-one in the U.S.; Jagger's parallel project, the title track of the movie *Ruthless People*, stalled at number fifty-one.

Characteristically, though, on the flight back to New York from

Detroit, when Jordan begged Richards to include him in the Berry documentary, Keith, who had taken to wearing T-shirts bearing the legend OBERGRUPPEN-FÜHRER (major general of the troops), tortured his new friend, saying that he wasn't the right man for the job.

The most memorable thing Keith could remember Chuck Berry ever saying to him was "Fuck off," and their history had been, to say the least, uneven. Berry's attitude toward the Stones' appropriation of his work had always been ambivalent, even though they had increased his sales all over the world and earned him countless royalties. Sometimes he would act grateful, name "Satisfaction" among his favorite songs, and say he loved them; at other times he would refuse to acknowledge their impact. In 1972 when Keith had guested on a couple of numbers during a Berry concert in Hollywood, Chuck had had him thrown off stage for playing too loudly (claiming he had not recognized him). In 1981 Chuck had punched Keith in the eye backstage at the Ritz in New York (using a similar excuse). In 1983 he had dropped a lit match down Keith's shirt at Los Angeles International Airport. As Keith saw it, "Every time him and me got in contact, whether it's intentional or not, I end up wounded."

Berry had never taken any direction from anyone—except, perhaps, the law. He had been driven deep inside himself by a dubious 1962 conviction under the Mann Act for transporting a fourteen-year-old girl across state lines for alleged immoral purposes, and had spent two years in a federal penitentiary. But his biggest beef was pecuniary. All the black musicians who created rock and roll in the mid-1950s, from Bo Diddley through Little Richard to Berry himself, continued to be robbed of millions of dollars by white promoters who had gotten them to sign away the majority of their songwriting and publishing royalties. Keith had no illusions about what he had gotten himself into.

RICHARDS: "Chuck doesn't give a shit. Chuck only thinks about himself. I like Chuck, but I feel sorry for him. He's a very lonely man. Also, after living that secluded one-man show for so many years, he probably wasn't prepared himself for how he was gonna act. He kind of played it by ear. I talked my way into it. Now get out of it."

On July 12, two days after returning to New York from the Franklin sessions, Richards flew to St. Louis to visit Berry in his home just outside the city in Wentzville. Behind Chuck's house was a large fun fair called Berry Park. Keith was amused by the fact that Chuck had an amusement park in his backyard, and by his favorite entertainment: Berry had two large video screens in his living room. One played whatever he selected. The other ran constant footage of naked white girls throwing pies at each other and falling over. Berry's legendary attraction to young white girls had been the thing that had gotten him into most of the trouble he'd encountered.

Keith was also introduced to Chuck's father: "It was a weird kind of honor, 'Meet my dad.' Sweet old guy, ninety-one years old, sitting there watching *The Flintstones* and eatin' his grits. Chuck goes, 'Dad, this is Keith Richards from the Rolling Stones. Been together longer than anybody else ever.' The old boy looks at me and goes, 'You're lookin' pretty good!' I said, 'Thank you very much, Reverend!'"

Rapping away like two old prizefighters flipping through photographs of grueling encounters, the two men found they were well matched. When Richards inquired about the availability of Berry's legendary collaborator, the great boogie piano man Stu had identified for him in 1962, Berry said there would be no problem getting him to join them—Johnnie Johnson played regularly in St. Louis. Then, turning to his video screen, he snapped, "Listen to this, Jack!" (Berry called everybody Jack) and slapped a tape of the January Rock and Roll Hall of Fame jam session into the machine. As they watched themselves on the screen, Chuck pointed to the drummer, Steve Jordan, and enthused, "This guy sounds pretty good." Not skipping a beat, Keith asked if he could use the phone. "Sorry about that one, Steve," he told the man who would soon become his new collaborator. "I'm at Chuck's, and if you still want to do it, you're in."

After two days in Wentzville, Richards flew back to New York and got together with Jordan: "I got the key member in Johnson. I knew nobody else was going to get Johnnie Johnson together with Chuck Berry ... I mean, you're talking Johnnie Johnson-Chuck Berry, you're talking Lennon-McCartney, you're talking Jagger-

Richards, you're talking those great rock and roll teams, Leiber-Stoller, except that Johnnie never got any credit or any money.

"I got back to New York with no bassist. Steve said, 'There's one guy who could pull this off. He plays with NRBQ. Joey Spampinato.' I realized he's the only cat I know who can play an electric bass and make it sound like Willie Dixon on an upright bass. Then I called Chuck Leavell, since he's the most tasteful guy on organ I can think of. And within forty-eight hours, I went from havin' nobody to, boom, havin' the whole unit I wanted. Suddenly I got an inkling that things were going well."

But when Berry visited Richards in Jamaica that August, Keith got an inkling of the kind of problems he was going to encounter. From the minute Keith picked Chuck up at the airport, Berry was like a fish out of water, flipping about enigmatically. One minute he was enthusiastic and entertaining, the next—poof!—he would withdraw into a stony silence, leaving the people around him wondering what they did wrong. Richards recognized the traits because they were similar to Jagger's. Both Berry and Jagger were control freaks who had distanced themselves from almost everybody for fear of being ripped off. "Fuck, millions of people have ripped me off and I don't give a shit," Richards told Stanley Booth. "If you can't get over that, you have a problem. I've worked with two of the toughest bitches of all time. That's why I could handle Chuck. 'You know who I've been working with the last twenty years? You're chicken feed!'"

"At times I become very hot and cold, moody and very schizophrenic," Berry explained. "It's really controlled schizophrenia, and I'm controlling it."

The new band met in Wentzville for two weeks of rehearsals in the second half of September.

RICHARDS: "Steve Jordan and I had been hanging for a couple of years and we'd appreciated each other because Steve doesn't mind black jokes and I don't mind white jokes. Steve is not really Chuck's kind of guy. If it's wrong, Steve will say so and not give a shit. Chuck Berry doesn't need to hear he's playing his own shit wrong, but Steve has the front and the balls, and he can play. And because he is of the same dusky-brethren persuasion, he could cut through things it would take me twice as long to do. Steve can undercut Chuck's bullshit, and there's a lot of it.

"Just before Stu died, without any real reason, he'd said, 'Keith, never forget Johnnie Johnson is still alive and playing.' There's an eerie feeling to that boogie Johnnie's got. His hands are like a bunch of overripe bananas. Sometimes I was so fascinated I actually stopped playing and just watched those great big bananas bouncing around doing this incredible brain surgery. Other times I had an eerie feeling that it was Stu playing, but at the same time I felt that he was up there, beaming down at me from his cloud: 'Well done, son.'"

Playing and forming a firm friendship with Johnson gave Keith a view of how Berry wrote his music. It soon dawned on Keith that many of Berry's more famous songs, such as "Sweet Little Sixteen," were traditional songs that Chuck had adapted by brilliantly updating the lyrics, while Johnnie had updated the music. To Keith, Chuck was the Shakespeare of rock and roll, but the songs were obviously collaborations, and he felt it was a sin that Johnson had never received any recognition, or money, for his efforts.

During rehearsals, for the first time, Keith gained the confidence to think about finding another band for himself.

RICHARDS: "The whole process of putting those bands together for Aretha and Chuck made me suddenly realize that I did have this ability that I never knew I had 'cause I'd never had to use it, to put certain guys together in the right situation and create a band. That if you gave me the right guys, in ten days I could give you a band that sounded as if they'd been together for two or three years."

However, as soon as Keith started suggesting unheard-of things to Berry, such as turning down his amplifier or playing a number differently, Berry either counterattacked or withdrew. Keith realized Berry's way of controlling people was to ride them ruthlessly into the ground. During the filming of rehearsals, as Keith churned into the opening chords of "Carol" (a Berry song the Stones had sold more copies of than Chuck), Berry cut him off three times, insisting, like a pedantic schoolteacher, that his pupil buckle down and get it right. Guitar players have notorious egos. Sweat dripped off the ends of their noses as they stood toe to toe. The band was silent and bug-eyed.

RICHARDS: "I played the straight man out of necessity. My job was to get both Chuck and the band together, even though I was dying to turn around and let him have it. Never mind that the cameras were present, but I knew if I allowed myself to rise to the bait, it would have fallen to pieces. When I went into the rehearsals I'd take a .38 bullet and actually chew on it.

"Most of the band, the guys behind me, are going, 'Keith in this situation is going to pull out the blade and just slit the motherfucker's throat.' I'm biting bullets because I'm trying to show the band that, in order to get this gig together, I am going to take some shit that I wouldn't take from anybody. I'm not gonna let Chuck get to me that much. Whereas anybody else, it would have been toilet time. Nobody can touch me in that way. In the film you can see me chewin'. I'm on the edge. At any moment I could have turned around and downed the motherfucker. But Chuck doesn't understand 'cause he doesn't deal with people. He's the only guy who's hit me and I haven't done anything about it. Far worse things have happened to me in my life than Chuck Berry trying to fuck with me."

On another occasion, when Richards suggested Berry adjust his amplifier so that a track they were recording would be properly balanced, Chuck took off his guitar and refused to play, and Keith ended up shouting. "If Chuck made a mistake, he was used to blaming it on the band," he said. "He's got such a powerful personality that he managed to get away with it. And if it takes shouting, fine. It ain't different from working with anybody else. If he's wrong, he's wrong, and you let the guy know it. 'Cause if you go around crawling, licking ass, 'Oh, Chuck, please, please,' you'd never get anything done, but under those frantic circumstances, you get to know someone a little better."

When Richards brought the band into St. Louis a few days before the October 18 show, he was still battling every step of the way. He knew that Berry would try to wrest control of the band from him once they hit the stage. For recording purposes, he removed control of Berry's amplifier without letting Chuck know by burying a slave amp three subbasements below the stage and putting Berry's guitar through a boogie amp. When Berry refused to sing during the dress rehearsal, making it impossible to balance his voice level, Keith kissed him on the cheek, pleading, "Just once," and Chuck whispered through one track. When a friend joked backstage, "What, no black eye?" Keith snapped, "I just hope I don't have to give him a white eye!" During the filming of the concert, Chuck tried to undo the months of painstaking preparation. "I mean, we rehearsed for ten days, got on stage, and boom, out the window!" Keith said afterward, laughing. "Totally different arrangements, some in different keys. Everybody's lookin' at me on stage and I just looked at them, you know—'Wing it, boys!'"

Under the broiling movie lights in front of a star-studded audience, including Marlon and Anita, Linda Ronstadt, Etta James, Julian Lennon, Eric Clapton, and Robert Cray joined Berry on several of his classics and helped pull off the best live Chuck Berry on record. By the end of six hours Keith had shed pounds, and his stage suit (similar to the one Andrew Oldham had forced him to wear in 1963) no longer fit. In the film's interview with him, which was conducted immediately after the show, Keith looked a little charred around the edges, sounding as if he'd been up for several days. His phrasing, which sounded as if it came from another time zone, was one of the hilarious highlights of the movie. He spoke affectionately about working with Chuck.

RICHARDS: "So I ordered the straitjacket—wait six to eight weeks for delivery—and if anybody was going to take it, the one I wanted it to be was me, not so much as a musical director as an S&M director, social director of the S&M band. When you're working with Chuck you've got to be prepared for anything, anytime. But I still can't dislike him. I love him and I love his family.

"I've done what I wanted for him. I think it's the best Chuck Berry live you're ever going to get. I can't see him doing it again. It's good. We both came out of it with a bit more respect for one another. Now I'm going to sleep for a month."

STEVE JORDAN: "It didn't really matter what Chuck put him through because Keith was going to pay that debt no matter how long it took. It was something that plagued Keith. He had to document the real thing before Chuck died, and he did. Maybe I'm reading too much into it, but having played with Keith before and after, I think he's more himself now, more comfortable, like he feels entitled to make his own mark."

Despite his new-won confidence and the success of his work with both Franklin and Berry, Richards still saw his job as holding the Rolling Stones together. Therefore, it came as a stunning blow when he discovered that Jagger planned to go on the road without the Stones on completion of his second solo album, *Primitive Cool*. "Mick's decision virtually folded up twenty years of the band," said Charlie Watts. "Keith took it very hard."

Ever since Keith taped tracks with Gram Parsons in 1971, friends had been after him to make a solo album. The Toronto sessions, which remained a favorite among his closest supporters, had galvanized Anita into criticizing him for not doing it. There had been persistent rumors that *Bad Luck* was coming out in 1979–1980. If this was not enough encouragement, Richards might have taken a hint from the titles of some of the five hundred Rolling Stones bootlegs, which included *Keith and His Cocksuckers*; *Keith Richards and His Rolling Stones*; *Keith Richards, Booze and Pills*; *Keith Richards Luvely Licks*; *Keith Richards Not Guilty*; *Keith Richards Worn and Frayed*; *Keith Richards, What a Feeling*; *Keith Richards International Inquisition*; *Keith Richards Keef Baby Keef*; *Keith Richards Sheik Baby Sheik*; and *Keith Richards Soul Survivor*. And yet, according to one source, Keith just couldn't face breaking away from his band and was plagued by the fear of working solo. It was a move that even his best friends feared might lead to disaster. "Nobody can have any idea what I went through when Keith went solo," said Freddie Sessler, who was now living a few blocks away from Keith in New York and seeing him regularly again. "No idea. I mean, he couldn't see the band breaking up. He lived for the Rolling Stones." Keith himself admitted it almost broke his heart.

"One night Keith started talking—and with great pain—about wanting to get the band together and how his whole life is the Stones and how the Stones come first and always will come first," remembered Terry Hood. "He was afraid to push Mick to the wall and say 'Mick, dissolve the band or keep the band' because he was afraid that Mick would say, 'Dissolve the band.' I mean, literally, Keith was like so destroyed."

In the first half of 1987, as rumors that the Stones really were breaking up persisted, the press constantly asked Keith what was going on. "Everybody likes things cut and dried, and with the Stones it never will be," Richards replied. "Whether it's all over or not is really up to how everybody in the band feels. This particular period is basically, I think, a reaction to twenty-five years of being forced to work together whether we like it or not. Luckily, we liked it. But, I mean, eventually it's gotta get to the point where you say, 'Hey, it's always been fun to work together, but now it's getting a little bitter here and there, and lines are bein' drawn.' So, better off, let's just give it a breather, and then we'll see how ridiculous it all is and work it all out. I mean, I love working with those boys, and I don't see us not pullin' it back together. Just give us a break and we'll come back for part two."

In July 1987 Richards signed a contract with Richard Branson's Virgin Records to do two solo albums. Making the decision to go solo had been delicate enough. Keith had been freaked out by all the dubious offers he'd received, telling one friend that he felt like a wounded zebra with a pack of hyenas snapping at his heels. When Richard Branson, who headed Virgin Records, approached him, he was relieved to discover somebody with whom he felt he could have a straightforward, productive relationship. Richards's only condition was that nobody interfere while he was making the record. Branson readily agreed to stay out of the picture until it was finished. "I know how nervous he was when he did his solo album, whether it would be a success or not," said Terry Hood. "He never really wanted that."

RICHARDS: "I started making records by saying, 'Do I like it? Does it turn me on?' And I refuse to be budged from that criteria. Really. If I start to think about what do they want to hear, then I say I'm out of here. That's not the way I've ever done it. The only times people have liked my stuff is when I've done it because I like it. I'll reserve that for my criteria for anything I do. If I start trying to second-guess people, then I may as well be Liberace or Lawrence Welk. That means I want to be a star, instead of having to be forced to be one."

"I'm exhausted!" he told Bill German during the first week of the project. "I've never worked so hard in my life. The Stones was easy compared to this." What undoubtedly saved his sanity was finding somebody else to work with. By now, Keith and Steve Jordan, hardened by the Berry wars, were becoming partners. When they began to meet in the spring of 1987 to talk about the record, Richards discovered that he and Jordan could write songs and produce together. "The beauty of Steve and myself finding each other at that particular time," he said, "was that it was a very natural changeover, because Steve and Charlie knew each other and respected each other's work."

As Steve Jordan said, "When you look Keith in the eye, you know you're not going to bullshit him, and when you are going to bullshit him, do not look him in the eye. There's only one way he likes to say things, and that's brutally honest. He's not going to preach to you but he does have a moral code of honesty and loyalty and sincerity."

During the recording sessions, Keith also developed a new way of making songs.

RICHARDS: "When you're in a band like the Stones, you're in your own little capsule and whatever goes on outside doesn't really count. You can actually live inside that capsule quite comfortably and so you miss a lot of opportunities to find out what else is happening. Steve was a great help to me in breaking out of that and finding different guys to work with and different ways to work. Once I started, I started to really enjoy doing it because I started to realize I could move in slightly different ways. Steve and I had started playing together in February and March of '87, just drums and guitar. We just kept knocking out stuff and slowly brought in the other guys as we started to build up some material.

"I'd written about thirty to forty songs, and one day I just looked to him for advice, saying, 'I can't find how to continue, I can't find more to hook onto, or an additional subject matter to write about.' Steve looked at me with this big grin and said, 'When in doubt, write about Mick,' because he knows it'll make the juices flow in me. Which means 'You Don't Move Me''s not exactly about Mick, but it's a kickoff point. It's about anybody in that position where you have a friend you feel you can't get through to, and you're trying to let them know."

As they accumulated songs, Keith slowly brought in other players. To L.A. session musician Waddy Wachtel, who would become his new guitar twin, he announced, "I'm doing it and you're in!" Bass player Charley Drayton and keyboard player Ivan Neville got the same message. "I was finding the nucleus of a band again, *another* band," he pointed out. "And to me that's essential. The whole joy of making rock and roll music is the interaction between guys playing, and trying to capture that on tape." Although Richards has always claimed that he does not differentiate between black and white, the fact that three of these musicians were black (Jordan, Drayton, and Neville) was not irrelevant.

On August 15 the X-Pensive Winos—as he had named the band after catching them chugging a bottle of Lafite-Rothschild behind the drum kit—checked into Le Studio in Montreal for two weeks of recording.

RICHARDS: "I like to take everybody away from the distractions of where they live to record. That way you don't have the old lady calling you up and goin', 'I just scalded my bum on something!' You say, 'Well, go see a doctor, honey. I'm three thousand miles away!' But also, I like to get the guys to live together. That's the way you get to be a band, 'cause all you're doing is eating, going to the studio, sleeping. These are friends of mine, and everybody is a friend of each other, so it's supportive. In rock and roll music that's a very important thing. The idea of hired hands to me is 'Ouch!'"

From the start the *Talk Is Cheap* sessions were intuitive and spontaneous. The Stones had gotten used to waiting while Keith diddled around, but when he stopped playing with the Winos they yelled at him, "Pick it up! Pick it up, man!" Nobody had nudged him like that for some time and he loved it. They recorded seven tracks in ten days. Richards began to get the feeling that this could be one of those joyous tasks rather than the old grind that the making of the previous two Stones albums had been. As the band tightened up, he found himself spontaneously blurting out songs. He could hear the voice of his Dartford Tech choirmaster, Jake Clair, urging, "Not like that, like this." Soon he was dreaming the songs. He woke up one night, picked up his guitar, and played "Make No Mistake" into a tape recorder. The next morning he started singing. "Oh, this is just a dream, make no mistake."

In between working with the Winos, Richards had been in Jimi Hendrix's Electric Lady Studios on West Eighth Street in New York mixing the *Hail! Hail! Rock 'n' Roll* film sound track and album (two distinctly different tasks). On September 15, 1987, he attended the film's premiere at the New York Film Festival at Lincoln Center. He watched from a private box with Chuck and Patti.

RICHARDS: "I suddenly realized we were coming to the point in the movie where I suggested that maybe Chuck didn't write the music, that Johnnie Johnson actually provided the melodies, which I'm still firmly convinced of. So I'm sitting there in the balcony and I realize that I want a parachute. I wanted to get the hell out of there. But he thought it all was great. Loved the fight [in which Berry refused to play and Keith shouted at him], saw it for what it was. Since then, he's been a sweetheart. Asked me to work with him again. And now that we broke the ice, I say why throw it away? Asshole that he can be, I still love him. I'm still fascinated by what he does. I wouldn't have missed it for the world."

When the film and record were released in October they were a terrific success for Berry, who received one of the top honors given to an American entertainer—his own star on Hollywood Boulevard. The critics also praised Richards's contribution.

Meanwhile, Jagger began to founder in his solo career. His album *Primitive Cool*, released in August, reached only number forty-one on the U.S. charts. Its single, "Let's Work," barely made the top forty. By Rolling Stones standards, it was a commercial failure and an embarrassment. Mick was reduced to taking feeble punches at Keith through his lyrics. "Mick is very bitter about the feud with Keith," a Jagger spokesman sniffed. "He's had a real go at Keith [on 'Kow Tow' and 'Shoot Off Your Mouth'] and hopes that he listens to the record and realizes the significance."

With the success of *Hail! Hail! Rock 'n' Roll* confirmed, Richards threw himself into the second half of his album with renewed vigor. He turned down an invitation to attend Atlantic Records' fortieth anniversary party, saying he was in the "vital middle section of the work." In March 1988, he embarked on a picaresque journey with Jordan, flying first to Memphis, then Montserrat, and finally Bermuda in search of the sounds he needed to complete it.

RICHARDS: "At the time of the album I happened to be listening to a lot of South African Soweto street music—which was intriguing me a lot, because it seems to me that Africa, which produced the rhythms and heartbeats of American music and especially rock and roll, was now throwing it back to us again with electric instruments! That's where the Soweto sound is at! And somehow this is where I got the idea for the accordion [played by Stanley 'Buckwheat' Dural] and fiddle [played by Michael Doucet] on 'Locked Away.' I knew that 'Locked Away' needed some more color on it. I guess the fact that I had been listening to Buckwheat's latest record and the South African music was critical, and it suddenly just clicked in my mind. I'd say, 'Why didn't I think of this months ago?'

"If there was an overall concept to this album, it was to keep it musical. The public, they're so sick of slick, push-button, drum machine records. There's nothing wrong with any of this high-tech stuff, the toy department stuff. It's just a matter of what you do with it. Steve and I were trying to get things up to the hardware department. I have more exact, more perfect or skillful takes of each of these songs, but the more you try to literally perfect them, the more you lose the instinctive thing. Instinct is what I want."

Keith's attention to detail was illustrated by his continuing search for the perfect guitar sound. Benjamin Verdery, the classical guitarist and *Guitar Player* writer, selected a number of guitars for Keith.

BENJAMIN VERDERY: "I got this mad call to help him pick out a guitar so I went to the guitar salon and played at least a dozen guitars. There was this old Manuel Velásquez, and it was such a sweetheart. Keith didn't have big hands, and this guitar had a rock player's neck, which is like a truck, big old thing. I met Keith at rehearsal and he was incredibly personable. I showed him two Ramirezes and he said, 'Come on, come on, show me the one you really like.' He tried it and just said, 'Awwww.' He fell in love with it. I couldn't help but think—Manuel Velásquez, if he only knew."

RICHARDS: "The truth is, I'm more interested in the roll than I am in the rock.

"The title was the only thing about the record that had a connection to the Stones. I wrote a song for *Dirty Work* called 'Talk Is Cheap,' but I didn't finish it. And I thought to myself, at that time, 'This is a great title for an album.' I forgot about it because I didn't finish the song. But I'd written 'Talk Is Cheap' and taken a couple of Polaroids, and Jane, luckily, had kept them for me. We were searching and searching for an album title and Jane went through her filing cabinet and found my little title box and found 'Talk Is Cheap.' "

In the summer of 1988, Richards posed for the album cover, chose his single, and did a round of interviews with every important publication in his field from *Rolling Stone* to *Guitar Player*. One night in a bar he ran into his old guitar roadie from the 1978 tour, Tom Edmonds, and invited him and a friend named Diane up to his apartment to listen to the new songs. "He pulled up two really nice chairs and set a table between us and said. 'Take your shoes off'," Edmonds recalled, "hooked up the stereo, and we sat there and smoked hash and drank beer and listened to his album over and over and over again. I mean, that's all there is for Keith. I don't care how many times he listened to that record, he was grooving."

"We were with him for thirty-two hours straight and we talked about everything from Bach to Verdi," recalled Diane. "He loves classical music and keeps his stereo blasting. After playing his demo tape over and over he switched from Keith Richards to Tchaikovsky and it just stayed on for hours and hours while we smoked hash and drank. Keith is a very interesting man. The toughest marshmallow I ever met. He was going through his knife collection. He's got an excellent collection of switchblades and he was pulling them out and whipping them around."

After a while they told Diane to go out and get them some coke. "I told Keith to go fuck himself and he looked as if he couldn't believe it," she sneered. "I said, 'Go get your own fucking drugs, man!' Then Tom and I looked at each other and went, 'Rick!' " They were referring to the guitarist Rick Derringer, whom Keith had not seen since the 1966 American tour. They called and asked him to bring some coke over. When Tom told Keith he was working in the studio with Rick, Richards retorted, "Isn't he that flash guitar player? I don't want to hear any of that Rick Derringer shit!" When Rick arrived, Keith told Tom, "Play my album," then asked Derringer what he thought of it. "Well, it's OK," the latter responded. "It could use some more guitars!" "I saw Keith tense up," Edmonds recalled. "Keith didn't like it. It pissed him off." "Tommy and I couldn't even say anything," added Diane. "We were watching them like it was a movie. It was like two boys in the third grade."

Talk Is Cheap was released on October 4, 1988. On October 27 it entered the American charts at number seventy-five. It would stay on the charts for twenty-four weeks, peaking at number twenty-four. It sold a million copies worldwide, doing no better than Jagger's album commercially, but nobody had expected it to. And whereas *Primitive Cool* had received extremely cool critical response, *Talk Is Cheap* garnered excellent reviews.

"If any fans doubted it was Richards' nuclear furnace fueling the world's greatest rock and roll band," wrote Charles Young, "they have now only to compare Keith's first solo album, *Talk Is Cheap*, with Mick Jagger's two solo albums. Keith's sounds like a great Stones album without Mick Jagger, and both of Mick's sound like he's up studio-musician creek without a paddle."

"*Talk Is Cheap* rings with life," read a review in *Guitar World*. "One of rock's most intriguing iconoclasts has finally issued the ultimatum . . . It's the sound of Keith rediscovering and challenging himself . . . He's coming out swinging again, and connects. Just like always.

"Although no other Stones played on it," the prestigious magazine concluded, "*Talk Is Cheap* was the best Stones album in 17 years."

The reviews cannot but have stung Jagger, whom Richards cut down in one of the album's songs, "You Don't Move Me," with the lines "What makes you so greedy/Makes you so seedy."

For the *Rolling Stone* interview with Anthony de Curtis, Richards turned up at Jane Rose's office sporting red-tinted shades, gray corduroy slacks, a white jacket, and his favorite T-shirt, which bore the legend OBERGRUPPEN-FÜHRER. After mixing himself a Rebel Yell-and-ginger-ale and lighting a Marlboro, he draped his jacket on the back of one of the chrome-and-leather chairs in the office's conference room and went to work. Listening to Richards talk about his vision of rock and roll as a music of lasting power and dignity, de Curtis was impressed. Summing up the interview, he wrote, "Richards provided a necessary vision for the nineties."

Keith based his opinion of the album on his usual criterion— whether he liked listening to it. As he put it: "There's very few records that you make, or at least that I've made, that you wanna hear by the time you finish it. You're just so full with it. It's the last thing you wanna hear. But this one—I don't know if it's because it's a novelty, my first solo album—but I actually sit around and enjoy listening to it, put it on while I'm taking a shower."

There was a mixed reaction from the other members of the band. "He's not Pavarotti, is he?" said Wyman. Watts was totally support- ive, describing it as the kind of record that had been eluding the Stones for some time—"full of great songs and innovation." Woody commented that it was very much as he thought it would be. As for Jagger, when Richards asked him if he would like to hear it he said, "Sure." But as soon as it was on Mick started gossiping about someone he had run into the previous day, in the midst of which Keith excused himself to take a piss. "I come out of the john," said Keith, "and he's dancing around the room. For a minute I watch him, and he's just enjoying it. So I went back to the john and slammed the door and walked out again, and he's just sitting on the couch. But that's Mick. I know the bloke. He's a very closed personality. I guess I saw him liking it when he didn't know I was looking. So that's cool."

MICK JAGGER: "I remember thinking that the drums were too loud. I know it was produced by the drummer, but a bit too obviously for my liking. But it was a good enough effort. The songs needed a bit more focus. They sort of meandered. And that's one of my jobs with Keith. I edit his songs and make the melodies better."

Despite his solo success, Keith persisted in talking about the Stones. "You cannot deny the Stones," he told Lisa Robinson in September 1988, the month the record came out. "Even if the Stones never play another note, Mick and I still have to deal with each other for the rest of our lives . . . We can't even get divorced; it would be easier to do that with an old lady than to do that with

Mick ... I see it as growing pains; whereas Mick was afraid the Rolling Stones could turn into some sort of nostalgia dead end, I see the Rolling Stones on the cutting edge of growing this music up and the only band in the position to do it. As I said to him, 'Listen, darling, this thing is bigger than both of us.'

In October, while Jagger toured Australia and Japan, Richards did a publicity tour of England, Spain, Italy, and Norway. In London he played the Smile Jamaica concert in aid of hurricane victims. Asked what he thought of Jagger's solo tour of Asia, Richards replied, "I thought it was very sad that a high percentage of his show was Rolling Stones songs. If you're going to do something on your own, do stuff off the two albums you did. Don't pretend you're a solo artist and have two chicks prancing around doing 'Tumbling Dice,' do you know what I mean? The Rolling Stones spent a lot of time building up integrity, as much as you can get in the music industry. And the way Mick handled his solo career jeopardized all that. That severely pissed me off."

Jagger naturally chose to see the rupture from a different point of view. "I have always felt the Stones were an unfinished thing," he said. "I never said I wouldn't work with Keith again. When he was slagging me off, it was just to get publicity for his record. I think it was the only way he could get any. Keith takes things more personally. He's had a more problematic life."

Though Jagger's U.S. tour was canceled as a result of poor sales, Richards's wasn't. In November and December he took the X-Pensive Winos to fourteen cities across America. It was the final step in his personal vindication. "It's an incredible pleasure to play with those guys," said Richards. "It's like the Stones in the early days. Nobody has any respect for anybody, except when they do well." "In each city," wrote his old friend Stanley Booth, who accompanied him on the tour and interviewed him for *Playboy*, "the audience leapt to its feet as soon as Keith appeared and stayed there rocking until the last note faded away."

If the outcome of the competition between the Richards and Jagger solo albums was not clear enough, *Rolling Stone* put the boot in definitively. "Keith looked like a 'vampiric aristocrat' whose singing was as raw and natural and appealing as his playing," wrote one critic. His show amounted to "definitive and essential rock and roll" and left little doubt about "who constituted the backbone of what was once considered the greatest rock and roll band in the world."

After the last show, Keith's forty-fifth birthday party was attended by five hundred of his best friends. Jagger did not come. Virgin Records' Phil Quartararo presented him with a gold record of the album and everyone in the room sang "Happy Birthday." "As he cut a birthday cake done in a solid gold record motif," concluded Stanley Booth, "Richards looked, in spite of a face etched in deep scars and wrinkles, like a man for whom things were just getting started."

26

Slipping Away
1989–1992

He feels that music is his life, and he's going to die on stage. That's what he's living under.

ANITA PALLENBERG, *from an interview with Victor Bockris, 1989*

"It had gotten to the point," said Jane Rose, "where Keith was having so much fun, he didn't want to do another Stones record. So I said, 'Go to Barbados, look Mick straight in the eye, and tell him it's over.'" Keith approached the scheduled two-week meeting in January 1989 tentatively, telling Patti that he'd be back in forty-eight hours or two weeks. When he got to Barbados, he dropped his bag outside his room. He was ready to leave at a moment's notice.

For the first few hours Keith and Mick screamed at each other, but, according to Richards, they soon found themselves rolling on the floor laughing about the many horrible things they'd been quoted as saying.

RICHARDS: "We needed to clear the air, which, as old mates, we're very good at. Then, when we got into that room and sat down with our guitars, something entirely different took over. You can't define it, it's the same thing that always happens. I just start banging out a little riff. He'll go, 'That's nice,' and he'll come up with a top line. The good thing is that once Mick and I actually settle down in a room to work, everything else goes out the window. On the third day I found myself unpacking. After four or five days Patti got through to me on the phone and said, 'Two weeks, then?' I said, 'Happily, yes.'"

The reunification was perfectly timed. On January 18, the Rolling Stones were inducted into the Rock and Roll Hall of Fame. The Glimmer Twins flew to New York to attend the ceremonies. They acknowledged the influence of Brian Jones, and mourned the loss of Ian Stewart. "By then we were on a roll," said Richards, "and nobody in their right mind breaks a roll."

In February the band gathered in Barbados.

RICHARDS: "I was driving up to the rehearsal joint, and I heard Charlie in there and I just sat in the parking lot for five minutes. He was so crisp, so tight, I thought, 'We've got the songs, we've got the drummer.' I was smiling, like, no problem.

"I think that the Rolling Stones collectively feel that the band is capable of doing more important work—maybe more important than we've done for twenty years. Mick and I—the front line—have been working far more consistently on our own stuff for the last two or three years than with the Stones in the last fifteen years. We're playing up to an incredible level. And why shouldn't we compete with the kids? It's time once again for somebody to kick over the traces, and if anybody can do it, it's the Stones."

In April the Stones recorded *Steel Wheels*. They played for up to fifteen hours a day.

RICHARDS: "It's a joy to come to work again! It's only when I have nothing to do that suddenly this aches and you've got a bit of a twinge there. But when you've got something to do, you ignore all that. I'd get up in the morning and feel like I'd just done fifteen rounds with Mike Tyson. Get out of bed and my knees would buckle. I'd be lying there on the floor and Mick would go, 'What's the matter with you?' 'It's Charlie man, I know it.' Charlie was not going to let me off the hook. I think he was a little pissed, too, that I'd gone off and played with Steve Jordan. Like he was telling me, 'I'll show you how it's done.'"

Keith continued to be the musical thread that wove the Stones together. "Almost Hear You Sigh" (for which Steve Jordan shared a writing credit with Richards and Jagger on *Steel Wheels*) and "Can't Be Seen" had both been composed for *Talk Is Cheap*. One weekend he knocked off "Mixed Emotions." Another morning he woke up to hear Jagger playing the core riff of "Continental Drift" and was reminded of Morocco. Instantly Keith and Mick decided to fly to Morocco and record the song with the same group of Joujouka musicians Brian Jones had worked with on his posthumously released record, *Brian Jones Presents the Pipes of Pan at Joujouka*, to commemorate the twentieth anniversary of his death. "It really pulled a string in me," Keith said. "I thought we needed something like this. It was the unification of what this band is about."

In Tangier they stayed at the palace of Prince Absalan, whose daughter, Saroya, vividly recalled their energy: "They had this idea of making a song in homage to Brian Jones but they had no idea of what they were going to do until they met the Joujouka people. They talked with the old man who had been a friend of Brian's and that was beautiful. The atmosphere was very magical. Very positive, no tension. They were working all the time they were there. The girl in charge said, 'Please don't tell anybody the Stones are here,' but at the end of the first day Keith said, 'Where is everybody? Your friends are not coming?' I said she said we weren't supposed to bring people here. Keith said, 'No! We want a party!' So I invited a lot of people and they just jammed. Keith had five bottles of vodka and was drinking and smoking and having a great time. Keith directed the music. Mick always went up to Keith. Both of them were very close. They were laughing a lot, taking pictures."

In April and May they mixed the album at Olympic Studios in London—"Putting the fairy dust on the bastard," Keith called it. "This music, it's certainly not Beethoven or Mozart. It's got nothing to do with intricacy. It's got to do with a bunch of guys making accidents together, spontaneity and an immediate form of communication." They hadn't made a record so quickly since the sixties.

While *Steel Wheels* was rolling, the Stones' organization was planning a series of tours that would, in the course of the next two years, take them around the globe. In the fall and winter of 1989 they would play the largest stadiums in the major cities in America. In February of 1990 they would make a ten-day stand in Tokyo. In the summer they would tour Europe.

The logistics of these tours put anything they had done in the past in the shade. They had two enormous stages built for the U.S. tour alone and hired a crew of 380 technicians to run the complex operation, but the major emphasis was on the sound. Their playing in football stadiums had been uneven on their three previous U.S.

tours. On this tour they could not afford to give one bad show. Everything had to be perfect.

Although Keith had managed to stay away from heroin since he had married Patti, he still ingested so much alcohol, hash, cocaine, and downers that many of his friends found it difficult to understand how he could talk, let alone perform. Mick was jogging five miles a day with an Olympic instructor. Concerned about Richards's health, Jagger sent Jerry Hall over to convince Patti to get Keith into shape. She got to Keith's house at eleven o'clock in the morning. Patti was making breakfast, orange juice with a lot of vodka in it. Jerry said, "Aren't you concerned about Keith? Don't you think he should slow down his drinking and get in shape for the tour?" Patti, drinking a Bloody Mary, said "No, no. He's in shape." Jerry said, "Don't you think he should maybe start doing some exercises to get ready for the shows?" "Yeah," Patti answered, "he's doing his finger exercises."

In July the Stones congregated at a girls' boarding school, Wykeham Rise, in Connecticut for six weeks of rehearsals. For the all-important man who would be at the controls of the soundboard throughout every performance they chose a twenty-five-year veteran of the road, Londoner Benjamin Lefevre, who was staggered to discover the Stones' complete catalog contained 369 titles on thirty-eight CDs. He arrived at Wykeham Rise two weeks into the rehearsals. "It was just delightful. It was like going back into the sixties, a little band rehearsing in the front room," he recalled.

BENJAMIN LEFEVRE: "The Rolling Stones for me is Charlie Watts and Keith Richards. It's a rhythm and blues band and there it is—the rhythm guitar and the beat of it. Jagger is a phenomenal performer, great lyricist, great singer, but the engine house where it all is generated from is Keith's rhythm guitar against Charlie's playing. Keith's the animal that feels like playing today or doesn't, and that's part of his essence, that's what he is, that's how he does his art."

Lefevre recognized a potential battleground between Jagger and Richards. The set was to include, among others, "Start Me Up," "Miss You," "Ruby Tuesday," "You Can't Always Get What You Want," "Paint It, Black," "Sympathy for the Devil," "Brown

Sugar," "Jumpin' Jack Flash," "Little Red Rooster," "2000 Light Years from Home," and "Satisfaction." They hadn't performed these classics together for seven years, but Jagger had played Stones material in Australia and Japan, so he came to the rehearsals with set ideas of how to reproduce their sound in stadiums.

BENJAMIN LEFEVRE: "Jagger had fallen into how modern music is achieved with the aid of technology vis-à-vis sequencers, samplers, automation. Mick was worried about Charlie's kit coming across. He said to me, 'We need a count-in click so we can get the tempo absolutely right. I hope you've got a lot of samplers and that we can trigger this and trigger that.' I said, 'I don't want to use anything like that, I really want to make Charlie's kit come across without resorting to that.'

"At the end of the day we didn't use any click tracks or any tempo-deciding devices. If we had, Keith would have totally ignored them anyway."

RICHARDS: "Look around and you'll see that there's very little out there with our feel for the music. Nobody cooks. Today everything is computerized. The kids think it's OK to sit in a little room by themselves and push buttons to get *Boom-pah, Boom-boom pah/ Boom-pah, Boom-boom pah*, but their music's not going to go anywhere except for that. There are absolutely no dynamics involved, no feeling, no passion. You can't get those things out of a machine."

BENJAMIN LEFEVRE: "At the end of rehearsal Keith asked about doing sound checks. I said for the first half-dozen gigs it would be of great technical importance for that to happen, but after that, technically it's not necessary. However, it would be really nice if we got to see you every day, if you got to see where you were going to play that day, if you didn't just arrive in the limo, walk on stage, play, walk back to the limo, and disappear again. It would be nice for the whole technical crew, all three hundred eighty of us, to have the feeling that they were concerned about every aspect of what we were doing. He just went, 'Right, put a pool table in the dressing room and we'll do it every day.' And every single city we played, the Rolling Stones came and did a sound check. Unheard of. Unheard of."

As Richards saw it, "With the technology it's no longer five people in this band—it's like three hundred."

In August, *Steel Wheels* was released. It would go to number three in the U.S. and number two in the U.K. "Its vitality derives from raw elements, a rhythm section that pumps and pulses like the heart of a great beast," wrote Tom Wheeler in *Guitar Player*. "To a significant degree the art of Rolling Stones records is an extension of the guitar sensibility of Keith Richards, who sketches motifs with bold, blotchy guitar strokes, and then extends the boundaries with strategically placed guitar tracks from foreground to horizon."

"The track which most plainly reveals that the group is not merely cruising on auto-pilot is a remarkable tour de force called 'Continental Drift,'" wrote David Sinclair in *Q*. "The ability to draw on the outside musical developments—R&B, disco, country, et al.—has always been one of the Stones' greatest strengths. Here, with the help of Moroccan Master Musicians of Joujouka, is their comment on World Music. Jagger melds his voice into an extraordinary approximation of quavering Eastern harmonic street bazaar freakout—the sort of thing the Pogues have been dabbling in recently, but which the Stones presumably remember from the original era of psychedelia."

In Keith's judgment, the new album was on a par with *Some Girls* and *Exile on Main St.* "It's the easiest thing in the world for me to work with the Stones," he said. "Mick and I work together perfectly. It's when we're not working that we have problems."

The song that received the most critical attention was the last cut on the second side, "Slipping Away," on which Keith sang the lead vocal. "The Stones know their audience," wrote Jay Cocks in *Time* magazine. "It's pretty much the same as it's always been, and it will be happy to see them. It will also be happy to know that the material on *Steel Wheels* is a lot like them—up to date but fundamentally unchanged. The band must know it too, because finally, on the last song, they face it. 'Slipping Away' is a song about—indeed, almost consumed by—a sense of impermanence, of loss, of lives sliding into compromise. It's about ending, it's about dying, and it's a great Stones song. So when 'Slipping Away' begins and the husky fragility of Richards' vocal takes instant hold, it is clear that this is more than just a good closer for a record. It's a political gesture, a way of dealing with all that friction, even as it's being moved out front. And it's something more, an envoi, the start of a long good-bye."

To Linda Keith, who had married the guitarist and producer John Porter and to whom Keith was now occasionally sending his love, Keith's voice was almost unrecognizable. "It changed so dramatically, the tone, the pitch, the elocution, but beneath the layers of onion skin peeling away I can still recognize the basis of his personality." To David Courts, Keith had "turned into the grand old man of rock and roll, and I think he's conscious of that feeling, so he's more relaxed."

Shortly before embarking on the U.S. tour, Keith had a physical checkup. "The bugger stuck electrodes all over my body, hooked up more monitors to me than the Stones use on stage, and told me I was—normal!" he exclaimed. "I mean, can you imagine anyone telling Keith Richards he was normal?"

At a press conference, a reporter charged, "Some rock critics have said that the only reason you're doing it is for the money." Richards replied, "The glory, darlin', the glory." When another reporter asked about the status of the Richards-Jagger feud, Mick wrapped his arms around Keith, who answered, "We both gave up masochism."

RICHARDS: "I guess we're obsessed with showing that we can still make a better record than we've ever made, and go out and perform it as well as we ever did. Whether or not we really do doesn't matter. It's just going for it and thinking the possibility is there. We simply have to look better and sound better than anyone out there.

"We asked ourselves, 'Why are we doing this? Do we really want to?' And the answer was, 'We have to.' Not from the money viewpoint so much as the fact that none of us was about to let the Stones drift away. I think there is this need for us to rise to the occasion. We're still looking for the ultimate Rolling Stones. We're never going to find it, but it's like the Holy Grail. It's the quest that's important, not finding it.

"My vision of the Rolling Stones was that this was the perfect point and opportunity, at our state and age, to carry on and mature and prove it. I played with Muddy Waters six months before he died, and the cat was just as vital as he was in his youth. And he did it until the day he died. To me, that is the important thing. I'll do this until I drop."

From August 31 to December 20, the Stones' organization put on a magnificent piece of rock theater in cities across the United States. The Stones often played the same venue for two to five days, and they performed in front of crowds ranging from 80,000 to 120,000 per night during their three-hour concerts.

"Everybody was playing better on this tour than they had perhaps ever played," wrote David Fricke and Robert Sandall. "Keith Richards' commitment to living rock and roll is surpassed only by his enormous enthusiasm for playing it. The frequent flash of that familiar grin was seen so often on the tour that there could be no doubt as to how much Keith was enjoying being back on stage with the Rolling Stones.

"From the slashing opening of 'Start Me Up' through to the steaming finale, 'Satisfaction,' Keith was on the case, particularly so during the two-song segment when Jagger left the stage to him. 'Happy,' his vocal debut on *Exile on Main St.*, was an obvious choice and crowd pleaser for Richards' solo spot.

"Either 'Before They Make Me Run' or 'Can't Be Seen' from *Steel Wheels*, provided the second number of the interlude before the Richards generator was back on line as the powerhouse behind the main performance."

Over the decades Richards's relationship with his guitar had become part of his legend. Through the sixties and seventies his lifestyle had made it nigh impossible for him to hold on to possessions. He had lost some of his favorite guitars in fires and frequent thefts. During the eighties he amassed a collection of some sixty guitars, many of which hung on the walls of his apartment like works of art. By then he had begun to give them names. An early-fifties Telecaster was dubbed Micawber. A 1958 Gibson Les Paul TV was nicknamed Tumbling Dice, or Dice. A classic Manuel Velásquez acoustic was called Guts, and a sunburst-finish Telecaster-style electric was Electric Guts. Others were named Malcolm and Gloria.

For Keith the tour was another triumphal procession. He screamed in and out of the theaters in a cavalcade of limousines or vans surrounded by an escort of up to one hundred motorcycle policemen. His children accompanied him to a number of the shows, enjoying the fireworks and the getaway in the end. Patti was never far from him. He often played with a pair of her panties stuffed in his jacket pocket. Jagger was the star of the show but Richards, as can clearly be seen in the IMAX film of the tour, was the one who enjoyed it. While Jagger worked his ass off, Richards was just thrilled by the sound of his music and its rapt, enthusiastic reception: "You can't compete with this. I can't explain the chemistry of it. Now we're back playing, getting paid a helluva lot of money to play our songs. To be a grouch in this position, you'd really have to be an asshole."

"Richards, whose guitar playing and onstage presence was always inspirational, seems more confident than ever," wrote Lisa Robinson. "The musical partnership between Richards and Jagger, enhanced by the extraordinary drumming of Watts, makes this still the best rock and roll music on stage today. With their publicized problems obviously in the past, Jagger and Richards can now get down to the business of performing live music. However divergent their lifestyles, on stage theirs is the quintessential symbiotic relationship of all time."

"After the show there would be a pattern," recalled keyboardist Matt Clifford. "We'd all rush into our vans and limos and go back to the hotel. Mick would go to his room and then sometimes he and I would go out to dinner or a nightclub or watch a movie. Keith and Ronnie would go to Keith's room and start a nightlong session, with friends smoking and drinking, a general party and very loud music, and they would often be joined by the horn players—real rock and roll."

RICHARDS: "Anybody that wants to walk into my room knows they can have a drink and listen to Otis Redding after the show. You've got to have a little light relief now and again. I've got to, anyway. That's part of the job! It's in the contract. The heavy drugs are out, of course. I'd be an idiot—probably wouldn't be here—if I hadn't cut them out. But I don't look to go through life being someone's image of Keith Richards. I know who he is. I'm inside him. The idea of partying for nine days in order to keep the image of Keith Richards up is stupid. That was Keith Richards then. Now I'll stay up just two or three days."

At the end of the tour, in Atlantic City, the Stones were joined on stage by Izzy Stradlin and Axl Rose of Guns 'n' Roses, the band that was often referred to as the new Rolling Stones. Despite lead guitarist Slash's claim, "I don't want to be another Keith Richards," Stradlin was clearly obsessed with his debt to Keith, as his memory of the backstage rehearsal reveals. "I'm sitting there playing acoustic guitar with Keith Richards, thinking, 'This is soooo cool.' The Stones are all asking me, 'Which song are you gonna do?' We'd chosen 'Salt of the Earth.' Nobody knew it! And I'm thinking, 'Fuck, you guys wrote it over twenty years ago!' It gave us an incredible insight into what our band could be like in ten years, if we're all still alive."

On February 5, 1990, Keith and the Stones were in Tokyo. They were due to commence playing their ten-night stand at Tokyo's Korakuen Dome on February 14. Richards was as big a star in Japan as he was in Germany. To the Japanese, Richards was the face and soul of rock and roll, and he often appeared on the covers of magazines or books about the Stones. Settling into the vast presidential suites of the finest hotels, the Stones were feted wherever they went. They watched the heavyweight championship fight in which Buster Douglas upset Mike Tyson from luxurious boxes at the dome. They rehearsed for a week, then played to fifty thousand reverential fans each night for ten nights. On the opening night, before launching into "Happy," Keith greeted the crowd by saying, "I feel better than Mike Tyson!" According to Stones film archivist James Karnbach, "Keith did two songs and the place went crazy."

At the end of April Keith was in France rehearsing for the European tour. On May 12, 1990, *New Musical Express* published a survey asking fifty of the leading guitar players in rock who their three favorite players were. Richards came second after Jimi Hendrix.

From May to August the Urban Jungle tour took the Stones from

Rotterdam to London. They played forty-nine concerts in twenty-seven cities. The tour required a whole new stage and a slightly different set of songs.

Singing "Can't Be Seen" and "Happy," Keith got as much attention as Mick. "Above all there is Keith Richards, materializing on the Wembley stage through a blast of flame to storm into the riff of 'Start Me Up,' " wrote Adam Sweeting in the *Guardian* about the London show. "Even now, something of the perilous tardiness of his time-keeping has the power to sandpaper your spine. It is Richards, with nerve-damage balletics, who conspires with the ineluctable Charlie Watts to conjure the Stones' inimitable excitement."

MICK JAGGER: "Keith and I seem to be getting on all right. The tour got all that out of our systems. We'd had enough. So we had a good time. We never had any major problems on the road, considering that we're both pretty volatile. We didn't have any rows or anything. The trouble with Keith is that he thinks all the noise we make is coming out of these little boxes on stage. He doesn't seem to realize that it's all being fed through an enormous PA hanging off the front of it. I made the mistake of telling him in Berlin that this was the largest crowd we'd ever played to, here or in America. The result was unbearable."

Anita visited Keith in Berlin.

ANITA PALLENBERG: "Being Keith Richards is a job and he's got it down to a fine art. He was preparing for a German interview, he was saying, 'No makeup, no makeup,' and the secretary was saying, 'You don't even want to brush your hair?' and he said, 'No, I know everything,' you know, and then she said, 'Oh, but Mick said that you're a child with this guy, he lays traps.' He says, 'I don't care about these traps. I can answer, I'm not like Mick. They can't catch me.' He was just sitting there reading this book about the Nazis. Nothing can change him. He's very sheltered and shuttered and that helps him keep it going. I opened the fridge and there was a shepherd's pie. He doesn't want anything from the outside. Everybody knows what he wants, what he likes, what he needs. I know that sometimes he wishes he didn't have to do the Keith Richards act, especially the drinking."

NICK KENT: "What worries me most about Keith is the drinking. I think he's drinking too much and as a result he's becoming very Peter O'Toole. But I was very impressed by the show. I went thinking, 'Well, I just hope they're home.' They did 'I Just Wanna Make Love to You' on the first night [in Paris] and it really separated the tourists from the purists."

In the tune-up room backstage in Glasgow, Keith picked up a guitar without looking. One of the strings wound around its head was slightly longer than normal and it pricked his finger. He said, "Oh, bollocks!" It was the middle finger of his left hand, which is one of the most important fingers in his chord shapes. He went on and played the two-and-a-half-hour show and the finger became swollen. By the end of the evening he was having difficulty. The finger got stiff and became infected. They had to break for five days while he recovered and two British concerts had to be rescheduled.

On August 19, at the invitation of Czechoslovakia's president, Václav Havel, the Rolling Stones performed to 107,000 people in an outdoor concert in Prague. The poster advertising the show declared, "The Tanks are Rolling Out and the Stones are Rolling In!" At two meetings with the Stones, Havel, who had recently appointed Frank Zappa a special cultural ambassador for Czechoslovakia, expressed his joy that the concert was taking place and spoke of the role that rock music played in the events leading up to Czechoslovakia's November revolution.

RICHARDS: "That was an amazing gig. A ticket also acted as a one-day passport for fans coming from Poland, Hungary, and Russia. I hate to see music being used as propaganda, which increasingly more it is. But then I think back and realize it has always been—national anthems and signaling.

"When it comes down to it, music evolved out of necessity, not out of pleasure. Somebody got lucky, whipped the other tribe's ass, and then they could use the music for fun for a little while because there's no competition. So you get the rockin' down: 'We won, we won.' You know, so you start to get those songs coming in, apart from just the signaling. And after that, there's this progression.

"Music's meaning to people is one of the great mysteries. Forget economics, forget democracy or dictatorships or monarchies. The most fascinating relationship is between people and music and how it can do what it does with no apparent sweat. Who knows what it can do? It's a beautifully subversive language because it can get through anything. I don't care if it's porous or bombproof or has a Star Wars shield over it—music will get through. That's my experience.

"Rock and roll is probably the best work the English have done since the Empire. We took it and ran with it . . . It was one of the biggest weapons the English had and they didn't know it. Music is one of the most powerful and insidious and subtle weapons. It can penetrate areas that no K.G.B or C.I.A. can possibly get to. It's a beautiful, armor-piercing weapon, man.

"A lot of the reason you've got major shifts in superpower situations in the past few years has to do with the past twenty years of music. You'll never get rid of nationalism and so-called patriotism, but the important thing is to spread the idea that there's really this one planet—that's really what we've got to worry about. And all these little lines that were drawn by guys hundreds of years ago are really obsolete. Music is the best communicator of all. In the long term, the most important thing that rock and roll's done, it's opened up people's minds about these things. 'Cause you can't stop that shit. You can build a wall to stop people, but eventually the music, it'll cross that wall."

At the end of the tours, Keith walked away with a conservatively estimated fifteen million dollars, not taking into account royalties on increased sales of the complete Stones catalog.

Richards once observed that his life fell into seven-year cycles. From 1962, when he first met Brian Jones, to 1969, when Jones died, marked the first. Nineteen sixty-nine, when he had his first child with Anita Pallenberg, to 1976, when his third child with Anita died, marked the second. The beginning of 1977, when he was busted for heroin trafficking in Toronto, to the end of 1983, when he married Patti Hansen, was the third. And 1984, when Patti became pregnant, to 1991, when the Stones completed their $200,000,000 world tour by releasing a live album, *Flashpoint*, delineated the fourth. By these calculations, 1998 ought to be a hell of a year for Keith Richards. Nineteen ninety-two was not a bad start for a new cycle. In January he finished mixing *Flashpoint* in London and recorded the new Stones single, "Highwire." On January 24 he flew to New York, where he produced and played on two tracks for Johnnie Johnson's solo album, "Tanqueray" (a song he composed with Johnson) and "Key to the Highway," on which he performed a powerful vocal, making the line "I'm going back to the bottom where I started from" sound like his autobiography.

Keith spent February on vacation in Antigua. On March 1 he was in New York filming the "Highwire" video. The song was released that month and caused some controversy in England when its lyrics were interpreted as critical of the Gulf War. He spent March in New York beginning work on his next solo album and playing with Ivan Neville and Steve Jordan. In April he flew to San Francisco to produce and play on "Crawlin' Kingsnake," a song for John Lee Hooker's next solo album.

RICHARDS: "John came on and did a couple of songs at the Stones' last gig in America, in Atlantic City. I'd heard a couple of his latest records, including the one he'd put out in '89, and I said, 'Nice job, John.' Then at the beginning of this year he calls up and says, "I'd really like you to do a track on this album.""

"He asked me what song I wanted to do. I said, 'I wanna do a song about a subject you're really interested in, John. Let's do 'Crawlin' Kingsnake.'""

"Keith Richards has a love for me, and he does everything for the love of music," said Hooker. "He's a lovely, lovely person. He's a superman. I love him. Oh yeah, he knows what the blues is. He came up to the house, we had a good time together, and played some good things."

In San Francisco he also wrote some songs with Tom Waits for his solo album.

TOM WAITS: "He's such a strong personality, a completely intuitive musician. He moves like an animal. He's just pure theater standing in the middle of a room and putting on his guitar and turning on his amp. All this stuff is irregular. He said to me, 'You do the same thing I do to them. You say, 'This verse is four bars and this one is eight and the next one is two. This turns around and goes back to the top? I thought we were going to release here! And now you're back and there's a short bar here and a little thing in six/eight? What the hell is going on here?' He's a killer, man. A great spirit. Like a pirate, and he's a complete gentleman."

On April 6, *Flashpoint* was released to favorable reviews. "The Rolling Stones are hardly an oldies act, not one more dinosaur pack led out to stadiums to graze," wrote Paul Evans in *Rolling Stone*. "Instead they've become what they always aspired to be—rockers with the staying power of roots musicians, veterans who continue to practice their art with skill and verve and undiminished soul."

In June, Johnnie Johnson's solo album, *Johnnie B. Bad*, was released. In September John Lee Hooker's *Mr. Lucky* came out.

In October Keith played with Bob Dylan and assorted Winos at the Guitar Legend Show in Seville's La Cartuja Auditorium in front of six thousand people. He got to Spain on Monday, the fourteenth, checked into the Tryp Colon Hotel, and began rehearsing on Tuesday. "It was great," he reported. "The production was good, there were nice people backstage, and nobody stole my guitars. One minute you're talking to Bo Diddley, the next minute you're talking to Les Paul. You never get that high a concentration of people playing one instrument at one time when you're doing a gig." One observer noted, "Richards charmed everyone backstage. They were in equal parts touched by his friendliness and impressed by his drinking—he never seemed to be without a glass of Jack Daniel's."

Richards was introduced at 11:00 P.M. by Bob Dylan as "one of my favorite players." They performed a version of "Shake, Rattle and Roll" that horrified Harold Steinblatt of *Guitar World*: "Dylan's rhythm work on 'Shake, Rattle and Roll' was far too loud and noticeably ragged. Richards forgot the lyrics and his own playing would not cause Django Reinhardt to lose any sleep. The best thing about Richards's singing and playing is their seemingly offhanded nature. But 'Shake' was no 'Happy' and it left me rattled, almost shattered." Fortunately, Keith recovered his bearings and did rousing versions of "Going Down," "Something Else," and "Connection" with Steve Jordan behind him.

While Richards was hopping around the world playing with his favorite musicians, the Rolling Stones machine fired impressively on all cylinders but one. Bill Wyman was in the wake of an embarrassingly short marriage and divorce from his gymslip mistress and rocking Lolita, Mandy Smith, and was once again threatening to leave the band. Some wondered if this might have been related to the publication of his autobiography, *Stone Alone*, in which he made it clear on every other page that he got the majority of the women and the minority of the money that flowed the Stones' way in the sixties. Keith, who Jane Rose claimed was disinclined to read books about the Stones, commented, "I've known Bill for so long that I could have pretty well written much of it myself. But, bless his heart, I know he's talking about leaving and I know he's had a rough time with Mandy; everyone knew it was a gigantic mistake, but what can you say? Anyway, we ain't doing anything this year, so hopefully he'll feel different in six months.

"Now, if we did go out on tour without Bill, I'm sure he'd be very pissed off and that's what I'm counting on. But then, Bill's from a different generation. For him success is going on *The Michael Aspel Show*. I think he's on his third menopause. Certainly can't be his first!"

Added Charlie Watts, "Bill can't leave the Stones. It's like joining the army. You can't get out."

In October the IMAX film of the world tour was released. The screen at each theater that showed the film was one hundred feet wide and sixty feet high. The music was loud. Keith attended a press conference for the film in November. Asked what he thought of it, he replied, "It's big." Asked what he thought of his appearance in it, Richards shot back, "Hey, man, I never like the way I look."

In November the Stones signed a new record contract with Virgin Records. For a reported forty-five-million-dollar advance starting in 1993 they would deliver three new studio albums and give Virgin the rights to their back catalog from *Sticky Fingers* onward. Considering the possibilities of releasing the back catalog in various formats, strong sales on the double-platinum *Steel Wheels*, and the two to three million records a year the catalog steadily sold, it was probably a good deal for Virgin. When the Stones had signed their first record contract in 1963, pop music was mostly a tax write-off for record companies. By 1992 it was a twenty-two-billion-dollar-a-year global business.

In December Virgin released *Keith Richards and the X-Pensive Winos Live at the Hollywood Palladium, December 15, 1988.* Ten thousand numbered copies of a boxed set that included a CD, video, and booklet quickly sold out.

RICHARDS: "It wasn't for public consumption. Jane said, 'Let's just have a record for ourselves, and you can see what you're doing up there.' That's the way it stayed for a few years. Jane got pumped up about it again, and I looked at it, listened to the audiotape, and thought it was pretty good, so the idea started forming about putting it together. And once you say, 'OK, let's take one step forward,' it often goes all the way, which it has."

The project was an unexpected success. In light of the Virgin deal, it got a lot of attention. "Mr. Richards looks as though he's having fun, and the music, raw and exuberant, has a naturalness that isn't always found in the Rolling Stones," read the *New York Times* review. Dimitri Ehrlich reviewed it for *Interview*: "His voice has been burnt to a growl, but Richards wears his age well. He still performs with a sexy, wounded lope, summoning edgy sentiments out of his instrument with a jaded effortlessness. With a cockroach's endurance, Richards has been able to keep time on his side, and he manages to imprint every recording he makes with a sloppiness that is both sublime and heartfelt."

RICHARDS: "One of the reasons I put this out was because there's so much crap around these days. If you really wanted to get upset about bootlegs, it would drive you mad, but my attitude is that, in a way, bootlegs are another indication that people like what you do. But people kept coming up to me, telling me they had bought this concert for seventy-five dollars, and all it was was a load of shit with the Winos screaming faintly in the background. I'm very happy with it. It has a flow. I like the atmosphere on it, and I love Sarah Dash singing 'Time Is on My Side,' which is the best version I've ever heard."

At award ceremonies in January 1992, Richards inducted the inventor of the electric guitar, Leo Fender, who had died in March, into the Rock and Roll Hall of Fame. Keith attended the ceremonies with Patti, Marlon, Jane Rose, and Andrew Loog Oldham. According to one witness, he "managed to wear his tux like a nightshirt and spit out one-liners like a nightclub comic." "I think the stroke of genius, really, was not his inventing the electric guitar," said Richards, "but inventing the amplifier to go with it. This is the Hall of Fame. Well, here's the fame. It's been a long haul.

"He gave us the weapon," Keith concluded. "Caress it. Don't squeeze it."

"What will save the Rolling Stones," wrote Jay Cocks in *Time*, "is that in a positive way, in a way that rock was never expected to tolerate, they are acting their age. The fan keeps coming back to 'Slipping Away' and thinks about the deaths in the band family. There was, famously, the passing of Brian Jones, one of the formative members and chief sybarites, overdosed in 1969, found dead floating in a swimming pool. And more recently, and just as crucially, there was Ian Stewart, the keyboard player, who died of a heart attack in 1985."

"There was," one friend ruefully pointed out, "really a trail of corpses behind Keith." Among those Cocks failed to mention were Michael Cooper, Gram Parsons, Tara Richards, Freddie Hauser's son, and Keith Harwood.

Death was no stranger to Keith in 1991. In March, Eric Clapton's four-year-old son, Conor, died when he fell out the window of his mother's high-rise apartment in New York. "Funnily enough," recalled Clapton, "the first person I heard from was Keith Richards. He wrote me a fantastic letter, and I called him right away. He just said, 'Well, I'm here, you know, if there's anything I can do . . .'"

In April ex-New York Doll Johnny Thunders overdosed in New Orleans. Jerry Nolan, the Dolls' drummer, recalled how very early one morning, a few weeks later in New York City, he saw Keith leaning against a wall reading and smoking a cigarette at the corner of Broadway and Tenth.

JERRY NOLAN: "He'd seen me first. He made a motion showing we knew each other. There was no one out—it was me and him. He gave me a typical limp English handshake and says, "Look, Jerry, I'm sorry. I know what it's like. I don't know what to say. I wish I had a poetic answer. But I will say one thing. Somehow, I don't know how, but somehow, hang in there. Stick to it. Don't give up."

In October the legendary promoter Bill Graham, who had his own ups and downs with the Stones, died in a helicopter accident. "That's the end of night-time helicopter flights for me, baby," Keith said.

"I've relied on accidents all my life," he once told an interviewer. "Everything I've ever planned has never worked out. I'm just something that accidents happen to. Some of them are good, and some of them are bad. Most of them are good, and the bad ones ain't killed me yet."

27

Hate It When You Leave
1992–1993

My music is about chaos. I suppose it reflects my life and probably everybody else's. Nothing happens quite when you think it's supposed to or when you want it to, but when it does, you've got to roll with it. You learn, and you get back up again and pick it up. It's very hard to explain, but I try to do the same thing with the lyrics that I do to the music—a juxtaposition that kind of slams you the wrong way here, and then suddenly it's in the right place. It's just like life.

KEITH RICHARDS, *from an interview with Jas Obrecht, 1992*

Nineteen ninety-two was an X-Pensive Winos and a perfect Keith Richards year. In January, Keith started out writing and recording songs for *Bone Machine* by Tom Waits, who recalled, "He's totally mystified by the music, like a kid. He finds great joy in it, and madness and abandon. He looks at the guitar, and his eyes get all big and he starts shaking his head." That same month, Keith began writing songs for his next X-Pensive Winos album, *Main Offender*, with Steve Jordan. He moved back into his East 4th Street apartment in New York so the two of them could work uninterruptedly. "With Steve, he's around the corner," Keith explained. "I'm at his place, or he's at my place. It's a very close thing—I've got an idea, boom, we can start on it right away.

"We sit around in a room with a couple of guitars and a drum kit or piano and a tape recorder and start talking about stuff—'Do you remember that great song Otis played?'—and wait to see where it drifts. You spend half the time having another beer and cracking up. It's one of those things where maybe I'm just playing background music to the telephone. And Steve says, 'That's nice. What are you doing there?' So it's a matter of recognizing things. And there you have an embryo, a germ of an idea. But you begin by sitting around with nothing." There was a continuity in the way he saw his songwriting that year.

RICHARDS: "I'm not an autobiographer. I write songs, I don't write a diary. I'm not baring my soul, I'm trying to distill things and feelings that I've had through my life and I know for damn sure that other people have had, and I try and evoke them. The only songs that interest me could mean anything to anybody.

"I can draw back now on a lot of my life. I can hit an emotion, I can put them together better now. Vulnerability is an interesting thing. I always like to suggest it, because it's in everybody. If you can open up, you can open up other people as well.

"You're not really writing each song as a contained piece; one song tends to influence the other. We tried to avoid making too much sense of this record. To me, ambiguity and provocation and mystery is far more powerful and important. It's kind of like life; you're not quite sure what's going on. I still keep going. It's to do with accepting things, being able to ride it and at the same time not cutting it off. If things don't hurt at all, you're numb, and that's the worst. My songs are about where to touch and when to touch, about not knowing, a bafflement. There's a time when you have to dig deeper, say a few things you wouldn't want to put into anybody else's mouth, and not just write something because it fits the image. Then you're just writing ads for yourself."

Keith found further continuity in the gathering together of the Winos. In February, the core of the band, Waddy Wachtel, Steve Drayton and Ivan Neville joined Richards and Jordan in New York and began to rehearse. Throughout the sessions and the *Main Offender* tours, Keith also employed the talents of Bernard Fowler, Sarah Dash, Babi Floyd and Bobby Keys. The recording sessions for *Main Offender* began on March 18 in the Site Studios in San Rafael, California, and lasted until April 1. Before leaving New York, Keith threw an early birthday party for Patti.

RICHARDS: "It was a real blessing to be able to rely on the same guys, because you can build, and grow, on what you did before. I learned an awful lot about what to do on this record by taking the Winos on the road in '88. That forged an identity for the band, and made me start to realize there was some potential beyond just making a record. We already felt like a band, just making the first record, but going on the road actually made us one. Playing live, we started to switch around on the instruments.

"I kept that experience in the back of my mind while I was doing *Steel Wheels*; I dredged it up when Steve and I were talking about the album last year. We wanted to utilize more of the talents of the band. Ivan can do everything. Charlie is basically a drummer, but he's also one of the best, most imaginative bass players I've ever played with.

"It only gets better when you start exploring the people you're working with. If you're working with people you only know vaguely you never really explore anybody's potential. What I like about making records is taking guys with different points of view and finding out if the focus ends up in the same place, if everybody's looking into that same spot. That's when it starts to happen."

Keith spent the summer overdubbing and mixing in New York. He added Waddy Wachtel to the production team, making the creative human sandwich that always seemed to bring out the best in him.

RICHARDS: "Bringing Waddy in on the production was the other big step. Steve and I are very good, but we're so close to it. We're black and white in more than the obvious ways, and Waddy was a great breakthrough. He's got a better-organized and more mathematical brain than Steve or I have. Steve's better, I'm the worst—I can come up with inspiration or ideas, but organization . . .

"One of the most encouraging things about working in music is that you don't think about people's differences. What you play, and the way you're playing it is the only thing that counts. It's very hard to comprehend that people have so much difficulty getting along out there, because with music it's always so easy. This is a funny line-up: the Jew, the black guy and the Anglo. We're a cross-section; it's a great three-way street. The way I think about it is that I'm working with New York guys. Charlie and Steve are from New York. Waddy's from Queens. Ivan and I are the odd men out; he's from New Orleans. I'm an honorary New Yorker."

As the summer progressed, Keith became so immersed in the

work he refused to change out of his worn grey jeans, denim jacket, buckle boots and bandanna until it was finished. He was staying up for days.

This biography came out in September. Keith became aware of its publication one morning when he left Jane Rose's office and saw a big blow-up of its cover in a bookstore window directly across the street. "There I was in the window. And I thought, hang on, I haven't even finished the album yet, the promotion's too early," he laughed. The positive criticism the book received in England and America indicated more than anything else just how much Keith Richards' image had changed for the better since he played *Live Aid* with Dylan in 1985. "While Richards' extravagant appetites may be life-threatening," wrote David Gates in *Newsweek*, "in the short term they seem the very reverse of self-destructive: they're self-perpetuating, self-exalting."

On September 6, Keith completed work on *Main Offender*, which was mastered on the 8th. With six-weeks of non-stop work behind him, Keith was driven back to Connecticut, where he collapsed in bed for a full week. Though on stage Keith remained the maverick icon, off stage, especially in his Connecticut estate, he projected quite a different image. "The scene outside the large house is evocative of some pastoral setting in the English country-side," wrote his old friend from the seventies, Lisa Robinson, who visited him in this bucolic new setting that month. "The grass is lush and very green, and neatly trimmed hedges, tons of flowers and a large vegetable garden are adjacent to a flagstone patio with a built-in backgammon table, all flanked by a large swimming pool. In a light, misty rain, the man in the trench coat and snappy, small-brimmed hat walks two large, frolicking dogs around the property in what could easily be a scene out of *Wuthering Heights*. Except this isn't Laurence Olivier on the moors. It's Keith Richards.

"Inside his wood-paneled, book-lined library, with its maroon velvet and leather furnishings, Richards—a voracious reader—has a sly twinkle in his eye. In this large and well-appointed house Richards says that, at last he's finally been able to 'unpack,' and to have a place where he can 'settle in.'"

Another visitor to Keith's estate, the writer Bryan Appleyard, told Keith that he had expected to meet the Prince of Darkness. Instead, he encountered "a bloke who could be bending my ear in an East End pub." An amused Keith responded, "Yeah, I know. I can be the guy on stage any time I want. Actually, I'm trying to get away from that guy. I would like to stay in touch with him. He was dealing with a lot of self-created problems . . . But I'm a very placid, nice guy—most people will tell you that. It's mainly to placate this other creature that I work."

Keith spent October 1992 doing publicity for *Main Offender*. After a quick trip to L.A. to film the album's videos, he flew to Paris on October 13 for five days of European interviews. By the 19th, he was back in New York to do a major Rockline radio phone-in program.

Main Offender was released on October 20. That night Keith did a signing at Tower Records on lower Broadway that drew three thousand people and created near-riot conditions. "Forget Dallas and JFK; where were you the first time you heard 'Brown Sugar'? Or 'Start Me Up'?" read the Virgin Records ad. "*Main Offender* is proof positive that the Riffmeister General is very much alive and kicking, from the gentle Caribbean lope of 'Words Of Wonder' to the chop of 'Wicked As It Seems.' There's a definite whiff or three of Detroit in 'Hate It When You Leave.' 'Runnin' Too Deep' is bad news for tennis rackets all over the land because even the terminally tone deaf will fancy playing it; ditto 'Will But You Won't.' *Main Offender* smacks irresistibly of a maestro just having a good time. Keith Richards hasn't let us down once in the last thirty years, and he certainly hasn't started now."

In light of the success of *Steel Wheels*, Richards was given, if anything, more attention for his second solo album. He appeared on the covers of twenty-three magazines internationally, was profiled in many mainstream publications and received massive airplay—as well as good television coverage throughout Europe, the U.S., Australia and Japan. "Most artists in our business lose their magic as the business changes and as the artists age," Phil Quartararo, the president of Virgin Records said. "Keith has not only retained his magic, he's gotten better. For people in Guns 'n' Roses and countless other bands that admire this guy, where else would they turn? Keith was the first purist, and he's one of the only remaining purists."

Now that Johnny Thunders was dead, the front-man in the running for Richards' crown was former Guns 'n' Roses guitarist Izzy Stradlin. When Stradlin came out with his own album, it was so Richards-influenced that one critic dubbed it the best of the new Stones solos.

RICHARDS: "I admire Izzy for having the balls and the independence to leave a big running number like Guns 'n' Roses. I've got all the best wishes in the world for him. Half of you is flattered. It'll take him a while to get the hang of it, though. The fact is, to do what I do, it's not necessary to emulate everything that I did to do it. It's like saxophone players who took dope because they thought that's how Charlie Parker did it. That's not the ingredient. Guys that don't really know me, they're more likely to be the child of my image. Chasing an image is a dangerous game. If you have a self-destructive nature and you've suddenly got a lot of bread and you're a rock star, it ain't gonna do you too much good if you don't get a handle on it real quick. There's not a lot of advice I can offer, but I won't pay for the funeral."

Keith and the Winos were scheduled to go on tour from November '92 to February '93. Having tried to get the Stones to tour South America since the seventies, Keith took a step in that direction in November when he flew down to Buenos Aires. After rehearsing for four days, the group played in front of 45,000 people on November 7.

RICHARDS: "It felt great! It always feels great. You can have a wrenched back or a fever and the last thing you want to do is schlep out there and play music, but the minute you go out there and play the first chord it happens. It's as close to magic as I can get."

Back in New York on the 9th, the band went into intense rehearsals for its European tour. In late November, they flew to Europe and commenced a journey that took them through Copenhagen, Cologne, London, Rotterdam, Paris, Barcelona, Madrid and then back to London. Keith had gone through something of a transformation in his performance since the *Talk Is Cheap* tour. His voice was stronger as a result of singing regularly, but his outstanding contribution continued to be the unique balance of his guitar playing. "Keith Richards' genius is in his fingers, as they flick brazen rhythmic guitar chords and barbed-wire leads," noted one sharp-eyed writer, Jon Pareles. "He also showed talent in his legs. Strolling as he played, suddenly pivoting, perching on one foot like a heron, tipping his ankles on the floor or finishing phrases with a high kick, Richards had body language to match his music: casual, sly, cocky and insolently graceful. Richards shows off not by showing off. He uses rhythm chords as a goad, not a metronome, slipping them in just ahead of a beat or skipping them entirely. The distilled twang of his tone has been imitated all over rock, but far fewer guitarists have learned his guerrilla timing, his coiled silences. When he switches to lead guitar, Mr. Richards goes not for long lines, but for serrated riffing, zinging out three or four notes again in various permutations, wringing from them the essence of the blues. The phrasing is poised and suspenseful, but it also carries a salutary rock attitude: that less is more, especially when delivered with utter confidence."

While Keith was in London, he attempted to hold a "summit" with Bill Wyman, who had been saying for the last few months that he was going to resign from the Rolling Stones. "I just need to sit down with the guy and say, I've just got to know now, man," Richards explained to a friend. "I've worked with him for thirty years, and I don't want to change the line-up unless really necessary. Bill's exactly what a bass player should be. You never have to look round and wonder what he's doing. He's solid as a rock. He's unobtrusive but he swings—which is one of the important things about the Rolling Stones. I certainly don't want to blackmail him— which I could do: I'd have to go back in the diaries, but I'd find something. But I don't want to drag a reluctant and unwilling Bill Wyman around on tour. I just have to find out, eyeball to eyeball." However, throughout Keith's visit to London, Bill avoided him. "I did everything but hold him at gunpoint," Richards exclaimed, but Wyman's decision held.

Keith flew back to New York to prepare for Christmas and New

Year. Anita and Marlon joined Keith and the Hansen clan for Christmas in Connecticut. On December 28, Keith and the Winos filmed a concert for television in Chicago. On the 31st, they played the Academy in New York, a small theater which held two thousand people. Pearl Jam opened. Bert, Angela, Anita and Jane were there, as were Johnny Ramone, John McEnroe and designer Marc Jacobs. "Having hung together since that first album, the nucleus of the X-Pensive Winos has evolved into a killer of a band with a punchy character all its own," wrote another keen observor, David Sinclair, "and while Richards may look and speak as if the fuse protecting his central nervous system has been tripped once too often, his playing has rarely been sharper. Although he has lived a life of fearful excess, Richards has emerged as a supremely centered individual, and it seems no accident that his keynote song, with which this show ended, should be called 'Happy'. The loving way he caressed his guitar, occasionally snapping both hands away as if the instrument were simply too hot to touch, and his relaxed demeanor on stage left an impression of a man taking immense satisfaction in plying his craft to the very best of his abilities."

Keith spent the first weeks of January 1993 rehearsing the Winos in New York. On the 17th their US tour opened in Seattle. They played twenty-two shows in fifteen cities, ending with five triumphant nights, February 19–24, at the Beacon Theater in New York.

As the *Main Offender* tour ended, Keith was already looking forward to getting together with his other band. Jagger and Richards were scheduled to meet and get to work on the next Stones project in March. Uppermost on Keith's mind was replacing Bill: "A rhythm section change in a band is a heavy-duty number, so we've got to find the right cat. I wouldn't be happy with somebody who is already a big name. I'd rather bring in somebody who can work their way in." Though Wyman's departure presented a problem for Keith, it in no way dampened his optimism about the future of the Rolling Stones, all of whom had strong solo projects in the works. As he looked forward to reuniting with the band, he reflected on where they were headed.

RICHARDS: "I'm happier now about the Stones than I have been for ten years because everybody's working, and I don't have to look with a sense of dread at taking six months to find out what happened to the greatest rock and roll band in the world.

"It's kind of like an adventure, the Stones. You can't give up now. Once you're in, you take it to the end. If you got off the bus now, you'd spend the rest of your life wondering where the end of the line was. We're the only ones here, so in a way there's a duty to see how far you can take it. I think there's a possibility of another golden period in the Stones somewhere."

In the end, whatever or whoever else came and went, it was the music that stayed with Keith.

RICHARDS: "Music, to me, is the joy, right? I love my kids most of the time, and I love my wife most of the time. Music I love all the time. It's the only constant thing in my life. It's the only thing you can count on. It could fall apart. It's a balancing act. But you can fall down and get up. I guess I got over my embarrassment over falling down in public a long time ago. That to me is what makes it interesting. You set yourself up for a fall but you know you can get up.

"I really feel for new bands that are coming up because these days you need a quarter of a million dollars before you can start. And with that big money the marketing men want to play it safe. And when you play it safe, the best you're going to come up with is something that's not bad. And we're not sitting here talking because the music is not bad. We're here because it is Fucking Great!

"Playing it safe is not what it's all about. This music is about beautiful fuck-ups. And beautiful recoveries."

Asked what epitaph he wanted on his tombstone, Richards answered, "He passed it on."

Source Notes

> I'm a Sagittarius, half-man, half-horse, with a license to shit in the street.
>
> KEITH RICHARDS, *from* Rock Lives *by Timothy White,* 1990

The primary source for *Keith Richards: The Biography* is the information he has provided about himself in the many interviews he has given throughout his career. Out of the thousands of hours of tape, five statements stand out: a lengthy interview conducted by the author of this book in August 1977 (shortly after Richards's arrest in Toronto, a major emotional turning point in his life) for *High Times*, published subsequently in *The Rolling Stones: The First Twenty Years* by David Dalton (New York: Knopf, 1981); an interview on August 19, 1971, with Robert Greenfield for *Rolling Stone*; a series of interviews with Barbara Charone, published in *Keith Richards: Life as a Rolling Stone* (New York: Dolphin/Doubleday, 1982); a series of interviews by Stanley Booth published in *The True Adventures of the Rolling Stones* (New York: Vintage, 1985); and an interview by Stanley Booth in October 1989 for *Playboy*.

The author conducted interviews for this book with: William Burroughs, Jim Carroll, Jonathan Cott, David Courts, Robin Denselow, Rick Derringer, John Dunbar, Tommy Edmonds, Marianne Faithfull, Bill German, Albert Goldman, Lil Wenglass Green, Dr. Joseph Gross, Clinton Heylin, Dieter Hoffman, Terry Hood, James Karnbach, Linda Keith, Nick Kent, Sheila Klein (Oldham), Joanna Larson, Benjamin Lefevre, Richard Lloyd, Gerard Malanga, Gered Mankowitz, John Michel, Barry Miles, Hervé Muller, Uschi Obermeier, Anita Pallenberg, Robert Palmer, Perry Richardson, Julio Santo Domingo, Princess Saroya of Tangier, Freddie Sessler, Terry Southern, Sandro Sursock, Michael Watts, and Chris Welch.

Other interviews and articles drawn on in this book are by Dan Acquilante, Felix Aeppli, Mandy Aftel, Brian Appleyard, Brad Balfour, Victoria Balfour, Lester Bangs, John Bauldie, Alan Beckett, Massimo Bonanno, Mike Bosso, Mark Boxer, Mick Brown, Hadine Brozan, Andy Bull, Geoffrey Cannon, Roy Carr, Barbara Charone, Robert Christgau, Jay Cocks, Nik Cohn, Ray Coleman, Ray Connolly, Jonathan Cott, Mike Curtin, Anthony de Curtis, David Dalton, Fredric Dannen, Stephen Davis, Stephen Dixon, Adrian Deevoy, Martin Elliott, Richard Elman, Pete Erskine, Paul Evans, Mick Farren, Timothy Ferris, Bill Flanagan, Alec Foege, Ben Fong-Torres, Andrew Franklin, David Fricke, Deborah Frost, Vic Garbarini, Simon Garfield, Bill German, Mikal Gilmore, Michael Goldberg, Albert Goldman, Bob Gruen, Sid Griffin, Brion Gysin, Pat Hackett, Chris Heath, Christopher Hemphill, David Henderson, Gary Herman, Christian Kämmerling, Nick Kent, Zoo Kennedy, Scott Kutina, Jon Landau, Betty Landman, David Langsam, Andreas Lebert, Mark Leyner, Kurt Loder, Gil Markle, Glen Matlock, Christine McAulife, Neil McCormic, Vincent McGarry, Richard Merton, Jim Miller, Barry Miles, Kiki Miyake, John Morthland, Charles Shaar Murray, Jerry Nolan, Philip Norman, Jas Obrecht, Robert Palmer, Jon Pareles, Jim Perogatis, Charles Perry, Steven Prokesch, David Quantick, Greg Quill, Geraldo Rivera, William Rees-Mogg, Robert Reinhold, Ira Robbins, Wayne Robbins, Lisa Robinson, John Rockwell, Robert Sandall, Tony Scaduto, Tony Scherman, Stephen Schiff, Karen Schoemer, Kevin Sessums, David Sheff, Doug Simmons, David Sinclair, Elsa Smith, Giles Smith, Joe Smith, Mat Snow, Bob Spitz, Penny Stallings, Dia Stein, Robert Sundall, Adam Sweeting, Derek Taylor, Lionel Tiger, George Trow, Steve Turner, George Tremlett, Paul Trynka, Craig Vetter, Andy Warhol, Chris Welch, Tom Wheeler, Bob Whitaker, Timothy White, and Charles Young.

They were published in *Circus*, British *GQ*, *Chicago Sun-Times*, *Creem*, *Details*, *Esquire*, *L'Événement*, *Forbes*, *Guitar*, *Guitar* [*The Magazine*], *Guitar Player*, *Guitar World*, *Hit Parader*, *House and Garden*, *The Independent*, *Interview*, the London *Times*, the London *Sunday Times*, *Los Angeles Free Press*, *Masters of Rock*, *Melody Maker*, *Modern Drummer*, *Musician*, *New Left Review*, *New Musical Express*, *New York Newsday*, *New York Post*, *New York Rocker*, *The New York Times*, *The New York Times Magazine*, *The New Yorker*, *Newsweek*, *Partisan Review*, *People*, *Playboy*, *Punch*, *Q*, *Rapid Eye*, *Record*, *Record Collector*, *Rip*, *Rock and Folk*, *Rolling Stone*, *Rolling Stones 1989 Tour*, *Rolling Stone Super Rock Spectacular*, *ShBoom*, *Smart*, *Spin*, *The Sunday Correspondent*, *Tatler*, *Time*, *Time Out*, *Trouser Press*, *Vanity Fair*, *The Village Voice*, *Vox*, *Weekend Guardian*.

The Rolling Stones Book, a monthly official fan magazine from August 1964–November 1966, and *Beggars Banquet*, the official Rolling Stones newsletter from 1984 through 1992, edited by Bill German, were particularly useful.

Secondary in importance to the interviews, but indispensable to any writer, are the numerous books about the Rolling Stones, particularly, in addition to the aforementioned, *Symphony for the Devil: The Rolling Stones Story* by Philip Norman (New York: Linden/Simon and Schuster,

1984), *Up and Down with the Rolling Stones* by Tony Sanchez (New York: New American Library, 1980), *The Rolling Stones: The First Twenty Years:* by David Dalton (New York: Knopf, 1981), *On the Road with the Rolling Stones, 20 Years of Lipstick, Handcuffs, and Chemicals* by Chet Flippo (New York: Doubleday, 1985), and *Blown Away* by A.E. Hotchner (New York: Simon and Schuster, 1990). Other books include:

Aeppli, Felix. *Heart of Stone: The Definitive Rolling Stones Discography, 1962–1983.* Ann Arbor, MI: Pierian, 1985.

Aftel, Mandy. *Death of a Rolling Stone: The Brian Jones Story.* New York: Delilah/Putnam, 1982.

Aldridge, John. *Satisfaction: The Story of Mick Jagger.* London: Proteus, 1984.

Ali, Tariq. *Street Fighting Years.* London: Collins, 1987.

Appleby, John. *30 Priory Street and All That Jazz.* Bristol, England: John Appleby, 1971.

Balfour, Victoria. *Rock Wives.* New York: Quill, 1986.

Bauldie, John. *Wanted Man: In Search of Bob Dylan.* New York: Carol, 1990.

Bego, Mark. *Aretha Franklin.* New York: St. Martin's, 1989.

Benson, Joe. *Uncle Joe's Record Guide: The Rolling Stones.* Glendale, CA: J. Benson Unlimited, 1987.

Berry, Chuck. *Chuck Berry: The Autobiography.* New York: Harmony, 1987.

Blake, John. *His Satanic Majesty Mick Jagger.* New York: Holt, 1985.

Bonanno, Massimo. *The Rolling Stones Chronicle.* New York: Holt, 1990.

Booth, Stanley. *Rhythm Oil: A Journey through the Music of the American South.* New York: Pantheon, 1991.

Botts, Linda. *Loose Talk.* New York: Quick Fox, 1980.

Brown, James, with Bruce Tucker. *James Brown.* New York: Thunder's Mouth, 1990.

Burdon, Eric. *I Used to Be an Animal but I'm All Right Now.* London: Faber and Faber, 1986.

Burgess, Anthony. *A Clockwork Orange.* New York: Norton, 1986.

Burroughs, William. *Naked Lunch.* Paris: Olympia, 1959.

Cahill, Marie. *The Rolling Stones: A Pictorial History.* New York: Mallard, 1990.

Carr, Roy. *The Rolling Stones: An Illustrated Record.* New York: Harmony, 1976.

Chambers, Iain. *Popular Culture.* London: Methuen, 1986.

Chambers, Iain. *Urban Rhythms.* London: Macmillan, 1985.

Christgau, Robert. *Any Old Way You Choose It.* Harmondsworth, England: Penguin, 1970.

Christgau, Robert. *Rock Albums of the 70s*. New York: Da Capo, 1990.

Chuck Berry: The Chess Box. Universal City, CA: Chess/MCA Records, 1988.

Cohn, Nik. *Rock from the Beginning*. New York: Pocket, 1970.

Coleman, Ray. *Clapton*. New York: Warner, 1985.

Connolly, Ray. *Stardust Memories: Talking About My Generation*. London: Pavilion, 1983.

Cooper, Michael. *Blinds and Shutters*, Guildford, England: Genesis, 1990.

Dalton, David. *The Rolling Stones*. London: Star/W. H. Allen, 1975.

Dalton, David. *The Rolling Stones: An Unauthorized Biography in Words and Photographs*. New York: Delilah/Putnam, 1979.

Dalton, David, and Mick Farren. *The Rolling Stones in Their Own Words*. London: Omnibus, 1980.

Dannen, Fredric. *Hit Men*. New York: Random House, 1990.

Denselow, Robin. *When the Music's Over*. London: Faber and Faber, 1989.

Des Barres, Pamela. *I'm with the Band*. London: New American Library, 1987.

Dixon, Willie, with Don Snowden. *I Am the Blues*. New York: Da Capo, 1989.

Dowley, Tim. *The Rolling Stones*. New York: Hippocrene, 1983.

Draper, Robert. Rolling Stone *Magazine*. Garden City, NY: Doubleday, 1990.

Edelstein, Andrew, and Kevin McDonough. *The Seventies*. New York: Dutton, 1990.

Ehrlich, Cindy. *The Rolling Stones*. San Francisco: Straight Arrow, 1975.

Eisen, Richard. *Altamont: Death of Innocence in the Woodstock Nation*. New York: Avon, 1970.

Eliot, Marc. *Rockonomics*. New York: Franklin Watts, 1989.

Elliott, Martin, *The Rolling Stones Complete Recording Sessions*. London: Blandfold, 1990.

Elsner, Constance. *Stevie Wonder*. New York: Popular Library, 1977.

Farren, Mick. *Rolling Stones '76*. London: Second Foundation, 1976.

Fitzgerald, Nicholas. *Brian Jones: The Inside Story of the Original Rolling Stone*. New York: Putnam, 1985.

Flanagan, Bill. *Written in My Soul*. Chicago: Contemporary, 1987.

Fong-Torres, Ben. *Hickory Wind: The Life and Times of Gram Parsons*. New York: Pocket, 1991.

Frame, Pete. *The Complete Rock Family Tree*. London: Omnibus, 1979.

Fricke, David, and Robert Sandall. *The Rolling Stones: Images of the World Tour 1989–1990*. New York: Fireside, 1990.

Frith, Simon. *The Sociology of Rock*. London: Constable, 1978.

Frith, Simon. *Sound Effects: Youth, Leisure and the Politics of Rock and Roll*. New York: Pantheon, 1981.

Gillett, Charlie. *The Sound of the City: The Rise and Fall of Rock 'n' Roll*. New York: Outerbridge & Dienstfrey, 1970.

Goldman, Albert. *Freakshow*. New York: Atheneum, 1971.

Goldman, Albert. *The Lives of John Lennon*. New York: Morrow, 1988.

Goodman, Pete. *Our Own Story by the Rolling Stones*. New York: Bantam, 1970.

Green, Jonathan. *Days in the Life: Voices from the English Underground*. London: Heineman, 1988.

Greenfield, Robert. *S.T.P.: A Journey through America with the Rolling Stones*. New York: Saturday Review/Dutton, 1974.

Griffin, Sid. *Gram Parsons*. Pasadena: Sierra Records and Books, 1985.

Gruen, Bob. *The Rolling Stones Featuring Keith Richards*. Tokyo, 1990.

The Guitar Player Book. New York: Grove, 1979.

Hall, Jerry, and Christopher Hemphill. *Jerry Hall's Tall Tales*. New York: Pocket, 1985.

Hall, Stuart, and Tony Jefferson. *Resistance Through Rituals*. London: Unwin Hyman, 1976.

Harker, Dave. *One for the Money*. London: Hutchinson, 1980.

Harris, Sheldon. *Blues Who's Who*. New York: Da Capo, 1979.

Henderson, David. *The Life of Jimi Hendrix*. New York: Bantam, 1981.

Henry, Tricia. *Break All the Rules*. Ann Arbor, MI: UMI Research Press, 1989.

Herman, Gary. *The Who*. New York: Collier, 1971.

Herman, Gary. *Rock 'n' Roll Babylon*. London: Plexus, 1984.

Hewison, Robert. *Too Much: Art and Society in the 50s*. London: Methuen, 1986.

Higham, Charles. *Errol Flynn*. Garden City, NY: Doubleday, 1980.

Hodkinson, Mark. *Marianne Faithfull: As Tears Go By*, London: Omnibus, 1991.

Hoffman, Dezo. *The Rolling Stones*. London: Vermilion, 1984.

Hoffman, Dieter. *Das Rolling Stones Schwarzbuch*. Vaihingen/Enz: New Media Verlag, 1987.

Jagger/Richards Songbook (cassette tape). London: The Connoisseur Collection, 1991.

Jasper, Tony. *The Rolling Stones*. London: Octopus, 1976.

Kael, Pauline. *Reeling*. New York: Warner, 1976.

Kamin, Philip, and James Kambach. *The Rolling Stones in Europe*. New York: Beaufort, 1983.

Kooper, Al, with Ben Edwards. *Backstage Passes*. New York: Stein & Day, 1977.

LaVere, Stephen C. *Robert Johnson: The Complete Recordings*. New York: Columbia Records, 1990.

Littlejohn, David. *The Man Who Killed Mick Jagger: A Novel*. New York: Pocket, 1977.

Longmate, Norman. *The Doodlebugs*. London: Arrow, 1981.

Luce, Phillip C. *The Stones*. London: Wingate/Baker, 1970.

Lydon, Michael. *Rock Folk*. New York: Carol, 1990.

Macphail, Jessica. *Yesterday's Papers*. Ann Arbor. MI: Pierian, 1986.

Mankowitz, Gered. *Satisfaction: The Rolling Stones, 1965–1967*. New York: St. Martin's, 1984.

Marchbank, Pearce, and Barry Miles. *The Rolling Stones File*. London: Essex Music/Music Sales, 1976.

Markle, Gil. *Rehearsal: The Rolling Stones at Longview Farm*. Worcester, MA: Gil Markle, 1981.

Marks, J. *Mick Jagger: The Singer Not the Song*. New York: Curtis, 1973.

Martin, Lisa. *The Rolling Stones in Concert*. Colour Library International, 1982.

Matlock, Glen, with Pete Silverton. *I Was a Teenage Sex Pistol*. London: Faber and Faber, 1990.

McRobbie, Angela. *Zoot Suits and Second Hand Dresses*. Boston: Unwin Hyman, 1984.

Melly, George. *Revolt into Style*. Harmondsworth, England: Penguin, 1970.

Miles, Barry. *The Clash*. London: Omnibus, 1978.

Miles, Barry. *The Rolling Stones: An Illustrated Discography*. London: Omnibus, 1980.

Miles, Barry. *Mick Jagger in His Own Words*. London: Omnibus, 1982.

Murray, Charles Shaar. *Shots from the Hip*. Harmondsworth, England: Penguin, 1991.

Norman, Philip. *The Life and Times of the Rolling Stones*. London: Century, 1989.

Palmer, Robert. *The Rolling Stones*. Garden City, NY: Rolling Stone/Doubleday, 1983.

Peelaert, Guy, and Nik Cohn. *Rock Dreams*. New York: Popular Library, 1973.

Phillips, John. *Papa John*. Garden City, NY: Doubleday, 1986.

Platt, John. *London's Rock Routes*. London: Fourth Estate, 1985.

Quant, Mary. *Quant*. London: Pan, 1967.

Quill, Greg. *The Rolling Stones Anniversary Tour*. Ontario: Kamin and Howell, 1989.

Ratcliffe, Stephen, and Leslie Scalapino. *Talking in Tranquility: Interviews with Ted Berrigan*. New York: Avenue B Books, 1991.

Rice, Jo, Tim Rice, Paul Gambaccini, and Mike Read. *The Guinness Book of British Hit Albums*. London: Guinness, 1983.

Rogan, Johnny. *The Byrds*. London: Square One, 1990.

Rolling Stone *Interviews 1967–1980*. New York: St. Martin's/Rolling Stone Press, 1981.

Rolling Stone *Interviews: The 1980s*. New York: St. Martin's, 1989.

Rolling Stone *Record Review*. New York: Pocket, 1971.

Rolling Stone *Rock Almanac*. New York: Collier, 1983.

Rolling Stones Anthology, Vol. 1. New York: Abkco Music, 1975.

The Rolling Stones Complete. London: Omnibus, 1981.

Rolling Stones Steel Wheels North American Tour Book. New York, 1989.

Roth, Arlen. *Rock Guitar for Future Stars*. New York: Ballantine, 1986.

Savage, Jon. *England's Dreaming*. New York: St. Martin's, 1992.

Scaduto, Tony. *Mick Jagger, Everybody's Lucifer*. New York: David McKay, 1974.

Schaffer, Nicholas. *The British Invasion*. New York: McGraw-Hill, 1983.

Shaw, Arnold. *The Rockin' '50s*. New York: Da Capo, 1987.

Smith, Joe. *Off the Record*. New York: Warner, 1988.

Southern, Terry, Annie Leibovitz, and Christopher Sykes. *The Rolling Stones on Tour*. Cheltenham, England: Dragon's Dream, 1978.

Spector, Ronnie, with Vince Waldron. *Be My Baby*. New York: Harmony, 1990.

Stallings, Penny. *Rock 'n' Roll Confidential*. Boston: Little, Brown, 1988.

Stevenson, Ray. *The Sex Pistols File*. London: Omnibus, 1978.

Taylor, Derek. *It Was Twenty Years Ago Today*. New York: Fireside, 1987.

Thomson, Elizabeth, and David Gutman. *The Dylan Companion*. New York: Delta, 1990.

Tiger, Lionel. *Men in Groups*. New York: Vintage, 1970.

Tremlett, George. *The Rolling Stones*. New York: Warner, 1975.

Trudeau, Margaret, *Beyond Reason*. Paddington, New York & London, 1979.

Turner, Tina, with Kurt Loder. *I, Tina*. New York: Avon, 1986.

Wale, Michael. *Voxpop: Profiles of the Pop Process*. London: Harrap, 1972.

Welch, Chris. *Hendrix*. London: Omnibus, 1972.

Weiner, Jon. *Come Together*. Champaign, IL: University of Illinois Press, 1991.

Weiner, Sue, and Lisa Howard. *The Rolling Stones A to Z*. New York: Grove, 1983.

Weinberg, Max. *The Big Beat*. New York: Billboard Books, 1991.

Whitburn, Joel. Billboard *Top 1000 Singles, 1955–1990*. Milwaukee: Hal Leonard, 1991.

White, Charles. *The Life and Times of Little Richard*. New York: Pocket, 1984.

White, Timothy. *Catch a Fire*. New York: Holt, 1989.

White, Timothy, *Rock Lives*. New York: Holt, 1990.

Wilson, Colin. *The Occult*. New York: Random House, 1971.

Wood, Ron, with Bill German. *Ron Wood*. New York: Harper and Row, 1987.

Woodward, Bob. *Wired*. New York: Pocket, 1984.

Wyman, Bill. *Stone Alone*. New York: Penguin, 1990.

Some of the most compelling images of Keith Richards come from the films *One Plus One* by Jean-Luc Godard, *Gimme Shelter* by the Maysles Brothers, *Cocksucker Blues* by Robert Frank, and 25 × 5: *The Continuing Adventures of the Rolling Stones* by Nigel Finch; and the photographs of Michael Cooper (*Blinds and Shutters*, Guildford, England: Genesis, 1990), Dezo Hoffman (*The Rolling Stones*, London: Vermilion, 1984), Gered Mankowitz (*Satisfaction: The Rolling Stones 1965–1967*, New York: St. Martin's, 1984), Bob Gruen (*The Rolling Stones Featuring Keith Richards*, Tokyo, 1990), Annie Leibovitz, and Ethan Russell.

I nicked a sentence from Albert Goldman's essay on Tom Forcade, and a sentence from an interview in Jon Savage's *England's Dreaming* both printed on pages 61 and 62 of this book. The account of Keith and Anita's drug cure with Dr. Paterson is based on an interview with and notes by Steve Turner. To all three gentlemen, thanks.

Every attempt has been made to track down the original sources of this book. If anybody whose work is quoted herein is not mentioned above, the author apologizes and would be glad to rectify the mistake.

Index

Discover more about our forthcoming books through Penguin's FREE newspaper...

Penguin
Quarterly

It's packed with:

- exciting features
- author interviews
- previews & reviews
- books from your favourite films & TV series
- exclusive competitions & much, much more...

Write off for your free copy today to:
Dept JC
Penguin Books Ltd
FREEPOST
West Drayton
Middlesex
UB7 0BR
NO STAMP REQUIRED

READ MORE IN PENGUIN

In every corner of the world, on every subject under the sun, Penguin represents quality and variety – the very best in publishing today.

For complete information about books available from Penguin – including Puffins, Penguin Classics and Arkana – and how to order them, write to us at the appropriate address below. Please note that for copyright reasons the selection of books varies from country to country.

In the United Kingdom: Please write to *Dept. JC, Penguin Books Ltd, FREEPOST, West Drayton, Middlesex UB7 0BR*

If you have any difficulty in obtaining a title, please send your order with the correct money, plus ten per cent for postage and packaging, to *PO Box No. 11, West Drayton, Middlesex UB7 0BR*

In the United States: Please write to *Penguin USA Inc., 375 Hudson Street, New York, NY 10014*

In Canada: Please write to *Penguin Books Canada Ltd, 10 Alcorn Avenue, Suite 300, Toronto, Ontario M4V 3B2*

In Australia: Please write to *Penguin Books Australia Ltd, 487 Maroondah Highway, Ringwood, Victoria 3134*

In New Zealand: Please write to *Penguin Books (NZ) Ltd,182–190 Wairau Road, Private Bag, Takapuna, Auckland 9*

In India: Please write to *Penguin Books India Pvt Ltd, 706 Eros Apartments, 56 Nehru Place, New Delhi 110 019*

In the Netherlands: Please write to *Penguin Books Netherlands B.V., Keizersgracht 231 NL–1016 DV Amsterdam*

In Germany: Please write to *Penguin Books Deutschland GmbH, Friedrichstrasse 10–12, W–6000 Frankfurt/Main 1*

In Spain: Please write to *Penguin Books S. A., C. San Bernardo 117–6° E–28015 Madrid*

In Italy: Please write to *Penguin Italia s.r.l., Via Felice Casati 20, I–20124 Milano*

In France: Please write to *Penguin France S. A., 17 rue Lejeune, F–31000 Toulouse*

In Japan: Please write to *Penguin Books Japan, Ishikiribashi Building, 2–5–4, Suido, Tokyo 112*

In Greece: Please write to *Penguin Hellas Ltd, Dimocritou 3, GR–106 71 Athens*

In South Africa: Please write to *Longman Penguin Southern Africa (Pty) Ltd, Private Bag X08, Bertsham 2013*

READ MORE IN PENGUIN

A SELECTION OF MUSICAL HITS

The Big Wheel   Bruce Thomas

'The former bass guitarist of Elvis Costello and the Attractions, Bruce Thomas has written about life on the road for a successful rock band with a drummer whose excesses fulfil our every expectation of every rock drummer and a singer whose behaviour remains utterly enigmatic throughout. Thomas is obviously a witty and perceptive man, who handles his one-liners well' – *20/20*

Sweet Soul Music   Peter Guralnick

'As important for what it says about America, class and race issues, and the sixties as for its outstanding musical insights. Sooner or later it is going to be recognized as a classic' – Robert Palmer in *The New York Times*

Shots from the Hip   Charles Shaar Murray

His classic encapsulation of the moment when rock stars turned junkies as the sixties died; his dissection of rock 'n' roll violence as citizens assaulted the Sex Pistols; his superstar encounters from the decline of Paul McCartney to Mick Jagger's request that the author should leave – Charles Shaar Murray's *Shots from the Hip* is also rock history in the making.

Mystery Train   Greil Marcus

'There has never been a more well-written, imaginative, scholarly, infuriating, crackling, gladdening book about rock music ... Greil Marcus uses a handful of modern popular artists ... to illuminate and interpret two centuries of the American Dream' – *Sunday Times*

Dylan: Behind the Shades   Clinton Heylin

'The most accurately researched and competently written account of Dylan's life yet ... Heylin allots equal space to each of the three decades of Dylan's career, and offers a particularly judicious assessment of his achievements in the post-conversion Eighties' – Mark Ford in the *London Review of Books*

READ MORE IN PENGUIN

A SELECTION OF MUSICAL HITS

Sinéad Jimmy Guterman

Sinéad O'Connor is internationally famous for her haunting, passionate vocals and outspoken political views. Here is the story of the woman and her music: from her unhappy early years in a broken home and a Catholic reform school to her triumphant arrival as a major pop star of the 1990s.

Stone Alone Bill Wyman with Ray Coleman

Ruthless, cynical, electrifying and exuberant – the Stones played a revolutionary soundtrack for the Sixties. Offstage, bass guitarist Bill Wyman has always been 'the silent Stone'. But here he gives us the intimate and gripping story of the 'bad boys' of British rock and the era they helped to shape.

Pet Shop Boys, *Literally* Chris Heath

'They have defined something intangible in an all-too obvious era of pop music. Their Englishness, their balance – and their cynicism – combine to produce an effect of brilliance, self-regarding and self-referential' – *Sunday Times*. 'Witty, straightforward and painstakingly precise ... a compelling read' – *Time Out*

The American Night Jim Morrison

'A hellfire preacher, part-terrified, part-enraged and mainly fascinated by the drawbacks that being merely human entails ... refreshing' – Robert Sandall in the *Sunday Times*. 'A great American poet' – Oliver Stone

Bare George Michael and Tony Parsons

'A fascinating study of fame, power, and insecurity ... *Bare* paints a picture of a modern-day folk-hero against the stark background of contemporary Britain. Funny and incisive ... *Bare* heralds a new chapter in celebrity biography' – *Arena* magazine

READ MORE IN PENGUIN

A CHOICE OF NON-FICTION

The Time Out Film Guide   Edited by Tom Milne

The definitive, up-to-the minute directory of over 9,500 films – world cinema from classics and silent epics to reissues and the latest releases – assessed by two decades of *Time Out* reviewers. 'In my opinion the best and most comprehensive' – Barry Norman

The Remarkable Expedition   Olivia Manning

The events of an extraordinary attempt in 1887 to rescue Emin Pasha, Governor of Equatoria, are recounted here by the author of *The Balkan Trilogy* and *The Levant Trilogy* and vividly reveal unprecedented heights of magnificent folly in the perennial human search for glorious conquest.

Berlin: Coming in From the Cold   Ken Smith

'He covers everything from the fate of the ferocious-looking dogs that formerly helped to guard East Germany's borders to the vast Orwellian apparatus that maintained security in the now-defunct German Democratic Republic ... a pithy style and an eye for the telling detail' – *Independent*

Cider with Rosie/As I Walked Out one Midsummer Morning
Laurie Lee

Now together in one volume, Laurie Lee's two classic autobiographical works, *Cider with Rosie* and *As I Walked Out One Midsummer Morning*. Together they illustrate Laurie Lee's superb descriptive powers as he conveys the poignancy of a boy's transformation into adulthood.

In the Land of Oz   Howard Jacobson

'A wildly funny account of his travels; abounding in sharp characterization, crunching dialogue and self-parody, it actually is a book which makes you laugh out loud on almost every page ... sharp, skilful and brilliantly funny' – *Literary Review*

READ MORE IN PENGUIN

A CHOICE OF NON-FICTION

The Time of My Life   Denis Healey

'Denis Healey's memoirs have been rightly hailed for their intelligence, wit and charm ... *The Time of My Life* should be read, certainly for pleasure, but also for profit ... he bestrides the post-war world, a Colossus of a kind' – *Independent*. 'No finer autobiography has been written by a British politician this century' – *Economist*

Chasing the Monsoon   Alexander Frater

'Frater's unclouded sight unfurls the magic behind the mystery tour beautifully ... his spirited, eccentric, vastly diverting book will endure the ceaseless patter of travel books on India' – *Daily Mail*. 'This is travel writing at its best. Funny, informed, coherent and deeply sympathetic towards its subject' – *Independent on Sunday*

Isabelle   Annette Kobak

'A European turned Arab, a Christian turned Muslim, a woman dressed as a man; a libertine who stilled profound mystical cravings by drink, hashish and innumerable Arab lovers ... All the intricate threads of her rebellious life are to be found in Annette Kobak's scrupulously researched book' – Lesley Blanch in the *Daily Telegraph*

Flying Dinosaurs   Michael Johnson

Hundreds of millions of years ago, when dinosaurs walked the earth, we know that there also existed great prehistoric beasts call pterosaurs that could fly or glide. Now you can make these extraordinary creatures fly again. *Flying Dinosaurs* contain almost everything you need to construct eight colourful and thrillingly lifelike flying model pterosaurs – from the pterodactylus to the dimorphodon.

The Italians   Luigi Barzini

'Brilliant ... whether he is talking about the family or the Mafia, about success or the significance of gesticulation, Dr Barzini is always illuminating and amusing' – *The Times*. 'He hits his nails on the head with bitter-sweet vitality ... Dr Barzini marshals and orders his facts and personalities with the skill of an historian as well as a journalist' – *Observer*

READ MORE IN PENGUIN

A CHOICE OF NON-FICTION

Riding the Iron Rooster Paul Theroux

Travels in old and new China with the author of *The Great Railway Bazaar*. 'Mr Theroux cannot write badly ... he is endlessly curious about places and people ... and in the course of a year there was almost no train in the whole vast Chinese rail network in which he did not travel' – Ludovic Kennedy

Ninety-two Days Evelyn Waugh

In this fascinating chronicle of a South American journey, Waugh describes the isolated cattle country of Guiana, sparsely populated by an odd collection of visionaries, rogues and ranchers, and records the nightmarish experiences travelling on foot, by horse and by boat through the jungle in Brazil.

The Life of Graham Greene Norman Sherry
Volume One 1904–1939

'Probably the best biography ever of a living author' – Philip French in the *Listener*. Graham Greene has always maintained a discreet distance from his reading public.This volume reconstructs his first thirty-five years to create one of the most revealing literary biographies of the decade.

The Day Gone By Richard Adams

In this enchanting memoir the bestselling author of *Watership Down* tells his life story from his idyllic 1920s childhood spent in Newbury, Berkshire, through public school, Oxford and service in World War Two to his return home and his courtship of the girl he was to marry.

A Turn in the South V. S. Naipaul

'A supremely interesting, even poetic glimpse of a part of America foreigners either neglect or patronize' – *Guardian*. 'An extraordinary panorama' – *Daily Telegraph*. 'A fine book by a fine man, and one to be read with great enjoyment: a book of style, sagacity and wit' – *Sunday Times*

READ MORE IN PENGUIN

A CHOICE OF NON-FICTION

1001 Ways to Save the Planet Bernadette Vallely

There are 1001 changes that *everyone* can make in their lives today to bring about a greener environment – whether at home or at work, on holiday or away on business. Action that you can take *now*, and that you won't find too difficult to take. This practical guide shows you how.

Bitter Fame Anne Stevenson

'A sobering and salutary attempt to estimate what Plath was, what she achieved and what it cost her … This is the only portrait which answers Ted Hughes's image of the poet as Ariel, not the ethereal bright pure roving sprite, but Ariel trapped in Prospero's pine and raging to be free' – *Sunday Telegraph*

The Complete Book of Running James F. Fixx

Jim Fixx's pioneering book has encouraged a sedentary generation to take to the streets. Packed with information for the beginner, the more experienced runner and the marathon winner, it explains the many benefits to be reaped from running and advises on how to overcome the difficulties. 'This book is a boon and a blessing to the multitudes who jog and run throughout the world' – Michael Parkinson

Friends in High Places Jeremy Paxman

'The Establishment is alive and well … in pursuit of this elusive, seminal circle of souls around which British institutions revolve, Jeremy Paxman … has written a thoughtful examination, both poignant and amusing' – *Independent*

Slow Boats to China Gavin Young

Gavin Young's bestselling account of his extraordinary journey in small boats through the Mediterranean, the Red Sea, the Indian Ocean and the Malaya and China Seas to China. 'A joy to read, engaging, civilised, sharply observant, richly descriptive and sometimes hilarious … a genuine modern adventure story' – *Sunday Express*

BY THE SAME AUTHOR

Warhol

This is the kind of book I like: it tells me the things I want to know about the artist, what he ate, what he wore, whom he knew (in his case ... everybody), at what time he went to bed and with whom, and, most important of all, his work habits' – *Independent*

'Bockris's biography is superbly done ... Here Warhol and the courageous and weird personalities around him speak without fear' – *Sunday Times*

'Brilliant ... kaleidoscopic, racy, exhaustively complete and utterly fascinating – *Evening Standard*